The Psychology of Evidence and Trial Procedure

The Psychology of Evidence and Trial Procedure

Edited by
Saul M. Kassin
Lawrence S. Wrightsman

 SAGE PUBLICATIONS Beverly Hills London New Delhi

For information address:

SAGE Publications, Inc.
275 South Beverly Drive
Beverly Hills, California 90212

SAGE Publications India Pvt. Ltd.
M-32 Market
Greater Kailash I
New Delhi 110 048 India

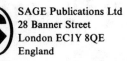

SAGE Publications Ltd
28 Banner Street
London EC1Y 8QE
England

Printed in the United States of America

Library of Congress Cataloging in Publication Data

Main entry under title:

The Psychology of evidence and trial procedure.

Includes indexes.
1. Evidence (Law)—United States.   2. Psychology,
Forensic.   3. Procedure (Law)—United States.
I. Kassin, Saul M.   II. Wrightsman, Lawrence Samuel.
KF8935.P75   1985   347.73′6   85-1688
ISBN 0-8039-2379-1

FIRST PRINTING

CONTENTS

Preface   7

I. INTRODUCTION

1. The Evidence and Trial Procedure:
The Law, Social Policy, and Psychological Research
WALLACE D. LOH   13

II. EVIDENCE

2. The Eyewitness
GARY L. WELLS   43

3. Confession Evidence
SAUL M. KASSIN and LAWRENCE S. WRIGHTSMAN   67

4. The Probity of the Polygraph
DAVID T. LYKKEN   95

5. The Defendant's Testimony
DAVID R. SHAFFER   124

6. Character Testimony
MARTIN F. KAPLAN   150

7. Survey and Field Experimental Evidence
JACOB JACOBY   175

8. Expert Psychological Testimony
EDITH GREENE, JONATHAN W. SCHOOLER,
and ELIZABETH F. LOFTUS   201

III. TRIAL PROCEDURE

9. Opening and Closing Statements
E. ALLAN LIND and GINA Y. KE   229

10. Questioning Witnesses
ELIZABETH F. LOFTUS and JANE GOODMAN   253

11. Jury Instructions
    AMIRAM ELWORK and BRUCE D. SALES   280
12. Issues in Trial Management:
    Conducting the Voir Dire Examination
    GORDON BERMANT   298

IV. CONCLUSIONS AND CONTROVERSIES

13. The Evidence on Evidence: Science and Law
    in Conflict and Cooperation
    PETER W. SPERLICH   325

Name Index   363

Subject Index   373

About the Contributors   379

PREFACE

In recent years, increasing numbers of psychologists have invested their energies and talents in evaluating various aspects of the legal system. Indeed, the remarkable growth of the interface between psychology and law has been well documented in *Annual Review of Psychology* chapters written by Tapp (1976) and, more recently, by Monahan and Loftus (1982). Psychologists have left no stones unturned in their quest to understand such diverse phenomena and processes as police and prosecutorial discretion, bail setting, plea bargaining and other out-of-court settlement procedures, trial advocacy, jury decision making, civil commitment, sentencing, and parole.

One phase of criminal and civil justice that has attracted considerable if not disproportionate amounts of attention is the courtroom trial. Perhaps it is its inherently theatrical appeal that is responsible for such widespread interest and curiosity. We can all evoke an image of "Perry Mason justice," of the maverick defense lawyer, the underdog in hot pursuit of the truth that will liberate his client, who persuades the trier of fact that the defendant is not guilty. And we can all evoke an equally lucid, well-worn image of "Henry Fonda justice" (*Twelve Angry Men*) in which the highly moral, principled, and fair-minded citizen stands alone on the jury, asserts his individualism, and ultimately persuades his eleven trigger-happy peers that there is a reasonable doubt about the defendant's culpability. Americans love a good trial and all its potential for dramatic glory. There are winners and losers, good guys and bad guys. The stakes are high, and can include billion-dollar antitrust awards in civil litigation as well as the death penalty in the criminal arena.

Ever since the publication of Hugo Munsterberg's *On the Witness Stand* (1908), psychologists and other social scientists have analyzed the trial process in depth in order to identify and understand the determinants of a judge's or jury's verdict. It is interesting that in the early, pioneering days of this interface, the emphasis was on evidence and procedure (the most notable examples are Whipple, 1909; Marston, 1924; Hutchins & Slesinger, 1928). Yet the more recent focus of psychologists' work has been on the nonevidentiary, extralegal biases that intrude upon judgments of guilt and liability. There are exceptions, of course. But reviews of the more recent literature on the trial process (e.g., several of the chapters in the edited volumes by Sales, 1981, and Kerr & Bray, 1982) would lead the naive reader to believe that verdicts are largely determined by the personality and prejudices of individual jurors, the size and composition of the deliberating body, the physical and interpersonal attractiveness of the litigants, pretrial publicity, and the like.

This shift in emphasis is disturbing in light of the fact that virtually all experts in the area agree that the overwhelming majority of verdicts is decided not by these extralegal factors, but by the strength, quality, and presentation of the evidence. Even Kalven and Zeisel, whose classic book *The American Jury* (1966) stimulated much of this recent research, stated flatly that their results "corroborate strikingly the hypothesis that the jury follows the direction of the evidence" (p. 161). So why the heavy emphasis on nonevidentiary factors?

One possibility was inadvertently suggested to one of us by a colleague who drew a distinction between "evidence," the stuff that judges and lawyers are interested in, and "psychological" factors, the substance of *our* discipline. This distinction, of course, is illusory. Perhaps it is maintained by those of us who believe it will create a special niche for psychological consultants to the legal community (i.e., lawyers may know about evidence, but we are uniquely equipped to provide information about the more hidden world of the decision maker). Perhaps not. In either case, evidence and the procedural rules that guide its presentation are heavily psychological in nature. Hearsay, eyewitnesses, confessions, character testimony, and polygraph test results are excellent examples. Indeed the rules of evidence and courtroom procedure upon which the conduct and flow of a jury trial is predicated were developed around a set of assumptions about human behavior (cf. Wrightsman, 1978). A second possible reason for the undue emphasis on extralegal factors is that they represent sources of error in the ideal system. As such, empirical verifications of their effects (for example, the finding that beautiful defendants are treated more leniently than their less attractive counterparts, or that authoritarian jurors are conviction prone compared to their egalitarian peers) are typically seen as failings of justice and, therefore, important to our social conscience. There is, in short, an implicit premium placed on demonstrations of nonevidentiary bias.

Currently, there are several books of varying levels available to those who are interested in the psychology of the courtroom trial. And, as reflective of the area, they typically cover the wide variety of topics mentioned earlier. In contrast to these sources, *this edited volume is devoted exclusively to evaluating the meat and potatoes of the trial drama and the single most important determinant of its outcome—the evidence and courtroom procedure.*

Plan and scope of the book. The book is divided into four sections. Within these sections, we are fortunate to have up-to-date chapters from notable experts in various specific topics. We open with an insightful overview and historical perspective on the laws of evidence and procedure as well as a definition of the empirical issues that should and often do concern psychologists.

The second section is devoted to the nuts and bolts of the psychology of evidence. Seven substantive topics were selected that are practically important, theoretically interesting, and always controversial. These are the eyewitness, confessions, the defendant's testimony, the polygraph, surveys and field experiments, character evidence, and the expert witness. These chapters were written with several goals in mind—to review the history and relevant laws that guide admissibility rulings, to evaluate the evidence in question for its competence (i.e., is it reliable and valid and, if so, under what conditions?) and credibility (i.e., how does the trier of fact perceive and weigh this type of evidence, and what impact does it ultimately have?), and to suggest, when possible, policy implications for trial judges (on the issue of competence and, hence, admissibility) and lawyers (on the question of credibility and its implications for trial advocacy).

The third section examines the major stages of trial procedure—opening statements and closing arguments, direct and cross-examination, and jury instructions. As in the evidence section, these authors approached their respective chapters with an eye toward certain goals—to describe the procedure in question and its intended function in the context of the trial as a whole, to evaluate the impact on the decision maker (most notably, the jury) of varying strategies that have been devised for its implementation, and to draw from this psychological analysis policy recommendations for judges (regarding trial management, e.g., how to administer jury instructions) and lawyers (regarding courtroom strategy, e.g., how to conduct a cross-examination). This section concludes with a chapter focusing on a special topic, one that is a current source of heated debate between the judiciary and the bar: the question of who should conduct the voir dire.

The volume closes with a provocative discussion of the role that psychology, as reflected in our various contributions, does and should play in the judicial process. This chapter touches on several important and recurring questions that are of interest not only to social scientists but to legal scholars and practitioners alike.

We expect this book to have the broad appeal one would naturally strive for in an interdisciplinary endeavor. Our contributors are leading scholars, and their chapters are not only broad in scope but written in nontechnical, accessible language. As such, this book should be of general academic interest to students, teachers, and researchers in law and the social sciences, and prove to be of great practical value to trial judges and litigators as well.

Acknowledgments. Any edited book is necessarily the joint product of the work of many people. As editors, we wish to thank each of our authors for their respective projects and for their efforts with us in bringing their chapters to fruition. We are also grateful to Terry Hendrix of Sage Publications for his support throughout this endeavor and to the entire production staff at Sage whose work is reflected, literally, on every page of this volume. Finally we each have our own social support networks, beginning with our wives, Carol and Lois, whose patience and tolerance for our lost weekends ultimately made this book possible.

—Saul M. Kassin
Lawrence S. Wrightsman

PART *I*
INTRODUCTION

CHAPTER 1

The Evidence and Trial Procedure

The Law, Social Policy, and Psychological Research

WALLACE D. LOH

"That which you hear me tell," said the Third Gentleman in Shakespeare's *The Winter's Tale, "*you'll swear you see, there is such unity in the proofs" (act 5, scene 2). The gentleman then described "many evidences" from which he inferred the proposition desired to be proved—namely, that the lost child was the king's daughter. In all of the Bard's plays, the words *proof* or *prove* recur some 350 times. Proof— the ratiocinative process of arriving at conclusions from available evidence—is part of everyday experience. Legal proof is simply a more formalized application of this universal mode of thinking. It is a process of persuading the trier to accept the conclusion derived from the facts found at trial. The procedural rules that govern proof in the courtroom constitute the law of evidence, the subject of this book.

This introductory chapter presents a conceptual overview of the law of evidence. The emphasis here is not on the technical rules themselves, seemingly more numerous than grains of sand, but on the history, general principles, and social policies that lie behind the rules. It provides the legal propaedeutics for much of the psychological research on evidence and procedure reported in detail in the ensuing chapters. To assess the legal relevance of psycholegal studies, it is important to see them in legal context, just as the contours of a visually

Author's Note: This chapter is a revised version of some sections of Chapter 9 of Loh (1984). The preparation of this chapter was supported by a summer research grant of the University of Washington Law School.

13

perceived figure takes shape against the ground in which the figure appears.

In the course of this exposition of the legal doctrines and their rationales, some pertinent empirical studies are also discussed. The purpose is to illustrate how such studies can help inform and evaluate the law. They stimulate reflection on the adequacy of certain legal preconceptions. They also provide a springboard for assessing some of the difficulties and prospects of applying psychological research to improving legal fact-finding.

THE FRAMEWORK

The Structure of Evidence Law

The rules of evidence "represent the most careful attempt to control the processes of communication to be found outside a laboratory" (Cleary, 1952, p. 282). Thus, the presentation of evidence in court for the purpose of legal proof can be examined in terms of a persuasive communications paradigm: Who says what, how, and with what effect. The plethora of rules prescribe, in essence, who can present the evidence, what evidence can be admitted, and how the evidence should be introduced. The target of the persuasion is the trier, either jury or judge. This communications analogy obviously oversimplifies the law of evidence, but it serves to highlight its basic structure.

First, there is a set of rules that pertains to communicators (i.e., witnesses). They set forth the qualifications for competency and capacity of ordinary and expert witnesses, and establish the limits for their support or impeachment upon questioning by counsel. There are also rules that prescribe the circumstances under which personal attributes of witnesses (e.g., community reputation, bad character) can be brought out at trial.

A second category of rules has to do with the nature and presentation of the communication. Some prescribe the form and scope of questions (e.g., direct versus leading inquiries) used to elicit evidence of a testimonial kind. Others structure the sequence or order of presentation of evidence by each side.

A third set of rules controls the admission or exclusion of evidence at trial. It constitutes the most substantial and important component of the body of evidence law. Evidence that is otherwise relevant to what is sought to be proved may nonetheless to be excluded on the basis of one of four rules: the hearsay rule—secondhand evidence is excluded because it is of questionable validity and might be overvalued by the jury; the relevance rule—evidence that is nonrelevant in the sense that its probative value is outweighted by the risks of prejudicial impact on the jury is inadmissible; the opinion rule—statements of opinion rather than fact from ordinary witnesses are excluded because such judgments belong to the province of the jury; and the privilege rule—evidence that is privileged (e.g., communications between attorney and client, clergy and penitent, or husband and wife) because they protect socially valued relationships is inadmissible. Each of these general rules has been finespun into a multiplicity of refined discriminations and exceptions that specify the conditions under which normally inadmissible evidence becomes admissible. The hearsay rule, for example, has some two dozen exceptions, more or less. It is these exceptions that make for the complexity of evidence law.

Finally, there are rules that guide the deliberations of the jury at the end of the trial, after all the evidence has been presented. These concern the standard of proof for evaluating the sufficiency of the evidence.

The importance of evidence law in the trial process is substantial. No matter how strong a litigant's case, he[1] is unlikely to prevail unless the supporting evidence can be made available to the trier. Evidence rules play a gatekeeping role in the courtroom—they condition if not control decision making by determining the evidence that will be admitted or excluded.

The Rationale of Evidence Law

"It is important to remember that all of the fundamental rules have some *reason* underneath," Wigmore (1935) taught. The reasons may not be sound in point of practical policy and they may be buried from sight, but they are there. "Therefore, to understand the reason of the rules is to be half way towards mastery of the rules deduced from these reasons" (1935, p. 5). The need for any rules to regulate the flow of communication in civil and criminal trials is said to rest on three rationales: practical necessity, the promotion of certain social values, and distrust of the jury.

There has to be some practical limits to the admissibility of evidence. Anything and everything cannot be considered if trials are not to be excruciatingly long and costly. Rules regarding relevance, for example, seek to prevent needless repetition of cumulative evidence and obfuscation of issues.

At trial, more is at stake than the truth of the matter in contest. Minimization of factfinding errors is not necessarily the *summum bonum* of litigation. Evidence law also serves to advance goals extrinsic to truth determination. Rules that exclude hearsay not only ensure that admitted evidence is reliable but also make trials appear fairer. If litigants and the public perceive the dispute resolution process as impartial, they are more likely to accept the legitimacy of the outcome. The protection of certain confidential relationships and the deterrence of police misconduct are examples of other values that are promoted by the exclusion of otherwise relevant and probative evidence.

The chief influence in the shaping of evidence law was the development of jury trials. The English law of evidence, according to Sir Henry Maine, "was in its origin a pure system of exclusion . . . which prevented large classes of testimony from being submitted to the jury" (in Wigmore, 1940, vol. 1, p. 30). The emergence of the modern jury trial in England around the sixteenth century caused judges to fear that their untrained, lay counterparts would be misled by false testimony and succumb to improper appeals to their emotions and sympathies. In its infancy, during the twelfth and thirteenth centuries, the jury was a self-informing group. Verdicts were based on information obtained in the vicinity rather than by what transpired in court. Over the course of the next two or three centuries, the process of trial was transformed, resulting in a corresponding change in the jury's role. The sworn testimony of witnesses gradually became the principal source of information and prospective jurors with preexisting knowledge of the dispute were excluded from passing judgment.

Initially, judges punished jurors for returning "erroneous" verdicts (especially in political cases of seditious libel). Jurors could be subject to *attaint*, a review of their verdict by a second jury. If the verdict was found demonstrably false, the original jurors were imprisoned or stripped of their personal property. The threat of attaint served to control verdicts. Once it became accepted doctrine that the jury is the sole judge of the facts and its verdict is final and sacrosanct (*Bushell's Case*, 1670), judges began to fashion other means to control and diminish jury discretion. The need for evidence rules is rooted in the jury's power of the general verdict and, in particular, the power of nullification.

Jury Nullification and Evidence Law

In criminal trials, the jury has the power of nullification, also called the jury's prerogative of leniency or jury sovereignty. This power implies the right to set aside the judge's instructions on the applicable law as well as the evidence presented in order to reach an acquittal verdict based upon the popular sense of fairness and the wisdom of the common man. The jury can ameliorate the harshness of the criminal law by interjecting communal morality into its secret deliberations.

Jury sovereignty is part of the broader and age-old issue of reconciling legal rules versus equitable results within the administration of justice. Law, by definition, embodies formal, relatively stable, and universal rules applicable in an impartial and equal manner to all. However, law also needs to be leavened by notions of equity; rules cannot always be applied woodenly if justice is to be done in a specific case. Whereas the judge provides uniformity in the administration of justice via adherence to precedents, the jury provides for individualization of justice. The power of nullification enables the jury to individualize the law without following or creating precedent—to render particularized justice without betraying the commitment to evenhanded application of law. In the protected privacy of its retirement, the jury in a criminal trial can supply the needed flexibility by "bending" rules and "finding" facts in order to do right in a given case.

In criminal cases, only a general verdict of guilty or not guilty is required. The jury need not divulge the reasons for its decision and acquittals are not reversible by the trial judge. Because of the general verdict, a jury can reach a result without following the substantive rules of law and even without giving weight to the evidence presented. When the medieval power of the courts to punish jurors for "incorrect" verdicts was repudiated in 1670, the jury was given in effect the power to find facts and apply the law according to its own conscience without fear of judicial reprisal.

In civil cases, the jury delivers a general verdict of liable or not liable. The court, however, can control the jury by ordering a new trial, by setting aside the jury's verdict if contrary to the preponderance of the evidence, or by instructing the jury to issue a directed verdict on behalf of one of the parties because the evidence clearly supports (in the court's judgment) the position of that party. The different values and the greater stakes present in criminal compared to civil trials make the jury in the criminal case far less accountable in any way for its general verdict. Two traditions, then, coexist in the jury. One is the unreviewable and unreversible power of the jury in criminal cases to acquit in disregard of law and evidence. The other is the legal practice and precedent of instructing juries in both criminal and civil cases that they must follow and apply the law to the facts that they determine. The jury can be seen as an institution for accommodating discretion and authority—for keeping equity and rule in equilibrium.

Another judicial safeguard created against jury arbitrariness was the regulation of the flow of information at trial. By crystallizing the wisdom of generations of professional decisionmakers in ready-to-hand rules, untrained citizens could be sheltered from the temptation of accepting uncritically any proffered evidence. The first treatise on evidence law was published in the early eighteenth century, after the modern trial by jury had been well-established. Such was the origin, and such the spirit, of evidence rules. "Judicial oversight and control of the process of introducing evidence to the jury gave our system birth; and he who would understand it must keep this fact constantly in mind" (Thayer, 1898, p. 181). The law of evidence is indelibly stamped as "the child of the jury system" (p. 266). In contrast, in nonjury proceedings judges have been and still are exempt from scrupulous subservience to jury trial evidence rules. The application of evidentiary rules of exclusion is relaxed when the capability of the trier is presumed.

Procedural Justice and Evidence Law

There is a unity of theme that underlies the corpus of evidence law. The rules are intended to increase the likelihood that adjudicative outcomes comport with the values of administrative efficiency, fairness, and reliable factfinding at trial. The values make up what might be called procedural justice. In our legal system, *how* a decision is rendered is as important as, and is inextricably tied to what the final disposition is. In different circumstances, each value may have a different priority, and one may sometimes be arrayed against the others. Speedy trials, for example, may promote cost-effective processing of cases but could work unfairness to certain litigants and enhance factfinding errors. Evidence rules may represent accommodations or compromises between these values. On the whole, evidence law—like other procedural law—is not merely a set of technical rules for managing the traffic of communication in court. It is more than a manual of trial etiquette. By controlling the process of proof, it provides the context for the application of the substantive law. The substantive law cannot be read except through the prism of procedure at trial.

Overview of the Chapter

The common law of evidence has been subject periodically to codification. The most recent and successful effort is found in the Federal Rules of Evidence (FRE), which became effective for all of the federal courts in 1975. Since then, the FRE have been adopted with some or no modifications by many states. In this chapter, the references to evidence law will be to the FRE. The specific issues chosen for discussion here—partly because there is empirical research that bears on them and partly because they implicate broader policy questions about the legal process—pertain to how the evidence is proffered (issue of order of presentation), what the evidence is (issues of admissibility and sufficiency), and the effect of the evidence on the jury after it has been filtered through the procedural rules (issues of the effectiveness and clarity of judicial instructions).

ORDER OF PRESENTATION OF EVIDENCE

Stages in the Presentation of Evidence

There are three principal stages in the sequence of proof-taking that are applicable generally to a civil or criminal trial. The first stage is the opening statement of the case. The party that bears the burden of proof—the side that has the responsibility of persuading the jury that the evidentiary proof proffered during the trial reaches the required level of probability: the plaintiff in a civil case, the prosecution in criminal case—has the first opportunity to outline its case to the trier of fact. (This exposition will focus on the criminal jury trial.) The prosecution begins with a general description of the facts of the case and a preview of the evidence that it will present later. There can be no argument on the merits of the case at this point. An attorney cannot attempt to persuade the jury to accept his version of the facts via the device of the opening statement.

After the prosecution completes its opening statement, the defense may also make a similar statement subject to the same constraints just noted, or defer it until after the prosecution has terminated the presentation of all of its evidence. In a criminal trial, the defense does not have the responsibility of proving innocence—that is presumed by law. Instead, it is the state that has the burden of proving guilt. For this reason, the defense may opt to waive its opening statement until after the prosecution has finished presenting its case. Such a deferral, however, seldom occurs in practice. By remaining silent at the outset of the trial, the defense allows the state to monopolize the opportunity to establish an initial rapport with the jury as well as its version of the facts of the case.

The second stage is the presentation of the cases-in-chief, first by the prosecution and then by the defense. The prosecution puts its case-in-chief (also called evidence-in-chief) by calling witnesses to testify, and by introducing real evidence (physical objects) and documentary evidence. The testimony is elicited by the prosecutor's questions on direct examination.

Any advantage the prosecution may have by presenting its evidence first is offset at least partially by the defense's right to cross-examine immediately after the direct examination of each witness is concluded. This right is part of the general right to confront one's accusers which is guaranteed by the Sixth and Fourteenth Amendments. The defense could elect not to cross-examine the state's witnesses; instead, it could call them later for examination during its case-in-chief. The more common practice is for prompt cross-examination to mitigate the impact of the direct testimony and to enable the defense to present its version of the facts before the prosecution completes its case-in-chief. It also permits the impeachment of the witness' credibility. So long as the direct and cross-examination of each witness is alternated, it is possible that neither party has a substantial advantage of position in the presentation of the cases-in-chief. After the defense's cross-examination of each witness, the prosecution can have another turn at bat if it wishes. It can conduct a re-direct for the purpose of bolstering or rehabilitating the witness before the jury; the defense, in turn, has the option of a re-cross.

The prosecution rests after presenting all of its evidence. By resting, the state says in effect that it has proved enough so that if the jury believes the evidence, it will render a guilty verdict. Now it is the defense's turn to present its case-in-chief, also denominated as evidence-in-defense or case-in-reply. It begins with an opening-statement, unless it was delivered at the first stage, and continues with direct examination on a witness-by-witness basis. These defense witnesses are then subjected to cross-examination by the prosecution and, again, there is the opportunity for re-direct and re-cross. After putting in its case, the defense rests.

The trial then proceeds to the third stage: the closing argument or summation. Up to this point, the communications to the jury have been mainly via witness testimony regarding evidence about the facts. Now, for the first time, the attorneys can address the jury directly for the purpose of persuasion. Commentary on the evidence rather than presentation of the evidence characterizes the summation.

Each side seeks to cast its case in the most favorable light possible. The presentation of evidence during the second stage is seldom done in a neat, orderly fashion: different witnesses testify at different times; the testimony is interrupted by objections, court rulings, recesses; the jury may forget evidence introduced at the beginning of a long trial. The summation enables the attorneys to organize and clarify the evidence for the jury, and to suggest reasonable inferences that could be drawn from it. They try to influence the jury to accept their respective version of the facts. They may point out extralegal factors to win the jury's sympathy (e.g., the defendant leaves behind a destitute family). The order of summation is prosecution-defense-prosecution; in some jurisdictions, the prosecution gives only one closing argument, after the defense completes its summation. The defense might try to anticipate some of the prosecution's summation arguments and rebut it in advance. The defense might also seek to remind the jury of its duties and the procedures of trial (e.g., that it is up to the state to prove guilt, rather than to the defendant to prove innocence). In a civil case, the defendant goes first and the plaintiff second. The plaintiff, then, has the right to have the first and the last word at a trial, a presumed advantage which is granted in order to compensate for shouldering the burden of proof.

Following the summation, the judge informs the jury as to the applicable law to the case at bar. (In some states, the court's instructions precede the attorneys' summation.) The instructions state the elements of the crime charged against the defendant, and the jury must find that the prosecution has presented evidence as to the each of these elements in order to return a conviction. The instructions also include general principles of the criminal law, such as the presumption of innocence, the standard of proof of beyond a reasonable doubt, and the importance of deciding solely on the basis of the evidence presented. In addition, the attorneys may submit to the judge proposed instructions on specific matters (e.g., cautionary instructions on the risks of eyewitness testimony). Finally, the jury retires to deliberate and render its verdict.

Gross Order and Internal Order of Presentation

Gross order refers to the overall order in which each side presents its respective case-in-chief. Internal order refers to the sequence in which evidence is presented by each side within its case-in-chief.

In a criminal trial, the prosecution traditionally proceeds first and the defense follows. The rationale for the gross order is related to the burden of proof. A plaintiff has to plead, produce evidence, and persuade the jury that more likely than not the defendant was negligent. If after examining the evidence the jury is in equipoise with respect to the ultimate issue of negligence (that is, it finds the evidence of each side equally persuasive), the plaintiff loses. The prosecution has to accuse, produce evidence, and persuade the jury beyond a reasonable doubt that the defendant is guilty. Again, failure to persuade at the requisite level results in loss for the prosecution. The party that shoulders the burden of proof bears the risk of nonpersuasion, but that same party is compensated by having the right to open and close the trial.

Each side can control the internal order of proof within its case-in-chief. The strongest or most important information may be presented last (climactic order) or at the outset (anticlimactic order). In a criminal case, the testimony of the defendant is usually one of the most important aspects of the defense. The Supreme Court has held that if a defendant opts to take the stand, he may choose to do so last, after all the other defense witnesses have testified (*Brooks v. Tennessee*, 1972). A defendant has the freedom to organize his internal sequence of proof so as to achieve maximum persuasive advantage of his own testimony.

A defendant can also control, at least in part, the gross order of trial by the prompt exercise of the right to confrontation. If he cross-examines a prosecution witness immediately after the witness's direct examination, he could nullify any "primacy" advantage of the prosecution. (If the first of two communications has a greater persuasive impact, it is known in the social psychological literature as a "primacy" effect. If the communication presented last is more influential, it is termed a "recency" effect.) Of course, if the defendant chooses to defer cross-examination until after the prosecution rests, any primacy effect from gross order remains intact.

Research on Order Effects

The effects of order in persuasive communications were the subject of extensive experimental study during the mid-1950s and early 1960s. On balance, the research yielded "no simple answer." "Sometimes primacy is found to operate, sometimes recency" (Saks & Hastie, 1978, p. 106). Interest in this area waned, but it was revived in the 1970s by the collaborative research of a lawyer, a social psychologist, and their associates, examining the effects of presentation order in the courtroom (Walker, Thibaut, & Andreoli, 1972). They recognized that the results from the earlier laboratory experiments could not be extrapolated directly to the courtroom because a trial consists of procedural and evidentiary features that are not duplicated in the typical social influence experiment. Their research, which sought a faithful although stylized representation of legal factfinding, showed a persuasive recency effect and a climactic effect for the prosecution. A subsequent study with "a more realistic simulation" found primacy effects (Pennington, 1982, p. 320). None of the foregoing simulations, however, included instructions on the burden of proof. This is a critical omission because, as noted earlier, the allocation of the burden is thought to neutralize the presumed advantages of order. To reconcile the discrepant results, the conditions under which a particular gross order or internal order are obtained remain to be specified.

ADMISSIBILITY OF EVIDENCE

The Basic Policy and Principle of Evidence Law

The basic policy of evidence law is to admit all evidence that would aid the truth-seeking function of a trial, unless there are valid reasons to exclude it. "The distinct tendency of the Federal Rules of Evidence is to admit rather than exclude" (Weinstein & Berger, 1976, pp. 105-110). The rationale is that anything that throws light on a controversy should be considered by the jury, subject to the judge's discretion to set reasonable bounds. This policy manifests a trust in the intelligence of the jury to reach a correct decision when all the facts are presented.

However, not all evidence can or should be admitted. The law of evidence consists primarily of exclusionary rules that determine admissibility. The principle that underlies the complex mosaic of exclusionary rules is evidentiary relevance. Only relevant evidence is admissible (FRE 402). Relevance refers to the probative value of evidence—whether there is a logical relationship between the evidence presented and the facts sought to be proven at the trial (FRE 401).

The trial judge determines relevance according to a balancing test: "Although relevant, evidence may be excluded if its probative value is substantially outweighed by the danger of unfair prejudice, confusion of the issues, or misleading the jury, or by considerations of undue delay, waste of time, or needless presentation of cumulative evidence" (FRE 403). At his discretion, the judge weights the probative value or relevance of the evidence against the probative dangers.

The notion of relevance needs to be distinguished from that of sufficiency. The two concepts reflect the division of labor between jury and judge. The jury decides the ultimate issue of the sufficiency or weight of the evidence—was enough evidence presented to satisfy the burden of persuasion? The judge decides the initial issue of relevance—does the particular evidence tend to establish or disprove the disputed factual matter for which it was offered? If it does not, the jury is not allowed to consider this evidence. If its relevance is disputable, judges usually let it in "for what it's worth" and let the jury decide.

As a result of dealing with countless factual circumstances involving relevancy, the courts over the years have formulated rules that standardize and thereby dispense with ad hoc balancing of probative value against prejudice. When similar situations arise repeatedly and the same decision is rendered in each case, the decisions eventually become hardened into rules to guide future instances.

The "Other Crimes Evidence" Rule

There is a large group of exclusionary rules that fall under the rubric of rules of relevancy. One such rule is the "other crimes evidence" rule: "Evidence of other crimes, wrongs, or acts is not admissible to prove the character of a person in order to show that he acted in conformity therewith" (FRE 404[b]). Thus, a defendant's past criminal record cannot be introduced in the prosection's case-in-chief to show his likelihood of committing the crime charged. A number of policy reasons underlie this rule.

One is the fear that a jury might overestimate the predictive relationship between past criminality and present conduct. As a general proposition there might be a relationship between these two factors, but it is hazardous to forecast propensity to crime in any particular instance. A second reason is the risk that a jury might be tempted to convict a defendant because he is an incorrigible offender, deserving of punishment. If a jury knows he is a "bad" person, it might not sympathize as much with him as with one without a record of past misdeeds, and therefore adjudge him by a lower standard of proof. Finally, there is the normative consideration, related to the presumption of innocence, that a defendant should be protected from inculpation by proof of former wrongdoings. It seems unfair to saddle a person forever with the record of the past, especially if one subsequently leads a blameless life.

As with nearly all legal rules, there are exceptions. One exception is to admit evidence of other crimes for the limited purpose of impeaching a defendant's credibility if he chooses to take the stand (FRE 404[a][3]). A defendant with a criminal record faces the dilemma of whether or not to testify. If he exercises his Fifth Amendment privilege, the jury will probably take into account his silence and draw adverse inferences from it, despite the fact that the prosecution and the judge are forbidden to comment on his silence and despite cautionary instructions by the judge to avoid drawing such inferences. However, if he waives his constitutional privilege, the prosecution is allowed to cross-examine the defendant and expose his prior record in order to impeach his trustworthiness. The risk to the defendant is that the jury, upon hearing the other crimes evidence, may use it for the unauthorized purpose of guilt determination. The judicial safeguard is the limiting instruction (FRE 105). If the defendant takes the stand, the court protects his interest by instructing the jury—upon request of the defendant—to consider it only for the authorized purpose.

Research on the Effectiveness
of Limiting Instructions

A fundamental premise of the limiting instruction would appear to be that jurors are able and willing to compartmentalize the evidence as directed. Common experience, however, suggests that this kind of mental process is less easily achieved than is assumed. One of the paradoxes of evidence law is that instructions are given despite the recognition by the legal community itself of their possible futility. Justice Jackson noted that "The naive assumption that prejudicial effects can be overcome by instructions to the jury . . . all practicing lawyers know to be unmitigated fiction" (*Krulewitch v. United States*, 1949, p. 453).

Social psychologists have put to the test the validity of these criticisms. The conflicting results from the different studies caution against drawing conclusions without an appreciation of the policies behind legal rules. In the typical experimental design, mock jurors listen to a taped criminal trial. Half of them are informed about the defendant's past record and half of them are not. A judge delivers limiting instructions to the first group. Several studies have found the instructions "futile." More convictions are rendered when the prior record is introduced than when it is not, regardless of the limiting instructions (Hans & Doob, 1976, p. 253). On this basis, some researchers have proposed a blanket exclusion on the admissibility of prior criminality. Others conclude that "the disturbing implication [of these studies is] that jurors will typically ignore or misunderstand instructions from the bench," and that in the area of evidence, "once again legal practice and scientific psychology are in conflict" (Saks &

Hastie, 1978, pp. 39, 63). However, there are other experiments that show the opposite result: Mock jurors who are given the limiting instruction render fewer convictions than those not so instructed. In a theft trial, 57 percent of mock jurors gave guilty judgments when a record of convictions (for crimes similar to the charge) was introduced without any instructions, compared to 35 percent guilty judgments when the same record was introduced with judicial instructions and to 27 percent guilty judgments in a control group not exposed to the prior record. The study concluded that mock jurors "do take account of a judicial instruction to disregard [past] convictions" (Cornish & Sealy, 1973, p. 222). Because of these "conflicting results," the effectiveness of these instructions is deemed "uncertain" (Davis, Bray & Holt, 1977, p. 337).

The evaluation of judicial instructions cannot be made solely on empirical grounds—on whether or not they have an impact on the jury. Apart from the issue of effectiveness, there are policy considerations that argue for the use or nonuse of these instructions.

Justice Jackson observed that evidence law appears "paradoxical and full of compromises" because it seeks to maintain a "balance between adverse interests" (*Michelson v. United States,* 1948, p. 486). Instructions can be seen as an attempt to balance competing interests in reliable factfinding and social values extrinsic to the truth function of trial. If the prosecution is allowed to introduce the prior record as part of its case-in-chief, there is the possibility of prejudicial impact on the jury. However, we know that many offenders are recidivists and that, as an actuarial matter, there is a high correlation between past and present conduct. To the extent that accurate factfinding is an important objective, evidence of prior crimes should be allowed as one of the pieces of information for the factfinder to consider. In European civil law countries, other crimes evidence is admissible to show a defendant's bad character or propensity to commit the crime charged.

What our law of evidence does, then, is to compromise between the extremes of unlimited admission and blanket exclusion. It strikes the balance between probative value and prejudice or unfairness by allowing the evidence for an intermediate purpose (to impeach credibility) but not the ultimate purpose (to establish guilt). The limiting instruction is a device by which the law lets the jury make the judgment. The jury can interject its notion of popular justice in the decision-making process. Under its power of nullification, it can bend the facts and thwart the law's commands in order to reach what it considers a right result.

As it turns out, the available data support the view that the limiting instruction helps to preserve this procedural equilibrium. The results are not really "conflicting." The study by Hans and Doob (1976) and the one by Cornish and Sealy (1973), when put together, show that admitting evidence of prior record is indeed a *via media* between unlimited admission and blanket exclusion. Conviction rates are highest under unlimited admission, lowest under complete exclusion, and in-between under limited admission. The question of the effectiveness of these instructions, then, depends on the comparisons that are made. Instructions on limitation are effective (in the sense of reducing guilty verdicts) when compared to the admission of the evidence without any instructions. They are obviously not effective or are less effective, however, when compared to the exclusion of the evidence. And this, perhaps, is precisely the Solomonic compromise that the instructions were intended to effectuate.

SUFFICIENCY OF EVIDENCE

The procedural and evidentiary rules that govern the trial process are intertwined. *How* proof is introduced at trial—namely, the gross order of presentation of evidence—is related to *how much* proof is needed to prevail. The sufficiency of the proffered evidence refers to the threshold of proof required by law.

Burden of Production and Burden of Persuasion

The burden of proof, although stated in the singular, entails two distinct and interrelated obligations: the burden of production and the burden of persuasion.

The first, known also as the burden of going forward with the evidence, is the responsibility of a party to produce enough evidence to satisfy a judge that the case is worthy of consideration by the jury. This burden is allocated initially to the party who pleads the existence of the disputed fact, normally the plaintiff or the prosecution. Its purpose is to ensure that juries are precluded from rendering verdicts in cases not grounded in evidence. It allows the judge rather than the jury to decide the case if the plaintiff or the prosecution fails to come forward with enough evidence to have a trial. Once enough evidence is produced, the second burden comes into operation. The plaintiff or the prosecution must persuade the factfinder that the evidence tendered reaches the required level of sufficiency.

Standard of Proof in Criminal Cases

The highest standard of proof in law—"beyond a reasonable doubt"—is constitutionally required for criminal conviction. By setting this threshold of persuasion, the law deliberately ensures that any error in the verdict is unidirectional, against the state. The premise is that type 1 errors (false positives) are less tolerable than type 2 errors (false negatives). The policy of the law is that it is better to risk letting the guilty go free than to risk convicting the innocent.

However, the law does not go so far as to require absolute certainty in the correctness of the verdict. One reason for the less than unequivocal measure of persuasion is that, in a trial, a decision must be rendered within the limits of the evidence adduced and within some reasonable time frame. In scientific factfinding, researchers can defer reaching conclusions while they gather more and more information until they reach the level of reliability generally accepted in the scientific community. In adjudication, however, to postpone a verdict until the evidentiary gaps are filled and all doubt is erased in the mind of the factfinder is both impractical and undesirable. A final authoritative judgment has to be rendered to settle the dispute, even if some uncertainty remains.

In other words, the law compromises the truth-finding function of trial. Reliability is one of the main values of procedural justice, but in practice something less than perfect reliability in factfinding is tolerated. Otherwise, social disputes might never get settled by the adjudicative process. This compromise is articulated in the formula for the standard of proof. The explication of this standard to the jury has been a perennial concern. It is an old maxim that all definitions are dangerous, and that definitions often need more explanation than the terms they explain. There have been literally hundreds of definitional attempts by the courts over the years. Some gild the lily in defining it; other simply declare that it needs no definition beyond what the words themselves imply (McCormick, 1972, sec. 339).

Standard of Proof in Civil Cases

The deprivation of property by civil liability infringes upon a less protected interest than the loss of life or liberty by criminal sanction. Consequently, a lower threshold of proof is expected in civil cases: Proof "by a preponderance of the evidence," sometimes phrased in terms of "more likely than not"—proof that leads a factfinder to find the existence of the disputed fact is more likely than its nonexistence.

Whereas the criminal standard is stated according to the amount of doubt in the mind of the factfinder, the civil standard focuses on the likelihood of the evidence. This likelihood is said to correspond to a subjective certainty of more than .50. If after evaluating all of the evidence the jury finds it split evenly, the plaintiff loses. By allocating the burden of persuasion to the plaintiff, a "tie" verdict is avoided. In practice, jurors and judges appear to translate the standard into a higher probability estimate. Surveys by Simon and Mahan (1971) show that jurors interpret it as .75, and judges as .55. The definition of "preponderance" has been a subject of extensive judicial ponderment. Some courts define it objectively as a determination of the balance of probabilities. Other courts deem the preponderance standard to be one of "common knowledge" and therefore in no need of explication (McCormick, 1972, sec. 339).

Research on the Comprehensibility of Instructions

If laypersons are to determine liability according to the applicable legal principles, those principles should be understandable to them. In some jurisdictions, trial judges write their own instructions to the jury, often selected from or based upon the proposed draft submitted by one or the other side in the case. In other jurisdictions, they rely on "pattern" or standardized instructions prepared by a blue-ribbon panel of judges, attorneys, and law professors. In both instances, these instructions "are often so archaic and unrealistic that . . . what the jurors hear is little more than legal mumbo jumbo to them" (Schwarzer, 1981, p. 782). This may appear puzzling in a profession whose members take pride in being wordsmiths.

The rationale for jury instructions sheds some light on why their lexical obscurity has long been regarded with equanimity by the bar and bench. Instructions are not merely a dispassionate exposition on what the law is. As indicated earlier, in the aftermath of *Bushell's Case* (1670) instructions became one of the principal means of limiting and guiding the jury's discretion—instructions served simultaneously to inform jurors (overtly) and to control jurors (covertly). Also, it is through a litigant's claim of error in the instructions that an appellate court is able to intervene and impose controls on both the trial judge's discretion and the jury's discretion. Instructions that are willfully ambiguous and periphrastic offer counsel a procedural peg on which to hang an appeal.

Recently, psychologists have begun to assess the comprehensibility of pattern instructions and rewrite them according to psycholinguistic principles. For example, in a series of experiments that represent the state-of-the-art in jury simulations, Severance and Loftus (1982) examined the ability of mock jurors to comprehend and apply pattern instructions (regarding inter alia reasonable doubt and the limited admissibility of evidence of prior convictions) and their revised counterparts. The pattern instruction on the standard of proof was as follows: "A reasonable doubt is one for which a reason exists. A reasonable doubt is such a doubt as would exist in the mind of a reasonable person after fully, fairly, and carefully considering all of the evidence or lack of evidence." The revised instruction read "A reasonable doubt about guilt is not a vague or speculative doubt but is a doubt for which a reason exists. A reasonable doubt is a doubt that would exist in the mind of a reasonable person after that person has fully, fairly, and carefully considered all of the evidence or lack of evidence." The revised version also added this new sentence: "If you are not satisfied beyond doubt that all elements of the charge have been proved, then you must find the defendant not guilty."

The studies found, as might be expected, fewer comprehension errors with the revised instructions. They also found significantly fewer guilty verdicts with the revised form. The authors suggest that increased understanding of the law "enhance[s] a just determination of guilty or not guilty." However, there is no inherent reason why psycholinguistic improvements in pattern instructions should reduce convictions. Also, it is not clear why this result is necessarily more "just." (Prosecutors typically do not go to trial unless they believe the defendant is actually guilty). It is possible that the revised version has a pro-defense bias. There was no independent assessment of the ideological tilt, if any, of the instructions. One might also speculate that the revision broadened the jurors' perceived scope of discretion in decisionmaking; in effect, it enhanced their power of nullification.

The thematic point to be made here is that the writing (or rewriting) of instructions is not simply a technical task. It is also a political process that implicates (unarticulated) normative choices under the guise of correctly stating the law. It is not by chance that committees responsible for drafting pattern instructions are composed of members who represent a spectrum of views. If improved clarity reduces conviction rates, the interests served are those of criminal defendants, not those of law enforcement and society generally. Assuming that the clarity can be calibrated, the determination of the degree of comprehensibility with which an instruction is drafted is an issue of policy rather than of science. Indeed, if clarity were the preeminent value, jurors could be informed by means of comprehensive lectures by judges (before and/or after the presentation of the evidence, together with an opportunity to ask questions) in lieu of brief instructions. The present system of instructions can be seen as the product of a series of practical, Solomonic accommodations between clarity versus ambiguity, judicial authority versus jury discretion, and uniform rules versus individualized justice. Rendering the instructions more understandable would upset the equilibrium.

Research on Quantification of Evidence and of Standards of Proof

Proof involves drawing inferences from the evidence. Since no conclusion can be drawn from facts without some step of inductive inference, all factual evidence is ultimately statistical and all proof is ultimately probabilistic. Lawyers have long been inclined to quantify the probability notions that lie inchoate behind legal evidence and the formulae of proof. It is hard to resist the lure of making factfinding more objective and precise by attaching numerical values to qualitative information.

Quantification has typically consisted of informal, homespun statistics, presented at the summation stage of the trial. In recent years, there have been more formal efforts to quantify the probative force of identification evidence and the measure of persuasion itself. In particular, Bayesian statistics has been proposed to aid the jury's factfinding. Based on the computation of conditional probabilities, it describes how subsequent probabilistic evidence (e.g., expert testimony that the odds that a palm print found on the murder weapon is similar to defendant's print is 1 in 1000) would alter a rational juror's initial, subjective estimate of guilt (say, .10) relying on other, qualitative evidence. (Applying Bayes's Theorem, the likelihood of guilt, given the palm print evidence, is .99, a drastic increase from the initial low estimate of .10; Finkelstein & Fairley, 1970). At trial, an expert would show the jury how to calculate the odds of the defendant's culpability, given probabilistic evidence (such as the palm print) linking the defendant to the crime.

Quantification of the probative evidence invites, directly or indirectly, quantification of the standard of proof. In fields as diverse as physics, genetics, insurance, economics, and gambling, it is well known that formal probability calculations provide more accurate predictions of outcomes than do intuitive reasoning about probabilistic information. Since all evidence is ultimately probabilistic, jurors also make probabilistic judgments although not in numerical terms. Whether the laws of probability are superior to unguided intuition in the courtroom setting is, in part, an empirical issue. Some social psychologists, relying on human information processing studies (which purportedly show that "people systematically violate the principles of rational decisionmaking when judging probabilities"), argue that the introduction of statistical models at trial is simply a matter of improving "decisionmaking technology" (Saks & Kidd, 1980-1981, pp. 131, 148).

Critics of trial by mathematics say there is something special about adjudicatory proof that makes probability calculus inapposite. Tribe (1971) argues that the appearance of precision that numbers convey may undermine the expressive purposes of trial. Beyond a reasonable doubt implies a subjective state of certitude. To permit the state to adjudge guilt without that requisite certainty would undercut public confidence in the criminal law. Declaring in advance the acceptable rate of false positives (.01 in the foregoing example) dehumanizes justice and diminishes respect for the individual. There is an ethical difference between unintended and officially tolerated wrongful convictions. In short, it may be the better part of wisdom to leave some matters unspoken.

There is another value in obscurity. The perceived legitimacy of adjudication depends in part on its authoritative finality. There needs to be closure in the settlement of disputes. Trial by ordeal may not have produced accurate results, but because of its "Judgment Day" quality, the outcome was respected by the medieval populace. Authoritative resolution may be more important than the ascertainment of truth, especially when the facts are uncertain. So long as the standard of proof is left ambiguous, the public can assume that it shares with the jury— which is supposedly representative of the community—common conceptions of the quantum of evidence needed to impose blame and punishment. The secrecy that surrounds jury deliberations fosters this assumption. Once the standard is quantified, others can question the verdict if they have a higher or lower subjective threshold of proof and the finality of adjudication is lost (Nesson, 1979).

It is beyond the scope of this overview to wade deeper into the debate on whether the laws of probability should be suspended in the courtroom. The conceptual point here is that the adoption of this "decisionmaking technology" takes on the characteristics of a value choice. In the pursuit of precision, there may be unintended or undisclosed purposes. Certain values are sacrificed when society permits sanctions to be imposed based upon statistical judgments, even when the figures are exceedingly accurate. The opposing contentions on the issue of the quantification of legal proof, as on the issue of the rewriting of jury instructions, engage thought on the nature and purposes of a trial.

METHODS OF PROOF

Inquisitorial and Adversarial Method

The law of evidence cannot be discussed *in vacuo.* An analysis of the rules that govern proof-taking at trial needs to take into account their original rationale—namely, to shelter the jury from misleading evidence—and also the nature of the method of proof itself—that is, an adversarial style of developing the evidence in court. If the origins of the Anglo-American law of evidence are found in the jury trial, its contours are shaped by the contested trial. In Western civilization, the quest for rational methods of adjudication has taken two forms: an inquisitorial approach in which the evidence is developed principally by the judge uninhibited by rules of evidence, and an adversarial approach in which the parties control the production of evidence and the judge is a neutral umpire who determines the admissibility of the evidence and instructs the jury in the applicable law. A key feature that distinguishes the two methods of factfinding are the evidentiary rules of exclusion. The choice of factfinder and assumptions about the factfinder's competence give rise to the need for these rules.

The inquisitorial method of factfinding grew out of the ecclesiastical courts. In the canon system of justice judges directed the gathering of evidence and were the sole arbiters. In modern continental procedure, the French criminal process is an archetype of the inquisitorial model. The central figures are the investigating magistrate (*juge d'instruction*) and the presiding judge at trial. The magistrate takes over the investigation of the case from the moment the arrest is made or the charge(s) filed. He gathers—unbounded by evidentiary restrictions—all probative evidence in a dossier that is sent to trial.

The trial itself is essentially a public recapitulation of the dossier. The judge, like the magistrate in the investigation phase, dominates the proceedings. Informed by the dossier, he interrogates the defendant and any other witnesses. There are no separate witnesses for the prosecution or the defense. Judicial interrogation is usually more like an informal conversation rather than a relentless cross-examination. Witnesses are asked to give a narrative account uninterrupted by questions or the invocation of exclusionary rules. The goal is to reconstruct the event in question. Afterward, the parties are allowed to question the witnesses in order to fill in the gaps or emphasize certain features of the testimony. Upon completion of the proof-taking, the parties offer summations of the facts and legal arguments.

In contrast to the active role of the continental judge in amassing and adjudicating the facts, the common law judge lets the parties control the investigation and development of the evidence. The paradigm of the adversary method is the keenly contested trial in which each party calls its own witnesses and seeks to present information favorable to its side. Factfinding unfolds by the rival use of witnesses. It is an article of faith among Anglo-American lawyers that "cross-examination is the greatest legal engine ever invented for the discovery of truth" (Wigmore, 1940, Vol. 5, p. 29). The judge, not having been exposed to a dossier, lacks the background information needed to participate directly in the adjudication. His role is limited to refereeing the contest by deciding what evidence should or should not be admissible. The trier, then, hears two alternating, one-sided presentations filtered through the sieve of evidentiary rules.

The foregoing are idealized portrayals of the two approaches. There are no purely inquisitorial or purely adversarial systems. It would not be realistic to ignore the inquisitorial elements in the American system. For example, American judges sometimes assume a proactive stance that belies the reactive umpire image. By the application of exclusionary rules and instructions on the law, they can influence the proceedings and restrain the jury. Conversely, continental processes do not faithfully conform to the inquisitorial model. At trial, attorneys sometimes play a more substantial role in the production of evidence than inquisitorial norms suggest. Despite the overlap between these two methods of proof in their day-to-day operations, epistemologically there are still clear differences in their central tendencies.

One implication of these procedural differences is the effect on the impartiality of the judge. The continental judge learns about the case from the dossier, which could lead him to form tentative pre-conceptions before the trial. Instead of discovering or reconstructing what happened, he may set out to confirm his a priori hypotheses. The Anglo-American judge would be disqualified if he had comparable prior knowledge. By leaving the production of evidence to the dialectics of partisan inquiry, he avoids the pitfalls of premature judgment.

Research on Methods of Proof

Debate over the relative merits of the Continental and the Anglo-American styles of proof-taking has raged for over a century. The arguments have been mostly speculative, resting on informed impressions and intuitive insights. In the 1970s, the social psychologist-lawyer team of Thibaut and Walker (1975) began "the first systematic attempt" to "define and clarify the nature of procedural justice through the applications of social psychological methods" (p. vii). In the epistemology of legal procedure, they have provided an empirical pied-à-terre. Several of their experiments purport to show that the sporting model of the adversarial process is "clearly superior" in terms of counteracting judicial bias, the satisfaction of the defendant with the trial outcome, and the perceived fairness of the proceedings.

Although innovative and imaginative, their research has not been immune to sharp criticism for its methodological and conceptual flaws. Subsequent experiments "contradict" their central assertion that the adversarial model is the preferred dispute resolution procedure (Austin, Williams, Worchel, Wentzel, & Siegel, 1981, p. 281). Even if there are differences in the factfinding effectiveness of the two methods, it cannot be said necessarily that one is "superior" to the other. Each method is embedded in a unique institutional context. The adversary approach is part of the larger common law tradition of individualized justice, case-by-case adjudication, and malleable decisional precedents. The inquisitorial mode is indistinguishable from the civil law tradition of standardized justice, uniform adjudication, and decisional standards based on precise, codified rules. It would seem only natural that these different systems of law should give rise to different methods of proof. Perhaps the more relevant issue for social research is not the comparative merits of the two methods but rather how each method can be improved in order to serve the interests of justice of its respective legal system.

SOME IMPLICATIONS FOR
PSYCHOLOGICAL RESEARCH

The leitmotif of this overview of the law of evidence and procedure is that legal proof, unlike scientific proof, is not merely an untrammeled cognitive exercise of determining what "is." It is also a judgmental process of determining what "ought" to be. The main purpose of the legal process is peaceful resolution of a dispute rather than the acquisition of information. Hence, more than truth-finding is at stake in a trial. In our adjudicatory system, reliability in determining the facts is an important, but not the only, ideal. The power of the jury to thwart the law and bend the facts in order to inject its notions of community morality is an example of the conscious sacrifice of truth to other values. Science makes no such concessions to competing considerations.

The commingling of the factual and normative aspects of legal factfinding has implications for psycholegal research. One implication is that because law has multiple and often conflicting ends, its operation cannot be tidily measured against any single ostensible purpose. There are multiple criteria for assessment. Thus, studies that question the effectiveness of limiting instructions are predicated on the assumption that fairness is the chief goal of trial. However, other ends are also served by the limited admission of a defendant's prior criminal record, such as the reliability of the guilt-determination process. Depending upon the criterion chosen, the efficacy of this legal practice can escape factual impeachment. The multidimensional nature of law should caution against too simplistic an approach to empirical evaluation.

A second and related implication is that psycholegal research is a good example of how values intrude in scientific inquiry. The days of any serious claim to a value-free social science are behind us. There is no immaculate conception of facts. All inquiry is selective; some facts are attended to and others are neglected. Empirical knowledge of the social order is interwoven with the beliefs and values one holds. A central teaching of the sociology of knowledge is that truth is not found in facts themselves, but in the way they are organized in relation to some interpretive scheme. In legal areas, issues of fact and issues of policy are separated by only a permeable membrane, and empirical researchers need to be attentive to their own ideological allegiances. Judge Bazelon (1982), an otherwise staunch proponent of applying social science to the law, has complained that "the main problem" with psychologists and other experts who recommend legal policy is that "they often do not expose the values underlying their choice of facts" and "often operate with hidden agendas" (p. 115). For example, efforts to redraft jury instructions could achieve the result—whether intended or not—of increasing the acquittals of criminal defendants. Research on eyewitness identifications is almost exclusively and obsessively preoccupied with the conditions of their unreliability, even though it is recognized that they are reliable under some conditions. In expert testimony, psychologists profess merely to "inform" the jury about scientific knowledge regarding the purported inaccuracy of eyewitnesses in general, but surely no one is so disingenuous as to believe that the scientific presentation is not an indirect means of casting doubt on the prosecution witness's testimony. Not surprisingly, surveys show that most attorneys see the expert testimony as "solely aimed at the acquittal of suspects" (Brigham, 1980, p. 318).

More generally, the psychology of trial evidence and procedure is consistent with the long-standing association between social science and liberal social-political values. The profession tends to attract those who are more interested in shaping the future than in preserving the past. Thus, teaching and research tends to focus on the "psychology of social change," not on the "psychology of the status quo." In areas of substantive law, too, psychologists have conducted research and offered expert testimony to challenge existing practices rather than to sustain them. School desegregation is an example in point. Some pro-integration psychologists, clad in sackcloth, have now conceded that they were "blinded by our ideology" at the time of the school desegregation cases in 1954, and that "A good deal of damage has been done by recommendations . . . based not on hard data but mostly on well-meaning rhetoric" (Gerard, 1983, p. 183).

Pro-criminal defense and liberal reform values color, expressly or surreptitiously, much of the psychological research on law. Unless there is greater self-awareness and disclosure of these values, researchers risk setting out to confirm what they already believe. Such openness may not always be feasible. Some researchers may not be conscious of the ideological scheme in which they operate, any more than fish are aware of the medium in which they swim. The adversary process can help expose these normative assumptions. This process, which Justice Holmes described as a miniature marketplace of ideas, ensures that opposing views are raised. It provides an institutional check on experts who might foist their preferences on policy in the guise of scientific expertise. Rivlin's (1973) idea of "forensic social science," wherein opposing scholars take on the task of marshalling evidence for one or the other side or a policy position, embraces an adversarial approach to social factfinding. Confrontation makes affirmative use of the inevitable bias of experts by exposing the subterranean premises of each side. Psychological research on the trial process should, itself, be subjected to the adversarial process.

A final implication is that the familiar plea for more and better empirical research will not necessarily lead to improved policy recommendations. Indeed, to the extent that evidentiary rules and procedures reflect moral choices and compromises, they need not be grounded on scientific proof. Data cannot resolve moral dilemmas, unless the "ought" capitulates to the "is." This is not to say, however, that empirical research does not have a role in shaping the law. Even normative conclusions are generated by an awareness of the facts. Psychological research can illuminate the different factual predicates of legal rules, thereby engaging thought on the adequacy of the law's preconceptions. Its role in policy is oblique rather than direct, heuristic rather than determinative. It cannot displace the normative judgments that are inherent in the law, but it can help make the law better informed. To paraphrase Thorstein Veblen, the outcome of psycho-legal research should be to provoke a second question where only one question was raised before.

NOTE

1. Here and throughout this chapter the masculine pronoun is used in a generic rather than literal sense unless the context indicates otherwise.

REFERENCES

Austin, W., Williams, T., Worchel, S., Wentzel, A., & Siegel, D. (1981). Effect of mode of adjudication, presence of defense counsel, and favorability of verdict on observers' evaluation of a criminal trial. *Journal of Applied Social Psychology, 11*, 281-300.

Bazelon, D. (1982). Veils, values, and social responsibility. *American Psychologist, 37*, 115-121.

Brigham, J. C. (1980). Perspectives on the impact of lineup composition, race, and witness confidence on identification accuracy. *Law and Human Behavior, 4*, 315-322.

Brooks v. Tennessee, 406 U.S. 605 (1972).

Bushell's Case, 124 Eng. Rep. 1006 (1670).

Cleary, E. W. (1952). Evidence as a problem in communicating. *Vanderbilt Law Review, 5*, 277-295.

Cornish, W. R., & Sealy, A. P. (1973). Juries and rules of evidence. *Criminal Law Review, 17*, 208-228.

Davis, J., Bray, R., & Holt, R. (1977). The empirical study of decision processes in juries: A critical review. In J. Tapp & F. Levine (Eds.), *Law, justice, and the individual in society*. New York: Holt, Rinehart & Winston.

Finkelstein, M. O., & Fairley, W. B. (1970). A Baysian approach to identification evidence. *Harvard Law Review, 83*, 489-517.

Gerard, H. (1983). School desegregation: The social science role. *American Psychologist, 38*, 869-877.

Hans, V. P., & Doob, A. N. (1976). Section 12 of the Canada Evidence Act and the deliberations of simulated jurors. *Criminal Law Quarterly, 18*, 235-253.

Krulewitch v. United States, 336 U.S. 440 (1949).

Loh, W. D. (1984). *Social research in the judicial process*. New York: Russell Sage Foundation.

McCormick, C. T. (1972). *McCormick on evidence* (2nd ed.). St. Paul, MN: West Publishing Co.

Michelson v. United States (1948). 335 U.S. 469.

Nesson, C. R. (1979). Reasonable doubt and permissive inferences: The value of complexity. *Harvard Law Review, 92*, 1187-1225.

Pennington, D. C. (1982). Witnesses and their testimony: Effects of ordering on juror verdicts. *Journal of Applied Social Psychology, 12*, 318-333.

Rivlin, A. M. (1973). Forensic social science. *Harvard Educational Review, 43*, 61-75.

Saks, M. J., & Hastie, R. (1978). *Social psychology in court*. New York: Van Nostrand Reinhold.

Saks, M. J., & Kidd, R. F. (1980-1981). Human information processing and adjudication: Trial by heuristics. *Law and Society Review, 15*, 123-160.

Schwarzer, W. W. (1981). Communicating with juries: Problems and remedies. *California Law Review, 69*, 731-769.

Severance, L., & Loftus, E. (1982). Improving the ability of jurors to comprehend and apply criminal jury instructions. *Law and Society Review, 17*, 153-197.

Simon, R., & Mahan, L. (1971). Quantifying burdens of proof. *Law and Society Review, 5*, 319-330.

Thayer, J. (1898). *A preliminary treatise on evidence at the common law*. Boston: Little, Brown.

Thibaut, J., & Walker, L. (1975). *Procedural justice: a psychological analysis*. Hillsdale, NJ: Lawrence J. Erlbaum.

Tribe, L. H. (1971). Trial by mathematics: Precision and ritual in the legal process. *Harvard Law Review, 84*, 1329-1393.

Walker, L., Thibaut, J., & Andreoli, V. (1972). Order of presentation at trial. *Yale Law Journal, 82*, 216-226.

Weinstein, J. B., & Berger, M. A. (1976). *Weinstein's evidence*. New York: Matthew Bender.

Wigmore, J. H. (1935). *A students' textbook on the law of evidence*. Brooklyn, NY: The Foundation Press, Inc.

Wigmore, J. H. (1940). *Wigmore on evidence* (3d ed.). Boston: Little, Brown.

PART **II**

EVIDENCE

CHAPTER 2

The Eyewitness

GARY L. WELLS

Several years ago a colleague asked me why I, a social psychologist, was doing research on eyewitness testimony. After all, he argued, it is experimental psychologists who are specialists in memory and they have been studying memory for nearly a century. Indeed, my colleague's observation was correct, but his argument contained an implicit false premise. He assumed that the important aspects of eyewitness testimony are merely functions of memory. In fact, however, much more is involved. Attitudes influence perception; social pressure influences what and how much people will report; beliefs people hold about memory determine how they will evaluate eyewitness evidence; verbal and nonverbal styles of testimony influence the credibility attributed to the eyewitness, and so on. Principles of memory are important in understanding eyewitness testimony, but to equate the psychology of eyewitness testimony with memory is to misconstrue the problem and overlook some of the most interesting phenomena, including the attitudes and beliefs that the potential juror holds about eyewitnesses. These are some of the things that will be discussed in this chapter.

This chapter is divided into five sections. The first two, which are brief, describe the nature of the problem and some of the legal background. The next section reviews research relating to eyewitness accuracy. How reliable are eyewitnesses? Obviously this is a complex question that can only be answered by reviewing the major variables that have been shown to affect eyewitness accuracy. The fourth section addresses the question of how adequately people can evaluate eyewitness testimony. The main concern in this section is to what extent the credibility that jurors attribute to witnesses is related to the accuracy of witnesses. The final section deals with practical perspectives and discusses two approaches to aiding the justice system in dealing with the eyewitness problem.

NATURE OF THE "EYEWITNESS PROBLEM"

Maurice Lovejoy, of Topeka, Kansas, served three months in jail on felony charges because an eyewitness identified him from a photo spread. Another man's confession eventually proved Lovejoy's innocence. For nearly two years Keith Carl, of Parsons, Kansas, cried out from a jail cell that he was innocent. Carl was imprisoned after a teenage girl testified that she was an eyewitness to an armed robbery and identified Carl as the perpetrator. Carl was released when another man confessed and provided definitive evidence that Carl was innocent. Lenell Geter, of Greenville, Texas, served 16 months in prison on the basis of five eyewitnesses' "positive" identifications of Geter and their attendant in-court testimony that he was the one who robbed a fried chicken restaurant. Although nine alibi witnesses, the NAACP, and extensive national media attention managed to get Geter a new trial, it was not until four of the five eyewitnesses identified a different person (from a photo array that did not include Geter's photo) that the prosecutor dropped charges against Geter.

A complete list of mistaken identifications is impossible to construct. Known cases of mistaken identification are likely to underestimate considerably the rate of misidentification because it is an unusual set of circumstances that fully exonerate someone who has been mistakenly identified. In addition, mistaken identifications that become known errors often do not result in false conviction, but the lives of the accused may be ruined nonetheless (e.g., see the cases of Father Pagano, in Ellison and Buckhout, 1981; Robert Dillen in Wells & Loftus, 1984). As will be discussed later, experiments show that false identifications often are associated with a great deal of confidence. Consider the case of Erwin Taylor, an Edmonton man who was murdered in 1982 by Claude Breton. Claude Breton had been beaten by a cab driver a year earlier and, while sitting in a bar, decided that Taylor was that cab driver. Breton went home, got a gun, came back and killed Taylor. Explained Breton's wife "I asked him how he knew it was the same man . . . he said 'It's him. I'll never forget him.'" Taylor, however, had never driven a cab and it was shown at a subsequent trial that Taylor could not have been the man who beat Breton.

A confident yet mistaken eyewitness identification represents a salient event in which to illustrate the "eyewitness problem." But the eyewitness problem is in fact a much broader issue. Eyewitnesses testify about more than just the identification of a perpetrator. Eyewitnesses also testify about time (e.g., how long did it take to get from point x to point y? what time did event x take place?), speed (how fast was car x going?), distances (e.g., how much room was there between the two cars?), sizes (e.g., was the object that person x was carrying large or small?), episodes (e.g., did he cock the rifle after it was handed to him or was it already cocked?), sounds (e.g., were the voices in the other room those of a male or female?), and so on. These memory reports may be as critical to the outcome of a case as are identifications.

The eyewitness problem is not merely a problem with eyewitnesses per se. In part it also is a problem with police practices and with jury beliefs. Consider, for example, a recent article in the Kansas City *Star*. This was a routine article reporting the fact that a convenience store had been robbed and an explanation by the police that "a description of the robber would not be released because the several eyewitnesses disagreed in their descriptions." Although the reluctance of police to release a description makes good sense, it raises an important question: What would the police have done had there been only one eyewitness? The answer is clear. On the opposite page was an eyewitness's description of a perpetrator in a separate case for which there was only one eyewitness. Apparently, the police understand eyewitness unreliability when eyewitnesses disagree among themselves. Of course, if there is only one eyewitness there is no chance for such disagreement and the testimony is accorded enough credibility to justify printing a description. Thus, the eyewitness problem is not to be understood merely as a problem with eyewitnesses, but also as a problem with how eyewitnesses are perceived and handled by police.

Finally, the eyewitness problem can be defined with regard to the behaviors of the triers of fact, namely jurors and judges. If jurors and judges were able to discriminate meaningfully between accurate and inaccurate eyewitness testimony, our concerns about inaccurate testimony would be lessened considerably. In general, then, the eyewitness problem is in fact a broad concern encompassing not only the issues of perception and memory of eyewitnesses, but also the assumptions and practices of police, jurors, and judges.   In recent years experimental social and cognitive psychologists have been approaching the eyewitness problem from several angles. Generally, these research approaches fall into three categories. First, there is research directed at the question of what variables tend to relate to eyewitnesses' accuracy with the goal of trying to estimate the extent to which eyewitnesses ought to be believed in various cases. The second approach to the problem is to find out how jurors evaluate eyewitness testimony in an attempt to see what processes lead them to believe false eyewitness testimony, as we know happens with some degree of frequency. Finally, there is a systems approach of trying to find ways to make eyewitnesses more accurate. Before discussing the research in these three areas, a brief legal overview is given.

LEGAL PERSPECTIVES

Eyewitness testimony often is referred to as direct evidence. In fact, however, not all eyewitness testimony is direct evidence. If, for example, an eyewitness testifies that she saw the defendant enter a building where an offense took place but did not see the defendant commit the offense, then the testimony is circumstantial. If, however, an eyewitness identifies someone as the person she saw committing the offense in question, then this is direct evidence. As direct evidence, eyewitness identification has a unique evidentiary status; specifically, if the eyewitness is correct then the defendant is guilty and if the eyewitness is wrong then the defendant is innocent. This type of isomorphic relationship between evidence and guilt is not achieved by any other form of evidence except, perhaps, confessions. Fingerprints, for example, indicate only that a given person touched a given surface.

Until recently, the law relied exclusively on the jury or judge to evaluate the reliability of eyewitness testimony without benefit of formal acknowledgment of the potential dangers in eyewitness testimony. It was not until 1966 that the U.S. Supreme Court agreed to review three cases involving issues of eyewitness identification evidence. These cases were decided in 1967 (*United States v. Wade*, 1967; *Gilbert v. California*, 1967; *Stovall v. Denno*, 1967). The *Wade* and *Gilbert* cases revolved around issues of the Sixth Amendment right to counsel. In both cases questionable lineup procedures had been conducted in absence of the defendants' attorneys. Although the Court ruled in favor of right to counsel, the Court later imposed limits on right to counsel by ruling that right to counsel does not apply to lineups conducted prior to the time police initiate criminal proceedings (*Kirby v. Illinois*, 1972). In *Kirby v. Illinois*, Kirby had been arrested but not charged at the time of the lineup. Further limits on right to counsel were made apparent when the Court ruled that photographic lineups do not allow the accused the assistance of counsel.

Stovall v. Denno (1967), decided on the same day as *Wade* and *Gilbert*, dealt with the issue of suggestive lineup procedures. The Court ruled that identification evidence must be excluded if the identification procedure was "unnecessarily suggestive and conducive to irreparable mistaken identification" (pp. 301-302). In the case of Stovall, the identification procedure was a "showup" (i.e., a one-to-one confrontation rather than a lineup), but the Court ruled that the identification should not be excluded in his case because the eyewitness, seriously wounded in the offense, could not visit the police station. Thus, the Court ruled that the showup was suggestive but not "unnecessarily" suggestive.

Further complicating the issue were several subsequent cases. In *Neil v. Biggers* (1972), for example, the Court shifted the emphasis from *procedure* (e.g., suggestive lineup practices) to *accuracy*. Specifically, the Court argued that it is the likelihood of mistaken identification that violates due process. The Court then listed five factors to be considered: the certainty of the eyewitness; the eyewitness's opportunity to observe; the eyewitness's degree of attention; the eyewitness's accuracy of prior description of the perpetrator; and the amount of time passed between witnessing and identifying.

Also in 1972 was a significant federal appellate case (*United States v. Telfaire*, 1972) involving the issue of cautionary instructions. In the *Telfaire* case the judge held that a trial judge must instruct the jury that identification testimony should be scrutinized carefully and received with caution if the defense counsel requests such instructions and the facts so warrant.

There are many other cases of some significance on the legal status of eyewitness evidence. The major cases discussed herein, however, capture the basic flavor of the way in which the legal system has handled the issue of eyewitness evidence. Three general observations can be made about the legal perspective on eyewitness evidence. First, almost all of the current legal perspective is based on the intuitions of the judges involved in the cases. The five *Neil v. Biggers* (1972) criteria, for example, are appealing at an intuitive level but are not in general agreement with empirical findings (see Wells & Murray, 1983). In addition, legal opinion on eyewitness evidence has been concerned almost exclusively with *identification* evidence. Finally, legal opinion regarding the role of expert testimony on eyewitness matters is ambiguous.

EYEWITNESS ACCURACY

In general, the accuracy of eyewitness testimony is determined by processes that occur at four stages. Three of these stages (acquisition, encoding, and retrieval) are traditionally accepted as part of classical memory theory. The fourth stage, communication, is unique to this chapter and has been added to handle a number of relevant issues and recent studies in eyewitness testimony.

Acquisition

The acquisition or encoding of information occurs at the time of eyewitnessing the event in question. Although the acquisition of event information may also occur later (e.g., if eyewitnesses interact later and share memories), such acquisitions are better relegated to the next stage (storage) and called storage additions or storage alterations. This is not to say that acquisition is isomorphic with the event. Indeed, what is acquired or encoded depends a great deal on processes such as attention, perception, and elaboration.

Generally, it is central, salient items rather than peripheral items that are better attended and perceived (e.g., Dristas & Hamilton, 1977; Myers, 1913). In addition, attention and perception generally are better if the event has a higher level of importance (Leippe, Wells, & Ostrom, 1978). On the other hand, extreme high levels of crime seriousness are likely to be detrimental to acquisition because high stress or high arousal leads to a narrowing of attention (Deffenbacher, 1983).

It is not only the nature of the stimulus or characteristics of the event per se that determine attention and perception. The interests, desires, wishes, and expectations of the witness also determine attention and perception. A study by Powers, Andriks, and Loftus (1979) illustrates how gender, which is correlated somewhat with interests, influences perception. In their study, male and female students watched a slide sequence of a wallet-snatching incident and then had their memory for details measured. Their results showed that males were more accurate than females on items dealing with the (male) thief's appearance whereas females were more accurate than males on items dealing with women's (e.g., the victim's) clothing or actions. The classic demonstration by Hastorf and Cantril (1954) that Dartmouth students and

Princeton students perceived different infractions in a filmed replay of a Dartmouth-Princeton football game attests to the influence of personal prejudices on perception.

Expectations also affect perception. In a simple demonstration of this, Bruner and Postman (1949) presented people with an array of playing cards in which certain cards had suit and color reversed (e.g., ace of diamonds was black). When later asked critical questions such as "how many aces of diamonds were there?" people responded on the basis of their prior expectations regarding the linkage of color and shape. For similar reasons, people judge orange-colored tomatoes to be redder than orange-colored lemons (Bruner, Postman & Rodrigues, 1951).

Faces can be encoded in a variety of ways, and the nature of the encoding has profound implications for the success or lack thereof at the point of retrieval. Considerable research indicates that cross-racial identifications are more difficult than within-race identifications (e.g., Elliott, Wills, & Goldstein, 1973; Malpass & Kravitz, 1969). Ellis (1975) presented evidence indicating that this may be due to encoding operations. Specifically, it appears that caucasians attend to eye color, hair color and hair texture when processing faces regardless of the race of the face. These cues are relatively nondiagnostic for purposes of discriminating between faces of blacks, which may account for the relatively poor performance of caucasians when they must later try to identify a previously-viewed black face.

The encoding operations performed by an eyewitness while viewing a face are linked intimately to the likelihoods of successful retrieval. Numerous studies have demonstrated the profound advantage of "global" encoding operations such as making trait judgments of a face (e.g., judging a face for honesty, kindness, sincerity or some other trait adjective) rather than feature judgments (e.g., judging the physical components of nose size, mouth shape and so on (e.g., Baddeley, 1979; Bower & Karlin, 1974; Winograd, 1976)).

The acquisition stage of eyewitnessing is a critical aspect of the final eyewitness product of communication (i.e., verbal statements such as "The stop light was red," "It took about three minutes," or "That's the man who robbed the store!"). Expectations, personal biases, stereotypes, the nature of the stimulus, interests, and cognitive processing strategies all influence the nature of the acquisition. But the acquisition stage has a unique status not shared fully by the other three stages. Specifically, acquisition or encoding operations are beyond the control of the criminal justice system. Although we can manipulate these acquisition variables in experiments (e.g., by varying the nature of the stimulus or the nature of the subject's interests), there is nothing we can do about controlling these variables in real eyewitness situations (see Wells, 1978).

Storage

The period during which the information is stored—sometimes called the retention interval—plays an important role in the accuracy of the eyewitness's eventual testimony. As everyone knows, memory performance declines as the retention interval gets longer (Ebbinghaus, 1885; Shephard, 1967). Theories of forgetting are numerous, but most relevant to eyewitness testimony are studies that show how memory reports change *systematically* as functions of "postevent information."

Postevent information refers to new acquisitions of information relating to the event, but these new acquisitions occur *after* witnessing the event. Postevent information comes from two sources: internal and external. Internal sources of postevent information often are discussed under the topic of reconstructive memory (Bartlett, 1932). Generally, any witnessed event is not only stored with some inaccuracies, but also is stored with incompleteness or gaps. A witness may remember a person as having had blond hair but, either because of a failure to attend or to encode, does not have information about eye color. In spite of this gap, eye color may become a part of what is placed in storage after the fact (postevent) through reconstructive processes. It is stereotypically less common to encounter a blond person with dark brown eyes than with light-colored eyes. The witness may, therefore, fill in this storage gap by recalling light-colored eyes. Indeed, experimental evidence indicates that reconstructed false memories can be indistinguishable from real memories in terms of the subjective certainty of the person (Wells, 1982). Along these lines, Shepherd, Ellis, McMurran, and Davies (1978) found that people recalled the *same* face differently depending on whether that face was described at the time as being that of a lifeboat captain versus a multiple murderer. Although the Shepherd et al. study was not designed to determine whether or not the effect occurred during storage (rather than at acquisition or retrieval), other research (e.g., Loftus & Greene, 1980) clearly shows that memory for faces is affected by events that occur during the storage stage.

Most of the work on postevent information has been concerned with external sources of postevent information. The leading work in this area has been conducted by Loftus (1979) and her colleagues. The general paradigm involves having people observe some event (e.g., a series of slides, a film, or a live event) and later exposing these witnesses to certain statements or questions that are varied systematically. It is these statements or questions that constitute the postevent information. Subsequently, witnesses are given a memory test and their memory reports are examined as a function of the postevent information (i.e., the previous statements or questions).

Consider, for example, a study by Loftus, Miller, and Burns (1978). People were shown a series of slides in which a red Datsun became involved in an accident with a pedestrian. For half of the viewers, the Datsun pulled up to a stop sign before becoming involved in the accident whereas for the other half of the viewers the sign was a yield sign. After viewing the event, half of the viewers in each condition were asked "Did another car pass the red Datsun while it was stopped at the stop sign?" whereas the other half were asked the same question with the word yield in place of the word stop. Sometime later, all viewers were shown two slides, one with a stop sign and one with a yield sign, and were asked to choose the one that they saw earlier. The results showed that subjects tended to choose the sign that was included in the question they were asked. Thus, for example, if they saw a stop sign but received the yield-sign question, they tended to think that they saw a yield sign in the original set of slides.

In addition to the effects of leading questions, there are other events that affect eyewitnesses during the retention interval. The common practice of having eyewitnesses search through a large number of mugshots is one such event. Brown, Deffenbacher, and Sturgill (1977), for example, exposed subject-witnesses to a live staged event and then had the witnesses view a large number of mugshots. Several days later the witnesses were shown a lineup that included persons involved in the original event, persons whose photographs were among the mugshots, and totally unfamiliar foils. The witnesses' task was to choose the persons who were involved in the original event. Brown et al's. results revealed that subject-witnesses rarely chose an unfamiliar foil, but were as likely to choose an "innocent" person whose face was seen only in the mugshots as they were to choose one of the actors who was actually involved in the original (live) event. Thus, even after an event has been encoded, the acquisition of subsequent information (as happens somewhat incidentally while viewing mugshots) can alter a witness's testimony regarding the original event.

Retrieval

Accurate eyewitness testimony depends not only on factors influencing the acquisition and storage of information but also the conditions of retrieval. Consider the following retrieval task: How many words can you recall that could fit the space and letter combination _ _ _ _ i _ _? Research indicates that people can recall several words in a 60-second period that could fit this space and letter combination. Suppose, however, people are asked how many words they can recall that fit the space and letter combination _ _ _ _ing. Although there are fewer words that can fit the latter situation than can fit the former, people easily recall many more words in a given amount of time in the latter case. In the case of _ _ _ _ing, we have created a retrieval condition that is conducive to recall whereas the case of _ _ _ _ i _ _ we have provided few cues to retrieval of relevant instances. Note, however, that the amount of information that people have in memory is the same in both of these examples—the examples differ only in the conditions of retrieval. Unfortunately, aspects of retrieval in eyewitness testimony are much more complex than this simple example would suggest.

There are two general types of retrieval traditionally identified in memory; recognition and recall. Recognition can be construed as a yes/no decision (or a series of yes/no decisions) in which the stimulus (e.g., face) in question is physically present. In recall, the stimulus to be recognized is not physically present but, instead, must be constructed verbally or pictorially (e.g., via the Identi-kit). Although it is commonly believed that recognition is superior to recall, there are conditions where recall succeeds when recognition fails (e.g., Tulving & Watkins, 1977).

Recall. There are numerous ways of taking eyewitness recall, each of which has implications for the completeness and accuracy of retrieval. *Open narrative* or free recall merely asks the eyewitness to describe what happened. Cues are almost totally absent. For example, the witness may be asked to describe "what happened on March 27, 1984." A *controlled narrative* or cued recall sets a more confined context for the question such as "describe Jane Miller's appearance when you saw her that day." *Closed questions* are more specific; Whipple (1909) has classified closed questions into four types: *determinitative,* such as "Was Jane Miller carrying a purse when you first saw her?"; *disjunctive* questions, such as "Was or was not Jane Miller carrying a purse?"; *expectative* questions, such as "Jane Miller was carrying a purse, wasn't she?"; and *implicative* questions, such as "Were you aware of the weapon that was in the purse Jane Miller was carrying?" The general rule that governs the way in which these different recall questions relate to eyewitness reports is that there is a trade-off between completeness and accuracy (e.g., see Marquis, Marshall, & Oskamp, 1972). In order of accuracy, open narrative is the most accurate followed by controlled narrative, determinative, disjunctive, expectative, and implicative. Completeness, however, is higher for closed questions followed by controlled narrative and open narrative.

Recognition. Recognition forms of retrieval typically concern identification of persons, usually the defendant. There are three main identification procedures used by police: mug-shot tasks, which are conducted when there is no specific suspect and may involve hundreds of photographs of faces; photo arrays, for which there is one or only a few suspects embedded among a relatively small number (e.g., 5 to 12) of distractor photos; lineups, also conducted when there is one or only a few suspects, each of which appear in person among distractor persons (usually 5 to 9 distractors). Generally, the difference in identification accuracy between live lineups and photo arrays is trivial (see Shepherd, Ellis, & Davies, 1982, chap. 12). Much more important are the procedures used and the structure of lineups and photo arrays. There is no evidence that the variables affecting identification accuracy are different for live lineups versus photo arrays, therefore the following discussion of testing or retrieval variables in identification is considered applicable to both.

Wells (in press) has proposed that a main source of error in lineup identifications is the tendency for eyewitnesses to choose a lineup member who best resembles the perpetrator. Wells termed this a "relative-judgment process" because it is the likeness of a given lineup member relative to others in the lineup, rather than the absolute similarity of the lineup member to the perpetrator, that drives the identification process. The danger of relative judgments is most apparent when considering situations in which the true perpetrator is absent from the lineup. When the perpetrator is not in the lineup, the relative judgment strategy will always produce a false identification. From this simple notion of relative judgments, two dangerous (poor) retrieval situations can be identified. First, identification procedures are poor if the situation explicitly or implicitly suggests that the true perpetrator is in the lineup. Research shows that such situations lead to high rates of false identification because witnesses fail to reject the lineup (i.e., say that the perpetrator is not present) when the lineup does not include the perpetrator (Malpass & Devine, 1981). A clearly superior identification situation exists when the eyewitness is explicitly forewarned that the perpetrator might not be present in the lineup. Comparing these two identification conditions, Malpass and Devine found that they yielded similar rates of accurate identification but the former situation produced a much higher rate of false identifications than did the latter situation.

Another implication from the relative-judgment conceptualization is that high (physical) dissimilarity among lineup members (especially between the suspect and the foils) increases the likelihood of false identification (Lindsay & Wells, 1980). Although the principle of similarity in lineups is understood intuitively at some level, it is in fact a more complex issue than it might appear to be. Consider, for example, the fact that high physical similarity among lineup members reduces the likelihood of accurate identifications in addition to reducing the likelihood of false identifications. Can we conclude, therefore,that higher levels of physical similarity increase eyewitness identification accuracy? The answer to this dilemma resides in the question of *how much* a given increase in similarity reduces false identifications relative to the reduction in accurate identifications. Experimental evidence indicates that the reduction in accurate identification rates is proportionately less than the reduction in false identifications as a function of a given increase in physical lineup similarity (Lindsay & Wells, 1980).

Encoding-retrieval interactions. A modern conception of memory (e.g., see Tulving & Thomson, 1973) has it that successful retrieval of memories depends on the extent to which cognitive operations at the time of retrieval are similar to (or overlap with) the cognitive operations involved in encoding. There are three important experimental demonstrations of this that are relevant to eyewitnessing. First, consider one of the leading-question studies mentioned earlier (Loftus, Miller, & Burns, 1978). In a replication of this study (Bekerian & Bowers, 1983) subject-witnesses observed a slide sequence of an auto-pedestrian accident that included a critical slide with a stop sign for half of the witnesses and for the other half showed a critical slide with a yield sign. Later a leading question was introduced, to wit: "Did a pedestrian walk in front of the red Datsun while it was stopped at the stop sign?" or "Did . . . the yield sign?" Thus, half of the witnesses were misled in the sense that they saw a stop sign but were asked a question in which a yield sign was presupposed, or vice versa. Bekerian and Bowers's study showed that the leading question produced errors in a later forced-choice task (where witnesses must choose between slides of a stop sign and a yield sign) only under certain conditions of retrieval. Specifically, the misleading question effect was eliminated when the retrieval task sent subject-witnesses through the original slide sequence up to the point of the critical (stop/yield sign) slide. This study, therefore, attests to the utility of the idea of "context reinstatement" or the notion of regenerating cognitive operations at the point of retrieval that mimic those involved in encoding.

Recent research on memory for faces shows how an *apparently* poor encoding might in fact be better than some other encoding depending on the retrieval task. Earlier, in the section on acquisition, it was noted that if people make trait judgments of faces (e.g., for honesty, kindness, and so on) their ability subsequently to recognize that face is much greater than if they were to make physical feature judgments (nose shape, size, etc.). However, it cannot be concluded that trait-judgment encoding tasks are superior forms of acquisition because, if the retrieval task is one of building the face from an Identi-kit, the physical feature encoding task procedures better face recall than does the trait encoding task (Wells & Hryciw, in press). The apparent reason for this stems once again from the idea of making retrieval operations similar to encoding operations. Specifically, the mental operations involved in the retrieval task of Identi-kit usage are similar to those involved in feature-judgment encoding.

Communication

The inclusion of a stage called communication is unique to this chapter and stems from the assumption that eyewitness memories can be retrieved even though they might not be communicated, and some of what is communicated does not proceed through the stages of encoding, storage, and retrieval. Consider some hypothetical examples of these phenomena. In the former instance, where a memory is retrieved but not communicated, an eyewitness might recall that a perpetrator had a scar over his left eye. The conscious retrieval of this memory may be accurate or not, but several things might make it more or less likely to be communicated to a police interrogator. Low confidence—uncertainty on the part of the witness that the memory is an accurate one—decreases the likelihood that the memorial retrieval of the information will be reported. Or, consider a situation in which a witness recalls that a letter opener was sitting on a victim's desk the morning of a brutal slaying. This memory might go uncommunicated, even though it is retrieved easily, because the witness judges the memory to be irrelevant or somehow unrelated to the case. Fear is another factor that tends to break the link between retrieval and communication. A witness might recognize a perpetrator in a lineup, for example, but fail to communicate the recognition for fear of reprisal.

Communications by eyewitnesses need not have their origins in acquisition, storage, and retrieval processes at all. The most obvious example of this is the mere act of lying. But even if we assume truthfulness and genuineness in eyewitness accounts, there are aspects of eyewitness testimony at the point of communication that do not have their origins in acquisition, storage, and retrieval processes per se. The most researched of these aspects is eyewitness confidence, an aspect of eyewitness testimony communications that has proven to be the single most important determinant of the credibility ascribed to eyewitnesses (Wells, Lindsay, & Ferguson, 1979).

Eyewitness confidence. Staged crime experiments indicate that the confidence that an eyewitness has in his or her ability to identify someone from a lineup is related to the likelihood that the eyewitness will attempt an identification (Malpass & Devine, 1981). This is interesting in light of research indicating that eyewitnesses are as willing to attempt an identification under poor witnessing conditions as they are under good witnessing conditions (Lindsay, Wells, & Rumpel, 1981). Thus, even though witnessing conditions affect memory accuracy profoundly, the effects of these conditions on confidence and the willingness to attempt an identification are weak or absent. Similarly, retrieval conditions, manipulated by Lindsay and Wells (1980) in the form of lineup biases, had profound effects on memory accuracy without corresponding effects on confidence or willingness to identify a person from a lineup. This research suggests that eyewitness confidence and the willingness to communicate a positive memory are not generated through the same encoding, storage, and retrieval processes that give rise to memory accuracy/inaccuracy. Instead, two sources of eyewitness confidence have been investigated. First, there is evidence suggesting that eyewitness confidence is in part a stable individual difference variable. Brown, Deffenbacher, and Sturgill (1977), for example, found that a given eyewitness's confidence when correct was correlated highly with that eyewitness's confidence when incorrect (whereas confidence when correct was not generally greater than

confidence when incorrect). In addition, there is evidence that eyewitness confidence increases as one mentally prepares to be cross-
examined (Wells, Ferguson, & Lindsay, 1981). Thus, eyewitness
confidence—an important parameter of eyewitness testimony communication—may be more of a social-personality process than it is a
memory (encoding, storage, retrieval) process. As such, it is not
particularly surprising that eyewitness identification accuracy and eyewitness confidence have been shown to have little or no relationship
(Wells & Murray, 1984).

   Response criteria. Confidence is not the only variable determining
whether an eyewitness will communicate a particular memory. There
are individual and situational differences that determine the willingness
of an eyewitness to communicate a recollection. The research of Ellis,
Shepherd, and Bruce (1973) indicates that age is one such factor.
Generally, it appears that children make significantly more errors of
commission and fewer errors of omission than do adults, suggesting a
lower criterion on the part of children for reporting a memory.

   Response criteria shift according to situational factors. Response
criteria can be manipulated directly, such as in a study by Hilgendorf
and Irving (1978) in which some eyewitnesses were told to use strict
criteria or to use loose criteria in deciding whether or not to say that
they recognized a lineup member. Loose criteria, of course, result in the
eyewitness reporting more about his or her recollection than do strict
criteria, and it is no surprise that loose criteria increase the amount of
false memories reported.

   One powerful situational variable that increases eyewitnesses' total
communication, presumably through a relaxation of response criteria,
is hypnosis (see Orne, Soskis, Dinges, & Orne, 1984). Indeed, modern
research indicates that hypnosis is better characterized as a treatment
for eyewitnesses that increases the amount of recollection an eyewitness is willing to communicate rather than a treatment that increases
the accuracy of testimony.

EVALUATING EYEWITNESS TESTIMONY

   How do jurors evaluate eyewitness testimony? To what extent are
jurors aware of the factors that lead to eyewitness errors? Research on
these questions is relatively recent and certainly is not as extensive as is
research on eyewitness accuracy. Nevertheless, there are now a
number of studies that have addressed this issue. Discussion of this

research begins with what may be the most important single factor determining the way jurors judge eyewitness testimony—namely, eyewitness confidence.

Confidence

A recent questionnaire study indicates that 75 percent of prosecutors and 73 percent of law officers believe that witnesses who are more certain also are more accurate whereas only 40 percent of defense attorneys hold such a belief (Brigham & Wolfskiel, 1983). Interestingly, experienced prosecutors were less likely to hold such a belief than were their less experienced counterparts. Among a survey of citizen-jurors, 67 percent believed that confidence and accuracy were related in eyewitness identifications (Yarmey & Jones, 1983). As discussed earlier, such beliefs conflict with a majority of the research findings, which show little or no relationship between eyewitness confidence and identification accuracy.

The results of the questionnaire studies do not, in and of themselves, tell us that people are seriously erring in their evaluations of eyewitness testimony. It could be, for example, that people believe there to be a positive relationship between confidence and accuracy but do not use such information in their evaluations of the credibility of a given eyewitness. A series of studies by Wells and his colleagues, however, indicates otherwise. Following staged thefts, unsuspecting eyewitnesess were presented with a lineup task. Those who made identifications were then questioned by someone who was blind as to whether the witnesses had accurately identified the thief or falsely identified an innocent person. These studies have shown consistently that subject-jurors who observe the questioning are much more likely to believe confident than nonconfident eyewitnesses (Lindsay, Wells, & Rumpel, 1981; Wells & Leippe, 1981; Wells, Ferguson, & Lindsay, 1981; Wells, Lindsay, & Tousignant, 1980; Wells, Lindsay, & Ferguson, 1979). Indeed, the confidence that a subject-juror ascribes to an eyewitness accounts for as much as 50 percent of the variance in subject-jurors decisions as to whether or not to believe the eyewitness's testimony (Wells, Lindsay, & Ferguson, 1979). Given the latter finding, there is little doubt that eyewitness confidence is the most powerful single determinant of the credibility ascribed to eyewitnesses. This is true in spite of the fact that these studies showed no relationship between eyewitness accuracy and the confidence ascribed to eyewitnesses.

Witnessing Conditions

Questionnaire studies suggest that people do not fully understand how some witnessing conditions affect eyewitness accuracy. Yarmey and Jones (1983), for example, found that 40 percent of their sample of citizen jurors thought that extreme stress would aid an eyewitness's ability to remember details of a witnessed event. In addition, only 33 percent of the citizen jurors indicated an awareness that eyewitnesses tend to overestimate the temporal duration of a crime. Citizen jurors fared slightly better in recognizing the fact that a caucasian will have a more difficult time identifying a black assailant than identifying a caucasian assailant, a belief endorsed by 43 percent of the respondents.

In general, there is little evidence supporting the idea that jurors are good at scrutinizing and taking appropriate account of witnessing conditions. In a study by Lindsay, Wells, and Rumpel (1981), witnessing conditions were varied in a staged theft experiment such that identification accuracy varied from 33 percent in the poor viewing conditions to 74 percent in the good viewing conditions. Subject-jurors then watched cross-examinations of these eyewitnesses in which the eyewitnesses' viewing conditions were described (in their own words) for the subject-jurors. Although subject-jurors took account of witnessing conditions in their tendencies to believe the eyewitnesses' testimony, the extent to which such account was taken was inadequate. In addition, witnessing conditions affected the extent to which jurors believed the eyewitness only when the eyewitness was relatively nonconfident. Confident eyewitnesses were believed at a high rate equally across witnessing conditions. This result appears to be highly reliable (Lindsay, Wells, & Rumpel, 1981; Wells, Lindsay, & Tousignant, 1980) and suggests that witnessing conditions may have little effect on the credibility jurors ascribe to confident eyewitnesses.

Further evidence that people may have little appreciation for conditions that lead to inaccuracy is a study by Kassin (personal communication, 1979). Kassin presented students with a summary of a study by Leippe, Wells, and Ostrom (1979) in which it was shown that a theft of a package believed by eyewitnesses to contain a calculator produced more accurate identifications of the thief than did the theft of a package believed to contain a pack of cigarettes. However, if witnesses learned the value of the package's contents after the thief had vanished, the value of the contents had no effect on accuracy. In Kassin's study, students were given a description of the study without the results and were asked to predict the results. The students' predictions bore no relationship to the results. In addition, students overestimated the levels of eyewitness accuracy in all conditions. Similar results have been obtained by Brigham and Bothwell (1982).

Testing Conditions

There is little evidence to suggest that people appreciate the role of testing conditions on eyewitness accuracy. A study by Wells (1984), using a prediction method similar to that of Kassin (1979), showed that students predicted eyewitness reports to be much more accurate under conditions of hypnosis than under control conditions, a common but erroneous assumption about hypnosis (see Orne, Soskis, Dinges, & Orne, 1984). Furthermore, the students expected hypnosis to provide more accurate eyewitness accounts even if the questioner used leading questions—a situation that has been shown to produce even greater levels of inaccuracy than either hypnosis or leading questions alone (see Putnam, 1979).

Biased lineups also appear to have little or no effect on subject-jurors' ascriptions of credibility to eyewitnesses. Lindsay and Wells (1980), for example, found that a lineup structure so biased that it yielded chance-level performance had no effect on the way subject-jurors ascribed credibility to the eyewitnesses' identifications even when the subject-jurors were shown a photographic reproduction of the lineup (see Lindsay & Wells, 1980, footnote 4). Similarly, subjects who were given a description of a staged vandalism study conducted by Malpass and Devine (1981) showed no appreciation for the effects of biased instructions on lineup identification accuracy (Wells, 1984). Malpass and Devine had shown that biased instructions to eyewitnesses yielded 78 percent errors under conditions where unbiased instructions yielded only 33 percent errors. Subjects gave equal estimates of error rates in these two conditions (16 percent and 18 percent, respectively).

Summary

There is no evidence supporting the view that people are good at evaluating the accuracy of eyewitness testimony under various conditions. But research on this issue is nascent and, therefore, strong conclusions should be withheld. Suffice to say that there is evidence that (1) the tendency for subject-jurors to believe eyewitness identification testimony is poorly related to the accuracy of the eyewitnesses' accounts; (2) eyewitness confidence is used by subject-jurors much more heavily than experimental data would warrant; and (3) numerous specific variables are misunderstood by people as regards the way they affect eyewitness accuracy.

PRACTICAL PERSPECTIVES

There are a number of implications of the findings from eyewitness research. At a general level, the current eyewitness literature can be used by courts to improve the instructions given to jurors. Typically, precautionary instructions are not given to jurors regarding eyewitness matters and those that are considered "models" (e.g., *United States v. Telfaire*, 1972) are not congruent with modern scientific evidence (see Greene, in press). The U.S. Supreme Court's main statement on eyewitness identification accuracy (espoused in *Neil v. Biggers*, 1972) also lags behind modern scientific evidence. Recent publications by eyewitness researchers have attempted to address discrepancies between eyewitness research findings on the one hand and the rules of thumb established by the courts on the other hand (e.g., see Wells & Murray, 1983). At this point, however, most of the practical application work is being carried on in the courtroom through the use of expert testimony.

Expert Testimony

Eyewitness researchers increasingly are being called on, usually by defense counsel, to give expert testimony regarding eyewitness reliability. Generally, research supports the conclusion that expert testimony regarding eyewitness matters lessens the impact of eyewitness identification testimony (e.g., Hatvany & Strack, 1980; Hosch, Beck, & McIntyre, 1980; Loftus, 1980; Saunders, Vidmar, & Hewitt, 1983; Wells, Lindsay, & Tousignant, 1980). Because eyewitness identification testimony usually is evidence for the prosecution rather than for the defense, it is not surprising that defense attorneys favor the idea of eyewitness experts much more than do prosecuting attorneys (see Brigham & Wolfskiel, 1983).

The fact that there is a respectable body of experimental literature on eyewitness testimony does not mean that eyewitness experts agree on the merits of expert testimony (e.g., see McCloskey & Egeth, 1983; Loftus, 1983). Although a seemingly good solution in some respects, experiments have shown that expert testimony might make jurors too skeptical of eyewitness evidence (Wells et al., 1980). Generally, there are three distinct positions that have been espoused regarding the use of expert testimony on eyewitness matters. First, there are those who argue that expert testimony should never be given by psychologists because it has not been proven to have positive effects on justice (McCloskey & Egeth, 1983). This position defines justice in terms of the ratio of conviction of the innocent to conviction of the guilty. An alternative position, espoused by Loftus, argues generally that jurors ought to be informed of all the factors known to affect eyewitness accuracy and that critics such as Egeth and McCloskey have placed too much emphasis on convicting the guilty and too little on protecting the innocent. A third position, espoused by Wells (1983), argues that psychologists may have an obligation to give expert testimony in cases where police procedures were especially poor (e.g., biased lineup, leading questions, or other system-variable concerns) because these are variables that the system can improve upon.

Improving Eyewitness Accuracy

An alternative method of applying eyewitness research that seems more palatable than expert testimony is the direct application of system-variable findings. Recall from the earlier section on acquisition that it was noted that the justice system could do nothing about acquisition variables. If cross-racial identifications are less reliable than within-race identifications, for example, the justice system cannot use such a variable to increase the accuracy of identifications. Generally, all factors surrounding a witnessed event, including characteristics of the witness and characteristics of the target (e.g., perpetrator), are uncontrollable in the real world, so their role in eyewitness reliability at best can be estimated. Hence, these variables have been termed estimator variables. On the other hand, lineup structure and interrogation methods are under the control of the justice system to some extent and thus have been termed system variables (Wells, 1978).

Given an understanding of the system-variable/estimator-variable distinction, it is easy to see how the findings discussed earlier under the headings of storage and retrieval can be used to help the justice system deal with the eyewitness problem. Unfortunately, it is not obvious as to how these findings can actually work their way into effective use by police and others who control many of the relevant variables. Research on lineup structure or question wording, for example, tends to be nested in mainstream academic psychology journals. Although a few of the journals and books supposedly are interdisciplinary, the rank-and-file police who conduct eyewitness interrogations and identification procedures cannot be reached through these social science outlets. Another source of information dissemination regarding system variables is through police training academies or through direct contact with police departments. Eventually, this would seem to be the most effective way to apply system-variable knowledge. At this point, however, two problems exist. First, there is a tendency for police departments to be suspicious of the intentions of experimental psychologists. Generally, they assume that the motive of an experimental psychologist is to hinder their operations and protect not only the innocent suspect but protect the guilty suspect as well. Equally problematic for getting police to adopt system-variable knowledge is the lack of incentive for change. Interestingly, one powerful source of incentive is the courts. If the courts became unwilling to accept eyewitness evidence under conditions where such evidence was obtained through poor system-variable practices (e.g., when there is evidence of leading questions or biased lineups), then police incentive to "do it right" would increase greatly. Indeed, it is this type of situation that led Wells (1983) to argue for a discriminating use of expert testimony—expert testimony that focuses on system-variable violations. Thus, there is the paradoxical argument that expert testimony, properly focused, might help increase the accuracy of eyewitness evidence that reaches the courts in subsequent cases.

REFERENCES

Baddeley, A. D. (1979). Applied cognitive and cognitive applied psychology: The case of face recognition. In L. G. Nilsson (Ed.), *Perspectives on memory research.* New Brunswick, NJ: Lawrence J. Erlbaum.

Bartlett, F. C. (1932). *Remembering.* Cambridge: Cambridge University Press.

Bekerian, D. A., & Bowers, J. M. (1983). Eyewitness testimony: Were we misled? *Journal of Experimental Psychology: Learning Memory and Cognition, 9,* 139-145.

Bower, G. H., & Karlin, M. B. (1974). Depths of processing pictures of faces and recognition memory. *Journal of Experimental Psychology, 103,* 751-757.

Brigham, J. C., & Bothwell, R. K. (1982). The ability of prospective jurors to estimate the accuracy of eyewitness identifications. Unpublished manuscript, Florida State University.

Brigham, J. C., & Wolfskiel, M. P. (1983). Opinions of attorneys and law enforcement personnel on the accuracy of eyewitness identifications. *Law and Human Behavior, 7,* 337-349.

Brown, E. L., Deffenbacher, K. A., & Sturgill, W. (1977). Memory for faces and the circumstances of encounter. *Journal of Applied Psychology, 62,* 311-318.

Bruner, J. S., & Postman, L. J. (1949). On the perception of incongruity: A paradigm. *Journal of Personality, 18,* 206-223.

Bruner, J. S., Postman, L. J., & Rodrigues, J. (1951). Expectation and the perceptions of color. *American Journal of Psychology, 64,* 216-227.

Deffenbacher, K. (1983). The influence of arousal on reliability of testimony. In B. R. Clifford & S. Lloyd-Bostock, *Evaluating witness evidence: Recent psychological research and new perspectives.* New York: John Wiley.

Deffenbacher, K., & Loftus, E. F. (1982). Do jurors share a common understanding concerning eyewitness behavior? *Law and Human Behavior, 6,* 15-30.

Dristas, W. J., & Hamilton, V. L. (1977). Evidence about evidence: Effects of presuppositions, item salience, stress, and perceiver set on accident recall. Unpublished manuscript, University of Michigan.

Ebbinghaus, H. E. (1885). *Memory: A contribution to experimental psychology.* New York: Dover.

Elliott, E. S., Wills, E. J., & Goldstein, A. G. (1973). The effects of discrimination training on the recognition of white and oriental faces. *Bulletin of the Psychonomic Society, 2,* 71-73.

Ellis, H. D. (1975). Recognizing faces. *British Journal of Psychology, 66,* 409-426.

Ellis, H. D., Shepherd, J. W., & Bruce, A. (1973). The effects of age and sex upon adolescents' recognition of faces. *Journal of Genetic Psychology, 123,* 173-174.

Ellison, K. W., & Buckhout, R. (1981). *Psychology and criminal justice.* New York: Harper & Row.

Gilbert v. California, 388 U.S. 263 (1963).

Greene, E. (in press). Judge's instruction on eyewitness testimony: Evaluation and revision. *Journal of Applied Social Psychology.*

Hastorf, A. H., & Cantrill, H. (1954). They saw a game: A case study. *Journal of Abnormal and Social Psychology, 49,* 129-234.

Hatvany, N., & Strack, F. (1980). The impact of a key discredited witness. *Journal of Applied Social Psychology, 10,* 490-509.

Hilgendorf, E. L., & Irving, B. L. (1978). Decision criteria in person recognition. *Human Relations, 31,* 781-789.

Hosch, H. M., Beck, E. L., & McIntyre, P. (1980). Influence of expert testimony regarding eyewitness accuracy on jury decisions. *Law and Human Behavior, 4,* 287-296.

Kassin, S. (1979). Personal written communication.

Kirby v. Illinois, 406 U.S. 682 (1972).

Leippe, M. R., Wells, G. L., & Ostrom, T. M. (1978). Crime seriousness as a determinant of accuracy in eyewitness identification. *Journal of Applied Psychology, 63,* 345-351.

Lindsay, R.C.L., & Wells, G. L. (1980). What price justice? Exploring the relationship of lineup fairness to identification accuracy. *Law and Human Behavior, 4,* 303-314.

Lindsay, R.C.L., Wells, G. L., & Rumpel, C. (1981). Can people detect eyewitness identification accuracy within and across situations? *Journal of Applied Psychology, 66,* 79-89.

Loftus, E. F. (1979). *Eyewitness testimony.* Cambridge, MA: Harvard University Press.

Loftus, E. F. (1980). Impact of expert psychological testimony on the unreliability of eyewitness identification. *Journal of Applied Psychology, 65,* 9-15.

Loftus, E. F. (1983). Silence is not golden. *American Psychologist, 38,* 564-572.

Loftus, E. F., & Greene, E. (1980). Warning: Even memory for faces may be contagious. *Law and Human Behavior, 4,* 323-334.

Loftus, E. F., Miller, D. G., & Burns, H. J. (1978). Semantic integration of verbal information into a visual memory. *Journal of Experimental Psychology: Human Learning and Memory, 4,* 19-31.

Malpass, R. S., & Devine, P. G. (1981). Eyewitness identification: Lineup instructions and the absence of the offender. *Journal of Applied Psychology, 66,* 482-489.

Malpass, R. S., & Kravitz, J. (1969). Recognition for faces of own and other race. *Journal of Personality and Social Psychology, 13,* 330-334.

Marquis, K. H., Marshall, J., & Oskamp, S. (1972). Testimony validity as a function of question form, atmosphere, and item difficulty. *Journal of Applied Social Psychology, 2,* 167-186.

McCloskey, M., & Egeth, H. (1983). Eyewitness identification: What can a psychologist tell a jury? *American Psychologist, 38,* 550-563.

Myers, G. C. (1913). A study of incidental memory. *Archives of Personality, 26,* 101-108.

Neil v. Biggers, 409 U.S. 188 (1972).

Orne, M. T., Soskis, D. A., Dinges, D. F., & Orne, E. C. (1984). Hypnotically induced testimony. In G. L. Wells & E. F. Loftus (Eds.), *Eyewitness testimony: Psychological perspectives* (pp. 171-213). New York: Cambridge University Press.

Powers, P. A., Andriks, J. L., & Loftus, E. F. (1979). Eyewitness accounts of females and males. *Journal of Applied Psychology, 64,* 339-347.

Putnam, W. H. (1979). Hypnosis and distortions in eyewitness memory. *International Journal of Clinical and Experimental Hypnosis, 27,* 437-448.

Saunders, D. M., Vidmar, N., & Hewitt, E. C. (1983). Eyewitness testimony and the discrediting effect. In S.M.A. Lloyd-Bostock & B. R. Clifford (Eds.), *Evaluating witness evidence.* New York: John Wiley.

Shephard, R. N. (1967). Recognition memory for words, sentences and pictures. *Journal of Verbal Learning and Verbal Behavior, 6,* 156-163.

Shepherd, J. W., Ellis, H. D., & Davies, G. M. (1982). *Identification evidence: A psychological evaluation.* Aberdeen, Scotland: Aberdeen University Press.

Shepherd, J. W., Ellis, H. D., McMurran, M., & Davies, G. M. (1978). Effect of character attribution on photofit construction of a face. *European Journal of Social Psychology, 8,* 263-268.

Stovall v. Denno, 388 U.S. 293, 302 (1967).

Tulving, E., & Thomson, D. M. (1973). Encoding and retrieval processes in episodic memory. *Psychological Review, 80,* 352-373.

Tulving, E., & Watkins, O. C. (1977). Recognition failure of words with a single meaning. *Memory and Cognition, 5,* 513-522.

United States v. Telfaire, 469 F.2d 552, D.C. Cir. (1972).

United States v. Wade, 388 U.S. 218 (1967).

Wells, G. L. (1978). Applied eyewitness testimony research: System variables and estimator variables. *Journal of Personality and Social Psychology, 36,* 1546-1557.

Wells, G. L. (1982). Attribution and reconstructive memory. *Journal of Experimental Social Psychology, 18,* 447-463.

Wells, G. L. (1983). *Expert testimony on eyewitness issues: Analysis of effects.* Paper presented at Eyewitness Conference, Johns Hopkins University.

Wells, G. L. (1984). How adequate is human intuition for judging eyewitness testimony? In G. L. Wells & E. F. Loftus (Eds.), *Eyewitness testimony: Psychological perspectives.* New York: Cambridge University Press.

Wells, G. L. (in press). The psychology of lineup identifications. *Journal of Applied Social Psychology.*

Wells, G. L., Ferguson, T. J., & Lindsay, R.C.L. (1981). The tractability of eyewitness confidence and its implications for triers of fact. *Journal of Applied Psychology, 66,* 688-696.

Wells, G. L., & Hryciw, B. (in press). Memory for faces: Encoding and retrieval operations. *Memory and Cognition.*

Wells, G. L., & Leippe, M. R. (1981). How do triers of fact infer the accuracy of eyewitness identifications? Memory for peripheral detail can be misleading. *Journal of Applied Psychology, 66,* 682-687.

Wells, G. L., Lindsay, R.C.L., & Ferguson, T. J. (1979). Accuracy, confidence, and juror perceptions in eyewitness identification. *Journal of Applied Psychology, 64,* 440-448.

Wells, G. L., Lindsay, R.C.L., & Tousignant, J. P. (1980). Effects of expert psychological advice on human performance in judging the validity of eyewitness testimony. *Law and Human Behavior, 4,* 275-286.

Wells, G. L., & Loftus, E. F. (1984). *Eyewitness testimony: Psychological perspectives.* New York: Cambridge University Press.

Wells, G. L., & Murray, D. M. (1983). What can psychology say about the Neil vs. Biggers criteria for judging eyewitness identification accuracy? *Journal of Applied Psychology, 68,* 347-362.

Wells, G. L., & Murray, D. M. (1984). Eyewitness confidence. In G. L. Wells & E. F. Loftus (Eds.), *Eyewitness testimony: Psychological perspectives.* New York: Cambridge University Press.

Whipple, G. M. (1909). The observer as reporter: A survey of the "Psychology of Testimony." *Psychological Bulletin, 6,* 153-170.

Winograd, E. (1976). Recognition memory for faces following nine different judgments. *Bulletin of the Psychonomic Society, 8,* 419-421.

Yarmey, A. D., & Jones, H.P.T. (1983). Is eyewitness testimony a matter of common sense? In S. Lloyd-Bostock & B. R. Clifford (Eds.), *Witness evidence: Critical and empirical papers.* New York: John Wiley.

CHAPTER 3

Confession Evidence

SAUL M. KASSIN
LAWRENCE S. WRIGHTSMAN

What could have more impact during the course of a trial than a revelation from the witness stand that the defendant had previously confessed to the crime? The truth is, probably nothing. Indeed Wigmore, in his classic treatise on *Evidence* (1970), asserted the opinion of several authoritative legal scholars that confessions rank as highest in the scale of evidence.

There are two bases for this appraisal. First, although estimates vary, there is reason to believe that confession evidence is introduced with astonishing *frequency* in the courts. A survey of deputy district attorneys in Los Angeles County, for example, revealed that confessions were given in 47 percent of the over 4000 cases reported (Younger, 1966). At the same time, the district attorney of New York City asserted that he planned to offer confession evidence in 68 percent of the homicide cases he had pending (see Kaufman, 1966). Kalven and Zeisel's (1966) extensive survey of trial judges indicated that, overall, "disputed" confessions (i.e., those that are denied or whose admissibility is challenged by the defense) arose in approximately 20 percent of the 3576 cases they had sampled nationwide.

In addition to the frequency with which confession evidence is received, a second reason for its importance is the obvious *impact* it can single-handedly exert on a defendant's fate. As McCormick (1972) put it, "the introduction of a confession makes the other aspects of a trial in court superfluous" (p. 316). Indeed over the years, several instances have surfaced of erroneous convictions based almost exclusively on uncorroborated confession evidence. In *Convicting the Innocent*, for example, Borchard (1932) reviewed 65 criminal cases, many involving individuals who were incarcerated or executed on the basis of confessions subsequently proved to be false (see also Frank & Frank's *Not Guilty*, 1957). The compelling nature of confession evidence has also been demonstrated on an empirical level. In a mock jury experiment, Miller and Boster (1977) had subjects read a description of a murder trial that included (1) only circumstantial evidence, (2) eyewitness testimony from either an acquaintance or a stranger, and (3) testimony alleging that the defendant had confessed to the police. It turned out that those subjects who received the confession evidence were more likely to view the defendant as guilty than the other groups, including those provided with the eyewitness identification.

THE RULES OF CONFESSION EVIDENCE AND PROCEDURE

Historically, confession evidence has provided a recurring source of controversy in American jurisprudence, as it simultaneously elicits both praise and suspicion. Is the alleged confession authentic? Can the testimony of paid informers, angry victims, and overzealous police officers be trusted? If so, was the defendant of sound mind, or could he or she have confessed to deeds that he or she did not commit? Was the defendant's statement coerced or induced by trickery during custodial interrogation? Was his or her constitutional privilege against self-incrimination violated? These questions illustrate and represent the complexity of the issues surrounding the use of confession evidence in court.

Before discussing the special rules that have evolved for the reception of confession evidence, we must first clarify what constitutes a confession. Traditionally, a confession was defined as "an acknowledgement, in expressed words, by the accused in a criminal case, of the truth of the guilty fact charged or of some essential part of it" (Wigmore, 1970, p. 308). This definition has been considered narrow in scope, as it excludes guilty conduct (e.g., fleeing from arrest), exculpatory statements (e.g., a self-defense explanation or apology) and other admissions (i.e., those that do not bear directly on the issue of guilt or fall short of an acknowledgment of all essential elements of the crime). These distinctions—particularly that between confessions and other admissions—had, in the past, enabled the courts to circumvent having to apply the stringent rules for introducing confession evidence when dealing with the other types of self-incriminatory statements (McCormick, 1972). However, because these distinctions are often subtle and difficult to make in individual cases (see Slough, 1959), and because the U.S. Supreme Court has indicated that coerced admissions are subject to the same constitutional safeguards as full confessions (e.g., *Ashcraft v. Tennessee*, 1944), today's accepted operational definition is, for all practical purposes, one that encompasses a relatively wide range of self-incriminatory behaviors under the label *confession*.[1]

A Historical Overview

According to Wigmore's (1970) historical analysis, the modern law's use of confessions has proceeded through a series of discrete stages. During the sixteenth and seventeenth centuries in England, there was no restriction, no doctrine about excluding confessions. All avowals of guilt were accepted at face value without discrimination. In fact, confessing was like pleading guilty, thereby precluding the need for a formal trial. Wigmore noted that at least through the middle of the seventeenth century, the use of physical torture to extract confessions was common and evidence so obtained was accepted without scruple. In contrast, by the nineteenth century there was a period during which the judiciary was generally cynical of all confessions and tended to repudiate them upon the slightest pretext. Two bases for this distrust of confessions were articulated—(1) that the process of procuring proof of an alleged confession through the testimony of an associate, informer, police officer, or victim, is of questionable reliability, and (2) even when the confession is a well-proved fact, it may have little diagnostic value (i.e., as an indicator of guilt) if it was the result of coercion or was induced by promises, threats, or other tactics of the "third degree."

During the twentieth century, confession evidence has been neither accepted nor rejected outright. Instead its admissibility has been determined on an individual basis by a rational consideration of the surrounding circumstances and the all-important requirement that it be proved voluntary. According to Wigmore, the outstanding development in recent years is the nationalization of confession laws, established through a series of U.S. Supreme Court decisions and founded upon the Due Process Clause of the Fourteenth Amendment (see also Stephens, 1973). Thus, in *Brown v. Mississippi* (1936), the court reversed a guilty verdict because of a confession that was received through physical brutality, and asserted that a trial "is a mere pretense where the state authorities have continued a conviction resting solely upon confessions obtained by violence" (p. 287; see also *Chambers v. Florida*, 1940).

In a nutshell, *voluntariness* had emerged as the primary criterion for the admission of confession evidence. The major task of recent years had thus become to articulate the theoretical rationale for this criterion as well as a procedural strategy for its implementation. Why are involuntary confessions excluded? Through the various Supreme Court decisions, essentially two types of reasons were advanced. First is the common law explanation that involuntary confessions, like testimony given while intoxicated or in response to leading questions, are untrustworthy and unreliable (see Wigmore, 1970; *Stein v. New York*, 1953). Accordingly, the operational test recommended for judges' rulings of admissibility is whether the inducement was sufficient to preclude a "free and rational choice" and produce a fair risk of false confession. The second rationale, first articulated in *Lisenba v. California* (1941), is that "the aim of the requirement of due process is not to exclude presumptively false evidence but to prevent fundamental unfairness in the use of evidence whether true or false" (p. 219). Both scholarly sentiment (McCormick, 1946; Paulsen, 1954) and subsequent case law (e.g., *Rogers v. Richmond*, 1961) have shifted toward this current emphasis on constitutionally-based procedural fairness, individual rights, and the deterrence of offensive police misconduct. As such, although involuntary confessions must be excluded if believed to be untrustworthy, that criterion is not enough—they must also be excluded if illegally obtained.

Current Status

Voluntariness is a difficult concept to operationalize since it requires inference about the suspect's subjective state of mind and embraces the dual concerns for trustworthiness and due process.[2] The Supreme Court, in fact, has evaded precise definition and stated in *Blackburn v. Alabama* (1960) that "a complex of values underlies the stricture against use by the state of confessions which, by way of convenient shorthand, this court terms involuntary, and the role played by each in any situation varies according to the particular circumstances of the case" (p. 207). The concept of involuntariness thus represents a summary expression for all practices that violate constitutional principles (e.g., the right to a fair trial, the privilege against compulsory self-incrimination) and can be determined only through a comprehensive analysis of the "totality of the relevant circumstances" *(Culombe v. Connecticut,* 1961, p. 606).

The catalog of factors that may be relevant to a determination of voluntariness covers a wide range. It includes characteristics of the accused (e.g., youth, subnormal intelligence, physical disability, mental illness, intoxication, illiteracy), the conditions of detention (e.g., delayed arraignment, inadequate living facilities, lack of access to counsel, friends, or other assistance), and—of course—the manner of interrogation (e.g., lengthy and grueling periods of questioning, physical abuse, deprivation of needs, threats of harm or punishment, advice, promises or reassurances, deception). Not surprisingly, the case law has been confusing and inconsistent, the courts have been burdened by numerous appeals for postconviction reviews of the voluntariness issue, and attempts at synthesis and generalization have met with little success. As Justice Frankfurter said, "there is no simple litmus-paper test" (*Culombe v. Connecticut*, 1961, p. 601).[3]

In the 1960s, the Supreme Court moved toward establishing more objective criteria for the admissibility of confession evidence. To that aim, the refusal of police to permit the accused to consult with an attorney was regarded as part of the relevant circumstances for judging voluntariness. In *Massiah v. United States* (1964), however, the Court ruled that if the accused has been indicted, all incriminating statements elicited by government agents in the absence of counsel are inadmissible.[4] Then in *Malloy v. Hogan* (1964), the Court broadened the exclusionary rules further by explicitly linking confession evidence to the privilege against compulsory self-incrimination. These decisions culminated in the landmark *Miranda v. Arizona* (1966) ruling in which the Court established broad, universally applicable guidelines for safeguarding the rights to remain silent and to counsel. It thus articulated the *Miranda* warnings and ruled that unless the accused is informed of these rights, all self-incriminating statements made are inadmissible.

For several years, the *Miranda* doctrine stood as a definitive and unambiguous safeguard against confessions induced or coerced through interrogation. More recently, however, the Supreme Court has limited its scope considerably (see Stone, 1977). In the latest development, in fact, the Court ruled that "overriding considerations of public safety" could justify a police officer's violation of the *Miranda* strictures (*New York v. Quarles*, 1984). One result of this decision is that, under certain circumstances, any self-incriminating statements elicited during questioning could now be admitted as trial evidence even if the suspect had not been apprised of his or her rights. A second result of this public safety exception to *Miranda* is the obvious forfeiture of a clear and objective criterion by which to judge the exclusion of confession evidence. As such, despite calls for the articulation of objective guidelines (White, 1979) in all likelihood the more subjective voluntariness criterion will take on added importance.[5]

COMPETENCE: THE PSYCHOLOGY OF POLICE CONFESSIONS

As our historical overview has shown, the exclusionary rules relating to confessions were based, from the outset, on the ethic of insulating our adversarial system of justice from the introduction of unreliable evidence. As Wigmore (1970) noted, although there is no way to determine the frequency of untrue confessions, it is reasonable to conclude "based on ordinary observation of human conduct, that under certain stresses a person, especially one of defective mentality or peculiar temperament, may falsely acknowledge guilt" (p. 329). In this section, we explore two questions—(1) what actually transpires behind the closed doors of the interrogation room, and (2) how competent or trustworthy is confession evidence?

Methods of Interrogation

The term *interrogation* is used generally to describe all questioning by police, regardless of whether it is conducted in custody or in the field, before or after arraignment. Despite the persisting controversy surrounding this aspect of criminal investigation, there is surprisingly little in the way of empirical documentation of interrogation practices.

In 1931, the U.S. National Commission on Law Observance and Enforcement published a report of its findings and confirmed the worst fear about police abuse, noting that the use of severe third degree tactics to extract confessions is "widespread" (p. 153). As examples, the commission cited as commonplace the use of physical violence, methods of intimidation adjusted to the age and mentality of the accused, fraudulent promises that could not be fulfilled, and prolonged illegal detention. In an effort to characterize the interrogation process as it might have changed since that time, the *Miranda* (1966) court—lacking direct observational or interview data—turned for evidence of what transpires to actual reported cases involving coerced confessions and to a review of the most popular manuals written to advise law enforcement officials about successful tactics for eliciting confessions (cf. Aubry & Caputo, 1965; Inbau & Reid, 1962; O'Hara & O'Hara, 1981). Essentially, the Court concluded from its inquiry that "the modern practice of in-custody interrogation is (now) psychologically rather than physically oriented" (p. 448),[6] but that the degree of coerciveness inherent in the situation had not diminished. The Court's specific substantive findings are described below.

The physical setting. To begin with, police manuals (most notably Inbau & Reid's *Criminal Interrogation and Confessions,* 1962) urge officials to employ a specially constructed room that is psychologically removed from the sights and sounds of the police station, and to maintain rigid control over the ecology of that interrogation room. The novelty of this facility is designed to give the suspect "the illusion that the environment itself is withdrawing further and further away" (Aubry & Caputo, 1965, p. 38). To further minimize sensory stimulation and remove all extraneous sources of distraction, social support, and relief from tension, the manuals recommend that the interrogation room be accoustically soundproofed and bare, without furniture or ornaments— only two chairs and perhaps a desk. Also critical, of course, is that the accused be denied communicative access to friends and family. Finally, the interrogator is advised to sit as close as possible to the subject, in armless, straightbacked chairs, and at equal eye level. Invading the suspect's personal space, it is said, will increase his or her level of anxiety from which the only means of escape is confession.

Manipulative tactics. Inbau and Reid (1962) described in considerable detail 16 overlapping strategies for eliciting confessions from initially recalcitrant suspects. From them, three major themes emerge. The first is to reconceptualize for the suspect the attributional implications of his or her crime by minimizing its seriousness (e.g., "I've seen thousands of others in the same situation") or by providing a face-saving external attribution of blame. The interrogator might, for example, suggest to the suspect that there were extenuating circumstances in his or her particular case, providing such excusing conditions as self-defense, passion, or simple negligence. Or, the blame might be shifted onto a specific person such as the victim or an accomplice. Inbau and Reid (1962) offered the following example of how such attributional manipulation has been used successfully as bait: A middle-aged man, accused of having taken indecent liberties with a 10-year-old girl, was told that "this girl is well developed for her age. She probably learned a lot about sex from boys . . . she may have deliberately tried to excite you to see what you would do." In another documented instance, Wald et al. (1967) observed a detective tell a breaking-and-entering suspect that "the guy should never have left all that liquor in the window to tempt honest guys like you and me" (p. 1544).

From an entirely different angle, an alternative strategy is to frighten the suspect into confessing. One way to accomplish this is by exaggerating the seriousness of the offense and magnitude of the charges. In theft or embezzlement cases, for example, the reported loss—and hence the consequences for a convicted defendant—could be increased. Another variation of the scare tactic is for the interrogator to presume to have a firm belief about the suspect's culpability based on independent, "factual" evidence. Police manuals are replete with specific suggestions about how to use what is referred to as the "knowledge-bluff" trick. The interrogator could thus pretend to have strong circumstantial evidence (e.g., the suspect's fingerprints at the scene of the crime), have a police officer pose as an eyewitness and identify the suspect in a rigged lineup, or even—through elaborate staging devices—try to persuade the suspect that he or she has already been implicated by an accomplice or another suspect. Another interesting technique, along similar lines, is to alert the suspect to his or her apparent psychophysiological and nonverbal indicators of a guilty conscience such as dryness of the mouth, sweating, fidgety movements, or downcast eyes.

The third general type of approach is based on the development of a personal rapport with the suspect. Referring to this as the emotional appeal, police manuals advise the interrogator to show sympathy, understanding, and respect through flattery and gestures such as the offer of a drink. Having established a friendly relationship, the interrogator might then try to persuade the suspect that confessing is in his or her own best interests. In a more elaborate version of this strategy, two detectives enact a "Mutt and Jeff" routine in which one comes across as hostile, and relentless, while the other gains the suspect's confidence by being protective and supportive. This technique is apparently quite common and was used in a case described by Zimbardo (1967).

In addition to these various specific strategies, the literature reviewed by the Supreme Court in *Miranda* contained several universally applicable rules of thumb, the most important of which is "an oppressive atmosphere of dogged persistence." Not surprisingly, the

Court concluded from its findings, that interrogation practices were inherently coercive.

Direct observational data. Are the admittedly indirect and poorly sampled data culled by the Supreme Court an accurate depiction of the interrogation process or do they portray only the most atypical and extreme forms of coercion? In an empirical study, Wald, Ayres, Hess, Schantz, and Whitebread (1967) observed 127 interrogations over the course of eleven weeks in the New Haven, Connecticut, Police Department. In addition to recording the frequency with which various tactics were used in these sessions, the investigators interviewed the police officers and attorneys involved as well as some exsuspects.[7]

Overall, this research revealed that one or more of the tactics recommended by Inbau and Reid (1962) was employed in 65 percent of the interrogations observed and that the detectives used an average of two tactics per suspect. The most common approach was to overwhelm the suspect with damaging evidence, to assert a firm belief in his or her guilt, and then to suggest that it would be easier for all concerned if the suspect admitted to his or her role in the crime. This latter plea was often accompanied by a show of sympathy and concern for the suspect's welfare. Most of the other methods cited in the manuals were also used with varying frequency, including the Mutt and Jeff routine, playing off other suspects, minimizing the seriousness of the offense, shifting the blame for the crime to external factors, and alerting the suspect to signs of nervousness that reveal a guilty conscience. The investigators reported that no undue physical force was used by the detectives, but they did observe the frequent use of promises (e.g., offers of lowered bail, reduced charges, and judicial leniency) and vague threats about harsher treatment. In three instances, suspects were told that the police would make trouble for their families and friends if they refused to cooperate.

Wald et al. (1967) concluded from their observations that the New Haven detectives employed most of the persuasive techniques listed by Inbau and Reid, thus justifying, to some extent, the Court's fears.[8] Indeed it is perhaps reasonable to speculate that because the mere presence of observers at the sessions could have inhibited the use of stronger forms of pressure, these results might even have underestimated the coercion employed during interrogation. Moreover, such tactics do not merely represent the abuses of an unenlightened, bygone era, as White (1979) cites similar kinds of advice in current police manuals and several such instances in recently reported cases.

Validity of Confession Evidence

As we noted earlier, judgments about the voluntariness and, hence, competence of evidence rest on two criteria—trustworthiness and procedural fairness. Earlier, we discussed the latter criterion. We focus now on the accuracy or trustworthiness requirement.

To measure the actual validity of confession evidence, one would ideally assess the combined frequency with which truly guilty suspects confess and truly innocent suspects do not. Two types of erroneous outcome are thus possible—those probably common instances in which guilty suspects fail to confess (misses in signal detection terms) and the probably rarer occasions when suspects who are innocent do confess (false alarms in signal detection terms). Because our accusatorial system of justice protects the individual's right to refuse self-disclosure, the first type of error obviously does not provide a basis for concern. The second category of error, however, does pose a serious problem for the courts. In assessing the trustworthiness of confession evidence, the question we must therefore ask is, What is the risk of false confessions?

Anecdotes and case histories. It is impossible to determine or even estimate the frequency with which people confess to crimes they did not actually commit. Is there a reasonable risk of false confessions? Although the layperson might find it difficult to believe, enough instances have been documented to suggest that concern over such a risk is justified (Barthel, 1976; Borchard, 1932; Foster, 1969; Frank & Frank, 1957; Munsterberg, 1908; Reik, 1959; Sutherland, 1965; Wigmore, 1937; Zimbardo, 1967; Note—*Indiana Law Journal*, 1953).

A perusal of the anecdotal literature suggests that it is useful to distinguish three psychologically distinct types of false confession— (1) voluntary, (2) coerced-compliant, and (3) coerced-internalized. *Voluntary false confessions*, those purposefully offered in the absence of elicitation, are on the face of it the most enigmatic of the three types. Why, for example, did over 200 people confess to the famous Lindbergh kidnapping? Apparently a "morbid desire for notoriety" could account for this episode as well as others in which numbers of false confessions are received for widely publicized crimes (see Note, *Indiana Law Journal*, 1953, p. 382). Other suggested motives for voluntary false confessions include the unconscious need to expiate guilt over previous transgressions via self-punishment, the hope for a recommendation of leniency, and a desire to aid and protect the real criminal. Then, of course, there are the innumerable instances in which false confessions are offered by individuals subsequently diagnosed as mentally ill and unable to distinguish between fantasy and reality (cf. Guttmacher & Weihofen, 1952).

In contrast to those occasions when individuals voluntarily initiate false confessions are those in which suspects confess through the coerciveness of the interrogation process. Within this category of *coerced false confessions,* a further distinction should be drawn. Psychologists have long recognized the importance of two conceptually different responses to social control attempts—compliance and internalization (see Kelman, 1958). Compliance may be defined as an overt, public acquiescence to a social influence attempt in order to achieve some immediate instrumental gain whereas internalization refers to a personal acceptance of the values or beliefs espoused in that attempt. Two meaningful differences between these closely related processes have been observed. First, although compliance is reflected in subsequent behavior only if it continues to have instrumental value, internalized behaviors persist over time and across a variety of situations. Second, it appears that whereas immediate compliance is most effectively elicited through powerful and highly salient techniques of social control, internalization is best achieved through more subtle, less coercive methods (see Lepper, 1982, for a self-perception theory explanation of this phenomenon).

In view of the foregoing distinction, it is clear that some false confessions may be viewed as *coerced-compliant,* wherein the suspect publicly professes guilt in response to extreme methods of interrogation, despite knowing privately that he or she is truly innocent. Reflecting the instrumental component of such conduct, Wigmore (1970) noted that one of the main reasons for distrusting confession evidence arises "when a person is placed in such a situation that an untrue confession of guilt has become the more desirable of two alternatives between which the person was obliged to choose" (p. 344). Historically, most of the false confessions extracted through torture, threats, and promises were probably of this type (e.g., the Salem witchcraft confessions of the seventeenth century). And, reflecting the nonpermanent character of "mere" compliance, such confessions are typically withdrawn and challenged at a pretrial voluntariness hearing.

A good example is the classic case of *Brown v. Mississippi* (1936) in which the defendants confessed after having been threatened by a lynch mob and whipped with steel-studded belts, and then maintained—upon appeal—that they had made false self-incriminating statements in order to escape the painful beatings and avoid further punishment.

It is also clear, however, that there are times when false confessions are *coerced-internalized*: when the suspect—through the fatigue, pressures, and suggestiveness of the interrogation process—actually comes to believe that he or she committed the offense. What is frightening under this stronger form of false confession is that the suspect's memory of his or her own actions may be altered, making its original contents potentially irretrievable.

As an illustration of how a suspect might come to internalize the events as suggested by the police, consider the following case, described by Barthel (1976). Peter Reilly, 18 years old, returned home one night to find that his mother had been murdered. He called the police who, after questioning him with the aid of a polygraph, began to suspect the boy of matricide. Transcripts of the interrogation sessions revealed a fascinating transition from denial through confusion and self-doubt (largely facilitated by the police officer's assertions about the infallibility of "the charts"), and finally to the statement, "Well, it really looks like I did it" and the signing of a written confession. Two years later, it was revealed through independent evidence that Reilly could not have committed the murder, that the confession that even he came to believe was false.

Psychological perspectives. Various theories have been brought to bear on the question, What is it about the coerciveness of interrogation that can cause innocent people to incriminate themselves? From a psychological standpoint, the coerced-compliant false confessions are readily explained by the individual's desire to escape an aversive situation and secure a favorable self-outcome. In these cases, the act of confession—compared to the consequences of silence or denial—is simply the lesser of two evils for a beleaguered suspect. But what about the more puzzling instances of internalized false confessions?

To account for this phenomenon, some observers have likened the interrogation process to hypnosis. Foster (1969), referring to the "station house syndrome," stated that police interrogation "can produce a trance-like state of heightened suggestibility" so that "truth and falsehood become hopelessly confused in the suspect's mind" (pp. 690-691). Since the state of hypnosis is characterized by the subject's loss of initiative, heightened capacity for fantasy production, confabulation, and reality distortion (e.g., an acceptance of falsified memories), and an increased suggestibility (e.g., in response to leading questions; see Hilgard, 1975), the danger of what appear to be internalized false confessions could provide a real source of concern. Indeed a study by Weinstein, Abrams, and Gibbons (1970) revealed that when a false sense of guilt is implanted in hypnotized subjects, they become less able to pass a polygraphic lie detector test.

Interestingly, Munsterberg (1908) had reported on a murder case in which the defendant was convicted and executed on the basis of a confession that might have been elicited through hypnotic induction. In 1906, a woman named Bessie Hollister was raped and murdered. Richard Ivens discovered the body and reported it to the police. Looking tired and disheveled, he was immediately suspected, placed under arrest, and interrogated. According to the police, although he initially denied the allegations, Ivens then confessed repeatedly, enriching the story on each successive occasion. At the trial, the prosecutor's case was centered around the confession. The defendant repudiated his statements and produced 16 unimpeached witnesses to substantiate his alibi. What, then, prompted the sudden shift during interrogation from denial to confession? According to Ivens, his only recollection of the session was of seeing a revolver pointed at him—"I saw the flash of steel in front of me. Then two men got before me. I can remember no more than that about it. . . . I suppose I must have made those statements, since they all say I did. But I have no knowledge of having made them" (Munsterberg, 1908, p. 169). As it turned out, the defense sought the opinion of several experts as to whether the confession could be explained through the use of hypnosis. Affirmative replies were received from many sources, including Hugo Munsterberg and William James.

From another standpoint, it has been suggested that internalized false confessions could result from a process of self-perception. Interested in "When saying is believing," Bem (1966) explored the idea that a false confession could distort an individual's recall of his or her own past behavior if the confession is emitted in the presence of cues previously associated with telling the truth (e.g., reassurance that one need not admit to wrongdoing). In an interesting experiment, subjects performed a task that required them to cross out a sample of words from a master list. Then, to establish two lights as discriminative stimuli for truth and falsity, subjects were asked general questions about themselves and instructed to answer them truthfully when the room was illuminated by a green light and to lie in the presence of an amber light. In the next phase of the procedure, the experimenter announced several words taken from the initial task. After some, he instructed subjects to lie and after others to tell the truth about whether they had previously crossed the word out—again while in the presence of a green or amber light. In the final step of the procedure, subjects were asked for each word to recall whether they actually had or had not crossed it out. The results indicated that false statements made in the presence of the truth light produced more errors in the recall of actual performance than either false statements made in the presence of the lie light or none at all. It thus appears that under conditions normally associated with telling the truth, subjects came to believe the lies they had been induced to tell.[9] In discussing the legal implications of this finding, Bem (1967) noted that "a physical or emotional rubber hose never convinced anyone of anything" and that "saying becomes believing only when we feel the presence of truth, and certainly only when a minimum of inducement and the mildest and most subtle forms of coercion are used" (pp. 23-24).

Generalization from Bem's laboratory research to the real-world process of criminal interrogation should obviously be made with caution. Still, anecdotal reports suggest the existence of internalized false confessions, and Bem's self-perception ideas provide at least a partial explanation of this phenomenon. Closely related, for example, is an interrogation tactic described by Driver (1968) of having the suspect repeat the story over and over, for "if duped into playing the part of the criminal in an imaginary sociodrama, the suspect may come to believe that he was the central actor in the crime" (p. 53).

CREDIBILITY: JURIDIC PERCEPTIONS OF CONFESSION EVIDENCE

As we noted earlier, confession evidence may be introduced in court if it is obtained via due process and passes the broad test of voluntariness. In judging the latter, a variety of factors are deemed relevant, including the defendant's state of mind, the detention conditions, and the methods of interrogation. In this section, we examine the credibility issue—what inferences do people draw from confession evidence, and what impact does it have on juridic decision making?

Procedure and the Jury's Function

In practice, most jurisdictions employ one of two general procedures for handling disputed confessions. In all cases, a special preliminary hearing is held in which a factfinder—usually the presiding judge—hears all the pertinent facts and determines the voluntariness and, hence, the competence of the confession evidence.[10] Under the California or "orthodox" rule, confessions found to have been coerced are entirely excluded, and those deemed voluntary are admitted with all the other evidence. Within this procedure, the jury's sole function is to determine the weight and credibility of the confession. Under the Massachusetts or "humane" rule, however, once a confession is admitted the jury is then instructed to make its own independent appraisal of voluntariness before considering its credibility and entering it into their evidentiary equation. This method thus increases the jury's role and the importance of its perceptions of voluntariness.[11]

A second procedural question that affects the jury's role is, By what standard of proof should the pretrial factfinder judge voluntariness? In the wake of the *Jackson v. Denno* (1964) prescription that the defendant is entitled to a preliminary hearing of admissibility, some states adopted the stringent criterion that voluntariness must be proven "beyond a reasonable doubt," whereas others sanctioned lesser standards, including proof by a mere "preponderance of the evidence." Since judges have been shown to translate the reasonable doubt criterion to mean an 89 percent certainty and the preponderance standard to mean only a 61 percent certainty (Simon & Mahan, 1971), this difference is noteworthy. In *Lego v. Twomy* (1972), the Supreme Court resolved this question in favor of the lesser standard, as it affirmed its faith in the jury's capacity to assess the truthfulness of confessions and to use those that are potentially unreliable cautiously.

An Attributional Analysis

The anecdotal literature is replete with case studies that collectively suggest that juries are often overwhelmed by confession evidence, that they place a good deal of faith in its probative value. Yet in *Lego v. Twomy* (1972), the Supreme Court asserted, "Our decision was not based in the slightest on the fear that juries might misjudge the accuracy of confessions and arrive at erroneous determinations of guilt or innocence" (p. 625).

Is this assumption well founded? How do jurors perceive evidence of a confession whose voluntariness is in question? Although psychologists have not focused directly on how jurors use such information, the inference process involved in such a decision is familiar to us via the social psychology of attribution. Essentially, we have a situation in which jurors are confronted with a verbal behavior whose causal locus is ambiguous. For example, if a suspect confesses in response to a threat made during an interrogation, that confession may be viewed either as reflecting his or her true guilt or as a means of avoiding the negative consequences of silence. Ideally, jurors employing Kelley's (1971) discounting principle would entertain at least a "reasonable doubt" about the accuracy of this kind of elicited confession (i.e., compared to one that is made in the absence of threat as a plausible cause). Indeed, research has demonstrated that observers use the attributional principle of discounting in a variety of contexts (e.g., Kruglanski, Schwartz, Maides, & Hamel, 1978).

On the other hand, a number of investigators have reported that perceivers characteristically fall prey to what has been called the "fundamental attribution error": They attach insufficient weight to situational causes and, instead, accept the dispositional implications of behavior at face value (see Jones, 1979; Ross, 1977). In a series of experiments, Jones and Harris (1967) had subjects read an attitudinal essay or hear a speech presumably written by another student. In one study, subjects read an essay in which the communicator either supported or criticized the unpopular Castro regime in Cuba. Some subjects were told that the communicator had freely chosen to advocate this position, while others were told that the communicator was assigned to endorse the position by an instructor. Results indicated that subjects in the no-choice condition clearly perceived the situational determinants of the communicator's opinion. Nevertheless, their impressions about the communicator's true belief were markedly influenced by the particular position he had espoused. In short, subjects did not dismiss the dispositional cause of a situationally determined opinion. This phenomenon has been replicated for several different essay topics and even when the salience of the situational cause is increased (Snyder & Jones, 1974; Miller, Jones, & Hinkle, 1981).

The parallels between this research paradigm and the coerced confession are striking. In both, the observer is faced with a verbal behavior that he or she may attribute either to the actor's true attitude or to the pressures of the behavioral situation. Yet, while the Supreme

Court assumes that jurors would discount an involuntary confession as unreliable and not allow it to guide their decisions, previous research suggests that jurors might not totally reject the confession when considering the actor's true guilt.

To complicate matters further, we have seen that the courts have defined coercion broadly to include a variety of circumstances, including—of course—*threats* of harm and punishment as well as *promises* of leniency and immunity from prosecution. Unfortunately, despite the law's treatment of these conditions as functionally equivalent, social psychologists have shown that observers attribute more responsibility and freedom to people for actions taken to gain a positive outcome than for the same actions if aimed at avoiding punishment (Bramel, 1969; Kelley, 1971). Apparently, as Wells (1980) has found, this attributional assymetry is related to a pervasive, often erroneous assumption that punishment exerts a more powerful effect on human behavior than does reward. The implications of this phenomenon for how jurors utilize different types of coerced confession evidence are clear. Specifically, they suggest that a confession that is made in response to a promise of mild treatment, leniency, or other favorable legal action (positive constraint) will be perceived by jurors to be more voluntary and hence as more indicative of guilt than one that followed a threat of continued interrogation, maltreatment, or harsh punishment (negative constraint).

What, then, do jurors believe about disputed confessions? To address this question and test the predictions derived from attribution theory, we conducted a series of mock jury experiments. In each, subjects read an abridged transcript of a criminal trial in which evidence of a confession and its surrounding circumstances was varied. They then rendered their verdicts and answered a series of case-related questions.

Relevant Mock Jury Research

To this point, it is clear that there are a multitude of important questions that can be raised about juries' views of confession evidence. As a starting point, we sought to investigate their perceptions of voluntariness and the verdicts that follow under the two most significant categories of eliciting circumstance—promises and threats.

Kassin and Wrightsman (1980). In our first experiment, subjects read a 25-page transcript of a criminal trial in which the defendant,

Ronald Oliver, was charged with transporting a stolen vehicle in interstate commerce. The transcript consisted of opening statements, the examination of three witnesses, closing arguments, and the judge's instruction to the jury.

Four versions of the trial were written. They were identical except for the inclusion and manipulation of a police officer's testimony in which it was revealed that upon arrest Ron Oliver confessed to having stolen the car. In a *no-constraint* condition, he confessed on his own initiative (i.e., without prompting). In a *positive-constraint* condition, Oliver confessed after being promised that "he would be treated well during his detention and that the judge would surely be a lot easier on him—maybe even a suspended sentence." In a *negative-constraint* condition, he confessed after having been warned that "he would be treated very poorly during his detention and that the judge would surely be very hard on him—maybe even the maximum sentence." Finally, in a *no-confession* version of the trial, it was revealed that the defendant flatly denied having anything to do with the crime.

Overall, we found that whereas 19 percent of the subjects in the no-confession version of the trial voted guilty, the conviction rate increased to 56 percent in the no-constraint confession group. This difference thus reaffirmed the time-honored suspicion that evidence of a prior confession has a measurable impact of juror decisions. The primary question we asked, of course, was whether or not subjects would discount a confession if induced by promises or threats. As it turned out, the answer is yes and no. When the confession was precipitated by a threat, the conviction rate increased only slightly, to 25 percent. When precipitated by a promise, however, it increased even further—to 38 percent. Presumably, these results were mediated by subjects' perceptions of the defendant's freedom of choice—positively constrained confessions are seen as more voluntary and therefore have a greater effect than negatively constrained confessions.

To test this mediation hypothesis, a second experiment was conducted using a stronger version of the Ron Oliver trial. This time, before rendering their verdicts, subjects in the three confession groups indicated whether they believed the defendant had confessed voluntarily and without coercion. As in the first experiment, the proportion of guilty verdicts was highest in the no-constraint confession condition at 78 percent, and lowest in the no-confession control group, at 11 percent. Compared to the latter as a baseline figure, the positively constrained confession significantly increased the conviction rate (50 percent), whereas the negatively constrained confession did not (22 percent). The voluntariness-judgment data, however, did not follow the same pattern. Whereas 94 percent of the subjects in the no-constraint group accurately perceived the confession as voluntary, this proportion was significantly reduced in *both* the positive and negative constraint conditions (39 percent and 22 percent, respectively).

Taken together, the foregoing results provide only qualified support for the ideal that jurors would discount coerced confessions as unreliable. When the coercive influence was operationally defined as a threat of harm or punishment, subjects fully discounted the confession evidence—that is, they viewed the confession as involuntary *and* they exhibited a relatively low rate of conviction. However, when coercion took the form of an offer or promise of leniency, subjects did not completely dismiss the confession. Under these circumstances, their judgments were internally inconsistent—they conceded that the defendant had behaved involuntarily but then voted guilty anyway. We have termed this latter result the "positive coercion bias."

Kassin and Wrightsman (1981). From a practical standpoint, this research suggests that positively coerced confessions, because they enter significantly into jurors' decisions, pose an evidentiary problem for the courts. Of course, one possible strategy for curbing this bias might be through the use of an appropriate cautionary instruction. Indeed, as we mentioned earlier, several states follow the Massachusetts procedure in which the jury is instructed to decide the voluntariness issue before rendering a verdict. Toward this end, two types of approved instruction are available to judges (see LaBuy, 1963; Mathes & DeVitt, 1965)—(1) a short form that simply directs jurors to reject any confession they believe to have been coerced, and (2) a longer version that actually defines both the positive and negative forms of constraint as coercive and, further, articulates the rationale that such elicited confessions are unreliable.

Does judicial instruction effectively limit jurors' use of positively constrained confession evidence? To address this question, we had some subjects read a version of a trial that included one of the two available forms of voluntariness instruction. The results replicated our earlier findings and, unfortunately, revealed that both sets of judicial instruction failed to mitigate the positive coercion bias. Why might subjects have been unaffected by the instruction manipulation? The simple answer is that, as a general rule, jurors are insensitive to judicial instruction (see Chapter 11 of this book). On a more specific level, recall that there are two reasons why coerced confessions are deemed inadmissible as evidence—(1) they are unconstitutional and procedurally unfair to the accused, and (2) they are unreliable and untrustworthy. Kalven and Zeisel (1966), citing real-world examples, suggested that "the jury may not so much consider the credibility of the confession as the impropriety of the method by which it was obtained" (p. 320). Yet it is clear that whereas the short instruction advanced no rationale, the long-form focused exclusively on the trustworthiness argument. Perhaps an instruction that emphasizes the fairness justification or what Kalven and Zeisel call the "sympathy hypothesis" would prove effective.

To test this idea, we conducted a second experiment for which we composed a due process instruction, one that emphasized the unfairness of even mildly coercive tactics. This time, subjects read an aggravated assault case in which the defendant pleaded self defense. In the various confession conditions, he admitted—upon arrest—that he had acted without provocation. In the no-confession control group, he maintained that he was afraid he was about to be attacked. The coercion manipulation was almost identical to that of our earlier experiments. In addition, subjects received either no instruction, the credibility instruction from the previous experiment, a due process ("fairness") instruction, or one that combined the two rationales. As before, the positive coercion bias was replicated. More important, although none of the instructional manipulations significantly affected verdicts, the instruction that appealed to both credibility and fairness considerations was at least partially effective as it significantly lowered the proportion of voluntariness judgments.

Kassin, Wrightsman, and Warner (1983). Before drawing any firm negative conclusions about the curative powers of voluntariness instructions, at least two important issues remained. First, can the *timing* of the instruction mediate its impact? In Kassin and Wrightsman's (1981) research, the judge's charge followed the presentation of evidence, as is common practice in most courts. Yet studies have shown that certain types of judicial instruction affect mock jurors' decisions only when they *precede* the evidence (cf. Elwork, Sales, & Alfini, 1977; Kassin & Wrightsman, 1979). Perhaps our subjects had tentatively decided on their *verdicts* before the instruction was delivered and so were subsequently influenced only in their *voluntariness* judgements. A second important question that remains is, Does the positive coercion bias persist or disappear after a jury deliberates and, if it persists, is judicial instruction any more effective a device at this group level? Kaplan and Miller (1978) have reported that jury discussion may correct for certain nonevidentiary biases. Yet our own research had focused on the beliefs and judgments of the individual, nondeliberating juror.

To investigate these possibilities, Kassin et al. (1983) had 102 five- and six-person juries read a version of the assault case, and receive the combined (credibility + fairness) or standard (i.e., no mention of voluntariness) instruction either before or after the presentation of evidence. The groups were then given 30 minutes to deliberate and arrive at a unanimous verdict. As it turned out, the conviction rate was somewhat lower in the positively constrained than unconstrained confession conditions (27 percent and 43 percent, respectively), although this difference was not statistically significant. When broken down by instruction condition, we found that although this pattern held for the uninstructed groups (41 percent and 49 percent), there was a significant difference among those groups that received the special charge (13 percent and 40 percent). In short, positively coerced confessions were rejected by juries who received the double-barreled voluntariness instruction.[12]

Summary and conclusions. Our research has shown that despite the courts' treatment of promises and threats as equivalent conditions of coercion, jurors react very differently to these two circumstances. When a suspect was said to have confessed in response to a threat of harm or punishment, even without signs of physical brutality, mock jurors fully rejected that evidence. When the inducement took the form of a promise of leniency, however, subjects were unable or unwilling to excuse the defendant completely and discount his or her confession. Under these circumstances, they tended to vote for conviction despite having conceded that the confession was, by law, involuntary. On the individual juror level, this phenomenon has proven to be quite robust and resistant to the effects of judicial instruction, even that which explicitly cites positive forms of constraint as coercive and potentially unreliable. On the encouraging side, our most recent study has shown that our own instruction, written to articulate both the credibility and fairness rationales, did eliminate the positive coercion bias among deliberating mock juries.

Our research represents a modest first step in understanding how juries view confession evidence in all its complexity. As such, several important questions remain unresolved. For example, why did mock jurors react so differently to the two types of constraint? Part of the answer, as suggested by Wells (1980), is simply that people view the promise of reward as a weaker form of behavioral inducement than a threat of punishment. Our own data provided mixed support for this hypothesis. In one study, we had subjects rate the degree of pressure exerted on the defendant to confess and found that these ratings were significantly higher in the negative- than positive-constraint situation. In the same study, however, we asked subjects to estimate the percentages of guilty and innocent people who would confess under the circumstances of the case they had read, and found that the promise and threat conditions were virtually identical on this measure.[13] Parenthetically, it is interesting to note that across constraint conditions, subjects estimated that 46 percent of truly guilty people and 36 percent of truly innocent people would confess. The latter figure is especially surprising because it suggests that people do clearly recognize the risk of false confessions (see Kassin & Wrightsman, 1981).

In addition to the empirical questions we have gleaned from the laws of confession evidence and procedure, innumerable others of conceptual interest to psychologists and of practical value to the judiciary await experimentation. For example, in recent years law enforcement officials have begun videotaping interrogation sessions for presentation in court. As such, the jury is enabled to view the confession and its surrounding circumstances directly rather than through the testimony of a witness (see Salvan, 1975). How might this procedural innovation affect jurors' perceptions of voluntariness and the inferences they draw from confession evidence? Based on the fact that people tend to attribute causality to that which is perceptually salient (see Taylor & Fiske, 1978), Lassiter and Irvine (1984) tested the hypothesis that judgments of voluntariness in videotaped confessions would be systematically biased by camera angle. A mock interrogation resulting in a confession was thus videotaped from three angles so that either the interrogator, the suspect, or both were visually salient. Subjects watched one of these versions of the episode. Sure enough, their judgments of coercion were lowest when the suspect was salient, highest when the interrogator was salient, and intermediate when the two were equally visible. In short, this seemingly trivial detail of procedure can, as attribution psychologists would predict, have a marked effect on juries' perceptions of confession evidence.

Implications for the entrapment doctrine. Finally, in the wake of the government's Abscam investigation as well as the recent, highly publicized John DeLorean trial, we would like to point out the implications of the issues discussed here for the related doctrine of entrapment. In *Sherman v. United States* (1958), the Supreme Court explicitly equated entrapment with positively coerced confessions. In both, the basic objective is actively to coax an individual into self-incriminatory behavior. The only meaningful difference is that in the case of solicitation the police disguise their identity and elicit nonverbal conduct that the suspect does not realize will be used toward his or her prosecution.

The entrapment doctrine has long been a source of jurisprudential controversy (cf. LaFave & Scott, 1972; Park, 1976). Was Abscam, for example, a fair investigation, or did it employ unjustifiably contrived methods not to prevent corruption but to create it? What conditions must be present for this line of defense to be relevant? Essentially, two positions have been advanced by the courts (*Sorrells v. United States,* 1932; *Sherman v. United States,* 1958). One position—a minority view referred to as the "objective" test—focuses exclusively on the propriety of investigatory methods, maintaining that entrapment occurs when police conduct is compelling enough to instigate a criminal act, even by an individual who is otherwise not ready and willing to commit it. The second view, favored by most courts and referred to as the "subjective" test, focuses instead on the defendant's state of mind. If the defendant was behaviorally predisposed, then the police are said merely to have afforded the opportunity to commit the offense. Within this framework, it is the jury that is responsible for evaluating the credibility of the entrapment defense.

How does the average citizen react to and interpret the defense of entrapment? There is anecdotal evidence to suggest that, as jurors, they react harshly to that line of justification (Kalven & Zeisel, 1966; see also Gershman, 1982, for a review of the Abscam verdicts). Indeed our attributional analysis and the discovery of a positive coercion bias in the use of confession evidence are entirely consistent with that characterization. Yet it is surprising that virtually no systematic research has addressed this important matter and the many practical issues it raises (e.g., how does the decision maker's perceptual set, as manipulated by the contrasting subjective and objective definitions, affect entrapment verdicts?).

CONCLUSIONS AND IMPLICATIONS

In the operation of our criminal justice system, confession evidence plays a vital role—it always has and, in all likelihood, it always will. As such, we have attempted to describe the behavioral dynamics of confessions, how they are handled by the courts, and how they are perceived by juries. To characterize our review of the literature, we would have to conclude that although confession evidence has attracted widespread attention from the legal community, it has virtually escaped scrutiny by academic psychologists, including those interested in forensic issues. We believe more time and energy should be devoted to understanding this important topic in all its brilliant complexity.

In particular, this chapter has suggested three general concerns toward which research efforts should be directed. First is the issue of accuracy. What precisely is the risk of false confessions under the varying circumstances and contingencies of interrogation? To date, this question is unanswerable as the uncorroborated anecdote is our only source of data. What is needed, therefore, is a creative experimental paradigm designed to provide at least an estimate of the problem. Ethical considerations notwithstanding, this paradigm would ideally involve providing subjects with an opportunity and incentive to commit a "crime" that is subsequently detected. Following this, subjects would be questioned under varying types and degrees of inducement to confess. The frequencies of true and false confessions, and nonconfessions as well, could thus be assessed (see Wells, 1980, method for measuring the effects of reward and punishment on rates of compliance with an aversive task). Alternatively, of course, a role-playing paradigm could be employed. That is, subjects could be asked to play the role of a truly guilty or innocent suspect in a mock interrogation session. As such, the frequency with which they break down and confess in response to prearranged prods and tactics could be observed (cf. Chapter 4 of this volume for a description of a similar methodology for studying the accuracy of polygraphic lie detection).

A second general issue in need of further research is that of credibility, or juridic beliefs about the accuracy of confessions. Our own research on perceptions of voluntariness for confessions elicited by promises and threats represents merely a first step toward understanding how people causally attribute and evaluate such evidence. What about other factors that enter into the "totality of the circumstances," factors such as the suspect's age, state of mind, or level of intelligence? How do jurors react to confession evidence that is obtained through the trickery and other tactics recommended by Inbau and Reid (1962)? And to what extent are all these judgments influenced by jurors' underlying philosophies about criminal justice—for example, whether they embrace a crime-control or due-process model of law enforcement? These and other important questions await further empirical research. Methodologically, jury decision-making paradigms are an obvious vehicle for addressing these credibility questions. An even more intriguing possibility is actually to measure peoples' ability to distinguish accurately between true and false confessions. This could be achieved by having subjects observe experimental interrogation sessions, as suggested earlier, and then judge whether the outcomes (confession or denial) are commensurate with the reality (guilt or innocence). Finally, we believe the issues raised by the psychology of confession evidence can be extended in important ways to other areas of the law. Their relevance to the entrapment doctrine was articulated earlier. Likewise, very similar questions are posed in the controversy about the voluntariness and coercion inherent in plea bargaining (cf. Brunk, 1979). To this point, we are long on questions, short on answers.

NOTES

1. The rules for admitting confession evidence to which we have alluded apply only to statements made by the criminally accused, not to admissions of a civil party or a criminal witness other than the defendant.

2. Voluntariness, for example, cannot be equated with the probable truth or falsity of the confession because the use of this definition could result in the failure to enforce the Due Process Clause of the Fourteenth Amendment (i.e., in instances where confessions are coerced but subsequently corroborated by additional testimony). Many courts had adopted a rule-of-thumb approach by which confessions were excluded if induced by a "threat" or "promise" or, in subjective terms, by "fear" or "hope." This definition is inadequate because it fails to account either for different degrees of inducement (and, hence, reliability) or for other tactics of coercive interrogation that do not involve promises and threats (e.g., prolonged detention). Still other courts defined voluntariness as a subjective state of mind and attempted to assess whether confession was free and rational or "the offspring of a reasoned choice" (*United States v. Mitchell,* 1944). As Justice Frankfurter noted, "because the concept of voluntariness is one which concerns a mental state, there is the imaginative recreation, largely inferential, of internal, 'psychological' fact" (*Culombe v. Connecticut,* 1961, p. 603).

3. As an example of the inconsistency, compare the following rulings reported in McCormick (1972). In one case, a confession was excluded because the interrogator told the defendant that the judge "would be easier on him." Yet in another, the confession was admitted despite it having followed the interrogator's promise that "it would go easier in court for you if you made a statement."

4. In *Escobedo v. Illinois* (1964), this principle was extended to include prearraignment stages of interrogation.

5. Most all courts follow a common law requirement that pretrial confessions be corroborated by independent evidence. Because of the number of exceptions carved out of that rule, however, and the laxity with which it has been interpreted, very few confessions are actually excluded by this legal safeguard (for a review, see Ayling, 1984).

6. Still, the Court was quick to point out that "the use of physical brutality and violence is not, unfortunately, relegated to the past" (p. 446).

7. The primary objective of this research was to assess the interrogator's compliance with and effects of the *Miranda* ruling. Since these findings are tangential to this chapter, they are not reviewed here.

8. Wald et al. (1967) also concluded that when these tactics were combined with a generally hostile demeanor and lengthy interrogation, they often appeared to be successful.

9. It is also interesting to note that the data provided support for the converse hypothesis that cues associated with falsehood can raise the subject's doubts about the validity of his or her true statements.

10. In cases where the defendant waives jury trial, opinions differ on the question of whether the same judge who resolved the voluntariness issue should also be permitted to determine guilt (see *Developments in the Law—Confessions*, 1966).

11. Until 1964, there was a third procedure known as the New York rule in which the judge was to exclude a confession as involuntary only if it was not possible that "reasonable men could differ over the inferences to be drawn." Guided by this lax standard, judges would thus admit questionable confessions on a conditional basis and then leave it to the jury to decide both competence and credibility. In *Jackson v. Denno*, the Supreme Court struck down this procedure as a violation of due process: "If it finds the confession involuntary, does the jury—indeed, can it—then disregard the confession in accordance with its instruction? . . . These hazards we cannot ignore" (p. 378).

12. The timing of the judge's instruction had a significant effect on verdicts (before evidence = 26 percent; after evidence = 45 percent) but did not interact with the other variables.

13. Another possible explanation of the positive coercion bias is that although jurors concede on an intellectual level that the confession was legally involuntary, they dislike and distrust a defendant who has shown a willingness to exploit the opportunity.

REFERENCES

Ashcraft v. Tennessee, 322 U.S. 143 (1944).

Aubry, A., & Caputo, R. (1965). *Criminal interrogation*. Springfield, IL: Charles C Thomas.

Ayling, C. J. (1984). Corroborating false confessions: An empirical analysis of legal safeguards against false confessions. *Wisconsin Law Review*, 1121-1204.

Barthel, J. (1976). *A death in Canaan*. New York: Dutton.

Bem, D. J. (1966). Inducing belief in false confessions. *Journal of Personality and Social Psychology*, 3, 707-710.

Bem, D. J. (1967, June). When saying is believing. *Psychology Today*, 1(2), 21-25.

Blackburn v. Alabama, 361 U.S. 199 (1960).

Borchard, E. M. (1932). *Convicting the innocent: Errors of criminal justice*. New Haven, CT: Yale University Press.

Bramel, D. (1969). Determinants of beliefs about other people. In J. Mills (Ed.), *Experimental social psychology*. New York: Macmillan.

Brown v. Mississippi, 297 U.S. 278 (1936).

Brunk, C. G. (1979). The problem of voluntariness and coercion in the negotiated plea. *Law and Society Review*, 13, 527-553.

Chambers v. Florida, 309 U.S. 227 (1940).

Culombe v. Connecticut, 367 U.S. 568 (1961).

Developments in the law—confessions. (1966). *Harvard Law Review*, 79, 935-1119.

Driver, E. D. (1968). Confessions and the social psychology of coercion. *Harvard Law Review*, 82, 42-61.

Elwork, A., Sales, B. D., & Alfini, J. J. (1977). Juridic decisions: In ignorance of the law or in light of it? *Law and Human Behavior*, 1, 163-189.

Escobedo v. Illinois, 378 U.S. 478 (1964).

Foster, H. H. (1969). Confessions and the station house syndrome. *DePaul Law Review*, 18, 683-701.

Frank J., & Frank, B. (1957). *Not guilty*. Garden City, NY: Doubleday.

Gershman, B. L. (1982). Abscam, the judiciary, and the ethics of entrapment. *Yale Law Journal*, 91, 1565-1591.

Guttmacher, M., & Weihofen, H. (1952). *Psychiatry and the law*. New York: W. W. Norton.

Hilgard, E. R. (1975). Hypnosis. *Annual Review of Psychology, 26,* 19-44.

Inbau, F. E., & Reid, J. E. (1962). *Criminal interrogation and confessions*. Baltimore: Williams & Wilkins.

Jackson v. Denno, 378 U.S. 368 (1964).

Jones, E. E. (1979). The rocky road from acts to dispositions. *American Psychologist, 34,* 107-117.

Jones, E. E., & Harris, V. A. (1967). The attribution of attitudes. *Journal of Experimental Social Psychology, 3,* 1-24.

Kalven, H., & Zeisel, H. (1966). *The American jury*. Boston: Little, Brown.

Kaplan, M. F., & Miller, L. E. (1978). Reducing the effects of juror bias. *Journal of Personality and Social Psychology, 36,* 1443-1455.

Kassin, S. M., & Wrightsman, L. S. (1979). On the requirements of proof: The timing of judicial instruction and mock juror verdicts. *Journal of Personality and Social Psychology, 37,* 1877-1887.

Kassin, S. M., & Wrightsman, L. S. (1980). Prior confessions and mock juror verdicts. *Journal of Applied Social Psychology, 10,* 133-146.

Kassin, S. M., & Wrightsman, L. S. (1981). Coerced confessions, judicial instruction, and mock juror verdicts. *Journal of Applied Social Psychology, 11,* 489-506.

Kassin, S. M., Wrightsman, L. S., & Warner, T. (1983). Confession evidence: The positive coercion bias, judicial instruction, and mock jury verdicts. Unpublished Manuscript.

Kaufman, I. (1966, October 2). The confession debate continues. *New York Times Magazine*, p. 50.

Kelley, H. H. (1971). *Attribution in social interaction*. Morristown, NJ: General Learning Press.

Kelman, H. C. (1958). Compliance, identification, and internalization: Three processes of opinion change. *Journal of Conflict Resolution, 2,* 51-60.

Kruglanski, A. W., Schwartz, J. M., Maides, S., & Hamel, I. Z. (1978). Covariation, discounting, and augmentation: Towards a clarification of attribution principles. *Journal of Personality, 46,* 176-189.

LaBuy, W. J. (1963). *Jury instructions in federal criminal cases*. St. Paul, MN: West.

LaFave, W., & Scott, A. (1972). *Handbook on criminal law*. St. Paul, MN: West.

Lassiter, G. D., & Irvine, A. A. (1984). Videotaped confessions: The impact of camera point of view on judgments of coercion. Paper presented at the Eastern Psychological Association, Baltimore.

Lego v. Twomy, 404 U.S. 477 (1972).

Lepper, M. R. (1982). Social control processes, attributions of motivation, and the internalization of social values. In E. T. Higgins, D. N. Ruble, & W. W. Hartup (Eds.), *Social cognition and social behavior: A developmental perspective*. San Francisco: Jossey-Bass.

Lisenba v. California, 314 U.S. 219 (1941).

Malloy v. Hogan, 378 U.S. 1 (1964).

Massiah v. United States, 377 U.S. 201 (1964).

Mathes, W. C., & DeVitt, E. J. (1965). *Federal jury practice and instructions*. St. Paul, MN: West.

McCormick, C. T. (1946). Some problems and developments in the admissibility of confessions. *Texas Law Review, 24,* 239-245.

McCormick, C. T. (1972). *Handbook of the law of evidence* (2nd ed.). St. Paul, MN: West.

Miller, A. G., Jones, E. E., & Hinkle, S. (1981). A robust attribution error in the personality domain. *Journal of Experimental Social Psychology, 17,* 586-600.

Miller, G. R., & Boster, F. J. (1977). Three images of the trial: Their implications for psychological research. In B. Sales (Ed.), *Psychology in the legal process*. New York: Halsted.

Miranda v. Arizona, 384 U.S. 436 (1966).

Munsterberg, H. (1908). *On the witness stand.* Garden City, NY: Doubleday.

National Commission on Law Observance and Enforcement. (1931). *Report on Lawlessness in Law Enforcement.* Washington, DC: Government Printing Office.

New York v. Quarles, 467 U.S., in press (1984).

Note. (1953). Voluntary false confessions: A neglected area in criminal administration. *Indiana Law Journal, 28,* 374-392.

O'Hara, C. E., & O'Hara, G. L. (1981). *Fundamentals of criminal investigation.* Springfield, IL: Charles C Thomas.

Park, D. (1976). The entrapment controversy. *Minnesota Law Review, 60,* 163-274.

Paulsen, M. G. (1954). The fourteenth amendment and the third degree. *Stanford Law Review, 6,* 411-437.

Reik, T. (1959). *The compulsion to confess.* New York: John Wiley.

Rogers v. Richmond, 365 U.S. 534 (1961).

Ross, L. (1977). The intuitive psychologist and his shortcomings. In L. Berkowitz (Ed.), Advances in experimental social psychology (Vol. 10). New York: Academic.

Salvan, S. A. (1975). Videotape for the legal community. *Judicature, 59,* 222-229.

Sherman v. United States, 356 U.S. 369 (1958).

Simon, R. J., & Mahan, L. (1971). Quantifying burdens of proof: A view from the bench, the jury, and the classroom. *Law and Society Review,* 319-330.

Slough, M. C. (1959). Confessions and admissions. *Fordham Law Review, 28,* 96-114.

Snyder, M., & Jones, E. E. (1974). Attitude attribution when behavior is constrained. *Journal of Experimental Social Psychology, 10,* 585-600.

Sorrels v. United States, 287 U.S. 435 (1932).

Stein v. New York, 346 U.S. 156 (1953).

Stephens, O. H. (1973). *The Supreme Court and confessions of guilt.* Knoxville: University of Tennessee Press.

Stone, G. R. (1977). The Miranda doctrine in the Burger Court. In *The Supreme Court Review.* Chicago: University of Chicago Press.

Sutherland, A. E. (1965). Crime and confession. *Harvard Law Review, 79,* 21-41.

Taylor, S. E., & Fiske, S. T. (1978). Salience, attention, and attribution: Top of the head phenomena. In L. Berkowitz (Ed.), *Advances in experimental social psychology* (Vol. 11). New York: Academic.

United States v. Mitchell, 322 U.S. 65 (1944).

Wald, M., Ayres, R., Hess, D. W., Schantz, M., & Whitebread, C. H. (1967). Interrogations in New Haven: The impact of Miranda. *The Yale Law Journal, 76,* 1519-1648.

Weinstein, E., Abrams, S., & Gibbons, D. (1970). The validity of the polygraph with hypnotically induced repression and guilt. *American Journal of Psychiatry, 126,* 1159-1162.

Wells, G. L. (1980). Assymetric attributions for compliance: Reward vs. punishment. *Journal of Experimental Social Psychology, 16,* 47-60.

White, W. S. (1979). Police trickery in inducing confessions. *University of Pennsylvania Law Review, 127,* 581-629.

Wigmore, J. H. (1937). *The science of judicial proof.* Boston: Little, Brown.

Wigmore, J. H. (1970). *Evidence* (Vol. 3). (Revised by J. H. Chadbourn.) Boston: Little, Brown.

Younger, E. J. (1966). Interrogation of criminal defendants—Some views on Miranda v. Arizona. *Fordham Law Review, 35,* 255-262.

Zimbardo, P. G. (1967). The psychology of police confessions. *Psychology Today,* June 1(2), 17-20, 25-27.

CHAPTER 4

The Probity of the Polygraph

DAVID T. LYKKEN

"I've been reading," said Flambeau, "of this new psychometric method . . . ; they put a pulsometer on a man's wrist and judge by how his heart goes at the pronunciation of certain words. What do you think of it?"

"I think it is very interesting," replied Father Brown; "It reminds me of that interesting idea in the Dark Ages that blood would flow from a corpse if the murderer touched it."

"Do you really mean," demanded his friend, "that you think the two methods equally valuable?"

"I think them equally valueless," replied Brown.

—G. K. Chesterton
The Mistake of the Machine (1913)

The courts of the United States are about equally divided in their stand on the admissibility of polygraph evidence. In at least 20 states,[1] polygraph examiners may testify as expert witnesses pursuant to prior agreement of the parties and, in Massachusetts and New Mexico, even over the objection of one party under certain circumstances. Appellate courts in about half of the states,[2] however, have ruled that polygraph findings are inadmissible even under stipulation. The attitudes of the federal courts have been similarly mixed. After a detailed analysis of the evidentiary status of polygraph results, the Eighth Circuit held, in *United States v. Alexander* (1975), that "the results of unstipulated polygraph examinations should not be admissible in evidence in criminal trial." This is the position of several other U.S. courts of appeal, including the District of Columbia Circuit, but the Sixth, Seventh, Ninth, and Tenth Circuits have yielded discretion to the district judge (cases cited in Abbell, 1977; see also Jones, 1979, notes 31, 32).

This disarray is understandable in light of the conflicting testimony that has been offered at the many evidentiary hearings on this issue. Most scientists who have taken the trouble to look into the question (and who are not personally involved in the polygraph business) find that the assumptions of the polygraph test are implausible and that the evidence for its validity is weak. Polygraphers, on the other hand, supported by the handful of practitioners who have scientific training, contend that the polygraph technique can be remarkably accurate, claiming validities of 90, 95, and even 99 percent. One spokesman for the polygraph industry, the celebrated defense attorney F. Lee Bailey, asserted recently on national television that out of every 100 tests administered, 96 are accurate 3 are inconclusive, and only 1 will be in error.

Two Types of Polygraph Examiner

The situation is further complicated by the fact that "the polygraph technique" is not a single entity to which a single numerical accuracy estimate could be, in principle, attached. Rather, there are numerous techniques that can be roughly sorted into two main categories, and two different types of polygraph examiner. Of the 8 to 10 thousand polygraphers in the United States, probably the majority subscribe to the views of Richard Arther[3] and the late John Reid,[4] who held that the examiner's "diagnosis" should be a subjective judgment based on the full array of information available to him or her, including not only the polygraph tracings but also the examinee's behavior before, during, and after the test, what the examinee says and how he or she acts. According to this view, the polygrapher's is a clinical art like that of an internist, a skill that ripens with experience.

The other principal school of thought, founded by Cleve Backster,[5] holds that polygraphers cannot claim to have special intuition or superior clinical judgment and that they should therefore base their conclusions entirely on the one source of information that is uniquely theirs—namely, the polygraph tracings, interpreted by a system of numerical scoring of the charts. Although this approach limits the examiner's range of speculation, one should not imagine that it eliminates the subjectivity of polygraph testing altogether. It is still the examiner whose manner and actions set the emotional tone of the proceedings, thereby determining the subject's confidence (or lack of it) that the test will be fair and accurate. While the examinee's confidence does not guarantee a valid result, lack of confidence can be fatal to the outcome. An innocent suspect who distrusts the test or the examiner is likely to be scored as "deceptive." Guilty suspects who have no fear of failure—who think that they can beat the test or know that the results will be suppressed if they fail—are likely to be scored as "truthful." Moreover, it is the examiner who selects the questions to be used in the test proper. It is probable, in fact, that the choice of questions alone can determine the test outcome, irrespective of the examinee's guilt or innocence.

Nevertheless, numerical scoring does ensure that different polygraphers are more likely to agree in their interpretation of the same charts and also prevents the examiner from resorting to ad hoc evaluations for the purpose of rationalizing preconceived opinions. A polygraph chart, on which "the needles move as subtly as Raskolnikov's soul" (Younger, 1966), is as complex and cluttered as any dish of tea leaves or a Rorschach card, allowing an examiner to read into it whatever he or she likes if allowed to do so. I have seen a clinical examiner interpret as "deceptive" charts that Backster would score as "truthful," on the grounds that the breathing was slow and regular, "indicating that the subject was attempting to 'beat' the test and, hence, must be deceptive." Another polygrapher, even more fancifully, decided that the subject, known to have served in military intelligence, "probably knew how to control his blood pressure." By thus discounting as self-induced the large control responses that would have required Backster to score the test as truthful," this examiner neatly turned it into evidence for deception! Numerical scoring helps to eliminate this sort of capricious and arbitrary interpretation.

Even the Backster method, however, does not yield a test for which one can make a single, stable estimate of accuracy. It is now generally agreed that the control question technique is biased against the truthful subject (OTA Report, 1983). This means that polygraph tests that are failed, ceteris paribus, are less accurate than those that are passed (although see the discussion below concerning base rates). Similarly, there is reason to believe (Orne, 1975) that tests administered by a "friendly" polygrapher, one hired by the examinee or the examinee's attorney and whose adverse findings, if any, will be kept in confidence, are more likely to produce favorable results than tests administered under adversarial circumstances. Finally, due to base-rate considerations to be discussed below, we know that the average accuracy of any selected subset of tests—for example, only those tests that are passed or only those taken pursuant to stipulation—is likely to be different than the accuracy of polygraph tests in general.

The Polygrapher as Expert Witness

As some courts have realized, the polygraph examiner as expert witness is in a unique position in that his or her testimony goes directly to the heart of the issue. While expert testimony often is important to a case—the cause of death was poison; the fingerprints on the glass were those of the defendant—the testimony of the polygrapher is dispositive. It remains for the finders of fact to evaluate the significance of testimony by the pathologist or the forensic scientist but, if they believe the polygrapher, the verdict is thereby decided. If they are to accept the accuracy claims of the polygraphers, our courts must eventually address the unsettling question of whether it is just, not to say economic or efficient, to continue to try criminal defendants at all in the traditional way. No one supposes the juries arrive at the correct verdict 99 or even 95 percent of the time, even after trials involving months of preparation and weeks of evidence presentation. If a more accurate result can be achieved by a polygrapher in two or three hours, the implications are obvious.

On the other hand, if these claims are thought to be exaggerated, how accurate is accurate enough? Pathologists and fingerprint experts do not always agree, and psychiatrists, so it would seem, almost never do. Especially in recent years, even the testimony of eyewitnesses is increasingly called into question. If polygraphers perform with an accuracy at least greater than chance, should not their testimony be admitted along with this other fallible evidence?

We can simplify the problem by at once excluding the type of 'clinical' polygrapher described above whose conclusions flow from a global and subjective judgment based not simply on the charts but also on the fact situation and on observations of the subject's demeanor and behavior. An expert witness is permitted to offer opinion testimony based on technical knowledge that is not available to a lay jury; how to score polygraph charts might qualify as specialized technical knowledge of the required sort. But judging the facts of the case and the credibility of witnesses is the responsibility of the trier of fact; the court does not recognize "experts" in these areas. Since clinical polygraphers do not base their conclusions solely on polygraph results, and cannot usually say themselves what weight they have given other factors, it would seem apparent that examiners of this persuasion must not qualify as expert witnesses within the traditional meaning of the term.

Problems remain with the other type of examiner, the examiner who employs numerical scoring. Even if polygraph tests could be constructed, administered, and scored by an objective computer, unless the results can be shown to be at least as accurate as juries are on the average, there is the danger that their admissibility would diminish rather than increase the likelihood of a just result. As Professor Tribe (1971) has pointed out, "Readily quantifiable factors are easier to process—and hence more likely to be reflected in the outcome . . . dwarfing softer variables." That is, in the deliberations of human decision makers, evidence that is simple and direct tends to be given greater weight than evidence that is complex or indirect. Polygraph evidence is invariably simple—"the defendant's denials were deceptive"—and, because it goes to the heart of the issue, invariably direct—"therefore, he is guilty."

Polygraph tests can be (and have been) scored by computers, but scoring is the least of the problems with the polygraphs as we know that numerical scoring by human hands and eyes is already reasonably reliable. Polygraph tests might also be administered by computer as well, although this has not yet been attempted. But, unique among psychological tests, the polygraph technique requires that the questions themselves be individually tailored to the particular case. We cannot foresee this responsibility being programmed into a computer. Since the outcome can be entirely determined by the choice of questions, the same individual can pass one test and fail another on the same issue. The much publicized case of John DeLorean is a recent example. The examiner hired by the defense found DeLorean to be "truthful" with p > .99 while the FBI polygrapher found him to be clearly "deceptive."

WHAT IS A POLYGRAPH TEST?

Let us establish first that there is no such thing as a "lie detector." Unlike Pinocchio, we are not equipped with an involuntary mechanism that triggers a distinctive response whenever we attempt intentionally to deceive. The polygraph instrument records breathing movements, changes in blood pressure, and electrical changes in the skin related to the sweating of the palms. No pattern of changes within or among these three variables has ever been shown to be uniquely associated with lying. Any polygraphic reaction that one might show when lying might equally show when truthfully denying a false accusation.

Daniel Defoe argued in 1730 that "there is a tremor in the blood of the thief . . . that, if attended to, will effectually discover him." But there may be a tremor in the blood also of the accused innocent; such tremors, whether in the blood or the breathing or the voice, are by themselves intractably ambiguous. William Moulton Marston, who appears to have coined the term *lie detector* more than 60 years ago, believed that lying is accompanied by a transitory increase in systolic or peak blood pressure and that this reaction is never associated with truthfulness. Some now argue that Marston was wrong on both counts. Yet it was Marston's systolic blood pressure test that figured in the first consideration ever given by a U.S. court to admitting into evidence the results of a psychophysiological test of veracity.[6]

The Relevant/Irrelevant Test

The field polygraph, with its several pens that could make continuous records of blood pressure changes plus breathing movements and, later, electrodermal responses, was invented by a California police officer, John Larson (1932), and his associate, Leonarde Keeler. With this development, instrumental lie detection entered its second phase. Larson and Keeler intermixed *relevant* or "Did you do it?" questions with *irrelevant* questions (e.g., "Do they call you John?"). Criminal suspects who displayed marked disturbance in reaction to the relevant (compared to the irrelevant) questions were subjected to intensive interrogation.

The polygraph shows that you are not telling me the truth about this matter, Eddy. The instrument doesn't lie so there's no point in your holding out any longer.

Not infrequently this tactic proved effective in inducing confessions. As the publicity about the lie detector enhanced its mystique, the polygraph's utility as a kind of bloodless third degree also increased. Those who have not been actually connected to a polygraph have difficulty realizing how vulnerable one feels, especially after the examiner runs the "stim" test.

The stim test, intended to stimulate the guilty subject's anxieties while reassuring the innocent, usually involves choosing a card from a special deck proffered by the examiner.

> Remember the number on the card you chose and then we'll see if the polygraph can find your number. I'm going to ask you a series of numbers now and I want you to answer "No" to each one. That means your answer to the question about *your* number will be untrue. Okay, here we go. Was your number 7?

The examiner invariably detects the chosen number quickly and accurately and a naive subject is then inclined to think that the machine can almost read his mind. He would be less impressed if he knew that the stim test is a trick involving marked or prearranged cards; the examiner would too often be wrong if he actually relied on the polygraph to detect the correct number (Reid & Inbau, 1977, p. 42, note 49).

All anyone can determine from the polygraph charts is that the subject was more disturbed by one question than he was by another. One cannot say why the question was disturbing, whether it evoked guilt or fear or indignation or, indeed, whether the reaction was produced by the question at all—a subject who bites his tongue or constricts his anal sphincter just as the question is asked can produce a response on the polygraph that cannot be distinguished from spontaneous emotional disturbance.

Relevant questions are accusatory questions and are likely to produce an emotional reaction in innocent as well as in guilty suspects. It seems likely that any given suspect would be *more* disturbed by such a question if he is guilty and so must lie than if he or she is innocent, but this does not help us because we have no calibration of how *this* subject responds when being either truthful or deceptive. There is no use in attempting to compare one person's polygraph chart with that of another because individual differences in emotional and physiological reactivity can be very large; Jones, when he lies, may respond less than Smith does when she is truthful.

There was astonishingly little attempt to assess the validity of the relevant/irrelevant (R/I) test over the years, perhaps because its usefulness as an inducer of confessions did not hinge on its actual validity but required only that the suspect could be made to believe in its validity. Moreover, as a polygraph examiner very seldom discovers after making a diagnosis whether he or she was correct or not, it was difficult for users of the R/I method to appraise the accuracy of the techniques objectively. Nevertheless, some practitioners gradually began to realize that too many innocent persons were "failing" the R/I test, that too many innocent suspects somehow found the "Did you do it?" questions more disturbing than the "Is today Tuesday?" questions even though in fact they had not "done it." Something new was needed if the polygraph technique was to be taken seriously as a test rather than as just a kind of psychological rubber hose.

The Control Question Test

In the late 1940s, John Reid (1947), an attorney turned polygrapher-investigator, invented the control question test (CQT) which, in one form or another, has become the standard technique of polygraphic lie detection. To the former list of relevant and irrelevant questions, Reid added a third type, misleadingly known as *control questions*. This appellation is misleading in that it invokes the idea of a scientific control which, in this context, would mean a stimulus equivalent in all respects to the critical or relevant question except for the one factor being tested. For example, suppose this suspect is being tested to determine if he is the man who shot Fred on May 18. The relevant questions will involve different ways of asking, "Did you shoot Fred on May 18?" Suppose that we manage to convince our suspect that he is also suspected of shooting another man, George, on January 5, that he is in equal jeopardy of being prosecuted for that crime. We do this although in fact the second murder is a fiction. Then when we ask the *control* question, "Did you shoot George on January 5?", we can be sure that our suspect's "No" answer is truthful. Now we have a genuine control in the scientific sense; we know that his emotional response to the control question is an estimate of what this suspect's reaction ought to be to the relevant question if he is also innocent of that crime. If, instead, he responds consistently more strongly to the "Fred" question we might take this as an indication that he is not as innocent of that crime as he pretends.

Reid knew of course that a polygrapher would seldom be able to get away with this sort of fiction and that a genuine control question would rarely be possible. Reid's alternative was to try to formulate questions about the suspect's past that would elicit false answers, whether the suspect was truthful about the relevant issue or not. Reid was not a psychologist and found it possible to believe that all lies are psychologically alike. If we ask our suspect, "Have you ever committed a crime for which you were not caught?" his answer will probably be "No" and that answer will probably be deceptive—after all, nearly everyone has committed some sort of crime. If our suspect is truthful about the relevant issue, then, Reid believed, he should be *more* disturbed about telling that control lie than he is by the relevant question. Therefore, if our suspect shows more physiological response to the relevant than to these control questions, we shall diagnose him as deceptive with a clearer conscience than we could using the R/I procedure.

Although this is clearly the sense of Reid's 1947 idea, the fact is that he never actually enunciated this simple scoring rule. Instead, his textbook (Reid & Inbau, 1977) is full of illustrations of actual polygraph responses given by guilty suspects to relevant questions. The implication is that each of these particular response patterns indicates deception specifically. The truth is that *no* particular polygraph response is specific to deception, that each of these suspects might have shown these same reactions to the relevant questions, possibly attenuated somewhat in degree, if they were innocent. To testify that a particular response "shows deception," is just talking through one's hat. I suspect that Reid had some faint awareness of this fact also since he always insisted that the diagnosis should *not* depend merely on the charts alone but that the skilled examiner should attend even more closely to the "behavior symptoms" displayed by the subject during the session. Reid and Inbau (1977, pp. 293-295) thoughtfully provide a list of symptoms that are "characteristic of the liar"—refusing eye contact, seeming nervous or hostile or "too friendly," and so on—for use by their clinical examiners.

The Backster Zone Comparison Test

It was Cleve Backster who provided a rationale for those modern examiners who prefer to use the polygraph as a test rather than as an interrogation technique. Although his background was in military intelligence, Backster, like Reid, was not shy about formulating sweeping psychological principles:

> A person's fear, anxieties, and apprehensions are channeled toward the situation which holds greatest immediate threat to his self-preservation or general well-being. (Backster, 1974)

This is the justification offered for taking Reid's control question procedure seriously as an actual test for deception. During a pre-test interview, the examiner formulates two or three questions referring to possible misdeeds in the suspect's past, ideally events that bear some thematic relation to the crime under investigation. In one real-life example, a murder suspect was asked, "Before the age of 26, did you ever intentionally hurt someone with a weapon?" and "Before you were 26, did you ever think of hurting someone for revenge?" Because the suspect answered both questions "No," the examiner *assumed* that both answers were lies. Following Backster's principle, he then also assumed that the suspect, if innocent of the murder, would regard these control questions as holding the "greatest immediate threat to his self-preservation," greater than the relevant question, "Did you shoot Fred?" The examiner therefore compared the average size of the polygraph responses to the relevant and control questions— comparing adjacent pairs of questions in the same "zone"—and, because this suspect seemed more disturbed by the questions concerning the murder for which he had been arrested, the examiner concluded that he was deceptive and, hence, guilty.

Another polygrapher independently reached the same conclusion and, hearing that these polygraph examiners had extensive experience and that (in their professional opinion) Floyd Fay lied when he denied his guilt, an Ohio jury found him guilty of aggravated murder and he was sentenced to life in prison. More than two years later the real killers were caught; they confessed and exonerated Fay (Cimerman, 1981). It is a coincidence that, during the same month in which Fay was released from prison, two other men, Larry Smith of Akron and James Mendoza of Milwaukee, both of whom also had been previously convicted of murder on the basis of polygraph testimony, also were vindicated and became free men.

The Preemployment Screening Test

In screening job applicants there is no specific issue that can be addressed redundantly by the relevant questions. Instead, the examiner wishes to inquire about a number of issues of interest to the potential employer: "Did you answer every question truthfully on your application form?" "Have you ever stolen money or materials from a previous employer?" "Have you ever used street drugs before work or at work?" "Do you have any unpaid debts that you have not already told me about?" "Do you know or suspect that you have any illness or disability that you have not acknowledged?" and so on. In this situation, the use of control questions is not feasible. Instead, the examiner employs a version of the R/I test, a series of relevant questions interspersed with two or three irrelevant ones. While it is expected that most of these questions may elicit some response from most job applicants, it is assumed that a truthful subject will respond about equally to all of them. When a particular applicant responds especially strongly to just one or two of the questions, it is concluded that he or she "has a problem" with that issue—in other words, that his or her denial is not truthful.

In 1983 a young professor of engineering at an eastern university was conducting certain secret researches for the Central Intelligence Agency (CIA). The time arrived when it was necessary for him to try out his method on data from the CIA files. This required that he receive CIA security clearance. No problems were uncovered in the extensive background investigation so an appointment was made for the final step, the standard CIA polygraph screening. One of the four categories covered in this screening is the area of sexuality. To the question, "In the past five years, have you had a homosexual experience?" the professor showed stronger physiological responses than he had shown to the other questions. Questioned about this, he assured the examiner that he was happily married and had always regarded his sexual inclinations as unexceptional. When the test was repeated, however, he again reacted to this question, now even more strongly. The examiner concluded that his denial of homosexual activity was deceptive and his security clearance was denied.

As is usually the case in real-life applications of the polygraph test, neither I nor the CIA polygrapher know for certain the "ground truth" about this professor's sexual orientation. Nor do I know why the CIA thought it appropriate to inquire into this matter. But I do know that about 95 percent of married men in their early 30s have *not* had a homosexual experience in the past five years. Therefore, the prior probability one should attach to the professor's denial of such experience is at least .95. After observing that his blood pressure increased or his breathing became more shallow following this question, the polygrapher's confidence in the professor's truthfulness must have fallen below 50 percent.

As a psychophysiologist of over 30 year's experience, I take these problems of psychological assessment seriously. If the professor had shown no reaction at all to the question, my posterior confidence would have been identical to that prior value of .95. Since he did in fact show some physiological disturbance following the question, and since this result is compatible with the hypothesis that the implied accusation was true, then my confidence ought to be to some extent reduced. How much it is reduced will depend upon how many other—and perhaps more plausible—explanations I can think of for his reaction. Perhaps the question surprised him or embarrassed him or irritated him, to mention just a few possibilities. After careful reflection, I now regard the truthfulness of the professor's denial as about 94 percent probable.

The Guilty Knowledge Test

A fundamentally different method of polygraphic interrogation can be used to detect not lying but rather the presence in the suspect's mind of *guilty knowledge* (Lykken, 1959, 1981; Iacono, Boisvenu, & Fleming, 1984). In some minority of important criminal cases the investigator can compile a list of facts that should be known to a guilty suspect but not to an innocent person who had not been present at the scene of the crime. Where this is possible, a kind of multiple-choice test can be constructed along the following lines:

Item 1. If you are the murderer, you will know where in the house we found the body. Where did we find the victim's body? Was it

  (1) in the bathroom?
  (2) on the staircase?
  (3) in the kitchen?
  (4) in the basement?
  (5) in a bedroom?
  (6) in the dining room?

Item 2. If you are the person who stabbed Wilson, you will recognize the murder weapon that we found in the house. I will show you six different knives, one at a time. Look at each knife as I show it to you. Which knife was used to stab Wilson? Was it

  (1) this one?
  (2) this one?
  (3) this one? and so on.

It is intended that each alternative will seem equally plausible to an innocent person who, therefore, should give his strongest physiological response to the correct alternative only by chance. Since the first alternative is never correct (because there is a tendency to react more strongly to the first item in any list), an innocent person should have about 1 chance in 5 of thus showing a "guilty" response on each question. If the items of information are independent, however, his probability of reacting selectively to the correct alternative on both items will be only $(.2)^2$ and, with 10 items, we can say that an innocent person will "hit" on all 10 less than once in 10 million times. More practically, if we classify as "guilty" those who hit on 6 or more items, we might expect to exonerate 99 percent of innocent persons while identifying the guilty about 97 percent of the time.

These impressive statistics depend, however, on assumptions that well may not be met in practice. They require the assumption that the incorrect alternatives in each item are intelligently selected so that they will all seem equally plausible to an innocent suspect. It is assumed also that the guilty person has, on the average, at least an 80 percent chance of recognizing the correct alternative. Further, if the guilty suspect produces augmented responses to incorrect alternatives by covert self-stimulation, this may increase the rate of false-negative errors. Finally, it must be assumed that the entire procedure is conducted in a fair and careful manner so as to avoid leading an innocent person into responding differentially to the correct alternatives. The questions should be spoken by someone who does not know the correct answers and cannot therefore inadvertently (or deliberately) give them away by emphasis or inflection. The suspect must not be exposed to the relevant information through new reports or in prior questioning. A fictional example of how the GKT might be properly used in police investigation is given in Lykken (1981, chap. 21).

THE ACCURACY OF THE POLYGRAPH

The paucity of scientifically credible research on the accuracy of these various forms of polygraph testing under real-life conditions is remarkable in view of the popularity of the polygraph in the United States. An exhaustive survey of the literature was recently conducted at the request of the Congress (OTA, 1983); this survey revealed that there is no evidence at all concerning the validity of the preemployment screening test, the type that is so widely used by federal security agencies.

It is generally agreed that the validity issue can properly be investigated only in the real-life situation because it is impossible in the laboratory to simulate the emotional concerns that affect the physiological reactions of persons—and especially innocent persons being tested under actual field conditions. This in turn presents the problem of defining a criterion of "ground truth." Laboratory volunteers can be simply instructed to lie or be truthful but this method cannot be used in the field. One approach has been to employ a panel of judges who review the final evidentiary dossiers, excluding those cases where they think the evidence too scanty to permit a firm conclusion. The second approach has been to obtain from file records cases where the person tested subsequently confessed his or her guilt or where the person tested was later cleared by the confession of someone else. Neither criterion is wholly satisfactory. Innocent persons sometimes make false confessions for purposes of plea bargaining after having "failed" a polygraph test and having been assured that the authorities were thereby unshakably persuaded of their guilt. Moreover, those guilty persons who later confess may not be wholly representative of guilty persons who do *not* confess.

Another requirement of an acceptable validity study, one that should be obvious yet one that has not always been honored, is that the tests to be included in the study must not be selected by examiners who have a vested interest in demonstrating their accuracy. A study reported in *Polygraph*, the journal of the American Polygraph Association (Stephens, 1982) illustrates this problem. The author, a polygrapher in Virginia, sent a questionnaire to all the licensed examiners in his state asking them how many of the polygraph tests they had administered in 1980 had been verified to their own satisfaction and, of these "verified" tests, how many had been proved correct. The average accuracy claimed by his respondents was 98.6 percent, a figure that has been since reported to committees of the U.S. House and Senate as if it were a scientific finding.

Another example is a study of the psychological stress evaluator (PSE)—a form of voice stress analyzer—that was reported at a U.S. Senate hearing in 1978 (Heisse, 1978) illustrates this problem. The author, head of an association of voice stress analysts, asked his members to submit PSE charts on "verified" cases so that they might be rescored by other members of the group. Heisse reported that the set of charts volunteered by his members, when rescored blindly by other PSE experts, proved to be 96.12 percent accurate. Other studies, by persons who do not make their living giving PSE tests, have shown that this instrument operates at an essentially chance level of accuracy (see Lykken, 1981, chap. 13, for details). It seems unlikely that Heisse's colleagues submitted for rescoring any verified charts that they had not themselves scored correctly.

Several studies conducted at the Reid polygraph firm in Chicago suffer from the same fatal defect; in each case the polygraph charts selected for evaluation were all chosen by polygraphers who scored them correctly in the first instance (Horvath & Reid, 1971; Hunter &

Ash, 1973; Slowick & Buckley, 1975; Wicklander & Hunter, 1975). When charts thus selected are rescored by other examiners, agreement with the original scoring tends to run at about 90 percent—but this is only an imperfect estimate of interscorer agreement rather than of test validity. Raskin (1976) asked 25 polygraphers to score independently a set of 16 verified charts, finding near-perfect agreement with the criterion among those examiners trained in the same method of scoring Raskin himself uses. But this is not surprising—and also not very informative—because these 16 charts were ones that Raskin had himself scored blindly without error. They were selected from a larger set of 51 charts on which Raskin's average accuracy was only 72 percent (Barland & Raskin, 1976).

Accuracy of the Clinical Polygraph Test

As we have already discussed, it is important to distinguish between the type of polygraph test in which the diagnosis is based solely on the charts, using numerical scoring so that other examiners would be likely to score the charts the same way, and "tests" in which the examiner bases his or her conclusion on the charts *plus* on impressions of demeanor and behavior *plus* an appraisal of the fact situation as he or she understands it, combining all this information subjectively so that it is impossible to determine how the different components were weighted. There is no standard terminology for making this distinction so I characterize the latter as "clinical" polygraph examinations.

The only study we have of the accuracy of these clinical examinations (Bersh, 1969) concerned lie tests administered according to the Reid method to Army personnel involved in criminal investigations. Evidentiary dossiers were evaluated by a panel of four judges. Where the panel was divided three to one, the prior test result agreed with the panel majority 75 percent of the time. When the panel was unanimous, agreement was 92 percent.

One problem with the Bersh study is that part of the same file of evidence on which the panel based its criterion judgment was available to the polygraphers at the time of the examination. For example, when the suspect confessed during the examination, this fact was reported to the panel. As Bersh admits, it is impossible to determine what part (if any) the actual polygraph results played in any given diagnosis as these tests were evaluated clinically. It is certain that to some extent, as in those cases involving a confession, the agreement between polygrapher and panel reflected merely the fact that persuasive extra-polygraphic evidence was available to both. The fact that agreement was highest when the panel was unanimous probably reflects this; if a fifth judge had reviewed the evidence at the time of the polygraph test, he or she might well have agreed with the panel about as much as the polygraphers did.

From an evidentiary point of view, another problem with the clinical polygraph test lies in the fact that there is no evidence at all that polygraph examiners as a group have any special expertise in evaluating case facts or in appraising the behavior and demeanor of a witness. These functions, in the law courts, are traditionally held to be the responsibility of the finders of fact—of judge and jury. Where some special technology can provide relevant information not otherwise available to the fact finders, a technician may be accredited as an expert witness and permitted to present his or her opinion based on that technology. But the opinions of clinical polygraphers are based only partly, if at all, on the technology of the polygraph, and the examiners cannot reliably determine how much their opinions were based on the polygraph charts and how much on other judgments and impressions for which they have no special competence. To permit a polygrapher of this persuasion to testify in court is equivalent to asking for the opinion of a police detective, as an expert witness, as to whether the defendant is guilty or innocent.

Accuracy of the Control Question Test

The only way to separate the examiner's clinical impressions from the purely polygraphic information is to have the charts scored blindly by an examiner other than the one who administered the test. There are three published studies of this type that seem to meet the criteria outlined above (Barland & Raskin, 1976; Horvath, 1977; Kleinmuntz & Szucko, 1982). In the Horvath study, for example, 56 polygraph charts verified by confession were selected without regard to prior scoring and submitted for independent rescoring by 10 polygraphers. Half of the persons tested had subsequently confessed their guilt while the other 28 had subsequently been proven innocent by the confession of other persons. Chance accuracy in this type of testing is 50 percent; considering that the subject either is lying or is not, one should be correct half the time just by flipping a coin. Horvath's examiners were correct 63 percent of the time overall. Kleinmuntz and Szucko's examiners did better, 73 percent, as did Raskin, who scored the tests

TABLE 4.1   Aggregated Results of the Three Credible Field Studies
of the Accuracy of the Control Question Test (CQT)

	Polygrapher's Diagnosis		Totals	
Status of Suspect	Truthful	Deceptive	N	Accuracy
Guilty	20	98	118	83%
Innocent	51	38	89	57%
Totals*	72%	72%	207	70%

NOTE: The charts of a total of 207 criminal suspects were scored independently
by a total of 14 trained polygraphers. Note that 43 percent of the innocent suspects
were classified as deceptive.
*Because the CQT is less accurate on innocent than guilty subjects, the average
accuracy obtained will vary with the proportion of the guilty in the sample. The
estimate of average accuracy shown in the right lower corner of the table, 70 percent
is independent of base rates of guilt and innocence.

administered by Barland an average 72 percent accuracy. When we
examine the fate of the innocent suspects we find that 49 percent of
them were erroneously classified as deceptive by Horvath's examiners
(37 percent in Kleinmuntz & Szucko and 55 percent by Raskin)—the
CQT is strongly biased against innocent and truthful respondents.
The results of the three studies are summarized in Table 4.1

Polygraph proponents, understandably embarrassed by these findings, have attempted to repudiate them. Raskin, for example, insists
that the polygraphers used by Horvath and by Kleinmuntz & Szucko
were incompetent (Raskin, 1984). Whenever polygraph results are
impeached, it is customary for the apologists to blame examiner
incompetence. The coauthor of the leading textbook of lie detection
asserted 20 years ago that 80 percent of examiners are incompetent
(Inbau, 1965), a view reasserted by Raskin in 1984. The alternative
possibility, of course, is that the technique itself is incompetent. Raskin
even dismisses his own study (Barland & Raskin, 1976) although it was
the centerpiece of his research project supported by the U.S. Justice
Department and the doctoral dissertation of his student, Barland. In
this case he says that the criterion was faulty because the dossiers that
the judges relied on were assembled by a "part-time Work Study
student" who had no experience of investigation—that is, who was
incompetent (Raskin, 1984). If we are to agree that the studies
summarized in Table 4.1 were inadequate, then we are forced to the
conclusion that, as is true for polygraph screening tests, there is no
credible scientific evidence at all as to the accuracy of the CQT or other
specific-issue tests under real-life conditions.

Base rates of lying: Effect on accuracy. It is easily seen that the accuracy of any diagnostic test will tend to vary for different subgroups depending upon the base rate of the condition (e.g., the proportion of liars) in the total group tested. Based on the summary figures in Table 4.1, the CQT correctly identifies 83 percent of the guilty and 57 percent of the innocent—a 70 percent accuracy overall. Because of this bias against the innocent person, it might be supposed that a CQT that is passed should be taken more seriously than one that is failed.

But suppose that the majority of the persons tested are in fact guilty and must lie on the test. It is widely believed that the vast majority of suspects actually brought to trial in our criminal courts are guilty; 80 percent would be a conservative estimate. It might be suggested that we should permit suspects who have passed CQT tests to introduce this fact in evidence at trial. Let us explore the consequences of this rule. Out of each 1000 suspects brought to trial, we shall assume that 800 are guilty. If all 1000 take the CQT, 57 percent (or 114) of the 200 innocent persons will pass. But 17 percent (or 136) of the 800 guilty persons will also pass. This means that, of the 250 passed polygraph tests introduced into evidence, more than half (54.4) percent will be in error.

Countermeasures: Beating the CQT. John Reid, the inventor of the control question test, was the first to illustrate how a sophisticated subject might effectively defeat it (Reid, 1945). Physiological reactions to the control questions can be augmented by many forms of covert self-stimulation, clenching the toes, biting the tongue, constricting the anal sphincter, and so forth. Examiners of the type who depend solely on the charts are required to evaluate as "truthful" any chart on which the control responses are systematically larger than those to the relevant questions.

I was consulted some time ago by a government employee with a high security clearance; for reasons that will become apparent I cannot reveal his name. He had failed a polygraph test administered by his agency in connection with a security investigation. Dismayed at this betrayal by a technique that, like most of his colleagues, he had trusted, this man had come upon a copy of my book (Lykken, 1981). In his first phone call, he anxiously inquired whether he might fly to Minneapolis the next day to talk with me "about Chapter 19." In that chapter I briefly discuss how one can defeat the polygraph through self-stimulation. My caller, his career and good name hanging in the balance, had decided that, since the test had cheated him by falsely branding him a liar, he would respond by cheating the test. I assured my caller that I had nothing more to add that would justify his trip to Minneapolis but asked him to report on the outcome of his second test.

When he called a week later, he no longer sounded like a hunted animal. He had passed the second test "with flying colors" and his worries were over. The only problem he reported was some difficulty "keeping a straight face." Again, I cannot say for certain that this man was truthful when he took the test and later when he talked to me. If he was not, he was an excellent actor and a very foolish spy—why should he have called me as he did if he was lying? A real spy, moreover, would have been trained in how to beat the polygraph without any help from me. Because they depend so heavily upon polygraph screening, U.S. security agencies have become careless about more laborious—and more trustworthy—methods of checking on their employees and protecting classified information (Lykken, 1984). The KGB knows that agents who can beat the polygraph have easy access to American secrets; it is said that they run a special training school in Poland for this purpose.

No one knows, least of all the polygraphers, how many KGB agents, psychopaths, sophisticated professional criminals, and others have managed to deflect suspicion or avoid prosecution by beating polygraph tests. My own guess is that the number of these *false negative* test failures is not nearly so great as the number of *false positives*—innocent persons who have lost jobs or reputations, who have been prosecuted or even convicted of crimes that they did not commit, or who have been led, sometimes by their own attorneys, to confess to some lesser offense in order to escape prosecution on some more serious charge.

I have in my files a letter from a polygraph examiner in Alabama recounting that he had been one of several persons suspected of planting a bomb in a police station. As he had refused to submit to a polygraph test to clear himself, he had been held without bail for a considerable time before finally being released for lack of evidence. He wonders whether I do not agree that he was wise to have refused the test on the grounds that, as a polygrapher himself, he would have probably failed although innocent.

He reasoned that an innocent person will pass the test only if the examiner succeeds in deceiving him in certain essential ways. The rigged stim test, designed to make the polygraph appear infallible, is one obvious deception. More subtle, but even more important, is the deception involved in leading the subject to believe that he might be in jeopardy if his answers to the control questions are not strictly true. My polygrapher correspondent knew, however, that the opposite is true, that his jeopardy would lie in *not* being concerned about the control questions. Knowing that the more he reacted to the relevant questions the more likely he would fail, he believed—I think correctly—that he *would* therefore have reacted just as he had been trained to expect a guilty suspect to react.

One can wonder that it did not occur to him to use his knowledge to beat the test by self-stimulation during the control questions. I think he was misled by the belief, common among polygraphers, that counter-measures are easily detected. This is true of unsophisticated attempts—breath-holding, moving in the chair, flexing the biceps under the blood pressure cuff—usually observed during the relevant questions, and these are the only attempts that, almost by definition, are detected. Many polygraphers are victims of their own mythology.

The credibility of the lie detector. In reviewing the short list of studies intended to determine how jurors react to polygraph evidence, it will be entertaining and perhaps instructive for the reader to try to predict the outcome of each study a priori. One approach has been to ask actual jurors what weight they gave to the polygrapher's findings in reaching their decision. In both of the published examples (Forkosch, 1939; Barnett, 1973), the jury's finding was consistent with the polygraph's results. When questioned later, did these jurors say that the lie detector had made up their minds for them, or did they claim that their decision had been based on all the evidence of which the polygraph had merely been a part?

Another approach (Koffler, 1957) has been to ask persons—for example, law students—how they would decide a particular case on the (nonpolygraphic) evidence, and then to ask how they might decide the same case given a polygraph result leading in the other direction *plus* an instruction that the polygraph is 99.5 percent accurate. Did these law students cling to their original decisions, or did they consider that this would be like acknowledging a defect of reason?

Suppose we question jurors who have actually reached a verdict without benefit of polygraph evidence and ask them how they would have voted if a polygrapher had testified for the party against whom their decision had been made. Now we are not merely changing the terms of a hypothetical example. Instead, we are trying to uproot a fixed decision based on real evidence using as our tool hypothetical evidence that, if accepted, would indicate that the juror's original judgment had been faulty. When Carlson, Pasano, and Jannuzzo (1977) attempted such a study with moot court jurors at the Yale Law School, they told some of their subjects that the lie detector was 70 percent accurate; of these jurors, how many decided that their first verdict had been wrong? Half of the jurors were told that the polygraph was 95 percent accurate; how many of these changed their minds? Since only this last result might be hard to predict on common-sense grounds, the answer should be revealed at once: 8 of 31 jurors decided that a test that was 95 percent accurate was more likely to be right than their own original decision.

Attempts to evaluate retrospectively or subjectively the weight of any particular form of evidence require the assumption that jurors operate on the basis of explicit decision rules that they can alter experimentally as one might try out a modification of a computer program. As most jurors do not reason in this manner, such methods seem doomed to result in murky ambiguity. The prospective or experimental approach is more promising but has its perils too. Cavoukian and Heslegrave (1980), for example, recruited subjects from visitors to the Ontario Science Centre and asked them to pose as jurors and render verdicts after reading case summaries. In two studies, both based on actual Canadian murder cases, the judgments of the posed jurors reading the actual evidence were compared with those of subjects whose case summaries included polygraph testimony favorable to the defendant. In the first experiment, less than half (48 percent) of the control jurors found the defendant "not guilty." Among the group who read that the defendant had passed a lie test, however, 72 percent voted "not guilty."

Cavoukian and Heselgrave's second experiment seems at first glance to be less interesting because most of the control jurors (86 percent of them) found for the defendant even without the polygraph evidence that, being favorable to the defendant, could not possibly therefore have had much additional impact; 90 percent of the jurors who also got the lie test results voted for acquittal. Two things about this study are intriguing, however. First, in the actual case on which it was based (*Regina v. Wong*, 1977), the only instance in which polygraph evidence had actually been admitted at trial in Canada, the real jurors found *against* the defendant (and, indirectly, against the polygraph expert). Apparently the written case summaries used in the experiment failed to convey certain adverse impressions that had influenced the real jury.

A second feature of this experiment provides a clue as to what some of these adverse impressions might have been. One group of mock jurors were given the case summaries and the polygraph evidence *plus* the testimony of an expert witness for the Crown who criticized the polygraph evidence and urged skepticism. This addition not only negated the positive effect of the polygraph but actually produced significantly more votes for conviction than the nonpolygraph evidence alone. One would like to see this unexpected finding replicated before making too much of it, but the possibility is worth noting that polygraph evidence may sometimes have the opposite effect to that intended. If the jurors do not trust the polygrapher who testifies, if they suspect (perhaps assisted by the testimony of an opposing expert) that the lie detector is being oversold, then they may conclude that the party relying on the polygraph must have a case weaker than it otherwise would seem to be.

Markwart and Lynch (1979) asked their mock jurors to render two verdicts, one after reading a four-page case summary and a second after participating in a 45-minute discussion with other mock jurors impanelled with them. The case facts and a 40-minute videotape of the judge's summary and charge to the jury were based on an actual murder trial conducted in Ontario. Four juries (42 people) heard the original facts, which included no polygraph testimony. About half of them (55 percent) tended toward a "not guilty" verdict prior to the group discussion. This almost even split suggests that the evidence was not dispositive in this case; indeed, after group deliberation, 88 percent of these control jurors concluded that there was a reasonable doubt of the defendant's guilt and voted for acquittal.

Here is the kind of situation where one might expect the polygraph to have its strongest impact, as in Cavoukian and Heslegrave's first experiment where addition of exculpatory lie test findings swung the majority from "guilty" to "not guilty." Four of Markwart and Lynch's mock juries heard the same case plus testimony that the defendant had failed the polygraph. Two-thirds of these 41 jurors voted to convict both before and after deliberation. Thus, the addition of the adverse polygraph produced a change from 12 percent to 66 percent deciding "guilty."

Four different juries were given testimony that the defendant had passed rather than failed the lie detector. Once again, the reaction to polygraph findings favorable to the defendant proved paradoxical. After deliberation, a significantly *smaller* proportion (59 percent) of these jurors chose a "not guilty" verdict than of those who received the same evidence *minus* the supposedly exculpatory lie test (88 percent).

Both of these mock jury studies suggest that, where the other evidence is inconclusive, polygraph evidence can determine the outcome in either direction. Both studies also suggest that the use of polygraph findings by the defense may be risky, however, and may actually weaken the rest of its case in the eyes of the jury. In the five reported cases (i.e., cases that had reached appellate courts) cited by Roper (1975) in which polygraph results had been admitted, the verdicts all coincided with the lie test findings. I am personally familiar with five additional cases, all involving the charge of murder, in which polygraph evidence was not rebutted by opposing expert testimony. Among these, the only instance where the jury failed to conform to the prior verdict of the polygraph was the one case mentioned above where the evidence was offered by the defense (*Regina v. Wong*, 1977).

The Accuracy of the Guilty Knowledge Test

It should be said at once that the accuracy of the GKT has not yet been assessed in a systematic way under real life conditions. I know of only a handful of instances in which it has been used in actual police work. Polygraphers are wedded to the various techniques of lie detection because they are so versatile while the GKT can only be used in certain instances of criminal investigation. And lie detection is (seems) so easy; just ask the question and see if the pens dance. To set up a competent GKT requires detailed and skillful investigation and few polygraphers are investigators.

The reason that analog studies (laboratory studies using simulated crimes and volunteer subjects) are not acceptable for purposes of estimating the accuracy of lie detection methods in real life is that one cannot simulate the kind and intensity of emotion experienced especially by innocent suspects. If the relevant question elicits strong anger rather than guilt, or if the control question elicits no emotion at all, in an innocent suspect, the CQT will likely fail. The GKT, in contrast, does not depend on the kind or degree of emotional response that is elicited. An innocent person may feel confident or frightened; in neither case is he or she likely to respond differentially to the correct alternatives because he or she does not know which ones they are. The guilty suspect, similarly, does not need to feel guilty or in fear of detection; hundreds of laboratory studies of the "orienting reflex" attest to the fact that perfectly calm individuals are likely to show stronger physiological responses to stimuli that are significant than to those that are not.

For these reasons, it can be argued that analog studies of the GKT do provide reasonable indications of how accurate the procedure might be in police applications *provided all of the necessary assumptions, listed above, are adequately met.* Eight laboratory studies[7] in which a total of 313 volunteer subjects were tested for guilty knowledge of a mock crime of which about half (161) of them were guilty are aggregated in Table 2. One of the virtues of the GKT is that one can predict how well it ought to work based on an evaluation of the items used. Five of the eight studies employed 6 items having 4 scored alternatives; one study used 10 items and two used only 5 items.

For a well-constructed GKT item with 4 alternatives, the probability that an innocent person will give his or her largest response to the correct alternative is about .25. Let us assume that a guilty suspect has a .80 probability of giving his or her largest response to the correct alternative. On these assumptions, we can calculate that 96.2 percent of the innocent should hit on 3 or fewer of the 6 items; the observed value shown in Table 2 was 96.7 percent. Similarly, we can compute that 89.1 percent of guilty suspects should hit on 4 or more items and thus be identified as possessing guilty knowledge; the observed value was 88.2 percent.

Use of the GKT as evidence at trial. The only instance known to me when the results of a guilty knowledge test were admitted into evidence at a criminal trial was related to me by an FBI examiner. He was particularly pleased by the experience because he had not been asked to give an opinion but merely to describe the results that spoke for themselves. For example, the bank robber had worn a solid-color stocking cap pulled down over his face. When the defendant had been asked, "What color was the cap worn by the robber? Was it black? red? brown? green? blue? gray?" his polygraph chart showed an obvious reaction only to "red," the correct color.

If polygraph examiners are to be allowed to testify in court, a reasonable precaution might be to limit their testimonies to a factual description of the tests and their results. That is, what questions were asked and what was the relative magnitude of the defendant's polygraphic response to each question. Thus, the polygrapher who testified for the prosecution in the Floyd Fay case would have merely

TABLE 4.2 Aggregated Results of Eight Analog Studies of the Accuracy
of the Guilty Knowledge Test

Status of Subject	GKI Diagnosis		Totals	
	Innocent	Guilty	N	Accuracy
Guilty	19	142	161	88.2%
Innocent	147	5	152	96.7%
Totals	89%	97%	313	93%

NOTE: Comparison with Table 4.1 shows that the GKT is more accurate over all
and far more accurate in identifying the innocent.

explained that he had asked Fay, "Did you shoot Fred on May 18?" and
"Before the age of 26, did you ever think of hurting someone for
revenge?" and that Fay had responded more strongly to the former
question. It is doubtful that the jury would have convicted Fay of
murder on the basis of that evidence. Unfortunately, however, that jury
never learned the details of the test or how it was scored; what they
heard was that the examiner had given thousands of polygraph tests
and in his opinion Fay had "shown deception" in response to questions
about his involvement in the murder.

Fay was in fact arrested at his home on the night of the killing before
any information had been released in the news. Fay might have been
given a guilty knowledge test that same night.

Fay, you are suspected of killing a friend of yours. If you are guilty, you'll
recognize the first name of the victim. Just sit quietly and repeat each
name after me. What is the name of the victim? Is it Bob? George? Jerry?
Pete? Fred? Bill?

What weapon was used in this killing? Was it an icepick? a pistol? a knife?
a shotgun? a club? a rifle?

The killer wore a ski mask over his face. What color was the ski mask?
Was it yellow? blue? red? green? brown? orange?

In the courtroom, the polygraph examiner might then testify that he had
asked, say, six such questions and that the defendant had given his
largest response to the correct alternative in each instance. The jury
then could decide what conclusions to draw from these facts. In Fay's
case, of course, the matter never would have gone to trial because there
is about a 96 percent probability that Fay would have passed a guilty
knowledge test and been cleared of suspicion at once.

CONCLUSIONS

Lie detection tests—interrogation techniques that attempt to diagnose answers as "truthful" or "deceptive" on the basis of the subject's involuntary physiological responses, whether measured by polygraph, voice stress analyzer, or otherwise—are undoubtedly useful as methods for inducing confessions from some guilty individuals. Their usefulness as actual tests, however, is questionable. They are based on psychological assumptions that are prima facie implausible. The control question polygraph test, generally regarded to be the most accurate of these techniques, is the only one for which we have credible scientific evidence concerning its validity in real-life applications. That evidence indicates that the CQT is wrong about one-third of the time over-all against a chance expectancy of 50 percent accuracy. The accuracy of the CQT in a particular application depends upon the base rate of lying in the population of persons tested. It can be shown that, if the CQT is 70 percent accurate in general, the accuracy of exculpatory tests offered in evidence by the defense may be actually less than 50 percent, the accuracy of a coin flip. The same conclusions apply to adverse findings resulting from tests taken under stipulation and pursuant to an offer by the prosecution to drop charges if the test is "passed."

The CQT is also dangerously biased against an innocent, truthful respondent who, if he or she is the only suspect tested, appears to have more than a 40 percent chance of being erroneously diagnosed as "deceptive." The CQT requires that the examiner succeed in deceiving the respondent in certain ways so that a sophisticated person (e.g., a polygraph examiner) cannot be successfully tested. In spite of such refinements as numerical or even computer scoring of the charts, the CQT is unavoidably subjective; it is very probable that an examiner can produce "passes" or "fails" almost at will by adopting a friendly or hostile manner and by tendentious selection of questions. On the other hand, it is clear that the CQT can be defeated by sophisticated guilty suspects using covert self-stimulation to augment their reactions to the control questions.

Because a polygrapher's conclusions inevitably go to the heart of any criminal case, and because they are so simple in concept, it seems likely that they will tend to be given undue weight in the deliberations of a jury of laypersons, especially in those cases where the other evidence is either complex or scanty. The two published studies that employed the mock jury paradigm both found that the unrebutted testimony of a polygraph examiner was sufficient to influence a majority of jurors in cases where the extrapolygraphic evidence was not dispositive.

There is a suggestion, however, that polygraph evidence entails a risk for the party that employs it. Where there is competent scientific rebuttal testimony, juries may interpret reliance on the polygraph as indicating that the party's case-in-chief is weaker than it otherwise might seem.

NOTES

1. States in which polygraph tests may be admitted into evidence subject to prior stipulation of the parties include the following: Alabama, Arkansas, California, Delaware, Florida, Georgia, Indiana, Iowa, Kansas, Nevada, New Jersey, North Dakota, Ohio, Oregon, Utah, Washington, and Wyoming.

2. These states are Alaska, Colorado, Hawaii, Illinois, Kentucky, Louisiana, Maine, Maryland, Michigan, Minnesota, Mississippi, Missouri, Montana, Nebraska, New Hampshire, New York, North Carolina, Oklahoma, Pennsylvania, South Dakota, Tennessee, Texas, West Virginia, and Wisconsin.

3. Richard O. Arther, who has a degree in police administration, has operated a polygraph business and a polygraph school (the National Training Center of Polygraph Science) in Manhattan since 1958.

4. The late John E. Reid, who was trained as a lawyer, operated both a polygraph firm and the Reid College for the Detection of Deception, both in Chicago.

5. Cleve Backster, who was in military intelligence during World War II, received his polygraph training from John Reid, as did Arther and most other polygraphers of that generation. In contrast to Arther, however, Backster, eventually rejected the Reid methods and established his own polygraph school in San Diego.

6. The case referred to here is *Frye v. United States,* 293 F. 1013 (D.C. Cir. 1923). In *Frye,* the appellate court ruled that, to be admitted as expert testimony, scientific tests or other evidence "must be sufficiently established to have gained general acceptance in the particular field to which it belongs."

7. The studies are Balloun and Holmes, 1979; Bradley and Warfield, in press; Davidson, 1968; Giesen and Rollison, 1980; Iacono et al., 1984; Lykken, 1959; Podlesny and Raskin, 1978; and Stern, Breen, Watanabe and Perry, 1981.

REFERENCES

Abbell, M. (1977). Polygraph evidence: The case against admissibility in federal criminal trials. *The American Criminal Law Review, 15,* 29-62.

Backster, C. (1974). The anticlimax dampening concept. *Polygraph, 3,* 28-50.

Balloun, K. S., & Holmes, D. S. (1979). Effects of repeated examinations on the ability to detect guilt with a polygraphic examination: A laboratory experiment with a real crime. *Journal of Applied Psychology, 64,* 316-322.

Barland, G., & Raskin, D. (1976). *Validity and reliability of polygraph examinations of criminal suspects.* (Report 76-1, Contract 75-NI-99-0001), Washington, DC: U.S. Department of Justice.

Barnett, F. J. (1973). How does a jury view polygraph examination results? *Polygraph, 2,* 275-277.

Bersh, P. A. (1969). A validation study of polygraph examiner judgments. *Journal of Applied Psychology, 53,* 399-403.

Bradley, M. T., & Warfield, J. F. (in press). Innocence, information, and the guilty knowledge test in the detection of deception. *Psychophysiology.*

Carlson, S. C., Pasano, M. S., & Jannuzzo, J. A. (1977). The effect of lie detector evidence on jury deliberations: An empirical study. *Journal of Police Science and Administration, 5,* 148-154.

Cavoukian, A., & Heslegrave, R. J. (1980). The admissibility of polygraph evidence in court. *Law and Human Behavior, 4,* 117-131.

Cimerman, A. (1981). "They'll let me go tomorrow": The Fay case. *Criminal Defense, 8,* 7-10.

Davidson, P. O. (1968). Validity of the guilty-knowledge technique: The effects of motivation. *Journal of Applied Psychology, 52,* 62-65.

Edwards, R. H. (1981). A survey: Reliability of polygraph examinations conducted by Virginia polygraph examiners. *Polygraph, 10,* 229-272.

Forkosch, M. D. (1939). The lie detector and the courts. *New York University Law Quarterly Review, 16,* 202-231.

Giesen, M., & Rollison, M. A. (1980). Guilty knowledge versus innocent associations: Effects of trait anxiety and stimulus context on skin conductance. *Journal of Research in Personality, 14,* 1-11.

Heisse, J. (1978). Hearings on *The Polygraph Control and Civil Liberties Protection Act* before the Subcommittee on the Constitution of the Committee on the Judiciary, U.S. Senate.

Horvath, F., & Reid, J. E. (1971). The reliability of polygraph examiner diagnosis of truth and deception. *Journal of Criminal Law, Criminology, and Police Science, 62,* 276-281.

Horvath, F. (1977). The effect of selected variables on interpretation of polygraph records. *Journal of Applied Psychology, 62,* 127-136.

Hunter, F., & Ash, P. (1973). The accuracy and consistency of polygraph examiner's diagnosis. *Journal of Police Science and Administration, 1,* 370-375.

Iacono, W. G., Boisvenu, G. A., & Fleming, J. A. (1984). Effects of diazepam and methylphenidate on the electrodermal detection of guilty knowledge. *Journal of Applied Psychology, 69,* 289-299.

Inbau, F. E. (1965). The case against the polygraph. *American Bar Association Journal, 51,* 857.

Jones, E. A. Jr. (1979). "Truth" when the polygraph operator sits as arbitrator (or judge): The deception of "detection" in the "Diagnosis of truth and deception." In J. Stern & B. Dennis (Eds.), *Truth, Lie Detectors, and Other Problems,* 31st Annual Proceedings, National Academy of Arbitrators.

Kleinmuntz, B., & Szucko, J. J. (1982). On the fallibility of lie detection. *Law & Society Review, 17,* 85-104.

Koffler, J. M. (1957). The lie detector—a critical appraisal of the technique as a potential undermining factor in the judicial process. *New York Law Forum, 3,* 123-158.

Larson, J. A. (1932). *Lying and its Detection.* Chicago: University of Chicago Press.

Lykken, D. T. (1959). The GSR in the detection of guilt. *Journal of Applied Psychology, 43,* 385-388.

Lykken, D. T. (1981). *A Tremor in the Blood: Uses and Abuses of the Lie Detector.* New York: McGraw-Hill.

Lykken, D. T. (1984). Trial by polygraph. *Behavioral Sciences and the Law, 2,* 75-92.

Lykken, D. T. (1984). Detecting deception in 1984. *American Behavioral Scientist, 27,* 481-499.

Lykken, D. T. (1984). Polygraphic interrogation. *Nature, 307,* 681-684.

Markwart, A., & Lynch, B. E. (1979). The effect of polygraph evidence on mock jury decision-making. *Journal of Police Science and Administration, 7,* 324-332.

Orne, M. (1975). Implications of laboratory research for the detection of deception. *Polygraph, 2,* 169-199.

OTA Report. (1983). *Scientific validity of polygraph testing: A research review and evaluation.* Washington, DC: United States Congress, Office of Technology Assessment.

Podlesny, J. A., & Raskin, D. (1978). Effectiveness of techniques and physiological measures in the detection of deception. *Psychophysiology, 15,* 344-359.

Raskin, D. (1976). *Reliability of chart interpretation and sources of errors in polygraph examination.* (Report 76-3, Contract 75-NI-99-0001), Washington, DC: U.S. Department of Justice.

Raskin, D. (1984). Testimony in *TSEU et al v. Texas Department of Mental Health-Mental Retardation et al.,* Austin, April.

Regina v. Wong. (1977). In *Canadian Criminal Cases.* (2nd ed., Vol. 33), p. 515.

Reid, J. E. (1945). Simulated blood pressure response in lie-detector tests and a method for their detection. *American Journal of Police Science, 36,* 201-204.

Reid, J. E. (1947). A revised questioning technique in lie-detection tests. *Journal of Criminal Law and Criminology, 37,* 542-547.

Reid, J. E., & Inbau, F. E. (1977). *Truth and Deception: The Polygraph ("Lie-Detector") Technique* (2nd ed.), Baltimore: Williams & Wilkins.

Roper, R. St. J. (1975). The search for truth at trial: An argument against the admission of polygraph test results at trial. *Polygraph, 4,* 119; 130-138.

Slowick, S., & Buckley, J. (1975). Relative accuracy of polygraph examiner diagnosis of respiration, blood pressure, and GSR recordings. *Journal of Police Science and Administration, 3,* 305-309.

Stern, R. M., Breen, J. P., Watanabe, T., & Perry, B. S. (1981). Effect of feedback of physiological information on responses to innocent associations and guilty knowledge. *Journal of Applied Psychology, 66,* 677-681.

Tribe, L. (1971). Trial by mathematics: Precision and ritual in the legal process. *Harvard Law Review, 84,* 1329-1393.

United States v. Alexander 526 F. 2d 161, 166 (1975).

Wicklander, D., & Hunter, F. (1975). The influence of auxiliary sources of information in polygraph diagnosis. *Journal of Police Science and Administration, 3,* 405-409.

Younger, I. (1966, December 31). A review of the first edition of Reid & Inbau, *Truth and Deception. Saturday Review.*

CHAPTER 5

The Defendant's Testimony

DAVID R. SHAFFER

> Jurymen seldom convict a person they like or acquit one they dislike. The main work of a trial lawyer is to make a jury like his client, or at least feel sympathy for him; facts regarding the crime are relatively unimportant. (Clarence Darrow as quoted in Sutherland & Cressey, 1966, p. 442)

> [Our] results corroborate strikingly the hypothesis that the jury follows the direction of the evidence. The highest acquittal rate is [in cases] where the defense . . . is the strongest, and . . . the . . . lowest acquittal rate is [in cases] where the prosecution evidence is the strongest. (Kalven & Zeisel, 1966, p. 161)

Our focus in this chapter is on the central figure in both criminal and civil trials—the defendant who stands accused of wrongdoing. Legal scholars and social scientists have long assumed that the outcome of many trials will largely depend on who the defendant is and what he or she chooses to say (or not say) when presenting a defense. As we see in the chapter's opening quotation, Clarence Darrow suggests that *extralegal* influences (i.e., those based on inadmissible evidence) such as the defendant's reputation, social background, or other attributes that affect juror sentiments toward the accused may contribute more to jury decisions than does the legal evidence itself. Among the many extralegal variables that are thought to affect lay juries' impressions of an accused and contribute to the verdicts they reach are the defendant's sex, race, and socioeconomic status, as well as his or her general attractiveness, moral character, and similarity to the jurors who are trying the case.

Just how powerful are these extralegal influences? Estimates vary depending upon the data base that one is considering. For example, archival analyses of criminal trials reveal that defendant characteristics such as gender, socioeconomic status, or race contribute very little, by themselves, to either jury verdicts or judges' sentencing decisions Hagan, 1974; Myers, 1979). However, race does become an issue in capital trials where black defendants who are convicted for the rape or murder of white victims are more likely to receive the death sentence than are either white or black defendants who have harmed black victims (Bowers & Pierce, 1980; Hagan, 1974; Wolfgang & Reidel, 1976). Kalven and Zeisel's (1966) analyses of more than 3500 trials indicate that defendants do *not* evoke strong positive or negative sentiments among jurors in roughly two-thirds of the cases they studied. And even when extralegal sentiments were strong, they were most likely to influence verdicts in close cases where the evidence clearly favored neither the defense nor the prosecution. In summarizing their findings from the Chicago Jury Project, Kalven and Zeisel state that "we find no cases in which the jury convicts a man, so to speak, for the crime of being unattractive" (p. 385). Indeed, one recent observational study of trial outcomes found no relationship between observers' ratings of the attractiveness of 74 criminal defendants and the verdicts rendered by juries trying their cases (Stewart, 1980; see also Kerr, 1982).

By contrast, the results of mock jury experiments suggest that extralegal sentiments play a much larger role in juridic decisions. In one study (Foley, Chamblin, & Fortenberry, 1979), 33 percent of the variability in hypothetical sentencing decisions was attributable to extralegal characteristics such as the race and socioeconomic status of the defendants. Other studies have found that mock juries attribute less guilt to defendants who are physically attractive, are of good character, or who express attitudes similar to those jurors hold (see Dane & Wrightsman, 1982).

Why the disparity in outcomes between actual courtroom cases and mock jury experiments? One reason may be that mock jurors typically receive abbreviated written or audiotaped versions of a trial— summaries that provide very little relevant evidence while focusing much more intently on extralegal factors than is normally true in actual trials. Indeed, several recent studies have found that the impact of extralegal sentiments on mock trial outcomes is attenuated or even eliminated as the legally relevant evidence becomes more reliable or clear-cut (e.g., Baumeister & Darley, 1982; Kaplan & Schersching, 1980). It is primarily in close cases where mock jurors express individual opinions without an opportunity to deliberate that their decisions are heavily influenced by extralegal sentiments toward the accused.

To this point, we may conclude that Clarence Darrow's sentiment hypothesis is an overstatement. However, the finding that extralegal sentiments contribute less to trial outcomes than does the weight of the evidence in no way implies that juror sentiments are unimportant. Kalven and Zeisel (1966) note that "sentiments about a defendant are rarely powerful enough to cause disagreement [with the judge] by themselves; rather they gain their effectiveness only in partnership with some other factor in the case" (p. 114). In this chapter, we will concentrate on one other factor that weighs heavily on juridic decisions both directly, in terms of its form and content, and indirectly, by virtue of its contribution to (or interaction with) various extralegal sentiments. That factor is the defendant's testimony.

THE DEFENDANT'S CONSTITUTIONAL RIGHTS AND PRIVILEGES

The framers of the United States Constitution took great care to protect criminal defendants against the arbitrary exercise of governmental power. The Sixth Amendment guarantees two basic rights: "In all criminal prosecutions, the accused shall enjoy the right to a speedy and public trial, by an impartial jury [and] . . . the right to have the assistance of counsel for his defense." The primary testimonial privilege granted an accused is the right against self-incrimination. This guarantee, as outlined in the Fifth Amendment, provides that "no person . . . shall be compelled in any criminal case to be a witness against himself."

During the tenth and eleventh centuries, defendants had few such rights and privileges under Anglo-Saxon law. Criminal courts (i.e., court officials) functioned as accusers, prosecutors, and triers of fact, and defendants were bound by the oath *de veritate dicenda*—a rule that required them to provide truthful answers to any and all interrogation, regardless of its content or relevance to the case. Clearly, this inquisitional oath was a model of self-incrimination that often presented an accused with the unenviable choice between contempt, perjury, conviction, or possible indictment for crimes unrelated to the offense under investigation (Berger, 1980). By 1352, "trial by jury" was becoming well established in English criminal law, and this method of adjudication was transported to the American colonies, serving as the foundation for guarantees provided under the Sixth Amendment (McCormick, 1972). It was not until the seventeenth century, however, that English courts acknowledged that self-incriminating testimony was inherently unjust and could not be compelled. This principle was gradually incorporated into the legal systems of the American colonies and served as the basis for the Fifth Amendment privilege against self-incrimination.

Use of the Fifth and Sixth Amendment privileges. Contrary to popular opinion, most criminal cases are not tried by jury. In fact, less than one-third of all criminal defendants stand trial; the remainder plead guilty in return for concessions from the prosecutor (Ebbesen & Konecni, 1982; Myers, 1979). And as approximately one-third of those who do stand trial opt to be tried by a judge, only 60-65 percent of felony prosecutions (or about 15-20 percent of all criminal cases) are actually decided by a jury (Kalven & Zeisel, 1966; Myers, 1979).

The primary means by which defendants invoke the privilege against self-incrimination is by declining to take the witness stand. This option was exercised by only 18 percent of the defendants sampled in the Chicago Jury Project, the clear majority (82 percent) deciding that it was in their best interests to testify (Kalven & Zeisel, 1966). However, Myers (1979) reported that 82 percent of the defendants in her sample did *not* testify as to their involvement in criminal activities (or lack thereof).

In deciding whether to testify, the accused and his or her counsel must consider a number of strategic factors, including the defendant's credibility as a witness and the believability of his or her testimony. Credibility is an especially important consideration. Once the defendant takes the stand, it becomes possible under certain circumstances for the prosecution to introduce evidence of prior convictions for the purpose of impeaching the defendant's credibility. Moreover, a decision to testify is often interpreted as a waiver of the privilege against self-incrimination, so that defendants who take the stand may not be allowed to invoke the Fifth Amendment in response to specific and potentially self-incriminating questions (Berger, 1980). Of course, the defendant must weigh these considerations against the potential costs of *not* testifying. Not only is an accused unable to give his or her interpretation of the facts by declining to take the stand, but jurors might also draw damaging inferences from the defendant's use of the privilege. As Kalven and Zeisel (1966) have noted, "The defendant . . . must know more about his alleged innocence than anyone else, and if he decides to withhold evidence [jurors are likely to assume] he must be doing so for a reason" (p. 144).

In sum, it is difficult to specify the percentage of trials in which defendants invoke the privilege against self-incrimination, for the incidence of its use undoubtedly depends on the jurisdiction, the nature of the offense, the defendant's background, and the believability of his or her version of the facts. Kalven and Zeisel's (1966) study revealed that defendants testify less frequently in murder and burglary trials than in other kinds of serious felony prosecutions (e.g., assault, narcotics, and rape cases). And the defendant's background does come into play, for those with previous criminal convictions are more likely to invoke the Fifth Amendment privilege than are their counterparts who have no record (Berger, 1980; Kalven & Zeisel, 1966). Previously convicted felons are particularly reluctant to testify when the evidence seems clear for acquittal; this is the circumstance under which counsel may see no reason for disturbing a favorable situation by allowing the defendant's record to be disclosed. By contrast, counsel's desire to present the defendant's version of the incident and avoid any adverse reaction to a claim of the Fifth Amendment privilege is likely to outweigh concerns about the credibility or believability of that testimony in cases where evidence is not especially favorable to the accused (Kalven & Zeisel, 1966).

In the pages that follow, we will look more closely at the contribution of the defendant's testimony to trial outcomes. First, we will focus on the content of that testimony—what the defendant says and the kind of defense that he or she may offer. Our attention then shifts to the critical issue of credibility, as we review what is known about the factors that judges and jurors are likely to consider when trying to determine whether a defendant is telling the truth. Finally, we will concentrate on what the defendant does not say—that is, the impact of a decision to "take the Fifth" on jurors' reactions to the accused.

WHAT THE DEFENDANT SAYS

As triers of fact, judges and juries must process the often contradictory testimony of several witnesses, consider the implications of physical and demonstrative evidence (if any), listen to competing theories offered by the defense and the prosecution to account for the facts, and then retire to weigh the evidence and decide which version of the facts is correct. Throughout a trial, the prosecutor may display contempt for the defendant and will strive to present a clear and simple explanation of the facts that points to conviction. By contrast, the goal of the defense attorney is to create *reasonable doubt* about the defendant's guilt. Counsel will typically display respect and sympathy for the accused while trying to show that the facts of the case are complex and their implications ambiguous. Viewed in this light, it should be apparent that both the substance and style of the defendant's testimony can be extremely important in determining the version of the facts that a judge or jury is likely to accept.

Evidence about a defendant's alleged confession was examined in Chapter 3 and will not be discussed here. The coverage in this section centers around three major kinds of testimony: (1) the defendant's denial of wrongdoing; (2) the defendant's explanation of the facts and circumstances surrounding the criminal act; and (3) the kinds of defense that are offered to account for an accused's actions and absolve him or her of criminal responsibility.

Effects of a Defendant's Denial

Is an accused well advised to take the stand and simply deny any involvement in the crime or complaint under investigation? Probably not. In a recent archival study, Myers (1979) assessed the contribution of both *evidential* (e.g., eyewitness testimony, defendants' statements about involvement, expert witnesses, recovered weapons) and *non-evidential* or extralegal variables (e.g., defendant demographics, prior legal histories, identities of victims) to verdicts rendered by juries in 201 felony prosecutions in Marion County, Indiana. The evidential variable that contributed most to verdicts was the defendants' testimony. Defendants who testified (typically denying their involvement or responsibility for harmdoing) were more likely to be convicted than those who did not testify.

Myers's finding is generally corroborated by the results of mock jury research. Shaffer, Sadowski, and Hendrick (1978) noted that a defendant's tearful denial of wrongdoing did not help his cause in a murder trial in which the evidence was highly equivocal. Moreover, Yandell (1979) reports that a person who makes exculpatory statements (e.g., by suggesting that he or she is not guilty before being asked) and who protests his or her innocence too vociferously is more likely to be judged guilty than is one who does not volunteer such information.

Attribution theory provides one explanation for judges' and jurors' skepticism about a defendant's denial of wrongdoing. According to Kelley's (1973) *discounting principle*, the role of any plausible cause for an event will be discounted (that is, viewed as less certain) if other plausible causes for the event are also apparent. In the context of a criminal trial, jurors are likely to perceive at least two plausible causes for a defendant's denial of wrongdoing: He or she may be innocent, or rather, may be lying in order to manipulate the triers of fact and gain an acquittal. If the evidence is ambiguous (as was the case in the Shaffer et al., 1978, study), judges and jurors may weigh these two causes as equally probable, and the defendant's denial should have little or no effect on their decisions. But if the weight of the evidence favors conviction (as in most of the trials sampled in Myers's archival study), or if the accused appears unnecessarily defensive by protesting too early or severely, the triers of fact are likely to infer that the defendant "doth protest too much" and must be attempting to manipulate their opinions.

The Defendant as an Interpreter of Facts

The discounting principle also suggests that defendants may not be very convincing when presenting an alibi or evidence of extenuating circumstances that might absolve them of responsibility for wrong-doing. In other words, the testimony of an accused is more likely to be discounted as self-serving than the same information provided by an impartial witness who has nothing to gain from its disclosure.

Frankel and Morris (1976) tested this hypothesis in a simulated plagiarism trial in which the defendant or an impartial witness testified about mitigating circumstances surrounding the offense. The major finding was that mock jurors recommended harsher sentences when it was the defendant who described the extenuating circumstances. By contrast, Suggs and Berman (1979) found that information about mitigating circumstances reduced the severity of mock jurors' sentences regardless of whether it was the defendant or an impartial witness who gave this testimony. The critical difference between these two studies was that Suggs and Berman's subjects believed that their judgments would have real consequences for the accused, whereas Frankel and Morris's jurors did not. Thus, it may be rather difficult for triers of fact to simply dismiss or discount a defendant's testimony when the decisions that they must reach have very real and important consequences for the accused.

Of course, the extent to which judges and juries are likely to discount a defendant's explanation of the facts will also depend on the amount of incriminating evidence that they have heard, the plausibility of the defendant's testimony, and the defendant's credibility as a witness. One variable that is thought to have a major impact on the defendant's credibility as a witness is his or her prior record. Although information about previous criminal convictions is generally inadmissible in court, the federal rules of evidence permit such evidence to be presented should the defendant elect to testify (see FRE 404b). Information about a defendant's background and record may then be introduced for the limited purposes of showing a motive for the crime or impeaching the credibility of the defendant's testimony. As such, the judge will generally instruct the jury that this evidence may be used only for these purposes, and is not to be taken as an indication of the defendant's guilt. Of course, the assumption that underlies these limiting instructions is that jurors can apply the evidence in the legally relevant way without drawing unauthorized inferences about the defendant's criminal culpability (Penrod & Borgida, 1983).

Kalven and Zeisel's (1966) analyses of verdicts from actual jury trials revealed that conviction rates were about 25 percent higher in cases where a defendant's prior record was introduced than in cases without such evidence. However, it is difficult to interpret these correlational data, for cases in which prior record information is introduced probably differ in many ways (e.g., nature of the offenses, strength of the evidence, willingness of the accused to testify) from those in which prior record evidence is not introduced. A number of researchers have held all other trial parameters constant in order to assess the causal impact of prior record information on the judgments of mock jurors. Their results are reasonably consistent: Jurors are more likely to convict an accused if they receive information about previous convictions than if they do not (see Penrod & Borgida, 1983, for a review).

Do these findings stem from jurors' reluctance to believe the testimony of a previously convicted felon? If so, triers of fact would be operating in a manner that the law permits. However, this does not seem to be what jurors were doing, for several investigators have found the evidence of a prior record influences jurors' verdicts without affecting their assessments of the defendant's credibility as a witness (e.g., Clary & Shaffer, in preparation; Wissler & Saks, 1982). Analyses of jury deliberations in two such studies revealed that statements about previous convictions were relatively infrequent, and when they occurred, they tended not to center around the credibility issue (Clary & Shaffer, in preparation; Hans & Doob, 1976). Instead, these juries were more likely to discuss a prior conviction (particularly one for a similar crime) as a basis for inferring that the defendant is the type of person who is capable of committing the current offense (see also Cornish & Sealy, 1973). So despite the legal rules and cautionary charges about the limited use of prior record information, it appears that jurors are apt to draw inappropriate inferences about the criminal propensities of previously convicted felons.

Special Classes or Categories of Defense

The law specifies sets of elements or conditions that must be true in order for a defendant to be found guilty of a crime. The two central aspects of criminal responsibility are committing an act prohibited by law (*actus reus*) and doing so with an evil intention or a criminal state of mind (*mens rea*). Ordinarily, a prosecutor will not be successful in convicting an adversary unless he or she is able to establish beyond a reasonable doubt that both of these conditions apply to the accused.

To establish mens rea, a prosecutor must show that the defendant chose to do evil "through his or her free will" (*United States v. Brawner*, 1972). When it is clear that the accused has committed a prohibited act, counsel will often try to convince the triers of fact to discount the defendant's criminal intentions by demonstrating that there were other plausible causes for his or her behavior. Among the more common (or celebrated) of these "discounting" defenses are the following.

(1) *Insanity.* Insanity is a legal term referring to a state of mind that would absolve a defendant of criminal responsibility for wrongdoing. The rationale underlying the insanity defense is that a person who is driven by irresistible impulses and/or is unable to distinguish right from wrong obviously lacks the capacity for free choice that must be established in order to prove criminal intent. Thus by legal definition, a defendant who is found to be insane cannot be convicted of a criminal offense (for an overview of the various legal definitions of insanity, see Hermann, 1983).

(2) *Intoxication.* The law has taken a firm stance against voluntary intoxication as an exonerating defense. Even if an accused was exceedingly drunk, the law will allow only that he or she was unable to form a specific intent (as in premeditated murder), but will still hold him or her liable for a lesser crime (e.g., manslaughter). Thus, drunkenness might be used as a mitigating factor to reduce the seriousness of a charge (Kalven & Ziesel, 1966).

(3) *Self-defense.* Intentional infliction of harm is excused under the special circumstance in which a person has been attacked and faces an immediate threat so dangerous as to make self-help the only practical

recourse. But such retaliatory violence is condoned only in the face of immediate threat when other legitimate alternatives (e.g., retreat) are not feasible, and only to the extent necessary to prevent or terminate the attack (LaFave & Scott, 1972).

(4) *Necessity and/or duress.* Outlawed conduct may be considered justifiable if the defendant believed it necessary for self-preservation (e.g., breaking and entering to take refuge from a blizzard) or to avoid a greater evil (e.g., assaulting a perpetrator to assist the victim of a crime). Closely related to the defense of necessity is that of duress. Here the defendant is claiming that he or she was forced by another party to commit criminal acts and hence, is really a victim rather than a criminal (LaFave & Scott, 1972). However, before the courts are likely to uphold this defense it must be established that the defendant could not have behaved otherwise without expecting imminent bodily harm or death.

(5) *Inadvertent conduct.* Anglo-American criminal law provides for very few instances in which nonintentional harmdoing is defined in criminal terms. In most jurisdictions, negligent or other nonintentional acts are not considered crimes if the victim is merely injured (although such injuries will often result in civil disputes). The major exception is negligent homicide, and even then, the prosecution must establish that the defendant acted with "gross," "wanton," or "willful" negligence before gaining a conviction. Of course, the defendants in these trials will typically argue that the act in question was either an unforeseeable accident or the result of simple rather than gross negligence.

(6) *Contributory fault of the victim.* Contributory fault is a defense based on the premise that the victim of a crime has in some way contributed to and is thus partially responsible for the defendant's actions. Although applicable to many kinds of offenses, contributory fault is often raised in forcible rape cases where the law recognizes but one issue in assigning criminal responsibility: whether or not the victim consented to have intercourse with the defendant at the time of the alleged offense (LaFave & Scott, 1972). If a defendant can show how a victim's actions (or inactions) could have contributed to the occurrence of sexual activities, he or she may be successful at convincing triers of fact to discount his or her own criminal intent.

After analyzing the outcomes of more than 3500 trials, Kalven and Zeisel (1966) concluded that jurors will often behave as the law allows by either totally or partially discounting a defendant's criminal intent after hearing plausible versions of these "discounting" defenses. In fact, juries are occasionally more lenient than the law allows when assessing the criminal intent of intoxicated defendants, those pleading self-defense, or those claiming that they were not grossly negligent in negligent homicide cases. Leniency toward a defendant may be especially probable when two or more plausible alternative causes appear to contribute to a defendant's actions. For example, Richardson and Campbell (1980, 1982) found that male perpetrators are judged less personally responsible for incidents of sexual assault or domestic violence if they were intoxicated at the time, and attributions of responsibility to the perpetrator were diminished even further if the victim was viewed as contributing to these incidents by being intoxicated herself.

Yet there is one defense that jurors find exceedingly difficult to accept: the insanity plea. Mock juries will typically reject insanity pleas and convict the accused, particularly if he or she has committed a very serious offense (Carroll, 1982; Simon, 1967). One explanation for this finding is that jurors believe that the notion of insanity as an absolving cause for wrongdoing is simply too lenient (Simon, 1967). Another related explanation is that a judgmental dimension equating insanity with "not guilty" and sanity with "guilty" presents jurors with a conflict that they will resolve by weighing evidence about the defendant's illegal actions more heavily than information about his or her mental state as they deliberate to a verdict (see McGlynn & Dreilinger, 1981).

Even when jurors in actual trials find defendants not guilty by reason of insanity, they are often uncomfortable with their decisions and feel that justice has not been served (Block, 1982). In recent years, several jurisdictions have changed the insanity defense by adding an alternative plea: guilty but mentally ill. Block (1982) suggests that this option improves the insanity statutes by allowing the trier of fact to place the blame for criminal conduct on the defendant (thereby rendering a "just" verdict) while also acknowledging the defendant's mental state as a contributor to illegal activities that perhaps should be treated by hospitalization rather than imprisonment.

FACTORS AFFECTING ASSESSMENTS OF THE DEFENDANT'S CREDIBILITY

It could be argued that the defendant is always a "witness," regardless of whether he or she elects to testify. Once a trial begins, the judge and jurors will periodically observe the accused, noting his or her demeanor and reactions to the evidence. Should the accused take the stand, the triers of fact must assess the plausibility and consistency of his or her testimony, and ultimately judge whether the defendant is telling the truth. Needless to say, the defendant's credibility or veracity is central to the trial process, and the ways in which defendants conduct themselves on and off the witness stand may be nearly as important to determining trial outcomes as the content of the evidence itself.

Appearance and General Demeanor

Fans of the *Perry Mason* series may recall that Mason's clients were nearly always well groomed, polite, and attentive during their appearances in court. This portrayal was hardly an accident, for defense attorneys generally believe that a defendant's appearance and demeanor are important. Polite and attentive behavior on the part of the accused is thought to promote a good impression. And one management consultant who specializes in such matters advises attorneys to have defendants dressed "quietly." Presumably, the best strategy is to "clean em up, cut their hair, and . . . no shiny suits or pinkie rings" (What to Wear in Court, 1974, p. 52). Henry Rothblatt (1979), a prominent criminal attorney, adds,

> Your client's style of dress should not deviate from his usual mode to the extent that he is uncomfortable and projects an unnatural, uneasy appearance. . . . Make sure your male client shaves every morning. . . . A female client should . . . use a minimum of make-up and style her hair conservatively. Obviously, alluring styled clothing should be prohibited. (p. 23)

Until recently, defendants who were unable to raise bail usually appeared in court dressed in prison uniforms. Of course, prison garb suggests that the defendant has remained in jail since the arrest which, in turn, may lead jurors to assume that the accused was denied bail because he or she is dangerous, unreliable, or untrustworthy. Several field studies have shown that defendants who remained in custody prior to and during the trial are more likely to be convicted and to receive harsher sentences than those who did not (Campbell, 1970; Doob, 1976). And in a tightly controlled mock jury study, Fontaine and Kiger (1978) found that a defendant standing trial in a prison uniform was judged more harshly than one who appeared in street clothing.

Although the Supreme Court has prohibited states from requiring a defendant to stand trial in institutional clothing (see *Estelle v. Williams*,

1976), it has also ruled that choice of attire remains with the defendant. Indeed, the court alluded to a common practice in Texas courts, where counsel often insists that a client wear prison garb "in the hope of eliciting sympathy from the jury" (p. 508). Clearly the available data suggest that this is a dubious strategy.

Does a defendant's general conduct or demeanor affect trial outcomes? In one mock jury study, Boone (1973) found that arrogant defendants were no more likely than their humble counterparts to be convicted of a violent crime. Verdicts were determined by the strength of the evidence, although the arrogant defendants were sentenced more severely when the jurors did convict. By contrast, Savitsky and Sim (1974) reported that a defendant's emotional demeanor can affect mock trial outcomes. Specifically, defendants who expressed distress and sadness during the proceedings were evaluated less harshly than those whose emotional states were neutral, happy, or angry. Finally, a field study by Parkinson (1979) is certainly relevant. Parkinson analyzed the transcripts of 38 actual trials, half of which resulted in acquittals and half in convictions. Her major findings were that acquitted defendants displayed more courtesy and deference, made fewer references to themselves, and spoke in more grammatically complete sentences than did defendants who were convicted.

Although the data are scanty at this point, they do suggest that a polite and serious demeanor, coupled with an apparent willingness to provide complete answers for questions (or at least to answer in complete sentences), help to create a desirable impression of the accused and perhaps make his or her testimony seem more credible.

Nonverbal Indications of Credibility and Veracity

In evaluating a defendant's testimony, the judge and jury recognize that the accused has a vested interest in the outcome of the trial and may be attempting to deceive them. How do triers of fact decide whether a witness is telling the truth? We are all probably aware of the folklore concerning the detection of deception. Presumably, restless behaviors (such as toe-tapping, fumbling with one's tie, picking one's fingernails), exaggerated gestures, faked emotional expressions, a tendency to be vague or to qualify one's answers, a failure to maintain eye contact, excessive swallowing, dryness of the mouth, and other physical symptoms such as blushing or perspiring can all interpreted as signs of deception and guilt (Kraut, 1978; Miller & Burgoon, 1982).

Over the past two decades, several investigators have probed the relationship between the emission of nonverbal behaviors by deceptive and nondeceptive communicators and the ability of recipients to discriminate deceptive from veridical statements on the basis of these cues (see Miller & Burgoon, 1982). Although there are some inconsistencies across studies, the literature indicates that deceptive communicators do emit several of the stereotypical signals of deception (e.g., excessive or exaggerated gestures, mannerisms symptomatic of anxiety, reticence, or negative affect, behaviors indicating vagueness or uncertainty, and incongruous reactions suggesting that external expressions contradict actual feelings). Moreover, observers in these studies tend to rely on many of these same cues to distinguish liars from truth-tellers (Miller & Burgoon, 1982). Thus it may not be surprising to learn that a witness who fails to maintain eye contact while testifying (a cue commonly read as "deceptive") is judged to be less credible than one who gazes directly at his audience when presenting his version of the facts (Hemsley & Doob, 1978).

The Importance of Vocal Cues and Language

Which behavioral cues do observers rely on most heavily in making judgments about veracity and deceit? While people claim that they are most attentive to a speaker's facial expressions, they actually rely more on vocal cues, especially as discrepancies among vocal, facial, and verbal messages become more pronounced (Miller & Burgoon, 1982; Rosenthal & DePaulo, 1979). Miller and Burgoon (1982) propose that

> facial cues [are] more relevant to judgments of positivity, while vocal cues seem to influence judgments of dominance. Perhaps detection of deception requires going beyond judgments of pleasantness or unpleasantness to evaluate other facets of expression, such as apparent confidence and assertiveness, which are gleaned from vocal patterns. (p 179)

Recent research by Lind and his associates suggests that the type or style of communication that occurs in the courtroom can influence jurors' assessments of a witness's credibility. Lind and O'Barr (1979) studied tape-recordings from actual trials and identified what they called "powerful" and "powerless" speech styles. Compared to the powerful style, powerless speech contains more frequent use of hedges (e.g., "kinda," "I think," "I guess"), hesitations (e.g., "well," "uh," "you know"), intensifiers (e.g., "very," "so," "I surely did"), gestures (e.g., using hands to indicate "over there"), hypercorrect grammar, and questioning forms of speech (e.g., using of rising intonation in declarative contexts). The researchers then had mock jurors listen to recordings of the same testimony delivered in either the powerful or powerless style. Those who were exposed to the powerful style perceived their witness to be more competent, dynamic, trustworthy, and convincing than did subjects exposed to the powerless delivery.

Lawyers are often advised to encourage their own witnesses to provide long answers while demanding brief responses from opposing witnesses (Keeton, 1973). Perhaps this is good advice. In a recent mock jury study Lind, Erikson, Conley, and O'Barr (1978) compared the effectiveness of "fragmented" and "narrative" styles of testimony. Witnesses who spoke in a fragmented style provided brief answers for a large number of questions, whereas those who spoke in the narrative style gave the same testimony, but in long, flowing answers to fewer questions. Mock jurors who heard the narrative testimony formed a more favorable evaluation of the witness than did those who heard the fragmented testimony.

In actual trials, defendants who elect to testify are much more narrative when questioned by their counsel under direct examination than when interrogated by the prosecuting attorney during cross-examination. This shift in testimonial style across different phases of the proceedings is particularly apparent if the defendant is on trial for serious offenses such as robbery or murder (Worley, 1978). The deception literature provides one explanation for these interesting findings: Communicators do tend toward brevity when engaging in unrehearsed deception (Kraut, 1978). Considering that responses to cross-examination are unrehearsed, it is tempting to conclude that the defendant's sudden brevity is an indication of deceit. On the other hand, let us recall that defendants become much more fragmented when cross-examined on serious charges. So it is possible that their brief and cautious answers under cross-examination are more a sign of high general anxiety or a concern about their great personal stakes in these trials rather than a true indication of any intent to deceive.

Observer Accuracy in Detecting Deception

Having discussed some of the nonverbal and paralinguistic cues associated with deception, we might wonder how accurate observers are when they use such information to estimate a communicator's veracity. Although many studies have addressed this issue, few of them correspond very closely to the circumstances that exist between jurors and witnesses in the courtroom. Nevertheless, the findings are sufficiently clear to make some cautious generalizations about the ability of jurors to determine whether a witness is lying or telling the truth.

After reviewing the literature, Miller and Burgoon (1982) concluded that

> despite knowledge of relevant cues, observers are not notably successful in detecting deception perpetrated by relative strangers. In attempting to determine whether a communicator was lying or telling the truth, observers in most studies were right about half the time, [the chance level]. (p. 191)

Is the average juror any more accurate when assessing testimonial veracity? Miller and his associates (1981) have conducted several mock jury studies to address this issue and to specify the kinds of information that might help jurors recognize deceitful testimony. The results of these experiments revealed that mock jurors were no more accurate than would be predicted by chance at identifying deceitful statements. Moreover, subjects who heard audio presentations of the evidence were no more successful in this regard than those who had only read a transcript of the proceedings. So while people tend to rely on vocal cues whenever a communicator's truthfulness is in doubt, the availability of such information does not enhance their ability to detect deceptive messages.

In view of the conventional wisdom about the ways in which liars reveal themselves through their nonverbal behaviors, why are observers (particularly mock jurors) not more accurate at detecting deception? There are at least two reasons. First, because mock jurors must generally suspect that deceit is a possibility, they are likely to interpret any unusual cue or gesture as a sign that the communicator is lying. Moreover, observers in these contexts are likely to have several nonverbal cues or gestures to interpret, particularly in the courtroom. Miller and Burgoon (1982) argue that many of the behaviors thought to signal deceit are precisely those we might expect from tense, anxious, and highly motivated criminal defendants—even those who may be innocent and are telling the truth. Thus, the courtroom is a setting in which a reliance on conventional wisdom about the detection of deceit "probably results in numerous faulty inferences, or misattributions of lying" (Miller & Burgoon, 1982, p. 186).

Since a jury may form distinct and often inaccurate impressions of witnesses on the basis of their nonverbal behaviors and linguistic styles, should we advise attorneys to coach their clients—to teach them to control their emotions and to use the more effective linguistic ploys when responding to interrogation? Clearly this may be interpreted by some as unwarranted intrusion on a judicial system that is hardly perfect but does function fairly well. By contrast, Vidmar (1984) favors the coaching strategy: If trial outcomes are to be decided on the basis of legally relevant evidence, then lawyers might use coaching to increase the credibility of witnesses, or at least to try to prevent jurors from basing credibility assessments on the witness's nonverbal mannerisms and methods of speaking.

WHAT THE DEFENDANT DOESN'T SAY: EFFECTS OF A FIFTH AMENDMENT PLEA

Acceptance of the right of a criminal defendant to decline to testify after being formally accused has been universal in the United States. If a defendant chooses not to take the stand, he or she can avoid all interrogation, and neither the prosecuting attorney nor the trial judge is allowed to inform jurors that they may draw a negative inference from the accused's reluctance to testify (see *Griffin v. California*, 1965; McCormick, 1972). However, the Supreme Court has ruled that judges may instruct jurors that they are to draw *no* adverse inferences from a defendant's invocation of the privilege, even if counsel specifically objects to this instruction (*Lakeside v. Oregon*, 1978).

A defendant's protection against self-incrimination could be compromised should he or she take the stand. Dean Wigmore's position (as cited in Berger, 1980) is that an accused's decision to testify amount to a waiver of the privilege with respect to all facts relevant to the offense being tried. This principle is easy to apply and is often used; yet it may run counter to the basic purpose of the privilege. As noted in McCormick (1972), "the privilege is not merely against taking the stand, and hence readily . . . waived *in toto* by taking the stand, but a privilege against self-incrimination. A rule of blanket waiver would not only discourage accused persons from testifying at all but would in effect make them prosecuting witnesses [should they testify]" (p. 280). Other legal scholars favor a less restrictive standard whereby "an accused who testifies forfeits his privilege only insofar as forfeiture is necessary to enable the prosecution . . . to subject his testimony . . . to scrutiny regarding its truth" (McCormick, 1972, p. 281). This less restrictive standard prevents the defendant from putting an entirely one-sided version of the facts before the jury while offering some protection from self-incriminating interrogation on matters about which he or she has not testified during direct examination. However, neither of these standards is universally accepted, and trial judges have a great deal of discretionary control in determining the scope of a defendant's testimonial privileges once he or she has taken the stand (McCormick, 1972).

Few points of law have generated as much controversy as the Fifth Amendment privilege against self-incrimination. From a purely legal standpoint, a Fifth Amendment plea does not allow an inference of either innocence or guilt since both guilty and innocent persons may have reasons to so plead. Staunch supporters of the privilege (e.g., Griswold, 1962) have argued for its continuance on the basis of the protections it affords an innocent party (e.g., safeguards against intimidation, coercion, or negative inferences that might result from a defendant's poor self-presentational skills; avoiding a waiver of the privilege with regard to future interrogation). Yet critics of the privilege have stressed that its invocation is self-defeating because the trier of fact cannot avoid drawing negative inferences about defendants who refuse to testify (see Hook, 1957; Packer, 1962). During congressional investigations of communist activities in the early 1950s, the refusal of witnesses to answer questions about their membership in the Communist party was generally interpreted as incriminating evidence (Berger, 1980). Indeed, while serving on the House Committee on Un-American Activities some 35 years ago, Congressman Richard Nixon offered his impression of the Fifth Amendment "protections" by cautioning one recalcitrant witness, "It is pretty clear, I think, that you are not using the defense of the Fifth Amendment because you are innocent" (as cited in Will, 1973).

Do jurors in criminal trials draw similar inferences about defendants who rely on the Fifth Amendment privilege? Kalven and Zeisel (1966) presumed so, although they provided no data to support their claim. Recently Shaffer and his associates have actually assessed mock jurors' reactions to Fifth Amendment pleas. In this program of research, mock jurors read and reacted to a transcript in which a male defendant was being tried for the armed robbery and murder of a storekeeper and the murder of the storekeeper's five-year-old granddaughter. The transcript consisted of several pages of testimony provided by a store clerk (who had been in the back room at the time of the shootings), a police ballistics expert, and the defendant (or the defendant's friend if the defendant had declined to take the stand). While questioning these witnesses, the prosecutor produced five pieces of circumstantial evidence that might seem to implicate the defendant. But under the cross-examination, the defendant (or defendant's friend) presented a seemingly plausible explanation for each piece of circumstantial evidence (c.f. Shaffer et al., 1978, for a more complete account of the testimony). Pretesting revealed that the weight of the evidence was balanced (i.e., it favored neither the prosecution nor the defense). Of central interest were jurors' reactions (i.e., assessments of the likelihood of guilt; verdicts rendered) to defendants who invoked the Fifth Amendment by either declining to take the stand or by refusing to answer one or more of the prosecutor's questions during cross-examination. Several control conditions were employed across studies, the most notable of which were the "confession controls" (i.e., where the defendant confessed to the crime while on the stand) and the "denial controls" (i.e., where the defendant denied the interrogative allegations when asked questions that might be construed as self-incriminating).

This research was designed to evaluate several hypotheses. Previous research conducted in nonjudicial settings had demonstrated that people who withhold information from others are perceived in *unit relation* with that information (Becker & Brock, 1966; Heider, 1958); the greater the apparent withholding of information, the stronger the assumed conjunction between the withholder and the probable implications of the information withheld. Application of these principles to the courtroom is straightforward. The more obvious it appears to jurors that the defendant is pleading the Fifth Amendment to withhold crime-relevant information, the stronger their assumption of unit relation between the defendant, the evidence withheld, and the probable implications of that evidence (i.e., the defendant must be guilty because presumably an innocent party would not withhold exonerating information). However, jurors should *not* assume a unit relation between the defendant and the crime if the withheld evidence is perceived as crime-*irrelevant* (e.g., information about the defendant's character or non-incriminating activities) even though these acts of evidence withholding might create very negative sentiments toward the accused. Finally, the discounting principle would lead one to believe that defendants who plead the Fifth on the advice of their attorneys would be judged less harshly than those who appear to invoke the privilege on their own. If jurors perceive the defendant's response as part of the counselor's overall defense strategy, they would have an alternative explanation for the Fifth Amendment plea and should be less likely to view it as a personal ploy to cover one's involvement in a crime.

For the most part, the results of this research are consistent with these hypotheses. In their initial experiment Shaffer et al. (1978) found that defendants who took the Fifth Amendment in response to a potentially incriminating question were judged as more likely to be guilty and deserving of conviction than their counterparts who simply answered this probe by denying their guilt. In a second study, Shaffer, Case, and Brannen (1979) found that the more crime-relevant information the defendant withheld (up to five invocations of the Fifth Amendment), the stronger the inferences were about his guilt and the more likely juries were to convict. However, this pattern did not hold for defendants who invoked the Fifth Amendment in response to crime-irrelevant interrogation. Finally, Shaffer and Sadowski (1979) found that a defendant who invoked the Fifth Amendment on the advice of his attorney was judged less likely guilty and less deserving of conviction than a counterpart whose decision to plead the Fifth was presumably self-initiated. Still, attributing the decision to one's counsel remained a dubious strategy, for defendants who did so were perceived as more likely guilty than those in a control condition who were never asked to respond to a leading question.

Would jurors react so negatively if a defendant invoked the Fifth Amendment by declining to take the witness stand? Shaffer and Case (1982) tried to answer this question by exposing mock juries to a trial in which the defendant either (1) declined to take the stand, (2) took the stand and invoked the Fifth Amendment in response to a potentially incriminating question, or (3) took the stand and provided an answer for this same question. The results were clear: Despite the equivocal nature of the legally relevant evidence against the accused, six of the nine juries that rendered unanimous verdicts in each of the Fifth Amendment conditions voted to convict the defendant whereas all of the juries rendering verdicts in the control condition voted for acquittal. Moreover, this bias against defendants who invoked the Fifth Amendment was apparent even though the judge had affirmed the defendant's right to so plead and had instructed jurors that they were to draw no inferences about the defendant's innocence or guilt from his use of this constitutional privilege. During the jury deliberations (which were recorded) approximately 80 percent of the comments made about the defendant's refusal to take the stand were negative in their implication (e.g., "An innocent person would plead his case"). Thus, it appears that many juries simply chose to disregard the judge's instructions[1] and act on the impression that an innocent person who has nothing to hide would probably not resort to such legal chicanery as a Fifth Amendment plea.

Is the bias against those who use the Fifth Amendment mediated by jurors' negative *sentiments* toward a person who so pleads? Apparently not. Shaffer and Case (1982) systematically manipulated juror sentiments toward an accused by providing information that he was either homosexual or heterosexual. This sexual preferences manipulation had a strong impact on juror sentiments (homosexuals being evaluated negatively) but no overall effect on their guilt ratings or the verdicts they rendered in groups. By contrast, the evidence-withholding manipulation had no effect on juror sentiments toward the accused but did influence their guilt ratings and verdicts (i.e., given the same evidence, jurors usually convicted defendants who declined to take the witness stand or who invoked the Fifth Amendment while on the stand, whereas they never convicted an accused who testified and answered all questions). In a second study, Shaffer, Case, and Brannen (1979) found that repeated use of the Fifth Amendment privilege created equally (and extremely) negative sentiments toward the accused, regardless of whether he was withholding crime-relevant or crime-irrelevant information. But only when the information withheld was potentially relevant to the present crime did the defendant's use of the Fifth Amendment privilege affect jurors' assessments of his criminal culpability. Taken together, these findings suggest that mock jurors are quite capable of weighing what the defendant does or does not say, deciding which information is relevant to their task as triers of fact, and then using this input to reach legal decisions that are not unduly influenced by their negative sentiments toward the accused.

Cautions and limitations. Although the findings we have reviewed indicate that mock jurors make negative inferences about defendants who plead the Fifth Amendment, we are hesitant to advise against the use of this constitutional privilege in all circumstances. Clearly, the use of the self-incrimination statute seems a dubious strategy in cases such as those presented in the simulations where the evidence was balanced. However, in her analysis of 201 felony prosecutions, most of which could be characterized as strong cases against the accused, Myers (1979) found that defendants who testified were more likely to be convicted than those who did not. So a decision *not* to take the stand just might be a prudent course for defendants who have very poor self-presentational skills and/or little if any credible evidence to present. Are previously convicted felons well advised not to testify in order to avoid the disclosure of their prior criminal activities? Defense attorneys think so, particularly if the evidence in the present case clearly favors acquittal (Kalven & Zeisel, 1966). And they may be right, for we have seen mock jurors use prior record information (particularly a prior record for a similar crime) as an indication that the defendant is the type of person who is capable of committing the current offense (Clary & Shaffer, in preparation; Cornish & Sealy, 1973). Furthermore, mock jurors do not automatically assume that the Fifth Amendment privilege is a shield for the guilty, for juror assessments of defendant culpability were always much stronger for an accused who admitted his guilt than for those who invoked the privilege any number of times. In fact, recordings of jury deliberations revealed that most jurors were quite aware that the Fifth Amendment privilege was designed to protect the innocent and is based on the premise that it is better to acquit a guilty party than to convict an innocent one (Clary & Shaffer, in preparation; Shaffer & Case, 1982). So it appears that jurors treat a claim of the privilege not so much as an admission of guilt, but as a piece of evidence in its own right that weighs heavily against the accused. And how heavily does it weigh? Our best guess is that the use of the privilege will produce few convictions when the legally relevant facts point to acquittal but is almost invariably a risky strategy whenever the evidence could be characterized as equivocal.

SUMMARY AND FUTURE DIRECTIONS

Unlike the eyewitness, the expert witness, and the complainant- or victim-witness (particularly in rape trials), the defendant as a witness has not been the subject of extensive, programmatic research. The literature that is available suggests that what the defendant says affects trial outcomes, particularly if he or she is able to present a plausible alibi or convince the trier of fact that extenuating circumstances (e.g., insanity, intoxication, the behavior of a victim) contributed to the acts in question. A simple denial of criminal actions or intentions is an ineffective strategy, and virtually anything a defendant says is likely to be compromised if he or she (1) has a previous criminal record for a similar offense; (2) does not appear appropriately serious, deferent, or concerned during the trial; or (3) emits any number of nonverbal or paralinguistic cues that jurors commonly interpret as indications of deceit. Moreover, defendants who rely on their constitutional "protection" against self-incrimination arouse suspicion among members of the jury, who will often assume that a decision to remain silent indicates that the accused must have something to hide. Thus, what the defendant chooses *not* to say may figure importantly in trial outcomes, particularly when the legally relevant evidence clearly favors neither the prosecution nor the defense.

Unfortunately, the literature we have reviewed centers almost exclusively on the defendant without seeking to determine how the substance or style of his or her testimony might be interpreted in light of other important courtroom parameters (e.g., the seriousness of the crime; the amount evidence for and against the accused; the credibility or competence of other witnesses). Moreover, a simple listing of testimonial variables that influence trial outcomes really tells us very little about the underlying causes of these effects. Consider, for example, that both a prior conviction for a similar offense and a decision to invoke the Fifth Amendment are biasing factors that we have characterized as *evidence* weighing heavily against the accused. Maybe so, but it is conceivable that the major impact of a prior record or a Fifth Amendment plea is to alter jurors' subjective weighing of other pertinent testimony, or perhaps simply lead to more careful scrutiny of that evidence and its probable implications. Indeed, there is some support for these assertions. While deliberating, mock juries evaluating a defendant who has invoked the Fifth Amendment subsequently spend more time examining the relevant facts and talk less about legally irrelevant information than do juries receiving the same evidence in a trial in which the accused has not claimed the privilege (Shaffer & Case, 1982). In addition, jurors tend to concentrate more on the connections between different pieces of evidence and are more negative in their assessments of these facts if they are discussing a case in which the defendant has declined to testify (Clary & Shaffer, in preparation).

In sum, we suspect that all categories of evidence are interactive and that a narrow focus on the defendant's testimony provides only a rough estimate of the impact of this information on trial outcomes. These observations are intended not to negate the value of our current knowledge but rather to call for research that assesses both the direct and indirect effects of different kinds of evidence. A best guess is that future advances in the psychology of courtroom testimony are likely to come from realistic and comprehensive mock trials (or from detailed analyses of actual trials)—studies that seek to determine the strategies or heuristics that judges and juries use when weighing, comparing, contrasting, and consolidating various categories of evidence as they draw the conclusions that underlie their verdicts.

NOTE

1. Does a judge's cautionary instructions to the jury call undue attention to the defendant's use of the privilege and thereby increase the chances of a conviction? Apparently not, for Clary (1978) found the juries instructed not to draw adverse inferences from a defendant's Fifth Amendment plea were no more likely to convict the accused than were juries receiving no judicial commentary on the meaning and use of the privilege.

REFERENCES

Baumeister, R. F., & Darley, J. M. (1982). Reducing the biasing effect of perpetrator attractiveness in jury simulation. *Personality and Social Psychology Bulletin, 8,* 286-292.

Becker, L. A., & Brock, T. C. (1966). Prospective recipients' estimates of withheld evaluation. *Journal of Personality and Social Psychology, 4,* 147-164.

Berger, M. (1980). *Taking the Fifth.* Lexington, MA: D. C. Heath.

Block, G. (1982). The Hinckley trial and the fallacious presumptions of the insanity defense. *ETC, 39,* 222-238.

Boone, J. S. (1973). The effects of race, arrogance, and evidence on simulated jury decisions. *Dissertation Abstracts International, 33* (12-A), 7018.

Bowers, W., & Pierce, G. (1980). Arbitrariness and discrimination under post-Furman capital statutes. *Crime and Delinquency, 26,* 563-635.

Campbell, J. J. (1970). *Law and order reconsidered.* Washington, DC: Government Printing Office.

Carroll, K. R. (1982). Factors affecting juror response to the insanity defense. *Dissertation Abstracts International, 42,* (7-B), 3029-3030.

Clary, E. G. (1978). *The effects of a defendant's prior record and evidence withholding on juridic judgments.* Unpublished master's thesis, University of Georgia.

Clary, E. G., & Shaffer, D. R. (in preparation). Another look at the impact of juror sentiments toward defendants on juridic decisions.

Cornish, W. R., & Sealy, A. P. (1973). Juries and rules of evidence. *Criminal Law Review, 17,* 208-228.

Dane, F. C., & Wrightsman, L. S. (1982). Effects of defendants' and victims' characteristics on jurors' verdicts. In N. L. Kerr & R. M. Bray (Eds.), *The psychology of the courtroom.* New York: Academic Press.

Doob, A. N. (1976). Evidence, procedure, and psychological research. In G. Bermant, C. Nemeth, and N. Vidmar (Eds.), *Psychology and the law.* Lexington, MA: D. C. Heath.

Ebbesen, E. B., & Konecni, V. J. (1982). Social psychology and the law: A decision-making approach to the criminal justice system. In V. J. Konecni & E. B. Ebbesen (Eds.), *The criminal justice system: A social-psychological analysis.* San Francisco: W. H. Freeman.

Estelle v. Williams, 425 U.S. 501 (1976).

Foley, L. A., Chamblin, M. H., & Fortenberry, J. H. (1979). *The effects of race, socioeconomic status, and personality variables on jury decisions.* Paper presented at the annual meeting of the American Psychological Association, New York City, September.

Fontaine, G., & Kiger, R. (1978). The effects of defendant dress and supervision on judgments of simulated jurors: An exploratory study. *Law and Human Behavior, 2,* 63-71.

Frankel, A., & Morris, W. N. (1976). Testifying in one's own defense: The ingratiator's dilemma. *Journal of Personality and Social Psychology, 34,* 475-480.

Griffin v. California, 380 U.S. 609 (1965).

Griswold, E. N. (1962). *The Fifth Amendment today.* Cambridge, MA: Harvard University Press.

Hagan, J. (1974). Extra-legal attributes and criminal sentencing: An assessment of a sociological viewpoint. *Law and Society Review, 8,* 357-383.

Hans, V. P., & Doob, A. (1976). Section 12 of the Canada Evidence Act and the deliberation of simulated juries. *Criminal Law Quarterly, 18,* 235-253.

Heider, F. (1958). *The psychology of interpersonal relations.* New York: John Wiley.

Hemsley, G. D., & Doob, A. N. (1978). The effect of looking behavior on perceptions of a communicator's credibility. *Journal of Applied Social Psychology, 8,* 136-144.

Hermann, D.H.J. (1983). *The insanity defense: Philosophical, historical, and legal perspectives.* Springfield, IL: Charles C Thomas.

Hook, S. (1957). *Common sense and the Fifth Amendment.* New York: Criterion Books.

Kalven, H., Jr., & Zeisel, H. (1966). *The American jury.* Boston: Little, Brown.

Kaplan, M. F., & Schersching, C. (1980). Reducing juror bias: An experimental approach. In P. D. Lipsitt & B. D. Sales (Eds.), *New approaches in psycholegal research.* New York: Van Nostrand Reinhold.

Keeton, R. E. (1973). *Trial tactics and methods* (2nd ed.). Boston: Little, Brown.

Kelley, H. H. (1973). The process of causal attribution. *American Psychologist, 28,* 107-128.

Kerr, N. L. (1982). Trial participants' behaviors and jury verdicts: An exploratory field study. In V. J. Konecni & E. B. Ebbesen (Eds.), *The criminal justice system: A social-psychological analysis.* San Francisco: W. H. Freeman.

Kraut, R. E. (1978). Verbal and nonverbal cues in the perception of lying. *Journal of Personality and Social Psychology, 36,* 380-391.

LaFave, W. R., & Scott, A. W. (1972). *Handbook on criminal law.* St. Paul, MN: West.

Lakeside v. Oregon, 435 U.S. 333 (1978).

Lind, E. A., Erickson, B. E., Conley, J., & O'Barr, W. M. (1978). Social attributions and conversational style in trial testimony. *Journal of Personality and Social Psychology, 36,* 1558-1567.

Lind, E. A., & O'Barr, W. M. (1979). The social significance of speech in the courtroom. In H. Giles and R. St. Clair (Eds.), *Language and social psychology.* Oxford, England: Blackwell.

McCormick's Handbook of the Law of Evidence (1972). E. Cleary (Ed.) St. Paul,MN: West.

McGlynn, R. P., & Dreilinger, E. A. (1981). Mock juror judgment and the insanity plea: Effects of incrimination and sanity information. *Journal of Applied Social Psychology, 11,* 166-180.

Miller, G. R., Bauchner, J. E., Hocking, J. E., Fontes, N. E., Kaminski, E. P., & Brandt, D. R. (1981). " . . . and nothing but the truth": How well can observers detect deceptive testimony. In B. D. Sales (Ed.), *Perspectives in law and psychology: Vol. 2. The trial process.* New York: Plenum.

Miller, G. R., & Burgoon, J. K. (1982). Factors affecting assessments of witness credibility. In N. L. Kerr & R. M. Bray (Eds.), *The psychology of the courtroom.* New York: Academic press.

Myers, M. A. (1979). Rule departures and making law: Juries and their verdicts. *Law and Society Review, 13,* 781-797.

Packer, H. L. (1962). *Ex-communist witnesses.* Stanford, CA: Stanford University Press.

Parkinson, M. G. (1979). *Language behavior and courtroom success*. Paper presented at the annual meeting of the British Psychological Society, Bristol, July.

Penrod, S., & Borgida, E. (1983). Lay rules and legal inference. In L. Wheeler & P. Shaver (Eds.), *Review of personality and social psychology* (Vol. 4). Beverly Hills, CA: Sage.

Richardson, D., & Campbell, J. L. (1980). Alcohol and wife abuse: The effect of alcohol on attributions of blame for wife abuse. *Personality and Social Psychology Bulletin, 6,* 51-56.

Richardson, D., & Campbell, J. L. (1982). Alcohol and rape: The effect of alcohol on attributions of blame for rape. *Personality and Social Psychology Bulletin, 8,* 468-476.

Rosenthal, R., & DePaulo, B. M. (1979). Expectancies, discrepancies, and courtesies in nonverbal communication. *Western Journal of Speech Communication, 1979, 43,* 76-95.

Rothblatt, H. B. (1979). The defendant—should he testify? *Trial Diplomacy Journal,* Fall, 21-24.

Savitsky, J. C., & Sim, M. E. (1974). Trading emotions: Equity theory of reward and punishments. *Journal of Communication, 24,* 140-147.

Shaffer, D. R., & Case, T. (1982). On the decision to testify in one's own behalf: Effects of withheld evidence, defendant's sexual preferences, and juror dogmatism on juridic decisions. *Journal of Personality and Social Psychology, 42,* 335-346.

Shaffer, D. R., Case, T., & Brannen, L. (1979). Effects of withheld evidence on juridic decisions: Amount of evidence withheld and its relevance to the case. *Representative Research in Social Psychology, 10,* 2-15.

Shaffer, D. R., & Sadowski, C. (1979). Effects of withheld evidence on juridic decisions II: Locus of withholding strategy. *Personality and Social Psychology Bulletin, 5,* 40-43.

Shaffer, D. R., Sadowski, C., & Hendrick, C. (1978). Effects of withheld evidence on juridic decisions. *Psychological Reports, 42,* 1235-1242.

Simon, R. J. (1967). *The jury and the defense of insanity*. Boston: Little, Brown.

Stewart, J. E., II, (1980). Defendant's attractiveness as a factor in the outcome of criminal trials: An observational study. *Journal of Applied Social Psychology, 10,* 348-361.

Suggs, D., & Berman, J. J. (1979). Factors affecting testimony about mitigating circumstances and the fixing of punishment. *Law and Human Behavior, 3,* 251-260.

Sutherland, E. H., & Cressey, D. R. (1966). *Principles of criminology* (7th ed.). Philadelphia: Lippincott.

United States v. Brawner, 471 F. 2d. 969 (D.C. Cir, 1972).

Vidmar, N. J. (1984). Social psychology and the law. In A. S. Kahn (Ed.), *Social psychology*. Dubuque, IA: Wm. C. Brown.

What to wear in court. (December 16, 1974). *Newsweek,* p. 52.

Will, G. (1973). Time for Nixon to answer. *Kent-Ravenna Record Courier,* June, 16.

Wissler, R. L., & Saks, M. J. (1982). *On the inefficiency of limiting instructions*. Paper presented at the annual meeting of the American Psychological Association, Washington, DC, August.

Wolfgang, M., & Reidel, M. (1976). Rape, racial discrimination, and the death penalty. In H. A. Bedau & C. M. Pierce (Eds.), *Capital punishment in the United States*. New York: AMS Press.

Worley, A. E. (1978). An examination of criminal defendants' verbal behavior under two types of courtroom interrogation procedures. *Dissertation Abstracts International, 38,* (9-B), 4547-4548.

Yandell, B. (1979). Those who protest too much are seen as guilty. *Personality and Social Psychology Bulletin, 5,* 44-47.

CHAPTER 6

Character Testimony

MARTIN F. KAPLAN

This volume emphasizes the contribution of evidence and testimony to the decisions reached in court. Testimony as to the character of the defendant is part of the family of testimony, although as we shall see it is often treated as a distant and unwanted relative. This chapter examines the conditions under which character testimony will be allowed to attend family gatherings, and how it must present itself to be allowed to remain. The rules governing character testimony are embedded in assumptions and justifications regarding the psychology of juror judgment; these will be taken in turn, with comment.

ADMISSIBILITY AND PRESENTATION OF CHARACTER TESTIMONY

Character testimony treads a thin line of admissibility. There are a number of *purposes* to which character testimony can be put: to establish a general characteristic or propensity to act in a criminal manner; to establish a general characteristic to be innocent of wrongdoing or to rebut the same; to establish a specific characteristic that is relevant to an element of the charged offense; and to impeach the defendant as witness. Moreover, there are a number of *types* of testimony: general reputation of the accused, personal opinion of the testifier, and specific acts. Not all purposes and types of testimony are admissible in court. In some instances, substantial discretion by the trial judge is required, causing admissibility variations between jurisdictions. The web of requirements and exceptions is indeed complicated.

To begin, character testimony is generally inadmissible (Waltz, 1983). That is, it is not considered in conformity with Rule 401 of the

Federal Rules of Evidence (FRE), which defines relevant or probative evidence as

> evidence having any tendency to make the existence of any fact that is of consequence to the determination of the action more probable or less probable than it would be without the evidence.

Subsequent rules and practices define the general limitations of character testimony with respect to probativeness.. FRE Rule 404A gives the general exclusionary principle:

> Evidence of a person's character or a trait of his character is not admissible for the purpose of proving that he acted in conformity therewith on a particular occasion.

In short, such testimony is not admissible for proving guilt. Both general character and specific traits are not probative for the specific instance at issue. That a person is generally disreputable or possesses the trait of violence does not inform about a violent act committed on any specific date. But there are exceptions to this exclusion, and these will now be considered.

Evidence of Good Character
and Rebuttal

FRE 404A permits testimony in behalf of a defendant's "good" character to show that he or she is unlikely to have committed a crime. This rule is in marked contrast to the prohibition on testimony intended to show "bad" character or criminal propensities. This exception has been upheld in appellate review (e.g., *Michaelson v. United States*, 1948). "Good-character testimony may be in the form of a single witness's personal opinions or of testimony as to general reputation in the community, but may not be given as to the specific acts or behaviors of the defendant (Rules 405A and 608A). Only if this exception is exercised can the prosecution elicit testimony aimed at proving bad character, but even then only by cross-examination of good-character witnesses and for rebuttal purposes only (Rules 404A and 608B). The reasoning for this constraint is that character statements cannot go unchallenged, and the prosecutor can challenge what was said by the witness in his or her testimony by bringing to the witness's attention instances of bad character (but see limitations to this below) in cross-examination and asking whether he or she is aware of these facts. The prosecutor may not produce independent or extrinsic evidence to rebut good character testimony as such would presumably tip the scales toward negative inferences about the defendant rather than the allowed discreditation of the witness. The principle here and generally is that negative testimony may never be introduced for the purpose of proving criminal character generally or in the charged instance, but it may be admitted to assess the credibility of friendly witnesses (Cleary, 1984; Waltz, 1983). Note that the preferred mode of testimony is general rather than specific; rules accept broad statements about general character in this exception and prohibit specific acts. This is because general reputation is considered to be the summation of many specific acts and is therefore more efficient as a source of testimony. To bring in specific acts opens the door to selectivity and can provoke side issues and disputes over specific content. The rules repeatedly caution against admitting evidence that would be distracting and time-consuming, which are considered the main drawbacks of specific-act testimony (Cleary, 1984).

Proof of Elements of Charge

A second exception to the general exclusionary rule is that character evidence may be admitted if it is probative for a particular element of the charge (FRE Rule 404B). This is the only instance in which character evidence can be used to prove complicity. The test is whether character is crucial to the issue at hand. McCormick (Cleary, 1984) comments that character may be crucial in two ways: It may provide circumstantial evidence for an issue in the case, or it may bear directly on a material fact or issue. The former is illustrated by *Carbo v. United States* (1963) in which a gangster was accused of using his violent reputation as a weapon for extortion. The prosecution was allowed to introduce testimony regarding his reputation as circumstantial evidence. The latter is articulated in FRE Rule 404B, which permits testimony that is used to show a particular plan, purpose, motive, opportunity, preparation, knowledge, or absence of a mistake or accident. So, where past acts show a similarity in methods of the crimes, they are admissible. Moreover, traits are admissible if they are part of the charge, as in libel or negligence, where malice and irresponsibility are respective elements (Cleary, 1984). Note that a fine distinction (lost perhaps on jurors) is made between character testimony that creates a proof that the *person* committed the crime and that which proves an *element* of the crime.

Certain civil cases make particularly important use of character testimony as an element of the case. In many instances, character *is* a material fact, as in defamation, where the accused may offer the defense that the plaintiff's character *is* as bad as he or she alleged, or in negligence, where it is shown that the defendant was unfit or allowed an unfit person to use a dangerous object or to assume a sensitive position. In instances where character is the fact, FRE and court practice prefer testimony regarding specific acts, which is presumed to be more probative to the specific behavior in question. In other instances, character is used circumstantially to prove another material fact. For example, in negligence cases, testimony may be offered to show that the person is (or is not) the sort to exercise care. Or, in an insurance case, testimony may bear on whether the deceased is or is not the sort to commit suicide. Note that character is not the fact in issue but may be circumstantially used as evidence for the fact at issue (e.g., careless driving or suicide). In circumstantial usage, where a general disposition is to be established, reputation and opinion testimony is preferred by the FRE over specific acts (Cleary, 1984).

Impeachment of Testimony

Perhaps the most frequently used exception for introducing character testimony is for impeachment of the credibility of other testimony. FRE Rule 608A allows character testimony in the form of personal opinion and reputation in the community in order to assess a defendant's credibility *as a witness,* but not, once again, as a perpetrator of the charged act. Rule 608B allows, on cross-examination, inquiry into past acts of misconduct, even if a conviction was not obtained, for purposes of impeachment. But extrinsic evidence of past acts cannot be introduced unless they were for crimes that were punishable by more than one year of imprisonment or involved dishonesty (Rule 609A). Should character evidence allowed for the purpose of impeachment be limited to attacks on the specific trait of truthfulness, or should it be allowed to include more general character information? The courts appear to vary on how far ranging the inquiry can be (Cleary, 1984). In any event, the use of opinion and reputation evidence to impeach the defendant as witness has been upheld (e.g., *United States v. Escobedo,* 1970).

It is clear at this point that any single piece of character testimony may be admissible for some purposes (witness impeachment and proof of relevant elements) and inadmissible for others (inference of general propensity, of commission of the charged act, or general prejudice against the defendant). FRE Rule 105 permits the admission of evidence that is competent for one purpose but incompetent for another. The prescribed protection against the unwanted effects is to "restrict evidence to its proper scope and instruct the jury accordingly." Thus, limiting instructions, in which the jury is informed of the admissible and inadmissible (i.e., improper) uses of the testimony and the inferences that can be drawn, are the remedy for potential prejudice. It is not an entirely naive remedy; FRE Rule 403 authorizes the courts to consider the overall prejudicial effect of the admitted evidence, and the power of limiting instructions to prevent such prejudice, relative to the probative value of the evidence. As such, judges have the discretion to exclude dual-purpose testimony if they believe that limiting instructions cannot tip the balance from prejudice to probativeness. In this regard, it should be noted that the courts generally consider evidence bearing on witness credibility to be particularly crucial for juries to receive (Cleary, 1984; Waltz, 1983).

Defendant's Past Record

A special mention should be made regarding the introduction of past record as character testimony. On the one hand, such information could be highly prejudicial. It could lead to an inference of general criminality, or to a specific inference of incrimination for the charged crime, or to a bias to convict and punish a bad person for past misdeeds regardless of his or her standing on the present charges. On the other hand, past record could be probative for certain elements of the present crime (e.g., by proving similarity of methods), and for assessing the defendant's credibility as a witness. The latter purpose is a legacy of the Old English principle that felons are incompetent to give testimony (Waltz, 1983). Once again, the court must weigh the undesirable versus the desirable effects of such disclosure in deciding whether to allow past record to be introduced. But even when admitted, there is still a decision to be made on how much detail to allow. If entered for the sole purpose of impeachment, should testimony be limited to an attack on the defendant's truthfulness or broadened to impugn his or her general character? If entered for the purpose of proving an element of the charge, should testimony be limited to a mere citation of past offenses or could it provide concrete details? If so, how much detail? As before, two balances must be achieved according to a composite of the relevant guidelines of the FRE. The probativeness for the particular purpose (impeachment or evidence of elements) must be balanced against potential prejudice, and also against the chance that the testimony may be misleading, time-consuming, and distracting. It may be, for example, that the introduction of details of past record might provoke unnecessary debate over the truth and meaning of events and accusations.

Another issue is that the introduction of past record or charges may serve to embarrass the defendant and ruin his or her reputation. Having him or her testify as to past record can be demeaning. Through the nineteenth century, as a corollary of the ban on self-incrimination, witnesses could avoid answering questions whose answers might degrade or deface them (Cleary, 1984). Today, the permissibility of such questions is at the court's discretion; FRE Rule 611A gives the court discretion to prevent the harassment or embarrassment of witnesses when cross-examined under Rule 608B, which allows inquiry into past acts in order to impeach testimony. The courts tend to be rather lenient in allowing questions on this score.

On the score of potential embarrassment and debasement, the danger is at least equally possible for testimony given to impeach the credibility of witnesses other than the defendant. In particular, the integrity of the plaintiff in rape trials has been of concern in instances where the defense has aggressively tried to impugn the testimony or motives of the victim. Here more than elsewhere the character of the plaintiff has formed a major part of the defense strategy ("defense of consent"), to the potential harm of the defendant's reputation. Recent "rape-shield" statutes are aimed at protecting the victim/witness from damage to character. Statutes range from barring all evidence of the victim's character for chastity to requiring preliminary hearings to screen evidence for relevance and harm (Cleary, 1984). Rule 412 of the FRE protects against harm to the victim's reputation by barring reputation and opinion evidence of past sexual conduct, but allowing evidence of specific incidents if they are relevant and their probative value outweighs the danger of prejudice (e.g., previous sexual relations with the defendant). It remains to be seen whether these statutes will serve as models for related limitations in the sorts of character testimony that will be allowed for defendants and witnesses in non-rape trials.

PSYCHOLOGICAL JUSTIFICATIONS AND ASSUMPTIONS

We now turn to the justifications and assumptions underlying the use and admissibility of character testimony. It bears repeating that the general rule is that such testimony is inadmissible. While at first glance this would seem to be treating character testimony differently than other types of evidence, in a basic way it is not. Loh (1984) notes that rules of evidence came into being in the eighteenth century when the jury became the sole judge of the facts and means were needed to control the flow of information to the jury and thereby limit their discretion. If prejudice is a precursor to discretionary use and distortion of the facts, it is understandable that severe limitations would be put on testimony that is assumed to distract from factual issues and increase juries' discretion. Character testimony—indeed any testimony—must meet the ideal criteria of probativeness for case issues (which are determined by the court) and of minimization of juror discretion (of which prejudice is one source). In practice and in the rules of evidence, admission is often a compromise between these dual criteria.

Given the general prohibition, psychological treatment of character testimony is best followed by considering the *exceptions* to the rule. Broadly speaking, there are two: probativeness for elements of the charge, and impeachment of testimony. These will be considered separately, although some of the issues overlap. In this section, a major issue that bears on both exceptions will also be treated: the distinction between testimony as to general character versus evidence of specific acts.

Elements of the Charge

Testimony regarding previous criminal acts or charges is admissible under certain circumstances but cannot be used to form an inference about a general propensity toward committing the charged crime. Such testimony can be used, however, to prove elements of that crime. In short, a witness can testify that the defendant is the sort of person who would use a certain method, or have a certain motive, and so on, but cannot say that he or she is the sort of *person* that would and did commit the crime. Although this prohibition may satisfy the rationale that admitted testimony should be probative, it may violate the proscription on prejudice—that is, such testimony may lead to an inference of general criminal tendencies and specific culpability for the charged crime. Regarding the former danger, attribution theory (e.g., Kelley, 1967) and research (e.g., McArthur, 1972) have demonstrated that showing a consistent history of some act will lead observers to infer the presence of an internal disposition toward that behavior. Note that one test of probativeness is whether past acts share commonalities with the present charge. Thus, testimony that is most probative for specific elements is also most likely to lead to the proscribed inferences of criminal propensity!

Turning to the danger of assuming culpability for the specific charge, it makes little sense, psychologically, to separate the end product from its elements. That is, a composite judgment of a defendant's guilt is an integrated function of the evaluations of various component pieces of information (i.e., the elements and evidence pertaining thereto). As our judgments of any characteristic of a person are formed by algebraically combining the evaluated elements (Anderson, 1981; Kaplan, 1982a), changing the incriminating value of any one element (e.g., motive) directly changes the whole. For example, observers average the strength of a suspect's motive with strength of his or her opportunity to commit the crime in assessing the likelihood of commission. If the strength of either motive or opportunity is increased or decreased, there is a corresponding shift in judgments of culpability (Kaplan, 1982b). Testimony does not bear on a single element without bearing on its end product—the ascription of guilt.

The foregoing discussion suggests that there is greater potential for prejudicial inferences than is assumed for testimony that is introduced as evidence for specific elements. But it also serves a sometimes necessary probative function, and the court must weigh the two potentials. Although there is no metric for weighing the two, courts face the dilemma that greater similarity between the charges and the acts addressed in the testimony enhances both inferences of general and specific criminality and of probativeness.

Impeachment of Testimony

Admission of character testimony for the purpose of impeaching testimony by the defendant or his or her character witnesses is based on at least two sets of assumptions. First, it is assumed that character for truthfulness may be inferred from the offered testimony, and further, that this character is proof of truthfulness *in this instance* (Waltz, 1983). Second, it is assumed that the testimony will not produce harm. Harm refers both to inducing a belief in the defendant's propensity toward crime generally and in this specific instance, and to otherwise interfering with the trial process (e.g., being misleading and time-consuming; see Lempert & Saltzburg, 1982). In short, as is true for testimony entered to prove elements of the charge, assumptions revolve around probativeness and harm.

Character for Truthfulness
and Impeachment

Character for truthfulness is considered relevant circumstantial evidence for assessing the truthfulness of present testimony. In turn, prior acts (e.g., criminal record) and general reputation may be used to establish this character for truthfulness. Note the sequence of reasoning: From specific acts (e.g., stealing) one may assume a general trait (dishonesty) and then deduce from that trait a situation-specific disposition (to lie under oath in the present instance). This reasoning is inconsistent with the spirit of the rules that apply to testimony offered in proof of specific elements, which disallow the inference based on character testimony that the defendant is more or less probable to have committed the crime charged in this instance. For impeachment purposes, the jury is permitted to infer an action in a trial issue (lying) from character, but for proof of the charge it is forbidden. The rules seem to waver on whether specific acts can prove a general propensity, and whether a general propensity can in turn be informative for particular behaviors (lying versus guilt) at issue in the trial. The question of the relationship and predictiveness of specific acts and general traits is taken up later. Here we will examine the particular issue of truthfulness.

The foregoing reasoning assumes that people behave consistently over time and across situations. If a defendant lied in the past, or more generally, engaged in "bad" acts, he or she is probably lying in the present instance. Or conversely, if he or she is generally truthful and has "good" character, he or she is probably telling the truth now. If we have learned one thing from years of personality research, it is that people are inconsistent in their behavior. Traits change over time, and the same traits operate differently in different contexts (Kaplan, 1981; Lempert & Saltzburg, 1982; Saks & Hastie, 1978). Moreover, behavior is greatly influenced by the external situation (Mischel, 1968). General dispositions, for truthfulness or whatever, are imperfect predictors of behavior in a particular instance—a phenomenon that is recognized by the FRE for proof of guilt but not for impeachment of testimony—but one must take situational constraints into account. One of the most cited conclusions in personality psychology is that honesty is situationally specific (Hartshorne & May, 1928). They placed children in a number of situations that lent themselves to cheating and lying. The children showed little consistency across situation in behavioral measures of honesty. That is, it was impossible to predict whether a child who cheated on an arithmetic test would also cheat on a spelling test. One can conclude that generally honest people lie on occasion, and generally dishonest people tell the truth now and then. We are dealing with a probabilistic assumption based on character and situation, and the jury has no idea of the probabilities (and neither do psychologists).

Potential for Harm and Its Remedy

The potential for prejudicial harm from character testimony is rampant. On appearances, defendants seem to have the advantage; they may present good-character testimony at their choice. However, this testimony must be with regard to general reputation only and may be rebutted by bad-character evidence in the form of both general reputation and specific acts. For several reasons, this arrangement swings the advantage away from the defendant.

First, information about specific acts may have a greater impact on jurors than does general reputation evidence despite the rule assumption that general reputation is better evidence because it is more inclusive and reliable (Cleary, 1984). Decision-making research (e.g., Tversky & Kahneman, 1974) suggests that people rely on specific instances more than general base-rates. For example, a car buyer will be more influenced by knowing that his neighbor has repair problems with his Volvo than by the consumer statistics, or base-rate, which show an excellent repair record. A number of factors favor the impact of the former information. Specific instances are more concrete, immediate, and vivid ("he lied in this instance in this way") compared to base-rate descriptions, which are abstract, distant, and pallid ("he lies more often than most people"); see Nisbett & Ross, 1980. General reputation testimony can be considered to be base-rate or probabilistic information in that it describes an individual's characteristic or standing in relation to the general incidence of that characteristic in the population. It is found repeatedly that people are not as affected by base-rate probabilities as they should be (Tversky & Kahneman, 1974). Moreover, people are insensitive to the greater reliability inherent in the larger sample size of summary data compared to single instances. Therefore, people will be overly impressed by specific acts because they are more salient and, according to the "availability heuristic" (Tversky & Kahneman, 1974), people estimate the probability that an object possesses a certain charactertistic by the ease with which a specific instance comes to mind. Specific acts evidence may be a powerful mediator of the assumption that many other instances of those acts exist, even in the face of contrary information of a general, base-rate nature.

The second reason why the defendant offering general reputation testimony is at a disadvantage is that the specific acts testimony is likely to be carefully selected by the advocate to be more extreme in nature than the general reputation testimony, and extreme information tends to carry greater importance (Warr & Jackson, 1975).

Third, negative information about an individual tends to be more believable than positive because it is more unexpected and hence violates behavioral norms (Hamilton & Zanna, 1972).

Fourth, negative information has a greater impact on our judgments than does positive. Impressions formed on the basis of positive information are less resistant to change by subsequent negative information than vice versa (Richey, McClelland, & Shimkunas, 1967). Negative information is more salient (noticeable) than is positive (Hamilton & Fallot, 1974). And, positive traits are discounted in the presence of negative (Hodges, 1974). Collectively, these phenomena are labeled negative salience and strongly suggest that any positive impression stemming from "good character" testimony can be more than offset by rebuttal. Although cross-examination gives the appearance of evenhandedness, this remedy has different import for positive testimony rebutted by negative than for the reverse.

If character testimony can do more harm for the defendant than good, what is the nature of this harm? Is it that juries would attribute to the defendant a general character disposition for criminal behavior? Attribution theorists (e.g., Jones, 1979) label as the fundamental attribution error the tendency to infer personal dispositions rather than situational events as the cause for observed behavior in others. Given a litany of past offenses, we are more likely to attribute them to a stable criminal character than to temporary and situational causes. The charged crime can then be seen as another manifestation of this disposition. Moreover, inferences of "bad" character may affect people's interpretation and processing of subsequent evidence (Hamilton, 1981). There is, therefore, evidence to support the fears of prejudice expressed in the FRE.

The main safeguard against harm (aside from denying admission) lies in limited admissibility instructions often read to the jury. In the legal community, there is some doubt as to the effectiveness of telling the jury they may use testimony for one purpose but not for another purpose, especially with strong psychological inferences. Loh (1984) cites case opinions by Justices Jackson, Frank, and Hand that are pessimistic, and McCormick (Cleary, 1984) is equally worried. And there is a good reason to worry. Impressions, once formed, are often quite resistant to change, despite subsequent instructions designed specifically to undermine the initial effect—this is termed "belief perseverance" (Ross & Anderson, 1982). For example, people who form impressions based on false data of the relationship between test scores and a person's subsequent performance retain those impressions even after disclosure of the false nature of the data. Making matters worse, there is a growing body of literature to suggest that a good many jury instructions, including those pertaining to limited use of evidence, are simply incomprehensible to the layperson (see review by Elwork, Hansen, & Sales, 1985). Finally, instructions have been shown to be ineffective—and even counterproductive—in related issues. These include instructions to disregard the defendant's character (Kaplan & Kemmerick, 1974) and attitudes (Mitchell & Byrne, 1973), pretrial publicity (Sue, Smith, & Gilbert, 1974), and inadmissible evidence (Sue, Smith, & Caldwell, 1973). Although the cited studies were of mock juries where instructions did not have the force of law, they are consistent and suggestive in their outcome. There may be conditions under which limiting instructions can be made more effective and where the impact of character testimony may be reduced, but their treatment will await the last section of the chapter.

General Character or Specific Acts

Generality versus specificity is an issue in two senses. There is a distinction with respect to the inference that is drawn by the jury, (i.e., general character of the defendant versus a specific trait disposition) and in the way in which that inference is proved (i.e., general reputation or opinion versus specific acts). The rules show a preference for specific traits (e.g., honesty, violence) but proved in a general manner (e.g., reputation). Note in this regard that admissibility of specific acts is provided for largely by common law, while reputation and opinion are endorsed by the FRE (Cleary, 1984). These preferences are based on assumptions that specific trait inferences and general testimony are both more probative than prejudicial. Questions concerning these two crucial criteria may thus be raised about the generality of the inferred trait and of the content of the *testimony*.

How specific must a trait be to be pertinent? To answer this, one would need to know the correlation between the specific traits for which testimony is offered and the target trait that is the element of the case or of impeachment. For example, if testimony shows that a defendant is unstable in his employment history, is this predictive of negligence in driving? Similarly, one would also have to know the correlation between the general characteristic and the target trait. Even if testimony establishes a general disposition toward negligence, does this predict negligence in driving, and in this particular instance? These correlations would not be readily available at trial, of course, but it can be said that they are generally low if the specific situations surrounding the behavior that is the basis of testimony and the target act are not taken into account (see discussion of interactionism below). However, people *believe* the correlations between traits are higher than they are. "Implicit personality theory" refers to the beliefs people have about which characteristics go together and which do not (Bruner & Tagiuri, 1954; Schneider, 1973). There are universal conceptions that if a person possesses certain characteristics, he or she will also possess certain other characteristics (Passini & Norman, 1966). Underlying these implicative relationships between traits is an evaluative good/bad dimension (Osgood & Tannenbaum, 1955). People see characteristics as going together on the basis of evaluative similarity (Rosenberg, Nelson, & Vivekananthan, 1968), a phenomenon that has been labeled the *halo effect* (Newcomb, 1931; Thorndike, 1920). Thus, there is a chance of overestimating the probativeness of a trait that has been testified to over a trait that is more pertinent. There is an additional danger that such overestimation (by the court in allowing such testimony and by the jury in drawing inferences from it) will take place along evaluative similarity lines. People who have negative traits, as evidenced by general testimony or by specific acts that lead to trait attributions, will be inferred to have negative traits that are probative even when the evidenced traits are not probative to crucial issues or to impeachment.

Should general character testimony be preferred over specific acts? The rationale is that general testimony is less prejudicial, misleading, time-consuming, and open to side issues that distract from main issues (Cleary, 1984). It is assumed to be more probative, reliable, and accurate than single, specific acts because it is the accumulation of many acts (Waltz, 1983). Note the contradictory exception, however, that specific acts are allowed for proving the trait of truthfulness (or untruthfulness) for purpose of impeachment.

McCormick (Cleary, 1984) disagrees, commenting on a speculative basis that the more general the testimony, the less probative and objective it is. The psychology of personality provides some substantive basis for evaluating existing practice. It suggests that the use of general dispositions, whether of character in broad terms or of a particular trait, is questionable for predicting an action in a particular situation (e.g., the charged act). We have seen that the trait disposition of honesty (or dishonesty) is not necessarily predictive of lying in a particular instance. More broadly, the issue is reflected in the question addressed by personality psychologists of whether trait dispositions are manifested consistently in behavior across a variety of situations (cross-situational consistency) or whether their effects depend on the particular situation. The latter view states that behavior in any instance is a joint function of traits and situations, so that a trait may be manifested in one situation but not in another. For example, mock jurors with biases toward judging defendants harshly convict more than those with biases toward leniency when trial evidence is ambiguous and unreliable but not when evidence is clear and reliable (Kaplan & Miller, 1978). In mainstream psychology, interactionism between traits and situations is now considered the rule for understanding behavior in specific instances (Ekehammar, 1974; Endler & Magnusson, 1976; Funder, 1983). On a related note, measures of temporary or transient dispositions (states) correlate more highly with other state measures of the same dispositional characteristic than with measures of the *trait*, or enduring characteristic, and higher than different measures of the trait with each other (Zuckerman, 1983). For example, two different measures of anxiety over taking a particular test (state) will correlate more highly with one another than they will with a measure of general anxiety, and this correlation between state measures will be higher than that between two measures of general anxiety (trait). This means that the best way to predict or postdict an individual's specific behavior or state at a particular time (which is what is most at issue in the trial) is through knowledge of his or her actions or states in similar situations (i.e., specific acts tied to specific situations). Enduring traits are not by themselves good predictors (i.e., are not probative) of an action or a tendency for an action (state) in a specific situation, nor do they have as great an impact on behavior as do states (Kaplan, 1981). Personality traits are most valid when they are observed in a series of specific manifestations, by different methods, and in situations similar to the one targeted for prediction. But this calls for information about a series and pattern of specific acts and states—information that is specifically limited by the FRE.

McCormick (Cleary, 1984) proposes a form of admissible evidence that approximates the sort of information that is considered to be most valid by personality psychologists. He suggests that the defendant's "habits" be inquired into rather than his or her character. Habit denotes a regular response to a repeated situation. In psychological terms, this is a situationally specific trait as opposed to a generalized disposition. We saw above that the former is more probative or predictive; McCormick comments that it will also be less prejudicial since it would not directly speak to a person's good or bad character. Such testimony is admissible by FRE Rule 406 to show that a defendant's conduct was in conformity (or not) with habit provided that it is shown that (1) the habit was regular, and (2) the situation of the crime was sufficiently similar to that in which the habit was displayed. Admission of specific act testimony in conformity with Rule 406 would seem to make sense in light of the dictum of interactionism between personality and situation.

In sum, the problem with character testimony is in the transition from a general disposition to a specific, targeted act. It does not matter whether the trait was derived by the jury from testimony on specific acts or by the witness from his or her own or others' integration of a series of acts. Although the latter form of testimony is inherently unreliable because we do not know how the acts were integrated into general reputation, what the acts were, or whether there was systematic distortion by the witness, what is more important is that inferences about traits that are consistent across situations and times are not very accurate. Compounding the problem is that the general character trait that is most closely implied from the testimony is often different than the target act (trial issue). For example, from testimony about an assault conviction a jury might infer a disposition of aggressiveness and criminality, which in turn is expected to be probative for the trial behavior of lying (or not) in testifying. More accurate inferences are drawn from specific acts consistently observed in similar situations to the one in question.

IMPACT OF CHARACTER TESTIMONY

Whatever the probative and prejudicial value of character testimony, it is bound to have some effect on verdicts. This last section examines the ability of jurors to detect inaccurate or deceptive character testimony, the impact of that testimony on their verdicts, and potential means of modifying the impact.

Detecting Testimony Credibility

What are the effects of deception on witness behavior? While no research on deception in character testimony can be found, a review of

studies of witness credibility in other types of testimony suggests a
number of indices that accompany lying or deception (Miller &
Burgoon, 1982). These include the following: speaking in broad and
sweeping generalities; fewer references to verifiable past events and
personal experiences; fewer factual statements; more references to
others ("them" and "they" rather than "we" and "us"); and fewer self-
references. Note that all are *encouraged* forms of character testimony—that is, all would be abundantly present if testimony were steered
toward general reputation and away from specific acts and the testifier's
personal opinion. Consequently, the behaviors accompanying deception would not be diagnostic for character testimony; detection would
be particularly difficult in this instance.

Are jurors able accurately to detect deception in character witnesses? Again, studies of this type of testimony are lacking. In fact,
relevant studies in any sort of testimony are sparse. In reviewing studies
of testimony and of interviews, Miller and Burgoon (1982) are pessimistic about jurors' abilities to detect deception. There is no evidence
that observers are aware of the effects interviewee deception can have
on their behavior or that observers can detect the behaviors when they
depart from the norm. Moreover, nonverbal (e.g., body and facial) cues
do not improve detection (Miller & Fontes, 1979) and may even distract
and lead to less accuracy (Maier & Thurber, 1968). Miller and Burgoon
(1982) conclude, "Observers are not very successful in detecting
deception perpetrated by relative strangers." Why this inaccuracy?
One possible explanation is that many of the behaviors signaling
deception also signal anxiety, which is expected to be natural in the trial
setting. Compounding matters for character testimony, many of these
behaviors are prescribed for the witness!

Impact of Testimony on Verdicts

The law, as reflected in the FRE, assumes that character testimony
will carry disproportionate weight. Indeed, many of the studies that will
be cited here show significant effects on verdicts. However, anecdotal
evidence in actual trials suggests otherwise. Kalven & Zeisel (1966)
surveyed judges in trials in which the jury decision either agreed or
disagreed with what the judge would have rendered. The judges
attributed 22 percent of the disagreements to extralegal factors
generally. But more to the issue, in only 10 percent of the cases where
the jury convicted when the judge would have acquitted did the judge
attribute the disagreement to jurors' knowledge and use of prior record.

And in most such instances, the other evidence in the trial was considered to be ambiguous. Thus, trial judges believed that the negative impact of character testimony was weak and limited largely to cases with "thin" evidence.

Experimental evidence suggests greater impact. Turning first to studies of prior and concurrent crimes, we find that mock juries are more likely to convict with testimony of a prior record, despite limited use instructions (Doob & Kirschenbaum, 1973; Hans & Doob, 1976). Refining this effect for prior record, there is evidence that prior convictions for crimes *similar* to the current charge increase convictions, but that prior crimes that are *dissimilar* to the charge decrease convictions (Sealy & Cornish, 1973). Moreover, the particular charge plays a role; prior convictions for a dissimilar crime increase convictions for an auto theft charge but not for murder (Wissler & Saks, 1982). Perhaps jurors are better able to conform to limited use instructions in more serious cases. Finally, the presence of concurrent charges, as in joined trial, increase conviction rates (Tanford & Penrod, 1982) by leading to an inference of criminal character (Tanford & Penrod, 1984). This confirms the fear that testimony as to alleged criminal acts can have a prejudicial effect. This effect can be complex; strong evidence in the joined charge leads to *less* convictions while weak evidence leads to *more* convictions in the target charge.

Studies of defendant characteristics are of two sorts—those that vary characteristics that are pertinent to case issues and those that address general character. The former applies, of course, to one of the admissibility criteria for establishing a case-specific fact. Borgida (1979) found that character evidence about the plaintiff's cautiousness affected his or her case favorably in a civil negligence suit when one witness testified, but hurt the plaintiff's case when several witnesses gave similar testimony. Repetition of testimony may have given the appearance of contrivance.

General character information has been varied through testimony regarding the defendant's social or physical attractiveness. Landy and Aronson (1969) reported longer sentences assigned to socially unattractive than attractive defendants, although subsequent studies established some limitations for this effect. Attractiveness affects conservative but not liberal mock jurors (Nemeth & Sosis, 1973), and its impact can be reduced by strong instructions on criteria for conviction (Weiten, 1980). Also, socially attractive defendants are treated more *harshly* when they have low justification for the convicted act compared to high justification or need (Izzett & Fishman, 1976).

Limitations also apply to the general observation that more lenient verdicts and sentences are accorded defendants holding attitudes similar to those of jurors (and therefore possessing positive characteristics). Attitude similarity affects high but not low authoritarians (Mitchell & Byrne, 1973). Deliberation reduces the effect of attitude similarity that is observed in predeliberation verdicts (Bray & Noble, 1978; Izzett & Leginski, 1974). The effect of physical attractiveness is also open to limitations. While male jurors judge an attractive opposite-sexed defendant more leniently, females are not influenced by physical appearance (Efran, 1974). And, the probative value of physical appearance cannot be ignored. Sigall and Ostrove (1975) found that attractive female defendants were more likely to be convicted of swindling, and less likely to be convicted of burglary, than their unattractive female counterparts. For the former charge, at least, attractiveness could be viewed as probative for method and ability.

The defendant's demeanor during testimony may be considered a factor in jurors' decisions. The defendant who shows remorse for his or her actions (Savitsky & Sim, 1974) or who has suffered in connection with the action (Austin, Walster, & Utne, 1976) will be given a reduced sentence.

Most of the foregoing studies of social and physical attractiveness had the deficit of not varying the content of the factual (i.e., non-character) evidence. When character and factual evidence are covaried—that is, when the evidence is varied to be either mildly incriminating or exonerating—the effect of factual evidence is considerably greater than that of character (Kaplan & Kemmerick, 1974). In combination with the cited limitations, this suggests that the impact of character testimony needs to be considered in context. Not all jurors are similarly affected by character testimony; sometimes such testimony is probative for the particular charge, the similarity between the testified character and charged act needs to be considered, deliberation can reduce impact, and importantly, the net effect of character may be relatively minor compared to that of factual evidence. These findings will figure prominently in the next section on the modification of character testimony impact.

What of the defendant who has read this chapter and wishes to avoid the pitfalls of testifying? Woe to him! Refusal to testify can increase the likelihood of conviction (see Chapter 5 of this volume). So, caught between a rock and a hard place, we turn to the question of how to minimize the effects of character testimony for that large majority of defendants who do offer testimony in their own behalf and for whom unfriendly testimony is given.

Reducing the Impact of
Character Testimony

A number of strategies for reducing the impact of potentially prejudicial effects of character testimony emerge from the preceding discussion. The concern here is not with the probative aspects of testimony, but with the prejudicial dispositions the testimony might create in the juror. These strategies lead, in turn, to a general model of the processing and utilization of evidence by jurors.

The impact of character testimony depends on the nature of the crime. Its impact is less for crimes of a serious than nonserious nature, which of course involve severe rather than mild consequences for the defendant (Wissler & Saks, 1982). Therefore, one strategy would be to impress the jury with the serious nature of the charge and the potential consequences of conviction.

The presence of related or joined charges increases the chance of conviction on a given charge by producing an inference of criminality. If joinder is unavoidable, potentially prejudicial inferences might be minimized by placing some distance between the charges (e.g., by emphasizing their dissimilarities).

Repeatedly the finding emerges that biasing effects from any source (e.g., inadmissible evidence, pretrial publicity, defendant character) are maximized when other available and admissible evidence is sparse or weak. Similarly, the remedial effect of instructions to disregard evidence should be strongest when there is an abundance of other probative evidence. For example, Kaplan and Miller (1978) convened jurors who were previously determined to have strong pro- or antidefendant dispositions. These trait biases affected verdicts in a mock trial when the evidence was characterized as argumentable and unreliable. But when the same evidence was portrayed as valid and reliable, the effects of trait biases vanished. The lesson in these findings is that when trial evidence is strong (whether for or against the defendant), reliable, and noncontentious, effects of biasing agents are reduced. Jurors are looking for answers to the questions posed by the trial. If admissible evidence can supply that answer, they will not resort to inadmissible evidence, character-based inferences, or preexisting biases.

Deliberation has a remedial effect on biases in juror decisions. When deliberation stresses the facts of the case, the effects of biasing agents are reduced (Bray & Noble, 1978; Izzett & Leginski, 1974; Kaplan & Schersching, 1981). The last resort for removing bias is in a properly conducted deliberation. It seems useful, then, to remind the jury of the need to discuss the admissible case facts and not the inadmissible inferences. To illustrate the role of deliberation in modifying the impact of unwanted elements, Kaplan and Miller (1978) produced negative *states* in jurors by subjecting them to obnoxious, histrionic, delaying, and other annoying behavior by the defense attorney in a staged trial (some readers may have observed such behavior in *opposing* attorneys). Other juries were exposed to the same trial, but without that source of annoyance. The effect of this negative state was to increase judgments of guilt made before deliberation. But after deliberation (which focused on discussion of trial evidence), the difference in judgment between the two sets of juries vanished). Deliberation remediated the state bias.

The social-psychological study of judgment provides a theoretical model for the remediation of unwanted elements, such as prejudice. Information integration theory (Anderson, 1981) is a general model of human judgment in which there are three fundamental steps in forming a judgment. First, each piece of information about the object to be judged is evaluated with respect to the judgment. A *scale value* is assigned to each piece, referring to its position on the judgment dimension. For example, testimonial evidence of a threat to the victim's life would likely have a high scale value on the dimension of defendant guilt (the target judgment), while evidence of a generally honest reputation in the community would have a low scale value for guilt (but high for truthfulness).

Second, each piece of information is assigned a *weight*, which refers to its subjective importance to the judgment. Independent of scale value, different sorts of information have different impacts (weights) on a given decision. For example, eyewitness testimony should carry a greater weight than character testimony. Weight is a joint function of reliabiity (i.e., credibility) and validity (i.e., probativeness) of the information.

Third, the various pieces of information—or, more correctly, their scale values—are integrated into a unitary judgment. A juror does not report a verdict on each piece of information in the case (motive, method, etc.) but reaches an integrated response ("guilty"). The scale values are integrated by an algebraic rule, most often by averaging, weighting each by its relative importance.

This model, presented briefly here, has been applied to the role of biases in social judgments (Kaplan, 1975) and their elimination under certain circumstances. Also relevant to the present discussion, the model has been successfully extended to judgment formation by jurors (Kaplan, 1977a) and particularly to reducing the impact of juror bias (Kaplan & Miller, 1978; Kaplan & Scherching, 1980). Recall that any piece of information that can potentially be used in judgment is given a scale value. This is true for evidence, admissible or not, biasing information intended for other purposes, and even for the juror's predispositions. Limited-use instructions and instructions to ignore biases, inadmissible evidence, pretrial publicity or the like will not affect the scale value for guilt. Negatively valued testimony does not take on a positive value through instructions; you cannot "make a silk purse out of a sow's ear." Instead, once information has been apprehended and evaluated, the question is whether you can reduce its impact or *weight*. Instructions are not entirely successful in reducing the weight of unwanted elements relative to legally probative information, especially when the latter is unreliable or weak. The weighted averaging principle suggests a means of reducing the impact of a given element without directly attacking that element. In a weighted average, the weights are relative to one another, so that any increase in the weight of one piece of information necessarily results in a decrease in the *relative* contribution of others. In short (at the risk of continuing our animal adages), there are two ways to "skin a cat." If impact cannot be reduced directly, it can be modified by increasing the impact of other elements. Such salutary effects have been demonstrated for reducing juror bias (Kaplan, 1982a; Kaplan & Schersching, 1980). One can use the relative weighting principle to combat potential prejudice aroused by character testimony through the presence of probative evidence, clearly and reliably presented. Note that biases have least impact, and instructions are most effective, when jurors also have strong and reliable evidence.

This analysis accounts for the role of deliberation in reducing the impact of biasing agents, including impermissible inferences from character testimony (Kaplan & Schersching, 1981). Prior to deliberation, the individual juror's judgment is based on an integration of scale values of trial evidence, character testimony, and preexisting biases. To the extent that the first mentioned element is not taken into account or does not have impact, the latter elements will affect this judgment. This individual judgment will likely have *not* integrated all potential facts due to forgetting, inattention during original presentation, and general limitations in information processing capacities. During deliberation jurors discuss the trial facts that influenced them, and thereby share information about the case. Each juror may be sharing information that was not incorporated by some other jurors in their original judgments, so that the judgment made after deliberation may integrate more probative evidence than the one before (Kaplan & Miller, 1977) and therefore show less impact of nonevidential or biasing factors (Kaplan,

1977b; Kaplan & Miller, 1978). Deliberation increases the pool of legally probative testimony to be integrated, reducing then the relative impact of proscribed elements, such as general or specific dispositional inferences arising from character testimony. The key to the remedial effect of deliberation is that it should elicit a considerable number and variety of facts that are probative and reliable, and that increase the set of information that is taken into account (Kaplan & Miller, 1977), while not dwelling on the prejudicial information. In short, the prescription is for full, open, and complete discussion of evidence.

SOME LAST THOUGHTS

This chapter has not treated the full range of defendant characteristics for which literature exists (e.g., race, sex, other socioeconomic and demographic variables). It has been limited to those that would be contained in character testimony and related cross-examination. For a full treatment of the entire scope of defendant characteristics, see Dane and Wrightsman (1982) and Chapter 5 of this volume.

This chapter has not proposed any policy, statutory, or rule changes. This is in keeping with the preferred role of social science (my preference, at least) to inform policymakers and legal practitioners on the likely social and personal effects of existing practices and to advise them of the probable consequences of proposed laws and policies (Kaplan, 1985). Social science is on its firmest ground when it *describes* behavioral effects of variables in the given system, but not when it *prescribes*. Here, I have tried to address the behavioral or judgmental consequences of character testimony vis-à-vis the concerns expressed in the FRE and in legal commentaries on the FRE. Assigning to these consequences scale values for social desirability and weights for priorities remains a task for the legal rule-makers.

REFERENCES

Anderson, N. H. (1981). *Foundations of information integration theory.* New York: Academic Press.

Austin, W., Walster, E., & Utne, M. K. (1976). Equity and the law: The effect of a harmdoer's "suffering in the act" on liking and assigned punishment. In L. Berkowitz & E. Walster (Eds.), *Advances in experimental social psychology* (Vol. 9). New York: Academic Press.

Borgida, E. (1979). Character proof and fireside induction. *Law and Human Behavior, 3,* 189-202.

Bray, R. M., & Noble, A. M. (1978). Authoritarianism and decisions of mock juries: Evidence of jury bias and group polarization. *Journal of Personality and Social Psychology, 36,* 1424-1430.

Bruner, J. S., & Tagiuri, R. (1954). The perception of people. In G. Lindzey (Ed.), *Handbook of social psychology*. Cambridge, MA: Addison-Wesley.

Carbo v. United States, 314 F.2d 718 (1963).

Cleary, E. W. (Ed.). (1984). *McCormick on evidence* (3rd ed.). St. Paul, MN: West.

Dane, F. C., & Wrightsman, L. S. (1982). Effects of defendants' and victims' characteristics on jurors' verdicts. In N. L. Kerr & R. M. Bray (Eds.), *The psychology of the courtroom* (pp. 83-115). New York: Academic Press.

Doob, A. N., & Kirschenbaum, H. M. (1973). Some empirical evidence on the effect of S.12 of the Canada Evidence Act upon an accused. *Criminal Law Quarterly, 15,* 88-96.

Efran, M. G. (1974). The effect of physical appearance on the judgment of guilt, interpersonal attraction, and severity of recommended punishment on a simulated jury task. *Journal of Research in Personality, 8,* 45-54.

Ekehammar, B. (1974). Interactionism in personality from an historical perspective. *Psychological Bulletin, 81,* 1026-1048.

Elwork, A., Hansen, D. A., & Sales, B. D. (1985). The problem with jury instructions. In M. F. Kaplan (Ed.), *The impact of social psychology on procedural justice*. Springfield, IL: Charles C Thomas.

Endler, N. S., & Magnusson, D. (1976). Toward an interactional psychology of personality. *Psychological Bulletin, 83,* 956-974.

Funder, D. C. (1983). Three issues in predicting more of the people: A reply to Mischel and Peake. *Psychological Review, 90,* 283-289.

Hamilton, D. L. (1981). Cognitive representations of persons. In E. T. Higgins, C. P. Herman & M. P. Zanna (Eds.), Social cognition: The Ontario symposium (Vol 1). Hillsdale, NJ: Lawrence J. Erlbaum.

Hamilton, D. L., & Fallot, R. D. (1974). Information salience as a weighting factor in impression formation. *Journal of Personality and Social Psychology, 30,* 444-448.

Hamilton, D. L., & Zanna, M. P. (1972). Differential weighting of favorable and unfavorable attributes of impressions of personality. *Journal of Experimental Research in Personality, 6,* 204-212.

Hans, V. P., & Doob, A. N. (1976). Section 12 of the Canada Evidence Act and the deliberation of simulated jurors. *Criminal Law Quarterly, 18,* 235-253.

Hartshorne, H., & May, M. (1928). *Studies in the nature of character: studies in deceit.* New York: Macmillan.

Hodges, B. H. (1974) Effect of valence on relative weighting in impression formation. *Journal of Personality and Social Psychology, 30,* 378-381.

Izzett, R. R., & Fishman, L. (1976). Defendant sentences as a function of attractiveness and justification for actions. *Journal of Social Psychology, 100,* 285-290.

Izzett, R. R., & Leginski, W. (1974). Group discussion and the influence of defendant characteristics in a simulated jury setting. *Journal of Social Psychology, 93,* 271-279.

Jones, E. E. (1979). The rocky road from acts to dispostions. *American Psychologist, 34,* 107-117.

Kalven, H., Jr., & Zeisel, H. (1966). *The American jury.* Boston: Little, Brown.

Kaplan, M. F., & Kemmerick, G. D. (1974). Juror judgment as information integration: Combining evidential and nonevidential components. In M. F. Kaplan & Schwartz (Eds.), *Human judgment and decision processes*. New York: Academic Press.

Kaplan, M. F. (1975). Information integration in social judgment: Interaction of judge and information components. In M. F. Kaplan & S. Schwartz (Eds.), *Human judgment and decision processes*. New York: Academic Press.

Kaplan, M. F. (1977a). Judgments by juries. In M. F. Kaplan & S. Schwartz (Eds.), *Human judgment and decision processes in applied settings*. New York: Academic Press.

Kaplan, M. F. (1977b). Discussion polarization effects in a modified jury decision paradigm: Informational influences. *Sociometry, 40,* 262-271.

Kaplan, M. F. (1981). State dispositions in social judgment. *Bulletin of the Psychonomic Society, 18,* 27-29.

Kaplan, M. F. (1982a). Cognitive processes in the individual juror. In N. L. Kerr & R. M. Bray (Eds.), *The psychology of the courtroom* (pp. 197-220). New York: Academic Press.

Kaplan, M. F. (1982b). *Putting mystery into social judgment: Evaluation of suspects in "whodunits."* Paper read at the meetings of the Midwestern Psychological Association, Minneapolis, MN.

Kaplan, M. F. (1985). A brief overview of the impact of social science on procedural justice. In M. F. Kaplan (Ed.), *The impact of social psychology on procedural justice.* Springfield, IL: Charles C Thomas.

Kaplan, M. F., & Miller, C. E. (1977). Judgments and group discussion: Effect of presentation and memory factors on polarization. *Sociometry, 40,* 337-343.

Kaplan, M. F., & Miller, L. E. (1978). Reducing the effects of juror bias. *Journal of Personality and Social Psychology, 36,* 1443-1455.

Kaplan, M. F., & Schersching, C. (1980). Reducing juror bias: An experimental approach. In P. Lipsitt & B. D. Sales (Eds.), *New directions in psycholegal research* (pp. 149-170). New York: Van Nostrand Reinhold.

Kaplan, M. F., & Schersching, C. (1981). Juror deliberation: An information integration analysis. In B. D. Sales (Ed.), *Perspectives in law and psychology. Vol. 2: The Trial* (pp. 235-262). New York: Plenum.

Kelley, H. H. (1967). Attribution theory in social psychology. In D. Levine (Ed.), *Nebraska symposium on motivation* Lincoln: University of Nebraska Press.

Landy, D., & Aronson, E. (1969). The influence of the character of criminal and his victim on the decisions of simulated jurors. *Journal of Experimental Social Psychology, 5,* 141-152.

Lempert, R. O., & Saltzburg, S. A. (1982). *A modern approach to evidence* (2nd ed.). St. Paul: MN: West.

Loh, W. D. (1984). *Social research in the judicial process: Cases, readings, and text.* New York: Russell Sage Foundation.

Maier, N.R.F., & Thurber, J. A. (1968). Accuracy of judgments of deception when an interview is watched, heard, and read. *Personnel Psychology, 21,* 23-30.

McArthur, L. Z. (1972). The how and what of why: Some determinants and causes of causal attributions. *Journal of Personality and Social Psychology, 22,* 171-193.

Michaelson v. United States, 335 U.S. 469 (1948).

Miller, G. R., & Burgoon, J. K. (1982). Factors affecting assessments of witness credibility. In N. L. Kerr & R. M. Bray (Eds.), *The psychology of the courtroom* (pp. 169-194). New York: Academic Press.

Miller, G. R., & Fontes, N. G. (1979). *Videotape on trial: A view from the jury box.* Beverly Hills, CA: Sage.

Mischel, W. (1968). *Personality and assessment.* New York: John Wiley.

Mitchell, H. E., & Bryne, D. (1973). The defendant's dilemma: Effect on jurors' attitudes and authoritarianism on judicial decisions. *Journal of Personality and Social Psychology, 25,* 123-129.

Nemeth, C., & Sosis, R. H. (1973). A simulated jury study: Characteristics of the defendant and the jurors. *Journal of Social Psychology, 90,* 221-229.

Newcomb, T. (1931). An experiment designed to test the validity of a rating technique. *Journal of Applied Psychology, 22,* 279-289.

Nisbett, R., & Ross, L. (1980). *Human inference: Strategies and shortcomings of social judgment.* Englewood Cliffs, NJ: Prentice-Hall.

Osgood, C. E., & Tannenbaum, P. H. (1955). The principle of congruity in the prediction of attitude change. *Psychological Review, 62,* 42-55.

Passini, F. T., & Norman, W. T. (1966). A universal conception of personality structure? *Journal of Personality and Social Psychology, 4,* 44-49.

Richey, M. H., McClelland, L., & Shimkunas, A. M. (1967). Relative influence of positive and negative information in impression formation and persistence. *Journal of Personality and Social Psychology, 6,* 322-327.

Rosenberg, S., Nelson, C., & Vivekananthan, P. S. (1968). A multidimensional approach to the structure of personality impressions. *Journal of Personality and Social Psychology, 9,* 283-294.

Ross, L., & Anderson, C. A. (1982). Shortcomings in the attribution process: On the origins and maintenance of erroneous social assessments. In D. Kahneman, P. Slovic, & A. Tversky (Eds.), *Judgment under uncertainty: heuristics and biases.* Cambridge: Cambridge University Press.

Saks, M. J., & Hastie, R. (1978). *Social psychology in court.* New York: Van Nostrand Reinhold.

Savitsky, J., & Sim, M. (1974). Trading emotions: Equity theory of reward and punishment. *Journal of Communication, 24,* 140-147.

Schneider, D. J. (1973). Implicit personality theory: A review. *Psychological Bulletin, 79,* 294-309.

Sealy, A. P., & Cornish, W. R. (1973). Juries and the rules of evidence. *Criminal Law Review,* April, 208-223.

Sigall, H. J., & Ostrove, N. (1975). Beautiful but dangerous: Effects of offender attractiveness and nature of crime on juridic judgment. *Journal of Personality and Social Psychology, 31,* 410-414.

Sue, S., Smith, R. S., & Caldwell, C. (1973). Effects of inadmissible evidence on the decisions of simulated jurors: A moral dilemma, *Journal of Applied Social Psychology, 3,* 344-353.

Sue, S., Smith, R. E., & Gilbert, R. (1974). Biasing effects of pretrial publicity on judicial decision. *Journal of Criminal Justice, 2,* 163-171.

Tanford, S., & Penrod, S. (1982). Biases in trials involving defendants charged with multiple offenses. *Journal of Applied Social Psychology, 12,* 453-480.

Tanford, S., & Penrod, S. (1984). Social inference processes in juror judgments of multiple-offense trials. *Journal of Personality and Social Psychology, 47,* 749-765.

Thorndike, E. L. (1920). A constant error in psychological ratings. *Journal of Applied Psychology, 4,* 25-29.

Tversky, A., & Kahneman, S. (1974). Judgment under uncertainty: Heuristics and biases. *Science, 185,* 1124-1131.

United States v. Escobedo, 430 F. 2d 14 (1970).

Waltz, J. R. (1983). *Introduction to criminal evidence* (2nd ed.). Chicago: Nelson Hall.

Warr, P., & Jackson, P. (1975). The importance of extremity. *Journal of Personality and Social Psychology, 32,* 278-282.

Weiten, W. (1980). The attraction-leniency effect in jury research: An examination of external validity. *Journal of Applied Social Psychology, 10,* 340-347.

Wissler, R. L., & Saks, M. J. (1982). *On the inefficacy of limiting instructions: When jurors use credibility evidence to decide on guilt.* Presented at the annual meeting of the American Psychological Association, Washington, DC.

Zuckerman, M. (1983). The distinction between trait and state scales is *not* arbitrary. Comment on Allen and Potkay's "On the arbitrary distinction between traits and states." *Journal of Personality and Social Psychology, 44,* 1083-1086.

CHAPTER 7

Survey and Field Experimental Evidence

JACOB JACOBY

Social scientists are increasingly being called upon to provide expert opinion and testimony regarding a widening spectrum of issues. In most instances, these experts testify from a base of accumulated knowledge and experience, often relying on the relevant scholarly literature. In a lesser, although increasing number of instances, they testify regarding research conducted specifically for purposes of the litigation at hand. This chapter addresses the question, How must research conducted specifically to address the legal issues at hand (i.e., primary research) be conducted for it to be admitted and given its due weight?

Although a university laboratory is the research environment of choice for most psychologists, primary research offered as legal evidence is not generally conducted in such settings. The term *field research* may be applied, despite the fact that a substantial amount of such research takes place at central location testing (CLT) facilities situated in shopping malls, which are essentially laboratory settings. Such field research encompasses both surveys and true experiments.[1] Although the unit of analysis need not involve human beings (see Loewen, 1982, chap. 9), our discussion is confined to those instances in which verbal reports are gathered from people serving either as survey respondents or test subjects.

WHEN PSYCHOLOGICAL PHENOMENA ARE RELEVANT

Although a legal issue may relate directly to the lay public, in a great many matters no concern need be given to what members of this public think, believe, or feel about the issue. For a select number of other issues, however, the layperson's state of mind represents the very heart of the legal issue. As an example, consider the matter of trademark infringement, where the key questions include the following:

(1) To what extent does a given mark (brand name, logo, etc.) or trade dress (i.e., package design) generate "secondary meaning" or confusion? That is, do consumers correctly or incorrectly associate that mark or dress with another mark or a particular source (i.e., manufacturer or sponsoring organization)?

(2) Given confusion, to what extent would disclaimers (such as might be placed on packages, labels, etc.) serve to dispell such confusion?

(3) To what extent does a mark (e.g., Kleenex) take on a generic significance such that, for a substantial number of consumers, that mark has come to represent the product category in its entirety (i.e., facial tissues) rather than a particular brand of the product that is manufactured by a single source?

At core, these questions relate to mental states. While experts relying on the scholarly literature and their own past experience might provide reasonable answers, these answers may not be equally applicable to each specific instance. Further, experts can and often do disagree. As such, there is no substitute for directly relevant empirical evidence. For these reasons, both attorneys and triers of fact are increasingly relying on primary research to assist in providing answers to the questions stated above.

THE HISTORY AND TREND OF FIELD RESEARCH

As early as 1930, legal scholars could be found arguing for the use of field research (Handler & Pickett, 1930). Admitting survey evidence, however, has posed many problems, the most significant of which has been a concern over violating the hearsay rule. As described below, the Report of the Judicial Conference Study Group on Procedure in Protracted Litigation that was adopted by the Judicial Conference of the United States in March 1960, along with several influential rulings—especially by Judge Wyzanski (*American Luggage Works v. U.S. Trunk Co.*, 1957) and Judge Feinberg (*Zippo Manufacturing v. Rogers Imports*, 1963)—shifted attention from the relatively fruitless concern over hearsay to a more productive focus on the conditions under which such research should be admitted and given weight.

In the decades since, an increasing number of surveys have been conducted and submitted. Indeed, primary research is becoming the rule rather than the exception in trademark infringement cases. Courts have even taken note of and sometimes ruled against parties on the grounds that they failed to submit a survey (e.g., *Mushroom Makers v. R.G. Barry*, 1977, p. 1231; *Information Clearing House v. Find Magazine*, 1980, p. 947; *Spring Mills v. Ultracashmere*, 1982, p. 1068; *NFL v. Wichita Falls*, 1982, p. 658; *Henri's v. Kraft*, 1983, p. 390). In *University of Pittsburgh v. Champion Products* (1983), which involved a claim of likely confusion stemming from the unauthorized use of University of Pittsburgh indicia on football replica jerseys, the court (making specific mention of the research that I conducted for plaintiff in *National Football League v. Wichita Falls Sportswear*, 1982), found a lack of proof by the university and suggested that a survey might have provided the critical evidence to sustain the claims of infringement. Rulings such as these have thus led Robin and Barnaby (1983, p. 436) to comment,

> It is a well-established rule of evidence that . . . *the failure to produce* a relevant document in its possession raises an inference that . . . the contents of that document would be unfavorable. There is no such rule involving *the failure* of a party *to create* evidence. Yet, there is a growing belief in the trademark bar that the failure of a trademark owner to run a survey to support its claim of likelihood of confusion gives rise to a similar adverse inference [italics added].

Clearly, the significance of survey research in trademark litigation has progressed a long way in a very short period. Because they illustrate many of the issues that need to be addressed when conducting primary field research for introduction in litigation, our discussion will focus on case law as this has evolved in regard to trademark issues.

FACTORS USED IN ESTABLISHING ADMISSIBILITY AND ACCORDING WEIGHT

While most surveys are routinely admitted, the majority are accorded little or no weight. This poor track record may be attributable to the fact that many researchers (and, one might infer, many attorneys as well) seem unfamiliar with what is required to establish admissibility and achieve weight. Rule 703 of the Federal Rules of Evidence (FRE), entitled the "Bases of Opinion Testimony by Experts," provides the foundation upon which surveys, public opinion polls, and field experiments can be introduced as evidence (see Weinstein & Berger, 1982). Together with evolving case law, this rule focuses attention on the criteria for admissibility and weight.

Establishing Admissibility

The most influential rulings in regard to the admissibility of case-specific behavioral research evidence were probably those by Judge Wyzanski in *American Luggage Works*, (1957) and Judge Feinberg in *Zippo* (1963). Both point to *necessity* and *trustworthiness* as the dual criteria for establishing admissibility.

> So long as the interviewees are not cross-examined, there is no testing of their sincerity, narrative ability, perception, and memory. There is no showing whether they were influenced by leading questions, the environment in which questions were asked, or the personality of the investigator. But where a court is persuaded that in a particular case all these risks have been minimized, that the answers given by the interviewees are, on the whole, likely to be reliable indicia of their states of mind, that the absence of cross-examination is not prejudicial, and that other ways of getting evidence on the same point are either impractical or burdensome, the testimony should be admitted. (*American Luggage Works*, 1957, p. 53)

Guaranteeing trustworthiness requires evaluating a study's methodology. As the factors used to assess trustworthiness are the same as are used to determine weight (*see Nestle*, 1983, p. 307), most courts routinely admit surveys and then consider their technical adequacy as a basis for assigning weight.

According Weight

First presented in the *Handbook of Recommended Procedures for the Trial of Protracted Cases* (Judicial Conference of the U.S., 1960, p. 429), essentially the same set of evaluative factors have been described in numerous places, including the *Manual for Complex Litigation* (1982, p. 116), McCarthy's *Trademarks and Unfair Competition* (1973, p. 509), and various court rulings. According to these sources, the offeror of a survey has the burden of establishing that

(1) the proper universe was selected and examined;
(2) a representative sample was drawn from that universe;
(3) a fair and correct method of questioning was used;
(4) the persons designing and conducting the survey were recognized experts;
(5) the data were accurately reported;
(6) the sampling plan and execution, the construction of the questionnaire, and the interviewing were conducted in accordance with generally ac-

cepted standards of objective procedure and statistics in the field of such surveys;
(7) the sampling and the interviews were conducted independently of the attorneys in the case; and
(8) the interviewers were adequately trained in the field, and had no knowledge of the litigation or the purposes for which the survey was to be used.

The next section illustrates how the courts have relied on these factors when deciding on admissibility and weight. This review is intended to assist researchers, attorneys, and triers of fact in designing, reporting, and evaluating primary research conducted for presentation as evidence in litigation. It should also be noted that these factors apply to primary research; the court may relax these standards for research not conducted with the explicit intent of being offered in the case at hand (*see Nestle v. Chester's Market*, 1983, p. 309).

CASE LAW BEARING ON ADMISSIBILITY AND WEIGHT[2]

Table 7.1 lists the cases reviewed and indicates how the court ruled regarding admissibility and weight.[3] Although not exhaustive, the listing does contain many of the more influential rulings involving surveys. In all, 44 separate cases involving separate comments on a total of 67 different surveys are cited. Several cases involve the submission of two or more surveys by one or both parties. In some cases the court admitted one while rejecting another. In several instances (see *Amstar v. Domino's Pizza*, 1980; and especially *Anti-Monopoly v. General Mills Fun Group*, 1982), the assessment of a survey's worth by the appeals court was completely contrary to that of the district court. Although the vast majority of the surveys were admitted, in only 14 out of 67 instances were they accorded substantial weight. What specific facets of these investigations did these courts, operating without juries, rely on when making their determinations? Unfortunately answers to this question must be accepted as tentative because judges generally do not comment upon all aspects of the studies that they review, nor do they always provide sufficient information to explain their opinions.

Employing the Appropriate Universe

It has become axiomatic in trademark case law that the key consideration in the design of a survey is whether the appropriate universe was tested (McCarthy, 1973, p. 500; Reiner, 1983, p. 374). More surveys are held inadmissible or given little or no weight for having employed an improper universe than for any other reason. As the court said in *NFL v. Wichita Falls*, "A survey of the wrong universe is of little probative value" (1982, p. 657). Clearly, if the issue concerns the secondary meaning attached to automobile oil filters, it makes no sense to assess the state of mind of a sixth-grade child.

The proper universe consists of all individuals whose mental states are relevant to the issue at hand. Sometimes this might encompass everyone residing in the United States. More often, it comprises a more narrowly defined group, usually circumscribed in terms of their purchase behavior, age, sex, or geography. The most influential discussion of this point probably appears in Judge Wyzanski's opinion in *American Luggage* (1957, p. 52) wherein it was noted that the universe selected for study may fail to be appropriate either because it excludes individuals whose state of mind is at issue or because it includes individuals whose state of mind is irrelevant. For example, in *General Motors v. Cadillac Marine,* where the issue concerned defendant's use of the name *Cadillac* on boats, the court opined, "The individuals among whom the poll was taken were not, in the vast majority of cases, 'purchasers' in any sense of the word. Indeed, many indicated they had no interest in boats at all" (1964, p. 737). This general requirement for appropriateness applies not only to the notion of "prospective purchaser" but to age, sex, geography, and experience as well.

Given the need to satisfy the court that the appropriate universe has been examined, perhaps the safest approach is to employ the "umbrella" procedure described by Reiner (1983), which I devised for the plaintiff in *NFL v. Wichita Falls* (1982). Briefly, in order to avoid the possibility that the court might reject the survey either on the grounds that the universe was too broad or too narrow, the study included both a broad umbrella universe (everyone aged 13 to 65 living within the 48 contiguous United States) as well as subuniverses consisting of prior purchasers, fans of professional football, and fans whose test setting contained a shirt representing their favorite NFL team. When the defendant argued that the only relevant universe was likely purchasers of NFL football jersey replicas, the judge was able to note that "separate data is available for prior purchasers of NFL football jersey replicas, 'fans' and 'fans plus' of NFL member clubs. Even defendant's own expert conceded that these groupings were likely potential purchasers of the NFL football jersey replicas" (1982, p. 658).

Various other factors can become relevant in defining an appropriate universe. Consider age. In *American Basketball Association v. AMF Voit* (1973, p. 446) the court held that a universe of males aged 12 to 23 who had played basketball within the past year was "too narrow to allow the survey to be given any substantial weight" because the universe of potential purchasers was substantially broader. On the other hand, in *WGBH v. Penthouse* (1978, p. 435), the court held that since the intended audience was 18- to 34-year-olds and the researcher "made no effort to be selective as to age or scientific interest of those surveyed," the survey universe was too broad, and thus "reduced the evidentiary weight to be accorded to its findings."

Geography is also relevant. For example, in *Sears v. Allstate Driving School* (1969, p. 18-19), the court held that "the universe selected . . . for this survey, the entire county of Suffolk, was too large. As 80 percent of defendant's business comes from within the 8- to 10-mile radius of the school, a more accurate sampling would have confined itself to this geographic area." The court in *Deere v. Farmhand* (1982, p. 258) was also critical of the geographic coverage, noting that "the responding panel members were randomly selected from the Doane nationwide panel despite the fact that Farmhand and Deere only compete in the midwest region of the country." In *James Burroughs Ltd. v. Sign of the Beefeater* (1976) the court deemed that a survey conducted within a 5-mile radius of defendant's restaurant assessed an appropriate universe.

In sum, field research must be based on an explicit description of the universe (or universes) of people whose mental states are at issue and about whom we intend to make a statement. Without this, the assessment cannot be meaningful. Further, the defined universe may either be completely inappropriate or, if appropriate (and with apologies to Goldilocks), too narrow, too broad, or just right.

Indeed, it is possible for the universe to simultaneously be too broad and too narrow. Consider plaintiff's study in *Frisch's v. Elby's* (matter pending) where the issue concerns whether restaurant patrons believe defendant's eastern Ohio "Family Restaurants" serve Big Boy hamburgers when plaintiff has exclusive rights to this mark in Ohio and defendant has rights in West Virginia. While the universe in this study is too narrow because it excluded teenagers (a substantial number of whom frequently purchase hamburgers), it is also too broad because it included a substantial number of people who said they rarely or never ate out, who were not hamburger purchasers/eaters, or who lived more than 10 to 15 miles from the supposedly infringing restaurants.

We conclude by emphasizing that our focus on the "prospective purchaser" is due to having confined our remarks to trademark infringement issues. Other domains of legal action (e.g., the impact of advertising, product liability) usually require different universes. To illustrate, the challenged claim in one recent ad substantiation case (*Litton v. FTC*, 1982) was that 76 percent of independent microwave oven technicians "recommend Litton." The study was found deficient by the Federal Trade Commission, which was affirmed by the appeals court, because the universe was confined to Litton authorized service agents, some of whom had "insufficient experience with other brands to respond accurately." The bottom line is that the responsibility for "defining the correct universe rests squarely on the researcher who must design the survey in light of the legal issues presented to the court" (Reiner, 1983, p. 372).

Sampling the Universe

It is sometimes possible to test all members of the relevant universe—for example, the case may involve a product only sold to 1260 firms in the nation, and we may be able to reach the purchasing agents at all these firms. However, most relevant universes are sufficiently large (e.g., "The universe of actual and potential purchasers of glue . . . is the adult population . . . of the United States," from *Loctite v. National Starch*, 1981, p. 251) so that assessing the mental state of all members of the universe becomes impractical. Under these circumstances, one selects a subgroup from the universe, tests it, and then generalizes the finding from this sample to the broader universe as a whole. These findings can be as accurate and valid as if we had tested the entire universe. The key consideration is the extent to which the sample *represents* that universe. All other things being equal, the greater the representativeness, the greater the accuracy of the estimate.

If only a sample is to be tested, then what plan will be used for determining just who will be included? Sampling plans are divided into two broad categories—probability sampling and nonprobability sampling. Probability sampling involves the random selection of elements (e.g., people) from the universe, where each element has a known probability of being selected. The major implication of this approach is that, if implemented according to plan, probability sampling virtually ensures that the elements that are selected do a good job of representing the universe as a whole, thus permitting relatively precise projections to that universe with a known degree of error. In contrast, while nonprobability sampling plans do not involve random selection and do

not provide estimates with a known degree of error, they can still provide fairly accurate estimates just so long as they are reasonably representative.
Samples do not have to be large.

The widely held belief that the accuracy of a sample is connected with its relative size to the universe is mistaken. A sample smaller than 1 per cent, taken from one universe, can be much more reliable than one comprising 10 per cent of another. To determine with equal accuracy the average age of the population of New York City and of Peoria, Illinois will require samples of equal size. (Zeisel, 1960, p. 329)

A more important consideration than size is the variability within the universe with respect to the factor of interest. To illustrate, assume that one wanted to know the average age of the members of two universes— the first consisting of all those individuals living in a particular city having a population of 800,000 and the second consisting of all 800,000 individuals living in nursing homes within the same state. Although the size of each universe is identical, there is likely to be much greater variability with respect to age when considering the population of the city than when considering the population of the nursing homes in the state. Hence, we would need a larger sample for determining the average age of the city residents than for determining the average age of the nursing home residents. One implication of this principle is that nonprobability sampling is more likely to provide accurate estimates of the universe when the members of that universe are relatively homogeneous with respect to the issue of interest.

Another relevant sampling issue is that, in theory, probability sampling requires one to begin with a list of each and every element within the universe and then sample from that list. Clearly, this is impossible to achieve with most universes of interest. Under these circumstances probability sampling thus entails going through a series of stages. For example, one might list all 50 states and then randomly select 10 in which to conduct a test (Stage 1). One might then list all the municipalities within these 10 states and randomly select 5 from each state (Stage 2). Next, one might randomly select a number of "points" for each municipality from which to begin interviewing (Stage 3). Finally, one might randomly select people living near each point (Stage 4). Although quite simplified, this illustration enables us to make several important points.

First, sampling is involved at each stage and, for each stage, this may be accomplished using either a probability or nonprobability plan. Thus one should not be misled when hearing that a particular survey is "a probability survey"—it is important to know at just which stages. As a case in point, in *Frisch's v. Elby's* (matter pending), plaintiff conducted a survey that was purportedly a probability study. Yet, while households were contacted via random-digit phone dialing (an accepted probability sampling procedure), the individuals within each household were selected using the question "I'd like to speak to a male/female at this number who is 18 years or older"—a decidedly nonrandom procedure that ensures that those who participate could only be reasonably representative of those individuals over 18 who happened to be home at the time that this call was placed. Most likely, this was the female head of household.

Relatedly, the term *random* does not necessarily mean the application of a probability sampling plan. As an example, consider *Toys "R" Us v. Canarsie Kiddie Shop* (1983, p. 1203) where a "random intercept" procedure was employed at three shopping malls in order to obtain a "randomly intercepted representative sample."

Another multistage sampling issue warranting comment is the trade-off between the number of sampling points and the number of individuals per sampling point. Consider doing a national probability study involving in-home interviews of 2000 respondents. Clearly it makes no sense to select one test point (say, St. Louis) and conduct all 2000 interviews at that point. By the same token, it would be very expensive and inefficient to conduct the study at 2000 points around the country. A reasonable intermediate approach would be to select 100 test points and conduct 20 interviews at each. These 100 points would provide satisfactory blanket coverage for the nation as a whole. Most marketing research, however, proceeds with many fewer points and a larger number of individuals to be tested at each point. A rule of thumb informally applied in the realm of advertising substantiation is that three of four different testing sites represent an absolute minimum for ensuring a minimal degree of representativeness. Trademark courts, however, have accepted as few as two (see *Exxon v. Texas Motor Exchange*, 1980, p. 507; *Brooks Shoe v. Suave Shoe*, 1981, p. 80; reaffirmed 1983, p. 855). One site has been deemed totally inadequate (*GM v. Cadillac Marine*, 1964, p. 737; *Jockey International v. Burkard*, 1975, p. 205).

Recent court decisions suggest increasing leniency toward non-probability surveys. For example, in *Litton v. FTC* (1982) the court stated that "a representative sample need not be a probability sample" and, using this more lenient definition, indicated it would permit Litton to employ a "properly selected 'judgment sample' or 'convenience sample' " (p. 372). In part, this leniency may stem from Rule 703, which requires that the facts relied on by an expert witness "be of a type reasonably relied on by experts in the particular field." Consumer and market researchers generally rely more heavily on nonprobability surveys, and commercial decisions of great consequence are often predicated upon the results of such surveys. This leniency may also stem from the recognition that conducting a probability study generally requires more time than a nonprobability study—time that may not be available to the researcher who must have his or her study completed before the assigned trial date, usually before the time of his or her deposition.

The leniency may also stem from the growing recognition that all research involves making trade-offs between various facets of the research process. For example, conducting a true probability study may require in-home interviewing, but the nature of the product (or the test environment for that product) may not admit to being transported. Under these conditions, the researcher may try to conduct an in-home probability study using photographs of the product, or may instead use authentic products and test these in a centrally located testing facility. As several courts have commented that using inauthentic stimuli considerably lessens the weight given to a study, both the researcher and the court might opt for a CLT facility in preference to an in-home probability study.

Our discussion thus far has focused on the plan for generating the sample. However, regardless of the plan that is ultimately employed, the necessary subsequent issue concerns implementation of that plan—specifically, how well does the obtained sample represent the universe of interest? Courts sometimes note plan versus implementation discrepancies and assign reduced weight accordingly (e.g., "most of the interviewees . . . appear to have had a higher than average educational and economic status, and thus did not constitute a representative cross-section of the consumer public," from *American Thermos v. Aladdin Industries,* 1962, p. 21).

In conclusion, the objective of sampling is to ensure that the subgroup tested is representative of the universe of interest. In the abstract, probability sampling generally offers a better approach for achieving such representativeness. However, other facets of the research design or the exigencies of the court calendar may dictate that one use a nonprobability sampling plan, and the trier of fact should not be hasty in reducing weight on these grounds. It is clearly better to have a nonprobability study conducted with members who are from the appropriate universe than it is to have a precise probability study conducted with respondents who are not.

Questioning: Appropriate and Unbiased

The rulings reviewed in Table 7.1 suggest that the courts raise two points regarding the questions posed to respondents: (1) Do these questions address the legal issues that are relevant to the case? (2) If so, are the questions posed in a clear and unbiased manner?

The first point is on par in importance with selecting the proper universe. Just as selecting the wrong universe is nonprobative, addressing the wrong issue is equally nonprobative. Yet in at least six instances the courts held that the questions that were posed actually addressed the wrong issue (e.g., *Duncan v. Royal Tops*, 1965; *Jockey International v. Burkhard*, 1975; *Loctite v. National Starch*, 1981; *Tomy v. P. G. Continental*, 1982; *Prudential v. Gibraltar*, 1982; *Anti-Monopoly v. General Mills*, 1981 [plaintiff's survey], 1982 [defendant's survey]; *Nestle v. Chester's Market*, 1983 [plaintiff's second and third surveys]).

This problem arises when the attorney either fails to clearly grasp the underlying legal issue or when there is unclarity in communicating the correct understanding to the researcher. Even when the attorney clearly communicates the issue, it may also surface because most researchers are sufficiently unfamiliar with legal nuances to allow important subtleties to go unrecognized and unattended. Another cause of the problem stems from trying to graft a questioning approach successfully used in a previous trial onto a current problem. "Merely duplicating a survey that was accepted in a previous trademark case is no assurance of relevance in another case" (*Nestle v. Chester's*, 1983, p. 310).

Given the legal profession's historical concern with phrasing questions, it is not surprising that the courts are quick to identify questionnaire construction flaws. Examples include citing leading questions (e.g., *GM v. Cadillac Marine*, 1964, p. 736; *Sears v. Allstate Driving*, 1969, p. 17-18; *LaMaur v. Alberto-Culver*, 1973, p. 614; *Union Carbide v. Ever-Ready*, 1975, p. 293; *Mennen v. Gillette*, 1983, p. 358); noting context, order, and sequence effects (e.g., *Sears v. All States Insurance*, 1957, p. 172; *Sears v. Allstate Driving*, 1969, p. 17); and even focusing on the meaning of single words (e.g., *WGBH v. Penthouse*, 1978, p. 435). Even when questions may seem acceptable, the responses they stimulate may be ambiguous and therefore accorded little weight (see *GM v. Cadillac Marine*, 1964; *Deere v. Farmhand*, 1982).

These problems are traceable to a sad fact of contemporary behavioral science research—that despite their great sophistication regarding such things as devising sampling plans and analyzing data, many researchers know pitifully little regarding the intricacies of questionnaire wording and construction. Some even neglect the fundamental axiom that, to extract valid data, questions must make sense to the respondent; otherwise the obtained data are likely to be meaningless. This important point surfaced in *Anti-Monopoly* when the issue was remanded to the district court with an invitation for that court to entertain new evidence. In commenting upon plaintiff's new survey, the lower court noted (1981, p. 453-454) that the questions used "were pulled, verbatim, from an illustration in the text of the appellate court opinion. . . . Plaintiff's expert, not a trained attorney, misconstrued the purpose of the illustration, which was to illustrate a point, not to suggest language for a scientific study."

By way of contrast, wording developed for the key question in *NFL v. Wichita Falls* (1982), and which has since employed elsewhere (e.g., *Figgie v. MacGregor*, matter pending; *U.S. Polo Association v. Ralph Lauren d/b/a Polo)*, attempts to ensure that the legal terminology and its significance is readily understood by the lay public. Specifically, it was believed that the younger and lesser educated members of the relevant universe would not understand the legal connotation of the terms *sponsored* and *authorized*. Hence, this author identified a set of synonyms and then examined the frequencies with which these appeared in printed matter directed to the general public (Thorndike & Lorge, 1944). These words and their frequency of occurrence (per million words of popular print) were as follows: authorize/authorization = 13; endorse/endorsement = 4; license = 22; permit/permission = 72 to 122; sponsor/sponsorship = 6. Given this tally, the following question was devised that incorporated both the language of the court and an explanation oriented to laypersons for those who might need it: "Did the company that made this shirt have to get authorization or sponsorship—that is, permission—to make it?"

Researcher Expertise

Contemporary social science research reflects many facets and intricacies, and it is rare for any single person to be competent in all aspects of the research process. Most researchers have extensive

TABLE 7.1 Field Research Submitted in Trademark Cases

Number	Parties (year)	Court[a]	Offeror[b]	Admitted	Weight
1	Sears Roebuck v. All States Insurance (1957)	A	P	no	little
2	American Luggage v. U. S. Trunk (1957)	D	P	yes	"not persuasive"
3	Jenkins Bros. v. Newman Hender & Co. (1961)	A	P	yes	little
4	American Thermos v. Aladdin Industries (1962)	D	D	yes	substantial
5	American Thermos v. Aladdin Industries (1962)	D	P	yes	substantial
6	Zippo Manufacturing v. Rogers Import (1963)	D	P	yes	little to none
7	GM Corp v. Cadillac Marine Corp. (1964)	A	P	no	—
8	Donald F. Duncan Inc. v. Royal Tops (1965)	A	P	yes	—
9	Humble Oil v. American Oil (1966)	D	P	yes	moderate
10	Humble Oil v. American Oil (1966)	D	D	yes	moderate
11	Sears Roebuck & Co. v. Allstate Driving School (1969)	D	P	yes	"little"
12	Burrough Ltd. v. Lesher d/b/a Beefeaters (1969)	D	D	yes	some
13	Am Basketball Assoc. v. AMF Voit Inc. (1973)	D	P	yes	not given "substantial weight."
14	LaMaur Inc. v. Alberto-Culver (1973)	D	D	yes	not "of significant assistance"
15	LaMaur Inc. v. Alberto-Culver (1973)	D	D	yes	not "of significant assistance"
16	Holiday Inns v. Holiday Out In America (1973)	A	P	yes	"little," "slight"
17	Grotrian-Steinweg v. Steinway & Sons (1973)	D	P1	yes	substantial
18	Grotrian-Steinweg v. Steinway & Sons (1973)	D	P2	yes	substantial
19	Union Carbide v. Ever-Ready (1975)	D	P1	yes	"little if of any weight"
20	Union Carbide v. Ever-Ready (1975)	D	P2	Yes	"little if of any weight"
21	Jockey International v. Burkhard (1975)	D	D	yes	little
22	National Football League v. Dallas Cap (1975)	A	P	yes	some
23	McNeil Laboratories v. Am. Home Products (1976)	D	D	yes	some
24	J. Burrough Ltd. v. Sign of the Beefeater (1976)	A	P	yes	substantial
25	Fremont v. ITT Continental Baking (1977)	D	D	yes	some
26	WGBH Ed. Foundation v. Penthouse (1978)	D	D	yes	little to none
27	Astatic Corp. v. American Electronics (1979)	D	P	yes	little to none
28	RJR Foods v. White Rock Corp. (1979)	A	D1	no	some
29	American Footwear v. General Footwear (1979)	A	D2	no	"rejected"
30	American Footwear v. General Footwear (1979)	A	P	yes	"rejected"
31	Amstar v. Domino's Pizza (1980)	A	P	yes	"substantially defective"
32	Amstar v. Domino's Pizza (1980)	A	D	yes	none

	Case	Court[a]	Party[b]		Weight
33	Exxon v. Texas Motor Exchange (1980)	A	P	yes	"great"
34	Loctite v. National Starch (1981)	D	D1	yes	none
35	Loctite v. National Starch (1981)	D	D2	yes	none
36	Scotch Whiskey v. Consolidated Distillers (1981)	D	P	yes	"great"/"particularly persuasive"
37	Anti-Monopoly v. General Mills (1981)	D	P	yes	none
38	Brooks Shoe v. Suave Shoe (1981)	D	P	yes	little
39	Brooks Shoe v. Suave Shoe (1981)	D	D	yes	considerable
40	National Football League v. Wichita Falls (1982)	D	P	yes	considerable
41	Tomy Corp. v. P. G. Continental (1982)	D	P	yes	irrelevant
42	Deere & Co. v. Farmhand (1982)	D	P	yes	none
43	Deere & Co. v. Farmhand (1982)	D	P2	yes	none
44	Anti-Monopoly v. General Mills Fun Group (1982)	A	D	yes	"no relevance"
45	Anti-Monopoly v. General Mills Fun Group (1982)	A	P1	yes	"compelling evidence"
46	Anti-Monopoly v. General Mills Fun Group (1982)	A	P2	yes	substantial
47	Levi Strauss v. Blue Bell (1982)	D	D	yes	considerable
48	Levi Strauss v. Blue Bell (1982)	D	P	yes	little
49	Prudential Ins. Co. v. Gibraltar Corp. (1982)	A	P	yes	none
50	U.S. International Trade Comm. v. Certain Cubes (1982)	A	P	yes	some
51	U.S. International Trade Comm. v. Certain Cubes (1982)	D	D	yes	none
52	Plus Products v. Plus Discount Foods (1983)	D	P	yes	"limited"
53	Toys "R" Us v. Canarsie Kiddie Shop (1983)	D	P	no	—
54	Mennen v. Gillette (1983)	D	P	yes	none
55	Aris Isotoner v. Fownes Bros. (1983)	D	P	yes	little
56	Aris Isotoner v. Fownes Bros. (1983)	D	D	yes	little
57	Nestle v. Chester's Market (1983)	D	D1	yes	some
58	Nestle v. Chester's Market (1983)	D	D2	yes	some
59	Nestle v. Chester's Market (1983)	D	P1	no	—
60	Nestle v. Chester's Market (1983)	D	P2	yes	"no bearing"
61	Nestle v. Chester's Market (1983)	D	P3	yes	none
62	Nestle v. Chester's Market (1983)	D	P4	no	—
63	Henri's Food Products v. Kraft (1983)	A	D1	yes	none
64	Henri's Food Products v. Kraft (1983)	A	D2	yes	some
65	Brooks Shoe v. Suave Shoe (1983)	A	P	yes	little
66	Brooks Shoe v. Suave Shoe (1983)	A	D	yes	considerable

a. D = U. S. District Court; A = U. S. Appeals Court
b. D = Defendant; P = Plaintiff

knowledge in some areas and only passing knowledge in others (e.g., many skilled survey researchers know little about designing experiments to assess cause and effect, and vice versa). Accordingly, "the researcher" often consists of a team of experts, each having unique skills and all working together under the direction of a principal investigator who maintains overall responsibility for the project.

The courts often allude to the expertise and prior courtroom experiences of those who designed or implemented the study. Sometimes these comments are favorable (e.g., *NFL v. Wichita Falls*, 1982, p. 658) and sometimes they are not (e.g., *Amstar v. Domino's Pizza*, 1980; *Toys "R" Us v. Canarsie Kiddie Shop*, 1983). These observations generally affect the weight rather than admissibility of the testimony so that even an error-plagued survey of 150 respondents "conducted by two college students as part of their summer employment" has been admitted (*GM v. Cadillac Marine*, 1964).

Accuracy of Report

Courts report being adversely moved by errors in categorization or tabulation (e.g., *GM v. Cadillac Marine*, 1964; *U.S. ITC v. Certain Cubes Puzzles*, 1982) even when the discrepancy is as small as the difference between 450 and 451 (see *Toys "R" Us v. Canarsie Kiddie Shop*, 1983). They are also adversely moved when the summarization and categorization of responses to open-ended questions is left to untrained personnel (see *Sears v. Allstate Driving*, 1969), or when the researcher claims more than is justified from the data (see *Loctite v. National Starch*, 1981, p. 251). Accordingly, researchers should (1) make certain that all responses to open-ended questions are recorded verbatim (*James Burrough v. Sign of the Beefeater*, 1976, p. 278); (2) remove all data evaluation and analysis from the hands of the field force; (3) fairly report the data, taking care not to claim that all neutral or ambiguous data support one's position and that what is reported is not only accurate, but also "truly reflective" (*GM v. Cadillac Marine*, 1964, p. 736); and (4) carefully proof all data (e.g., tables, tests of statistical significance) provided on discovery or introduced at trial.

Accordance with
Generally Accepted Standards

Testimony at deposition and trial often refers to the application or misapplication of "accepted standards," yet the published rulings rarely mention such standards. When comments do surface, they rarely refer to any specific standard. This reflects several factors.

First, research typically involves numerous choice points at which judgment must be exercised, and it is often not possible to maintain that one particular choice is necessarily and in general superior to another. This is particularly true when design trade-offs need to be made so that it is not feasible to simultaneously optimize on all desiderata.

Second, many aspects of research design admit to no hard and fast standard. The situation is analogous to the courts wrestling with the question, What percentage of consumer confusion is sufficient for establishing infringement? While 80 percent is clearly sufficient and 2 percent clearly insufficient, the courts speak with different voices on findings of 10 percent to 20 percent. Similarly, while a 90 percent response rate is clearly satisfactory and a 25 percent response rate is not, researchers take a variety of positions with respect to 60 percent.

A third reason is that many disciplines are involved in field research (e.g., sociology, psychology, statistics, marketing, advertising, and communication, to mention but a few) and there are a corresponding number of scholarly organizations whose principles and perspectives are relevant. However, beyond having codes of ethics, these organizations choose not to promulgate research standards. In some respects, this is a boon. Imagine the chaos that might result if they devised standards, and these standards were in disagreement on certain key issues.

In contrast to the scholarly organizations, three of the major professional organizations having members involved in survey/advertising/marketing/consumer research have issued guidelines. These are (1) *The Standards for Reporting Public Opinion Research* and *The Code of Professional Ethics and Practices* (n.d.) published by the American Association of Public Opinion Research and subscribed to, via written oath, by each of their members; (2) the *Guidelines for the Public Use of Market and Opinion Research* (1981) published by the Advertising Research Foundation; and (3) the *Guidelines for Conducting Forensic Research* (1983) published by the Council of American Survey Research Organizations. Yet, insofar as can be determined, none of these guidelines has ever been cited in court.

Nature of Attorney Participation

While the desideratum that "the sample design and the interviews were conducted independently of the attorneys" appears in the *Handbook of Recommended Procedures* (1960, p. 429) and McCarthy's *Trademarks* (1973, p. 509), inexplicably, it does not appear in the *Manual for Complex Litigation* (1982, p. 116). Clearly, the neutral unbiased nature of the research is suspect if attorneys, as interested parties, become involved in making crucial decisions regarding research design, implementation, or interpretation. On the other hand, researchers generally would not know exactly what questions to ask or how to phrase them without some understanding of the legal issues involved. Thus, the question is not whether attorneys should be involved but, rather, when and in what capacity they should participate.

Three of the reviewed rulings mention attorney input. In one (*Duncan v. Royal Tops*, 1965, p. 665), a plaintiff witness "testified that preparation of the survey questions was a 'joint venture' with plaintiff's attorneys and that the latter proposed the key survey question ultimately used." Ruling that this question addressed the wrong issue, the court never discussed the issue of attorney participation. In two other instances, judges have looked disapprovingly at attorney participation. In *Mennen v. Gillette* (1983, p. 357) the court commented that "the independence of the design was suspect." In *Brooks Shoe v. Suave Shoe* (1981, p. 71), the court explicitly mentioned that the plaintiff's survey failed to meet the criteria set forth in *The Handbook of Recommended Procedures*, commenting, "The survey was designed and to a degree supervised by Plaintiff's attorney who is not, and does not claim to be an expert in the field of conducting or designing surveys."

It appears to me that the most acceptable and appropriate strategy is for the attorney to explain the legal issue to the researcher, who is then responsible for developing the detailed research design and specific questionnaire items. These are then discussed with the attorney to ensure that they are responsive to the issues in dispute. While the researcher might then make modifications, he or she should nonetheless maintain final authority over the basic integrity of the specific design and questions involved.

The most egregious breach of this desideratum that I know of surfaced in *U.S. v. General Motors* (matter currently under consideration) in which I served as a consultant and expert witness for GM. In this case, the Department of Justice attorneys devised and administered a phone interview to consumers who had complained to either GM or the National Highway Traffic Safety Administration regarding rear wheel brake lock-up. The list of "questions" was simply a rambling collection of more than 50 open-ended phrases (e.g., "What is problem . . . use their words") that was preceded by specific, prejudicial instructions to the attorney/interviewer (e.g., "Use the witnesses' words as much as possible so as not to appear 'coached.'") Aside from the obvious lack of

training as either researchers or interviewers and the biased introduction, the conflict of interest stemming from having attorneys be both
advocates and researchers is likely to introduce, consciously or
unconsciously, serious biases in the postinterview "creation" of an
affidavit. While the court has not yet ruled on this study, if such an
investigation were proferred by an academic or commercial researcher
it would be laughed out of court. Consideration of this case leads quite
naturally to a discussion of the final guideline employed in evaluating
admissability and weight.

Interviewers: Level of Training and Awareness of Issues

This last category refers to the level of training of the field force (i.e.,
the individuals who actually interface with and collect the data from the
respondents) and whether they are aware of the identity of the client
paying for the study and/or the objectives of the investigation. On this
latter issue what is technically known as a double-blind procedure (i.e.,
one where both respondent and interviewer are blind as to the study
objectives) should be employed.

Court rulings rarely mention the training issue. In *GM v. Cadillac
Marine* (1964, p. 734) the court noted that the survey was conducted by
two college students but failed to indicate how this affected its
deliberation. In another instance, the court commented, "The women
who conducted the telephone interviews were low paid, part time
employees . . . rather than professional public opinion researchers.
Their brief training period did not even include their observation of a
simple interview. . . . this training deficiency is particularly relevant
when weighing the results" (*Sears v. Allstate Driving*, 1969, p. 116). The
courts have also been relatively reticent regarding double-blind administration, occasionally lauding its presence (e.g., *Scotch Whiskey v.
Consolidated*, 1981, p. 641) and finding serious fault when it is absent
(*Toys "R" Us v. Canarsie Kiddie Shop*, 1983, p. 1204).

ADDITIONAL ISSUES

Several additional issues need to be touched on even if, due to space
limitations, only briefly.

Authenticity

A number of courts have stressed the need for authenticity in both
respondent motivation and testing conditions. The focus on authentic

motivation may be traced to Judge Wyzanski's ruling in *American Luggage v. U.S. Trunk* (1957, p. 53):

> Another and most significant reason why the evidence of the poll is inadmissible . . . is that under the substantive law the issue is not whether the goods would be confused by a casual observer . . . but . . . whether the goods would be confused by a prospective purchaser at the time he considered making the purchase. If the interviewee is not in a buying mood but is just in a friendly mood answering a pollster, his degree of attention is quite different from what it would be had he his wallet in his hand. Many men do not take the same trouble to avoid confusion when they are responding to sociological investigators as when they spend their cash.

In the same case, Judge Wyzanski also objected to the use of inauthentic stimuli, specifically, using photographs of products rather than the products themselves (1957, pp. 52-53). Other courts have since pointed to one or both types of inauthenticity as influencing their rulings. Examples include *GM v. Cadillac Marine* (1964, p. 737); *Sears v. Allstate Driving* (1969, p. 18); *American Footwear v. General Footwear* (1979, p. 613); *Deere v. Farmhand* (1982, p. 257); *Toys "R" Us v. Canarsie Kiddie Shop* (1983, p. 1204); and *Mennen v. Gillette* (1983, p. 357).

These rulings notwithstanding, a certain degree of inauthenticity can be tolerated and is sometimes unavoidable. Photographs can be employed when it would be physically impossible to transport or recreate the product or environment (see *Exxon v. Texas Motor Exchange*, 1980). Moreover, research usually involves trade-offs so that satisfying one desideratum may mean sacrificing another. This is particularly evident when attempting to conduct large-scale probability sampling—a facet of research design that is generally in conflict with generating authentic marketplace conditions. When all other criteria used for evaluating admissibility and weight are applied and the survey is deemed acceptable on these grounds, then inauthenticity may be disregarded (see *Scotch Whiskey v. Consolidated*, 1981, p. 639).

Finally, as I and others have noted (e.g., Boal, 1983, p. 406), knowing that they are in some sense being tested, survey respondents may pay more attention and take greater care to avoid confusion than they ordinarily would when buying frequently purchased low cost products.

Surveys Versus Experiments

Both the *Handbook for Recommended Procedures* (1960, p. 426) and *Manual for Complex Litigation* (1982, p. 112) use the terms *poll* and *survey* interchangeably to refer to "the interrogation of part of the population whose views or attitudes are deemed relevant to the litigation." Consistent with this definition, we have used the term *survey* to encompass any research in which verbal reports are gathered from respondents. Such usage, however, is technically incorrect and masks exceedingly important issues that go to the very heart of a study's trustworthiness.

Surveys are only one type of research strategy, and not all the research that is proferred, admitted, and heavily weighed is a survey—despite the penchant of judges and attorneys for calling it such. For example, the studies that this author conducted for the plaintiff in *NFL v. Wichita Falls* (1982) and for the defendant in *U.S. Polo Association v. Ralph Lauren* (pending) were actually "field experiments." The technical distinction between "survey" and "experiment" embraces considerably more than just nomenclature.

Surveys and experiments serve completely different purposes. A survey is generally the preferred strategy if one's purpose is to identify and describe *associational* relationships—such as is reflected by the question, What is the level of secondary meaning or confusion associated with brand name X? In contrast, experiments are virtually the only strategy capable of assessing *causative* relationships—such as is reflected by the question, Does brand name X cause consumers to be confused as to product or source of manufacture? According to the Lanham Act, the proper focus in trademark cases is on marks that are "likely to *cause* confusion, or to *cause* mistake [italics added]." As such, experimental research becomes the necessary paradigm in this type of case.

Also note that the *random assignment* of respondents to conditions that is necessary for experiments is not the same as the *random selection* necessary for probability surveys. Although the same study might reflect both (e.g., *NFL v. Wichita Falls,* 1982), random assignment is the more important requirement when one's interest is in establishing cause and effect.

These considerations move us toward the most fundamental of all scientific issues—namely, are the proferred findings and interpretations valid (that is, trustworthy)? Unfortunately, a thorough discussion of the nature and types of validity, the trade-offs between them, and the procedures for ruling out threats to each type of validity are well beyond the scope of this chapter. Accordingly, we leave this task for another forum.

Beyond Universes of People
to Other Facets of Measurement

Another issue sorely in need of attention is the deeper meaning associated with the concept of the universe. Courts have been quick to note that in order to extrapolate a study's findings to the universe of people whose state of mind is relevant, the sample upon which the assessment is conducted needs to be reasonably representative of that universe. What the courts (and, unfortunately, too many researchers) fail to recognize is that there are many sorts of universes involved in *any* assessment and that a representative sampling needs to be done for each universe of interest (see Cronbach, Gleser, Nanda, & Rajaratnam, 1972).

For example, if the plaintiff argues that the defendant's advertising is likely to cause confusion and if said advertising appears almost equally on TV, the radio, and in print, then if the objective is to extrapolate from the test to the extant universe of advertising the plaintiff's study needs to test advertising from each of these media. On the other hand, if defendant's advertising appears solely or primarily in one medium, then ignoring the others is of little practical consequence.

By the same token, suppose the plaintiff's advertising appeared in a single medium (e.g., print). Suppose, further, that plaintiff used eight different print ads during the preceding 12 months. Assessing reactions to only one of those ads would result in interpretive difficulties: Were the findings characteristic of all the defendant's advertising or were they simply a function of the unique characteristics of the particular ad that happened to be selected for the test? It was for this reason that, when assessing whether or not there was a likelihood of confusion between *American Savings and Loan v. AmeriFirst Savings and Loan* (1983), I employed eight different newspaper ads placed by the former institution and five different newspaper ads placed by the latter, newspapers being the only medium in which these firms competed. Thus, when a number of media or advertisements are involved, it is preferable to select more than one exemplar of each using some defensible sampling plan. This same advice applies when the mark in question appears on more than one product, as is the case for some firms (e.g., General Electric) and designers (e.g., Halston). Unless there is ample reason to assume that what is found with one of these products will necessarily apply across the board to all other relevant products, all (or a reasonable sampling of) the products in question should be employed for adequate generalizability (e.g., *Levi Strauss v. Blue Bell,* 1982).

CONCLUDING OBSERVATIONS

More needs to be said regarding how the courts have, could, and should use primary research. Suffice it to conclude with two basic points.

First, just as designing a field study for litigation requires that the researcher understand legal issues if he or she is to devise a useful study, a proper appreciation for the findings and their limitations requires that attorneys and judges acquire an improved understanding of the research process. Such an understanding would enable them to evaluate research with a critical eye and to recognize that it is often flawed in some way. The question is not whether a study is imperfect but whether its flaws are "fatal"—so significant that nothing of worth can be gleaned from the data. Assuming all other facets of the research were of sufficiently high quality, it might be possible to cull the appropriate respondents from a universe that is too broad, while a narrow universe might still address enough of the proper universe to be meaningful. In short, to avoid throwing babies out with the bath water and to be better able to make proper and equitable judgments, judges who are entrusted to evaluate field research need to acquire a sounder foundation in the practice of behavioral science research.

Second, the set of factors relied on for evaluating trustworthiness and assigning weight are essentially unchanged from when they were first introduced 25 years ago (see *Handbook for Recommended Procedures,* 1960). The time seems ripe for their revision. While it is desirable to reduce redundancy (as between points three and six, and between portions of points six and eight) and improve the clarity of the existing factors,it seems imperative that the set be updated to reflect the advances in scientific thinking and practice made during the intervening 25 years.

NOTES

1. The courts, legal scholars, and attorneys have erroneously labeled all field research "surveys" or "public opinion polls." This suggests a failure to comprehend the fundamental distinctions between surveys and experiments and the different functions served by these research strategies. Both for ease of explication and so as not to detract from our exposition by introducing new terminology, we use the term *survey* throughout most of our discussion. However, the concluding section discusses the ramifications of the failure to appreciate this critical distinction.

2. I am grateful for the assistance of Messrs. Robert L. Raskopf, Esq. (of Townley & Updike, New York) and J. Paul Williamson, Esq. (of Arnold, White and Durkee, Washington) in gathering these materials.

3. Note that none of these cases involved jury trials. Further, it is sometimes not entirely clear from the judge's published opinion whether the survey was rejected or, if admitted, the amount of weight accorded. Except for the phrases that are surrounded by quotation marks, the categorizations in Table 7.1 therefore represent a certain amount of inference and judgment on the part of the author.

REFERENCES

Advertising Research Foundation (ARF). (1981). *Guidelines for the public use of market and opinion research.* New York: ARF.

American Association for Public Opinion Research (AAPOR). (n.d.). *Standards for reporting public opinion research;* and *Code of professional ethics and practice.* Princeton, NJ: AAPOR.

American Basketball Assn. v. AMF Voit, Inc., 177 *U.S.P.Q.* 442 (U.S.D.C., S.D.N.Y.), (1973).

American Footwear Corp. v. General Footwear Co. Ltd., 204 *U.S.P.Q.* 609 (U.S.C.A., 2d Cir.), (1979).

American Luggage Works, Inc. v. United States Trunk Co., Inc., 158 *F. Supp.* 50 (U.S.D.C., D. Mass.), (1957).

American Savings & Loan Association of Florida v. AmeriFirst Federal Savings & Loan Association, State of Florida, Division of Administrative Hearings. March 21-25. Miami, Florida, (1983).

American Thermos Products Co. v. Aladdin Industries, Inc. 207 *F. Supp.* 9 (U.S.D.C., D. Conn.), (1962).

Amstar Corp. v. Domino's Pizza, Inc., 205 *U.S.P.Q.* 969 (U.S.C.A., 5th Cir.), (1980).

Anti-Monopoly, Inc. v. General Mills Fun Group et al., 611 *F.* 2d 296 (U.S.C.A., 9th Cir.), (1979).

Anti-Monopoly, Inc. v. General Mills Fun Group et al., 515 *F. Supp.* 448 (U.S.D.C., N.D. Cal.), (1981).

Anti-Monopoly, Inc. v. General Mills Fun Group et al., 216 *U.S.P.Q.* 558 (U.S.C.A., 9th Cir.), (1982).

Aris-Isotoner Gloves, Inc. v. Fownes Brothers & Co., No. 81 Civ. 3573 (U.S.D.C., S.D.N.Y.), (1983).

Astatic Corp. v. American Electronics, Inc., *U.S.P.Q.* 411 (U.S.D.C., N.D. Ohio), (1979).

Boal, R. B. (1983) Techniques for ascertaining likelihood of confusion and the meaning of advertising communications. *The Trademark Reporter* 73(4), 405-435.

Brooks Shoe Manufacturing Co., Inc. v. Suave Shoe Corp. 533 F. Supp. 75 (U.S.D.C., S.D. Fla.), (1981).

Brooks Shoe Manufacturing Co., Inc. v. Suave Shoe Corp. *PTC Journal*, December 17, p. A-8, 1981.

Brooks Shoe Manufacturing Co., Inc. v. Suave Shoe Corp. 716 *F.* 2d 854 (U.S.C.A., 11th Cir.), (1983).

James Burrough Ltd., Inc. (& Kobrand Corp.) v. Sign of the Beefeater, Inc. (& Montgomery Ward & Co., Inc.), 540 *F.* 2d 266 (U.S.C.A., 7th Cir.), (1976).

James Burrough Ltd. (& Kobrand Corp.) v. William Lesher, d/b/a Beefeater's (& Doubl L. Washington) Inc., 309 *F. Supp.* 1154 (U.S.D.C., S.D. Indiana), (1969).

Council of American Survey Research Organizations (CASRO). (1983). *Guidelines for conducting forensic research.* Port Jefferson, NY: CASRO.

Cronbach, L. J., Gleser, G., Nanda, H., & Rajaratnam, N. (1972). *The dependability of behavioral measurements: Theory of generalizability for scores and profiles.* New York: John Wiley.

Deere & Co. v. Farmhand, Inc., 217 *U.S.P.Q.* 252 (U.S.D.C., S.D. Iowa), (1982).

Donald F. Duncan, Inc. v. Royal Tops Manufacturing Co., 343 *F.* 2d 655 (U.S.C.A., 7th Cir., reh. denied 11/14/65), (1965).

Equilink Corp. d/b/a MacGregor Athletic Products v. Figgie International, Inc. (Pending before Judge John E. Aprizzo, U.S.D.C., S.D.N.Y.)

Exxon Corp. v. Texas Motor Exchange of Houston, 628 F. 2d 500 (U.S.C.A., 5th Cir.), (1980).

Figgie v. MacGregor (opinion in preparation).

The Fremont Co., et al. v. ITT Continental Baking Co. 199 U.S.P.Q. 415 (U.S.D.C., S.D.N.Y.), (1977).

Frisch's Restaurants, Inc. v. Elby's Big Boy of Steubenville, et al. (in progress) U.S.D.C., S.D. Ohio. Docket nos. 81-3095/3098.

General Motors Corp. v. Cadillac Marine & Boat Co., 226 F. Supp. 716 (U.S.D.C., W.D. Mich.), (1964).

Grotrian, Helfferich, Schulz, Th. Steinweg Nachf v. Steinway & Sons, 365 F. Supp. 707 (U.S.D.C., S.D.N.Y.), (1973).

Grotrian, Helfferich, Schulz, Th. Steinweg Nachf v. Steinway & Sons, 523 F. 2d 1331 (U.S.C.A., 2d Cir.), (1975).

Handbook of recommended procedures for the trial of protracted cases. (1960). Judicial Conference of the United States. 25 F.R.D. 351.

Handler, M., & Pickett, C. (1930). Trade-marks and trade names—an analysis and synthesis. Columbia Law Review, 30, Part 1, 168-201; Part II, 759-788.

Henri's Food Products Co., Inc. v. Kraft, Inc., 220 U.S.P.Q. 386 (U.S.C.A., 7th Cir.), (1983).

Holiday Inns, Inc. v. Holiday Out in America, 481 F.2d 445 (U.S.C.A., 5th Cir.), (1973).

Humble Oil & Refining Co. v. American Oil Co., 259 F. Supp. 599 (U.S.D.C, E.D. Mo.), (1966).

Information Clearing House, Inc. v. Find Magazine, 492 F. Supp. 147, 209 U.S.P.Q. 936 (U.S.D.C., S.D.N.Y.), (1980).

Jenkins Bros. v. Newman Hender & Co., Ltd., 289 F. 2d 675 (C.C.P.A.), (1961).

Jockey International, Inc. v. Burkhard d/b/a/ Chapella-Brawn Co., et al., 185 U.S.P.Q. 201, (1975).

LaMaur, Inc. v. Alberto-Culver Co., 179 U.S.P.Q. 607 (U.S.D.C., D. Minn.), (1973).

Levi Strauss & Co. v. Blue Bell, Inc., 216 U.S.P.Q. 606 (U.S.D.C., N.D. Calif.), (1982).

Litton Industries, Inc. v. FTC, 676 F. 2d 364. (U.S.C.A., 9th Cir.), (1982).

Loctite Corp. v. National Starch and Chemical Corp., 211 U.S.P.Q. 237 (U.S.D.C., S.D.N.Y.), (1981).

Loewen, J. W. (1982). Social science in the courtroom. Lexington, MA: Lexington Books/D. C. Heath.

Manual for complex litigation (5th ed.). (1982). St. Paul, MN: West.

McCarthy, J. T. (1973). Trademarks and unfair competition (Vol. 2). Rochester, NY: Lawyers Co-operative Publishing Co.

McNeil Laboratories, Inc. v. American Home Products Corp., 193 U.S.P.Q. 486 (U.S.D.C., D. New Jersey), (1976).

The Mennen Co. v. The Gillette Co., 220 U.S.P.Q. 354 (U.S.D.C., S.D.N.Y.), (1983).

Mushroom Makers, Inc. v. R. G. Barry Corporation, 580 F. 2d 44, 47, 199 U.S.P.Q. 65 (CA 2 1978), affd. 441 F. Supp. 1220, 196 U.S.P.Q. 471 (S.D.N.Y. 1977), cert. denied 200 U.S.P.Q. 832 (U.S. 1979).

National Football League Properties, Inc. v. Dallas Cap & Emblem Mfg., Inc. 327 N.E. 2d 247 (26 Ill. App. 3d 820), (1975).

National Football League Properties Inc. et al. v. Wichita Falls Sportswear, 532 F. Supp. 651 (U.S.D.C., W.D. Wash.), (1982).

The Nestle Co., Inc. v. Chester's Market, Inc. et al., 219 U.S.P.Q. 298 (U.S.D.C., D. Conn.), (1983).

Plus Products v. Plus Discount Foods, Inc., 722 F. 2d 999 (U.S.C.A., 2d Cir.), (1983).

Plus Products v. Plus Discount Foods, Inc. & the Great Atlantic & Pacific Tea Co., Inc., 564 F. Supp. 984 (U.S.D.C., S.D.N.Y.), (1983).

The Prudential Insurance Co. of America v. Gibraltar Corp. of Calif. et al., 217 U.S.P.Q. 1097 (U.S.C.A., 9th Cir.), (1982).

Reiner, J. P. (1983). The universe and sample: How good is good enough? *The Trademark Reporter, 73*(4), 366-375.

RJR Foods, Inc. v. White Rock Corp., 603 *F. 2d* 1058, (1979).

Robin, A. & Barnaby, H. B. (1983). Trademark surveys—heads you lose, tails they win. *The Trademark Reporter, 73*(4), 436-445.

Scotch Whiskey Assn. v. Consolidated Distilled Products, Inc., 210 *U.S.P.Q.* 639 (N.D. Ill.), (1981).

Sears, Roebuck & Co. v. All States Life Insurance Co., 426 *F. 2* 161 (U.S.C.A. 5th Cir.), (1957).

Sears, Roebuck & Co. v. Allstate Driving School, Inc., 301 *F. Supp.* 4 (U.S.D.C., E.D.N.Y.), (1969).

Springs Mills, Inc. v. Ultracashmere House, Ltd. 532 *F. Supp.* 1203, 215 *U.S.P.Q.* 1057 (S.D.N.Y. 1982), revd 689 *F. 2d* 1127, 217 U.S.P.Q. 298 (CA 2 1982).

Thorndike, E. L. & Lorge, I. (1944). *The teacher's word book of 30,000 words.* New York: Columbia University.

Tomy Corp. et al. v. P. G. Continental, Inc. et al., 217 *U.S.P.Q.* 1367 (U.S.D.C., S.D.N.Y.), (1982).

Toys "R" Us, Inc. v. Canarsie Kiddie Shop, Inc. d/b/a Kids "R" Us, 559 *F. Supp.* 1189 (U.S.D.C., E.D.N.Y.), (1983).

Union Carbide Corp. v. Ever-Ready Inc., 392 *F. Supp.* 280 (U.S.D.C., N.D. Ill.), 1975).

U.S. Polo Association v. Ralph Lauren (opinion in preparation).

U.S. v. General Motors Corp., in U.S.D.C., District of Columbia (Civil Action No. 83-2220), (1984).

U.S. International Trade Commission. In re Certain Cube Puzzles, 219 *U.S.P.Q.* 322 (1982).

University of Pittsburgh v. Champion Products Inc., 529 *F. Supp.* 464 (WDPa. 1982). Affd. in part and revd. in part 686 F2d. 1040, 215 *U.S.P.Q.* 921 (CA 3 1982), cert. denied 103 S Cp 571 (1982), on remand BNA's *PTCJ*, Volume 26, No. 639, P. 279 (WDPa. 6/23/83).

Weinstein, J. B., & Berger, M. A. (1982). *Weinstein's evidence, Vol. 3.* New York: Matthew Bender.

WGBH Educational Foundation v. Penthouse International, 203 *U.S.P.Q.* 432 (U.S.D.C., S.D.N.Y.), (1978).

Zeisel, H. (1960). The uniqueness of survey evidence. *Cornell Law Quarterly, 45,* 322-346.

Zippo Manufacturing Co. v. Rogers Imports, Inc., 216 *F. Supp.* 670 (U.S.D.C., S.D.N.Y.), (1963).

CHAPTER 8

Expert Psychological Testimony

EDITH GREENE
JONATHAN W. SCHOOLER
ELIZABETH F. LOFTUS

Do you really think that the social scientists have discovered something new? Go home and ask your grandmother from Poland or your uncle from Armenia, who didn't get past third grade. Ask them and you'll have the answer. Grandmother will tell you, uncle will tell you, "Sure, perception is different, memories falter, speech fails, bias and prejudice must be allowed for, and liars exist." (Younger, 1979, p. 52)

In the courtroom, we offer expert testimony not because our views are recently come from Sinai but because in law and in fact, our knowledge ... exceeds that of laymen by a considerable margin, and will probably aid the trier in search for truth. If our knowledge is not yet perfect, neither is it trivial or useless for these purposes. (Rosenhan, 1983)

Courtroom verdicts have historically been based on case-specific evidence in the form of testimony from witnesses who have firsthand knowledge of relevant facts. Equally influential, however, can be the testimony of an expert witness—someone who by training or education is qualified to give an opinion in the courtroom. Recently courts have stretched their use of evidence to include expert psychological testimony about general aspects of human behavior and performance. The purpose of such testimony is to help judges and jurors more effectively evaluate the psychological factors that may be involved in a particular case. For example, if an eyewitness alleges to have seen the color of a defendant's jacket on a moonless night, it may be useful for an expert witness to describe the general lighting conditions necessary for

Authors' Note: The writing of this chapter was facilitated by grants from the National Science Foundation.

various colors to be observed. With this additional psychological information, jurors are presumably better able to evaluate the credibility of that witness's testimony.

The presence of psychologists in the courtroom has generated considerable controversy among members of the legal profession, as well as among psychologists. While some people urge that this testimony be admitted in court (Loftus & Monahan, 1980; Arnolds, Carroll, & Seng, 1981; Walker, Thyfault, & Browne, 1982; Thar, 1982; Rosenhan, 1983), others argue that it is inappropriate and should be excluded (McCloskey & Egeth, 1983; Younger, 1979). Critics of the use of psychological testimony question its validity, its impact on the jury, its moral implications, and whether psychologists can offer any useful knowledge that jurors do not already have. In this chapter we discuss various types of expert psychological testimony, describe the criteria that have been used to determine their admissibility, and outline a number of arguments that have been used to support and to criticize their use in court.

The applicability of psychology to the law has been appreciated since the turn of the century (e.g., Munsterberg, 1908), but psychological findings did not enjoy a breakthrough in terms of making their way into court until the famous 1954 desegregation case of *Brown v. Board of Education*. In a footnote to that decision, the works of seven contemporary social scientists were cited as suggesting the harmful effects of segregation on black children.

Since then, psychologists have provided expert testimony on a number of different legal issues including, but not limited to, the following:

- the mental state of a defendant, and whether he or she is competent to stand trial or was sane at the time the crime was committed;
- the degree of neurological impairment incurred by a victim in an accident disability case;
- the degree of mental retardation and acceptability of certain psychological treatment or therapies for individuals in various civil matters;
- employment discrimination class actions;
- the effects of bilingualism in children;
- sentencing recommendations;
- community standards on obscenity;
- the effects of prejudicial pretrial information;
- trademark infringement and fraudulent advertising suits;
- the reliability of eyewitness testimony;
- the degree of psychological trauma suffered by a victim of violent crimes; and

- the typical behavioral pattern of abused women and children (Perlin, 1977).

Some of these topics—particularly the ones involving determination of a person's mental state—fall squarely within the expertise of clinical psychologists or psychiatrists. Typically, a clinician or psychiatrist interviews or examines someone and then details in court the opinion that he or she has formed on the basis of that interview. This kind of expert testimony can be distinguished from the testimony of research psychologists who more typically describe the results of certain empirical studies that bear on the issues involved in a particular case. These experts may or may not actually interview parties in the case. The opinions of these psychologists are based on the results of their own and others' research—work that is presumably relevant to the particular case being litigated. Therefore, while clinicians often have opinions about a specific individual and may be asked to state those opinions in court, research psychologists are more likely to describe how people in general, given these circumstances, would behave. The researcher is usually not asked for—and is rarely able to provide—an opinion about psychological factors that had a definite impact on the case. Rather, he or she provides information to jurors so that they can decide for themselves what role these psychological factors might have played.

In this chapter, we focus on the expert testimony of research psychologists rather than clinicians because certain debates, such as the probative value of the testimony, arise whenever a research psychologist is called to the stand and because a substantial body of literature examining clinical testimony is already available (Brodsky, 1977; Brodsky & Robey, 1973; Ziskin, 1975). Specifically, we will discuss the role of the expert witness in eyewitness identification cases, battered woman homicide cases, and rape cases. All of these experts provide testimony based upon experimental data. First we describe what an expert can offer in each of these three areas, and second we discuss the issue of admissibility and the legal community's general reaction to this type of testimony. The issues involved in determining admissibility of expert testimony are surprisingly similar in these three realms; they are so similar, in fact, that a comparison of the controversies and outcomes involved may shed light on ways to resolve future controversies about expert testimony.

PSYCHOLOGICAL TESTIMONY
ON EYEWITNESS IDENTIFICATION

In May 1984 a young man named Joe Morton was tried in Reno on several counts of armed robbery. Morton's identity was made known to the police through a secret witness program instituted in Nevada. Morton maintained that he had been framed, that only by coincidence did he bear any resemblance to the robber, and that he was innocent. At trial, the defense moved to introduce the testimony of an expert witness—a psychologist trained in cognitive and social psychology—to discuss factors that could have influenced the eyewitnesses' identifications. Although the expert was not allowed to testify before the jury in this case, Morton was acquitted and subsequently freed. In other cases, experts on the topic of eyewitness identification have been allowed to testify, and the Arizona Supreme Court recently ruled that a lower court erroneously excluded an expert's testimony (State v. Chapple, 1983).

Research bearing on eyewitness performance comes both from specific studies utilizing an eyewitness paradigm and from psychological research on more general memory and perceptual processes. These studies have allowed psychologists to reach a number of general conclusions about eyewitness performance, and certain findings are commonly discussed by psychologists who testify in an eyewitness case. Although these findings are generally agreed upon by many researchers in the psychological community (see Yarmey & Jones, 1983), the validity and generalizability of some of these conclusions is not universally accepted (McCloskey & Egeth, 1983). We address this issue in more detail below.

A number of recent studies have documented the misconceptions many people have about eyewitness accuracy (Loftus, 1979; Brigham, 1981; Deffenbacher & Loftus, 1982; Wells, 1984). These studies, as well as research in the field of memory and perception, have led to the involvement of experimental psychologists as expert witnesses in cases that turn on eyewitness testimony. A psychologist is more likely to testify for the defense in criminal cases, but for either side in civil cases, in order to dispel certain myths that may exist in jurors' minds and to educate the judge or jury about the factors that influence eyewitness reliability.

Several factors or issues are commonly mentioned in expert testimony about eyewitness performance. They include the following:

(1) *The schematic nature of memory.* There is a wealth of literature indicating that people often do not remember specific details but rather

encode a general schema or abstraction about a particular event (Bartlett, 1932; Bransford & Franks, 1971; Cofer, 1973; Flagg, Potts, & Reynolds, 1975). Moreover, these schema are formed according to people's expectations about what they think should have occurred (Allport & Postman, 1958).

(2) *Forgetting over time.* The classic forgetting curve shows that forgetting over time increases dramatically at first and then gradually levels off (e.g., Ebbinghaus, 1964; Underwood, 1945). While the exact shape of the curve may depend on the type of information being recalled, forgetting curves are invariably monotonic in nature (Loftus, 1982).

(3) *Cross-racial identification.* A number of experiments have suggested that people are generally more accurate at identifying people who are of the same race as themselves than people of a different race (Malpass & Kravitz, 1969; Lindsay & Wells, 1983).

(4) *The impact of anxiety.* Deffenbacher (1983) reviewed 21 studies and concluded that people are most likely to remember an event when they are moderately anxious. Very high and very low anxiety levels reduce the likelihood that a person will accurately recall an event.

(5) *The impact of misleading information.* It is commonly observed that memories for events can be changed as a result of misleading questions (Loftus & Palmer, 1974; Loftus, Miller, & Burns, 1978). For example, subjects will recall and even describe in detail a nonexistent yield sign after hearing the question "How fast was the red Datsun going while it was stopped at the yield sign?" (Schooler, Gerhard, & Loftus, 1984).

(6) *The relationship between confidence and accuracy.* Although some studies have revealed a small relationship between confidence and accuracy, many others have observed little or no relationship between how accurate someone is and how confident they are in their memory (Deffenbacher, 1980).

(7) *Biased identification techniques.* A number of different types of line up and identification techniques have been shown to bias witnesses and increase the likelihood that an innocent person will be mistakenly identified (Loftus, 1979; Malpass & Devine, 1983).

(8) *Weapon focus.* A number of studies in perception indicate that people fixate longer on novel objects than on familiar objects. Additionally, when people see a weapon, they spend a disproportionate amount of time looking at it and consequently are less able to recall other aspects of the event (Loftus, Loftus, & Messo, 1984).

(9) *Individual differences in eyewitness ability.* Various studies have indicated that, contrary to popular belief, average eyewitnesses are no worse than the police at recognizing criminal suspects (Clifford, 1966). Individual differences due to the age of a witness are often observed (Yarmey & Kent, 1980; Loftus & Davies, 1984).

(10) *Overestimation of eyewitness ability.* A number of jury simulations have suggested that jurors tend to overestimate the reliability of eyewitnesses (Wells, Lindsay, & Ferguson, 1979; Wells, Lindsay, & Tousignant, 1980). Some studies have also shown that overestimation

can occur even when the eyewitness has been discredited—that is, even after hearing that "the victim had 20/400 eyesight," subject jurors still believe the witness (Cavoukian, 1980; Loftus, 1974; Saunders, Vidmar, & Hewitt, 1983).

These examples represent a sampling of the issues that a psychologist could discuss when testifying about eyewitness performance. (For a more thorough description, including an example of an actual trial transcript, see Loftus, 1979.) Generally, an expert witness will not mention all of the above factors, but only those that are relevant to the case at hand. For example, if the case involves a frightened clerk who was robbed at gun point by a janitor, the expert is likely to discuss weapon focus and the effects of anxiety on memory. He or she is not likely to discuss the memory abilities of a police officer, however. Additionally, the expert does not assert an opinion about whether a particular witness is accurate. Instead, the expert provides generalizations about eyewitness performance, leaving it to the jury to decide whether these factors have affected the witness's recollection.

PSYCHOLOGICAL TESTIMONY ON THE BATTERED WOMAN SYNDROME

Beverly Ibn-Tamas shot and killed her husband shortly after an altercation during which he threatened her with a pistol. Mrs. Ibn-Tamas testified at trial that her husband had beaten her many times over the course of their 3½-year marriage and that she was afraid for her life when she shot him. At trial, the defense offered the testimony of a psychologist who had conducted research on the topic of battered women to inform the jury about the characteristic mentality and behavior of these women. Although the trial judge refused to admit the expert testimony and Ibn-Tamas was convicted, the conviction was overturned on appeal, in part because the higher court determined that the expert testimony should have been admitted (*Ibn-Tamas v. United States*, 1979). The admissibility of this type of evidence is controversial; some courts freely admit it, others patently exclude it (Cross, 1982).

The term *battered woman syndrome* is used to describe a pattern of severe physical and psychological abuse inflicted upon a woman by her mate. Psychologists have conducted long-term studies of battered women and have developed theories to account for their predictable pattern of behavior (Walker, 1979).

A research psychologist is occasionally called upon to testify as an expert witness in battered women homicide trials. One common defense in these cases is the claim of self-defense—that the battered woman had to defend herself against abuse by her husband or partner. A requirement of this self-defense claim is that the woman must have experienced a reasonable fear of imminent danger. What happens, then, when battered women kill their husbands when the men are asleep, unarmed, or inattentive, as is often the case? Can they no longer use the self-defense argument? Because the traditional self-defense claim may be an inadequate defense for the battered woman defendant, many of the defendants have attempted to introduce expert testimony relating to the reasonableness of their belief of imminent harm. A psychologist would testify about the cyclical nature of most battering relationships using information gained from several relevant empirical studies. The expert might attempt to show how perceptions become distorted as a result of continuous physical abuse and how a woman could indeed fear for her safety even when confrontation is not imminent. The hope is to educate jurors and judges so that some prevalent myths about battered women are dispelled and so the battered woman defendant's claim of self-defense can be fairly evaluated.

Several studies of battered women have been conducted in recent years (Gelles, 1980; Goodstein & Page, 1981; Langley & Levy, 1977; Walker, 1979), and certain conclusions about the battering relationship and the woman involved have resulted. Some issues that an expert witness might discuss are presented below.

The cyclical theory of battering. Walker (1979) was the first to describe the three-phase cycle typical of many battering relationships. The first phase is characterized by minor abuse and tension buildup. The woman often attempts to calm her attacker to keep the beatings from worsening, but these attempts are usually unsuccessful and the incidents increase in number and severity. The second phase of the cycle—the acute battering stage—is characterized by severe and often brutal beatings. If one of the parties in a battering relationship is killed because of the beatings, it will invariably happen during this period. The third phase of the cycle is characterized by calm and loving behavior on the part of the batterer as well as his pleas for forgiveness and promises never to beat the woman again. The woman's hopes that her mate's behavior will change are reaffirmed, and women who have decided to leave often change their minds at this point.

Learned helplessness. Although battered women may, in theory, have some control over their situations, in reality they seem to become passive and helpless. They have learned through experience that the battering cycle is a process beyond their control and that nothing they do will change their situation. The battered woman lives in what some psychologists have termed a state of learned helplessness (Seligman, 1975).

Minimized consequences of violence. One result of this state of learned helplessness is a change in the woman's perception of the consequences of violence. The constant fear with which these women live often numbs them to the consequences of their actions. In fact, some women do not realize they have killed their husbands until so informed by the police.

The concept of the battering cycle and the resultant psychological effect of learned helplessness can explain how a battered woman perceives her situation. A psychologist testifying about the battered woman syndrome typically explains these theories to the judge or jury, trying to educate the decision makers so they can better evaluate the claim of self-defense.

PSYCHOLOGICAL TESTIMONY ON THE RAPE TRAUMA SYNDROME

The issue of rape trauma syndrome arose in the case of *State v. Saldana* (1982). A Minnesota woman alleged that she was raped by Saldana, but delayed a day in reporting the rape. At trial, the prosecution offered testimony from a psychologist who had counseled the rape victim for a 10-day period, beginning 10 days after her alleged rape. The expert testimony was offered in rebuttal of the defendant's claim that intercourse had been consensual.

The expert described the victim's reactions and testified that in her opinion, a criminal offense had occurred and the victim was telling the truth. Reasoning that an expert has no special ability to discern the truth, the Minnesota Supreme Court held that admission of this testimony was erroneous and overturned the defendant's conviction. Since then, several courts have allowed expert witnesses to testify about rape trauma syndrome; other courts have excluded this testimony (Ross, 1983).

A sizable literature suggests that rape produces a characteristic pattern of psychological, behavioral, and somatic reactions on the part of a victim and that these reactions are similar to the reactions of victims of other violent crimes (Burgess & Holmstrom, 1974; Hilberman, 1976; Symonds, 1976; Burgess, 1984). One difference is that the reactions are often more pronounced in rape victims than in others because the act of rape involves a personal violation described by one psychologist as "the ultimate violation of the self" (Hilberman, 1976, p. 436). This pattern of behavioral, psychological, and physical reactions has been termed *rape trauma syndrome.*

While psychologists, psychiatrists, and some lawyers and judges have come to view rape as an act of violence, others perceive it as a sexual act. Consequently, the legal response to a woman's allegation that she was raped has historically been to require corroborating evidence. The reasoning goes that if a woman was not secretly desirous of a sexual relationship, she would fight to the death in resisting such an attack. It is believed that if her accusation were true, corroborating evidence would be readily available.

What happens when a victim alleges that she has been raped but there is no evidence of her resistance, and when, as is often the case, there has been some association before the rape between the victim and the defendant? Presented with such a case, jurors are rarely impressed by emotional trauma. Instead they often apply an assumption-of-risk philosophy in judging the prerape conduct of the victim, and tend to acquit the defendant (Kalven & Zeisel, 1966):

> The jury, as we come to see it, does not limit itself to [the issue of consent]; it goes on to weigh the women's conduct in the prior history of the affair. It closely, and often harshly, scrutinizes the female complainant and is moved to be lenient with the defendant whenever there are suggestions of contributory behavior on her part. (p. 249)

In recent years, expert psychological testimony has been used by prosecutors to educate jurors in rape cases, to dispel certain myths they may have about the sexual nature of a rape, and to describe the psychic terror that may have caused a victim to submit in order to survive. Psychologists who testify in court typically discuss the pyschological impact of rape on its victims; in particular, their behavior before and during the assault, and their postrape psychological responses.

Behavior during the assault. Research has shown that the rape victim's response during an assault is similar to that of victims of other violent crimes (Burgess & Holmstrom, 1974; Symonds, 1976). Their primary objective is survival; the sexual nature of the assault is secondary. Consequently, rape victims react to the peril in predictable ways. The characteristic form of resistance is verbal, not physical, and most rape victims submit to their aggressors in the hopes that they will survive the attack.

Postrape psychological response. Research has also identified predictable patterns of postrape psychological adjustment in rape victims (Sutherland & Scherl, 1970; Burgess & Holmstrom, 1974). In the period immediately after the assault, a number of physical symptoms may be present (including physical trauma, sleep disturbances, muscle tension, and intestinal problems). Psychologically, the pervasive feelings are those of fear and anxiety. In the long-term reorganization phase, the rape victim attempts to regain control of her life but her behavior may still be pervaded by fear. The development of specific phobic reactions is common.

Expert testimony in rape trials could be used either to corroborate the testimony of the victim or to provide indirect education to the jury. A psychologist who testifies that rape victims typically respond to the violent rather than the sexual aspect of an assault could corroborate the victim's contention that a rape occurred although there was no sign of resistance. Similarly, a competent expert who has interviewed the victim can testify to a diagnosis of rape trauma syndrome when certain symptoms are present. In both of these roles, the expert provides the judge or jury with information that can be used to more fairly assess the prosecution's claim of forcible rape.

ADMISSIBILITY OF EXPERT TESTIMONY

Certain issues are central to determining the admissibility of any expert testimony, although different emphases may be put on these questions depending upon the particular kind of testimony offered. Traditionally, four basic requirements govern the admissibility of expert testimony (*United States v. Amaral,* 1973):

(1) The subject matter must be beyond the common understanding of the average juror or must assist the juror in understanding the evidence;

(2) the expert must be sufficiently qualified so that his or her opinion or inference will aid the jury;

(3) the evidence about which the expert testifies must be scientifically reliable and generally accepted in the scientific community; and

(4) the probative value of the evidence must outweigh its prejudicial effect.[1]

Even when these requirements are met, it is still within the trial judge's discretion to allow an expert witness to testify; he or she casts the ultimate vote in the admissibility election.

In the next section, we discuss the debate over the admissibility of these three kinds of expert testimony. More emphasis is placed on testimony about eyewitness behavior than about other kinds of expert advice because a great deal more research and writing has been done in this area and because an important controversy over the validity of this testimony has been generated within the psychological community. We examine the claims of McCloskey and Egeth (1983) that expert psychological testimony on eyewitness behavior should not be offered in court, as well as the counterclaims by other psychologists (Loftus, 1983; Wells, 1983, 1984) that this testimony is helpful. Because the usefulness of other kinds of expert testimony has not been a subject of controversy in the psychological literature, much of our analysis will describe the *legal community's* reaction to the eyewitness expert. However, since the issues in this area are applicable in other realms, we will weave together these different types of testimony and attempt to address the validity of each.

Does expert testimony assist the juror in understanding the evidence? Is the subject matter beyond the ken of the average juror?

Before these questions can be addressed, a more fundamental question must be answered: What do jurors commonly know? It is not immediately apparent whether certain issues are within the ken of the jury, although several recent studies have examined jurors' common understanding of eyewitness behavior (Deffenbacher & Loftus, 1982; Brigham & Bothwell, 1983; Yarmey & Kent, 1980). Deffenbacher and Loftus administered a questionnaire to students and to residents of Washington, D.C., half of whom had previously served on a jury in a criminal trial. Overall, typical performance was above chance level but was not high in absolute terms. Only half of the items were responded to relatively accurately. Deffenbacher and Loftus suggest that "jurors' intuitions might stand further edification regarding the vagaries of eyewitness behavior" (p. 24) and argue that expert testimony might improve the situation.

Brigham and Bothwell (1983) make the same point. In their study, prospective jurors were given descriptions of two previously conducted research studies on eyewitness behavior and were asked to predict the number of correct identifications made by subject-witnesses in those original experiments. Prospective jurors greatly overestimated the accuracy of experimental witnesses. Brigham and Bothwell concluded that the chance of finding 12 jurors who were sufficiently informed about the reliability of eyewitness testimony was remarkably slim.

Taken together, these studies suggest that jurors may hold certain misconceptions about eyewitness behavior. Moreover, they lend weight to the argument that expert testimony, if admitted, could serve to clarify these misconceptions and to make jurors more aware of the factors that influence the eyewitness and of how these factors operate. In their recent, influential article, McCloskey and Egeth (1983) take issue with this point of view. One argument they advance is that psychologists' knowledge of eyewitness performance is not beyond the common understanding and experience of the average juror. In particular, they question the assertion that uninformed jurors tend to overestimate the accuracy of eyewitness testimony (Loftus, 1974; Wells et al., 1979; Wells et al., 1980) and make several points about this alleged overestimation.

They argue that although a few studies suggest that jurors may overestimate the accuracy of witnesses, other studies indicate that jurors can be quite skeptical of eyewitness testimony (McKenna, Mellot, & Webb, 1981; Hosch, Beck, & McIntyre, 1980) and some research has shown that jurors will become more skeptical as a result of discrediting information (McCloskey, Egeth, Webb, Washburn, & McKenna, 1983; Weinberg & Baron, 1982). Second, they point out that cases of wrongful conviction do not necessarily demonstrate overestimation on the part of jurors. According to McCloskey and Egeth, mistakes will always occur, and if jurors were any more skeptical they might make more mistakes by allowing a disproportionate number of guilty people to go free. They also argue that studies showing that subject-jurors believe witnesses more often than they should (given the average accuracy of witnesses) have measured the wrong variable. The critical issue should not be belief rates but rather whether or not *conviction rates* are overly affected by eyewitness testimony—an issue that is often unaddressed. Finally, they suggest that even if jurors do occasionally forget to be skeptical of eyewitnesses, defense attorneys have plenty of opportunity to point out witnesses' deficiencies during cross-examination and in closing arguments.

McCloskey and Egeth's arguments are well articulated, but a number of psychologists have responded with compelling rebuttals. First, although some research has failed to demonstrate that jurors overestimate the accuracy of eyewitness testimony, this does not invalidate those studies in which this tendency has been observed. Instead of discounting these latter studies, researchers should ask, "How do they differ from the others?" and "What are the situations that are most and least likely to promote juror skepticism?" (Loftus, 1983). As a case in point, a recent study conducted by Saunders, Vidmar, and Hewitt (1983) suggests that whether jurors adequately consider discrediting information may depend on the strength of that information. Apparently, mild discrediting, such as mentioning the witness's poor eyesight, is insufficient to discredit the witness. Thus, jurors' failures to consider adequately the limitations of eyewitnesses appears to be a problem that should not be dismissed.

A second rebuttal suggests that while it is of interest to consider the effects of eyewitness testimony on conviction rates, the fact remains that a number of studies have revealed a dramatic disparity between the belief rates of subject-jurors and the accuracy rates of the witnesses whose testimony they observed. This disparity suggests that overbelief is a problem in at least certain circumstances (Wells, 1983).

Finally, it may be naively optimistic to suggest that lawyers can adequately point out the shortcomings of eyewitness testimony. A lawyer's remarks are invariably perceived as being motivated by the partisan interests of his or her client. Moreover, attorneys do not have the scientific credentials to give their opinion the credibility that follows from expertise. Finally, lawyers may engender negative reactions in the jury if they are overly rigorous in challenging the testimony of witnesses, particularly if the witness is also a victim (Loftus, 1983).

Ultimately, arguments about juror overestimations of eyewitness testimony boil down to a disagreement over how much evidence is necessary to make a psychological generalization. McCloskey and Egeth feel that the evidence is insufficient:

> The available evidence fails to show that jurors are overly willing to believe eyewitness testimony. This does not mean that jurors exhibit an appropriate amount of skepticism toward eyewitness testimony. Our point is simply that contrary to the claims of many psychologists and lawyers . . . juror overbelief in eyewitnesses has not been demonstrated. (1983, p. 555)

Clearly, some evidence for juror overbelief does exist, even if it is not sufficient to convince McCloskey and Egeth. As Loftus observes,

> Herein lies the major point of disagreement. How long should we continue doing research and how much data must we amass before we feel comfortable with application of that research. On this issue, reasonable people will and surely do disagree. (1983, p. 576)

In sum, eyewitness experts have argued about the extent to which psychological is beyond the common knowledge of jurors and whether jurors are overbelieving of eyewitnesses. Analogous questions can be asked about jurors who might hear other types of expert testimony.

Is expert testimony on the battered woman and rape trauma syndrome beyond the ken of the average layperson? Can expert testimony assist jurors in understanding evidence in these trials? Unfortunately, there are no studies of jurors' common understanding about battered women and rape victims, so it is difficult to say whether their assumptions conform to what psychologists know about these clinical phenomena. It is conceivable that jurors may reason the way the prosecutor in the case of *Ibn-Tamas v. United States* (1979) did. He suggested that the "logical reaction" of a battered woman would be to either call the police or leave her batterer. If jurors had this misconception, they could perhaps be aided by the testimony of an expert indicating that for various psychological reasons or fear of reprisal, battered women generally cannot leave.

The requirement that expert testimony be beyond common knowledge has been at the core of much debate over whether to allow experts to testify on these issues. Courts that have admitted testimony from an expert on the battered woman syndrome have done so in part because it will help jurors understand and evaluate the evidence. For example, the Supreme Court of Georgia in *Smith v. State* (1981) reasoned that

> the expert's testimony explaining why a person suffering from battered women's syndrome would not leave her mate, would not inform police or friends, and would fear increased aggression against herself, would be such conclusions that jurors could not ordinarily draw for themselves.

On the other hand, some courts have excluded testimony because of the assumption that juries are capable of understanding and deciding for themselves whether a defendant has proved self-defense and that expert testimony will not help them in that regard.

There is a similar dearth of information about jurors' commonsense understanding of rape trauma, although one recent study shows that jurors have many misconceptions about a rape victim's perceptions and behavior (Borgida & Brekke, 1984). As in battered woman cases, the issue of helpfulness to the jury has been controversial in cases that involved rape trauma syndrome. Some courts have reasoned that this evidence is within jurors' common knowledge (e.g., *State v. Saldana*, 1982) and others have decided that while jurors may have opinions about the common reactions of rape victims, these opinions may be wrong and an expert should therefore be allowed to testify about this matter. This debate would be clarified by further study of what it is that jurors already know about battered women or rape victims. If it is determined that jurors' commonsense understanding is at odds with research findings, then psychologists should not hesitate to offer testimony and trial judges should seriously consider admitting that testimony in hope of aiding the fact finder.

IS THE EXPERT WITNESS ADEQUATELY QUALIFIED?

There has not been a great deal of controversy over the qualifications of a potential expert witness. Most critics of expert psychological testimony question what the expert might say and not his or her ability to have an informed opinion. One general concern about the selection of expert psychological witnesses has been raised, however. Haward (1981) and Loftus (1983) discuss the potential problems resulting from lawyers' and judges' lack of awareness of the differences in training between one branch of psychology and another. As a result of their naivete, lawyers may ask their "pet" psychologist to testify on areas with which they are generally unfamiliar. In such situations, the psychologist may indeed be unqualified. In other instances, a person with education or experience in one field may be improperly asked to offer an opinion in an area outside of his or her expertise. For example, in *People v. White* (1980), a physician in internal medicine who had had "occasion to treat battered women" (p. 1072) was not allowed to testify on battered woman syndrome. Even though this doctor had treated battered women, he did not have special psychological expertise in the area and therefore could not be qualified as an expert witness. In general, however, because an expert must undergo cross-examination, it is not advantageous for an attorney to try to qualify an ill-prepared person and thus the expert's qualifications are rarely at issue.

DOES EXPERT PSYCHOLOGICAL TESTIMONY CONFORM TO A GENERALLY ACCEPTED SCIENTIFIC THEORY?

The concern here is that expert testimony without a recognized scientific basis may mislead or deceive juries. Without general scientific acceptance, that testimony would merely reflect a personal opinion. For this testimony to be admitted, it must be generally accepted as valid by other researchers in the field. Are these established theoretical bases for different types of psychological testimony, and do these theories merit the inclusion of the expert's advice at trial? Not surprisingly, the answers to these questions depend on whom one asks.

We first review psychologists' assessments of the validity of research on eyewitness behavior. As before, discussions about the validity of research on which other types of expert testimony are based will lag behind as there has been little attention to this question.

McCloskey and Egeth (1983) argue that almost anything an expert might tell a juror about eyewitness performance is either obvious or unwarranted. Specifically, they question many of the commonly cited "facts" regarding eyewitness testimony, they are skeptical of the alleged minimal relationship between confidence and accuracy because studies outside of the eyewitness area indicate a strong relationship between these two variables, and they question conclusions about weapon focus because of the small amount of research on this topic. Also, they question the alleged impact of anxiety on memory because there seems to be no systematic way to compare the anxiety levels induced in different studies and even cite a few studies that they view as evidence against the widely accepted notion that memories fade with time. One could infer from these remarks that there is considerable lack of scientific consensus in the eyewitness area.

There have been two major responses to McCloskey and Egeth's attacks on the validity of eyewitness research. It has been pointed out that many conclusions about eyewitness unreliability are based not only on specific studies but also on an entire history of cognitive, perceptual, and memorial research. This long history of research on, say, memory has prompted one researcher to state, "When an occasional study comes along that fails to show a decline in memory, even with a relatively long retention interval, I am interested, but it would take much more for me to completely revise my view" (Loftus, 1983, p. 569). Similarly, although there may be only a few studies that explicitly demonstrate the problem of weapon focus, there is a substantial body of literature indicating that people generally tend to focus on unusual or highly informative objects (e.g., Antes, 1974; Loftus & Mackworth, 1978).

The consensus among experts in the field is a second response to challenges to the validity of eyewitness testimony. A recent study by Yarmey and Jones (1983) asked 16 psychologists with one or more publications in the area of eyewitness performance various questions regarding eyewitness identification. Their results suggested that generally experts agree on most of the issues that are commonly discussed in court.

This issue of the validity essentially reduces to a question of how sure one needs to be about the state of the scientific literature before he or she is willing to testify about a particular finding. Even when a psychologist is certain that his or her findings are valid, there is still a personal decision that must be made about whether to testify to these findings. As one psychologist who responded to the Yarmey and Jones's (1983) questionnaire commented, "I would not 'swear to' any of the answers, not even the ones supported by my own data" (p. 38).

In the areas of battered woman and rape trauma syndromes, there has been little consensus about the validity of the available research and about whether that research can form the basis for an expert's opinion. Some courts have argued that the existence of these syndromes is well documented in the scientific literature and therefore that an expert be allowed to testify about them at trial (e.g., *State v. Marks,* 1982). Other courts have decided that because syndrome evidence has not been reliably established or documented by psychologists, the expert should not be permitted to testify (e.g, *State v. Saldana,* 1982). Interestingly, discussions of whether syndrome evidence is a sufficiently developed concept center on trying to decide at what point scientific principles become generally accepted as valid by other researchers in a particular field. Obviously this is a judgment call; it mirrors the controversy that exists in the eyewitness area. Until sufficient data are amassed to convince even the most demanding judge that the research is reliable, some psychologists will be allowed to testify because their opinions seemed based on generally accepted scientific consensus and others will be excluded because that scientific acceptance seems lacking.

DOES THE PROBATIVE VALUE OF EXPERT TESTIMONY OUTWEIGH ITS PREJUDICIAL EFFECTS?

Testimony has probative value if it is important to the determination of guilt or innocence. It has prejudicial effects if it misleads or biases the jury. It is important to keep in mind that this test must balance these competing influences. Simply demonstrating that a particular piece of evidence may have probative value or prejudicial effects is insufficient in and of itself to warrant the acceptance or exclusion of that evidence. Evidence with some probative value may still be excluded if there is sufficient potential for prejudice. These two factors pertain to the admissibility of expert psychological testimony and to the impact that such testimony may have on a jury.

In what ways could expert testimony be probative? When eyewitness testimony plays a major role in a case, there is the danger that an innocent person could be convicted. Considering that some studies have shown that jurors regard eyewitness testimony with little skepticism, expert testimony could increase the likelihood that jurors will carefully scrutinize the eyewitness account and, as a result, could decrease the likelihood of a wrongful conviction. Alternatively, it could help jurors discriminate between accurate and inaccurate eyewitness accounts. In terms of its prejudicial impact, there is the possibility that research evidence could bias or mislead the jury. It could cause jurors to become overly skeptical.

McCloskey and Egeth (1983) conclude that the potential harm of presenting expert testimony on eyewitness performance outweighs the possible benefits. We break their discussion into two parts: evidence for the probative value of this type of expert testimony, and evidence for its prejudicial effects.

McCloskey and Egeth acknowledge that various studies indicate that jurors' ability to discriminate accurate from inaccurate witnesses is not very good (Lindsay, Wells, & Rumpel, 1981; Wells et al., 1979). They argue, however, that no research yet demonstrates that providing jurors with testimony about eyewitness performance improves their ability to discriminate accurate from inaccurate witnesses. To buttress this point, they refer to Wells et al.'s (1980) failure to find differences between the overall discriminatory ability of subject-jurors who had received expert testimony and those who had not.

There are a number of responses to this critique. First, McCloskey and Egeth base their conclusions on a single study in which the expert testimony provided to some jurors consisted of only general information about eyewitness performance. Had subject-jurors received more explicit information (for example, that there is a minimal relationship between confidence and accuracy), their performance might have been better (Loftus, 1983). In fact, in a recent study reported by Wells (1983), subject-jurors were provided with just such information and showed significant improvement in their discriminatory ability. Thus, there now exists at least some evidence that expert testimony can facilitate juror discrimination.

A second point relates to the empirical observation that expert testimony decreases the likelihood that a subject-juror will believe a witness (Hosch, Beck, & McIntyre, 1980; Loftus, 1980; Wells et al., 1980). Even if expert testimony does not improve overall discrimination, it still may help by changing the nature of the mistakes that jurors make. Considering that eyewitnesses in criminal cases generally assist the prosecution's case, information that decreases the likelihood that jurors will believe inaccurate witnesses will also decrease the likelihood that innocent people will be convicted—that is, it will minimize a mistake that is generally considered far worse than letting a guilty person go free. Thus, even if expert testimony does not change the total number of mistakes that jurors may make, it can still reduce the worst type of mistake—the conviction of an innocent person.

Although McCloskey and Egeth find little evidence for the probative value of expert testimony about eyewitness performance, they see two ways in which it might have detrimental effects on juries. First, if jurors are already appropriately skeptical without expert testimony, then expert testimony may make them overly skeptical. Second, providing testimony about certain variables may cause jurors to overemphasize their importance and once again decrease their overall effectiveness.

Psychologists responding to these criticisms point to several inconsistencies in McCloskey and Egeth's logic. Wells (1984) points out, for example, that they argue that eyewitness testimony does not have much impact on the outcome of trials (McCloskey and Egeth cite studies by Chen, 1981, and Myers, 1979, in this regard). If this is true, then discrediting such testimony should also have little effect.

There are other inconsistencies in McCloskey and Egeth's reasoning. Throughout their article they suggest that the average juror has a sophisticated understanding of eyewitness performance, is appropriately skeptical of eyewitnesses, and generally has a low opinion of psychologists. If all of this is true, then why should jurors abandon their skepticism and disregard their understanding of eyewitness performance just because they hear expert testimony from a person whose profession they question? McCloskey and Egeth may be trying to have their cake and eat it too.

Similar problems arise when trying to weigh the probative versus prejudicial effects of other kinds of expert psychological testimony. In the area of the battered woman syndrome, possible prejudice could arise from labeling the murder victim a "batterer" or from the overly sympathetic effect that this testimony could engender in the defendant's favor. These possibilities must be weighed against the value of the expert's testimony in helping jurors evaluate the defendant's claim of self-defense. Because no one has studied the impact of this testimony on jurors, it is difficult to define a general balance between the two extremes.

With regard to rape trauma, the problem of prejudice arises if expert testimony is seen as attacking the character of the defendant. This possibility must be weighed against the benefit to jurors of information that may help them evaluate the issue of consent. Conceivably, recent kinds of testimony—specifically testimony that addresses *victim* behavior rather than *defendant* behavior—could tip the balance toward probativeness and away from prejudice, although this assumption has not been tested empirically.

How will these issues be resolved? Should experts be allowed to testify as long as their testimony has not conclusively proven to be prejudicial? Even if expert testimony is not prejudicial, is it appropriate to introduce if it has only questionable probative value? These questions seem to be decided on a case-by-case basis now. There are, however, certain safeguards that trial judges can take to ensure that prejudice does not outweigh probative value. For example, a cautionary instruction to jurors that expert testimony constitutes only one source of the available evidence might minimize its prejudicial effects.

WHAT IS THE PROPER ROLE OF AN EXPERT WITNESS?

Although the admissibility criteria subsume many of the issues surrounding the use of expert testimony, there are some other subtle points that need to be considered. McCloskey and Egeth argue, for example, that having psychologists testify in court will inevitably produce nasty battles of the experts, with each side reducing the credibility of the other. According to McCloskey and Egeth, this display of confict would hurt the reputation of the psychological profession by "creating (or sustaining) the impression of psychology as a subjective, unscientific discipline and of the psychologist as a 'gun for hire'" (1983, p. 559). One response to this criticism is that other scientific disciplines have been able to engage in courtroom disputes without causing undue harm to their respective professions. In addition, Wells (1984) suggests that by refusing to give expert testimony, psychologists may actually reduce the public's view of their profession by reinforcing the impression that psychologists are unable or unwilling to do research that has an applied value.

Whether expert psychological testimony affects the public's opinion of psychology is an empirical question that could be addressed by a well-designed survey study. Ultimately, however, the answer to this question will depend upon the manner in which the expert testimony is presented. A number of psychologists, judges, and lawyers, in an effort to avoid the potential "gun for hire" attitude, have suggested that psychologists routinely serve as "impartial" educators of the court

(Kogan, 1977; Pacht, Kuehn, Bassett, & Nash, 1973). According to this position, expert witnesses scrupulously avoid taking sides and instead try to present all the evidence on both sides of the issues. Proponents of this approach believe that by presenting both sides of the debate, battles of the experts will be reduced and jurors will receive a fairer assessment of the psychological knowledge of the issue.

Others have criticized this idea (Diamond, 1973; Perlin, 1977; Schofield, 1956), arguing that the legal system is designed for information to be presented in an adversarial manner. They assert that it would require a superhuman to avoid taking some position. They argue that expert witnesses should present their opinion (i.e., take a side) and perhaps even prepare a position for or against a certain proposition. It is assumed that alternative interpretations of the data will surface during cross-examination.

As a third opinion, Wells et al. (1980) suggest that psychologists should develop a standard form of expert advice that could be routinely delivered to triers of fact. The advantage of this approach is that it would avoid both the conflict and cost associated with hiring expert psychologists.

Having reviewed the debate over the proper role of expert psychological testimony, we wonder whether there exists an impartial and objective assessment of the issue. Both adherents and critics of psychological testimony have rather compelling scientific arguments to bolster their cases, and clamorings on both sides of the issue have been persistent and articulate (recall the comments of Younger and Rosenhan).

Ultimately it seems that personal values may decide how these issues will be handled. Psychologists must decide for themselves how much evidence is necessary before they can make generalizations about human behavior and whether even more evidence is required before such generalizations should be offered in court. Their decisions might be affected by answers to questions such as, How much worse is it to convict an innocent person than it is to let a guilty person go free? or, Should I feel a moral obligation to apply my research, or for that matter, not to apply my research? These questions are ones that science alone can never resolve.

Whenever diverse disciplines interact, each inevitably learns from the other. The relationship between psychology and law is no exception. Psychologists who testify in court—whether they describe eyewitness unreliability, battered women, or rape trauma syndrome—often experience conflict because of the dramatic differences they perceive between the adversarial nature of the courtroom and the education nature of academia (Camper & Loftus, 1984). Perhaps psychologist may learn from interacting with the law that psychologists are more adversarial that they often care to admit. In considering whether their research is applicable to the law, psychologists have been found to realize that their options are not absolute. Rather, they include personal values that often go without being identified explicitly. Understanding and articulating these underlying values is perhaps the single most important thing that psychologists can do to help resolve the controversy surrounding their expert testimony. Some psychologists will undoubtedly conclude that it is inappropriate for them to testify in court. Others will decide that they have valuable information that should be shared with the legal system. If psychologists follow their consciences and openly admit these predispositions, jurors will recognize that experts, like themselves, have personal opinions. It is the jurors' task to decide whether to buy that expert advice and just how much it's worth.

NOTE

1. The legal principles used to determine admissibility vary with each jurisdiction and with the particular testimony offered; i.e., some states rely on the *Dyas* test in deciding the admissibility of battered women expert testimony *(Dyas v. United States* 1977). This test requires that (1) the subject matter of the testimony is beyond the ken of the average layperson; (2) the expert have sufficient knowledge or experience in the field to make it appear that his or her opinion will aid the trier-of-fact; and (3) the state of the art of the field be such than an opinion can be formed by an expert. Other jurisdictions refer to Rule 702 of the Federal Rules of Evidence. This standard is somewhat more lenient than the *Dyas* test. It requires only that (1) the expert be qualified through skill, knowledge or experience; and (2) the expert be able to help the trier of fact understand the evidence or determine a fact in issue. Even if the testimony falls within the understanding of the average juror, an expert is still allowed to testify if that testimony adds to jurors' understanding of the evidence. In the eyewitness area, courts have generally looked to the requirements set out in *United States v. Amaral* (1973), while in the rape trauma syndrome cases, Rule 702 is the norm. The requirements outlined in this paper closely approximate those described by Rule 702.

REFERENCES

Allport, G. W., & Postman, L. J. (1958). The basic psychology of rumor. In E. E. Maccoby, T. M. Newcomb, & E. L. Hartley (Eds.), *Readings in social psychology* (3rd ed.). New York: Holt, Rinehart & Winston.

Antes, J. R. (1974). The time course of picture viewing. *Journal of Experimental Psychology, 103,* 62-70.

Arnolds, E. B., Carroll, W. K., & Seng, M. P. (1981). The admissibility of expert testimony on the issue of eyewitness identification in criminal trials. *Northern Illinois University Law Review, 2,* 59-85.

Bartlett, F. C. (1932) *Remembering: A study in experimental and social psychology.* New York: Macmillan.

Borgida, E., & Brekke, N. (1984). Psychological research on rape trials. In A. Burgess (Ed.), *Research handbook on rape and sexual assault*. New York: Garland.

Bransford, J. D., & Franks, J. J. (1971). Abstraction of linguistic ideas. *Cognitive Psychology, 2,* 331-350.

Brigham, J. C. (1981). The accuracy of eyewitness evidence: How do attorneys see it? *Florida Bar Journal,* (November), 714-721.

Brigham, J. C., & Bothwell, R. K. (1983). The ability of prospective jurors to estimate the accuracy of eyewitness identifications. *Law and Human Behavior, 7,* 19-30.

Brodsky, S. (1977). The mental health profession on the witness stand: A survival guide. In B. Sales (Ed.), *Psychology in the legal process*. New York: Spectrum.

Brodsky, S., & Robey, A. (1973). On becoming an expert witness: Issues of orientation & effectiveness. *Professional Psychologist, 3,* 173-176.

Brown v. Board of Education, 347 U.S. 483 (1954).

Burgess, A. (Ed.). (1984). *Research handbook on rape and sexual assault*. New York: Garland.

Burgess, A., & Holmstrom, L. (1974). Rape trauma syndrome. *American Journal of Psychiatry, 131,* 980-986.

Camper, P. M., & Loftus, E. F. (1984). The role of psychologists as expert witnesses: No more Daniels in the lions den. *Law & Psychology Review.*

Cavoukian, A. (1980). *Eyewitness testimony: The ineffectiveness of discrediting information*. Paper presented at the meeting of the American Psychological Association, Montreal, August.

Chen, H. T. (1981). *Disposition of felony arrests: A sequential analysis of the judicial decision making process*. Unpublished doctoral dissertation, University of Massachusetts.

Clifford, B. R. (1976). Police as eyewitnesses. *New Society, 22,* 176-177.

Clifford, B. R., & Scott, J. (1978). Individual and situational factors in eyewitness testimony. *Journal of Applied Psychology, 63,* 352-359.

Cofer, C. N. (1973). Constructive processes in memory. *American Scientist, 61,* 537-543.

Cross, M. B. (1982). The expert as educator: A proposed approach to the use of battered woman syndrome expert testimony. *Vanderbilt Law Review, 35,* 741-768.

Deffenbacher, K. A. (1980). Eyewitness accuracy and confidence: Can we infer anything about their relationship? *Law and Human Behavior, 4,* 243-260.

Deffenbacher, K. A. (1983). The influence of arousal on reliability of testimony. In S. Lloyd-Bostock & B. R. Clifford (Eds.), *Evaluating witness evidence: Recent psychological research and new perspectives*. New York: John Wiley.

Deffenbacher, K. A., & Loftus, E. F. (1982). Do jurors share a common understanding concerning eyewitness behavior? *Law and Human Behavior, 6,* 15-30.

Diamond, B. L. (1973). The psychiatrist as advocate. *Journal of Psychiatry and Law, 1,* 5-21.

Dyas v. United States, 376 A 2d 827 (1977).

Ebbinghaus, H. E. (1964). *Memory: A contribution to experimental psychology*. New York: Dover. (Originally published in 1885)

Federal Rules of Evidence. (1975).

Flagg, P. W., Potts, G. R., & Reynolds, A. G. (1975). Instructions and response strategies in recognition memory for sentences. *Journal of Experimental Psychology: Human Learning and Memory, 1,* 592-598.

Frazier, P. & Borgida, E. (1984). *Rape trauma syndrome evidence in court*. Unpublished manuscript.

Gelles, R. J. (1980). Violence in the family: A review of research in the seventies. *Journal of Marriage and the Family, 42,* 873-885.

Goodstein, R. K., & Page, A. W. (1981). Battered wife syndrome: Overview of the dynamics and treatment. *American Journal of Psychiatry, 138,* 1036-1044.

Haward, L. (1981). *Forensic psychology*. London: Batsford.

Hilberman, E. (1976). Rape: The ultimate violation of the self. *American Journal of Psychiatry, 133,* 436-437.

Horowitz, I. A., & Willging, T. E. (1983). *The psychology of law.* Boston: Little, Brown.

Hosch, H. M., Beck, E. L., & McIntyre, P. (1980). Influence of expert testimony regarding eyewitness accuracy on jury decisions. *Law and Human Behavior, 4,* 287-296.

Ibn-Tamas v. United States, 407 A 2d 626 (D.C. Ct. App), (1979).

Johnson, C., & Scott, B. (1976). Eyewitness testimony and suspect identification as a function of arousal, sex of witness and scheduling of interrogation. Paper presented at the meeting of the American Psychological Association, Washington, D.C., September.

Kalven, H., & Zeisel, H. (1966). *The American jury.* Boston: Little, Brown.

Kogan, J. D. (1978). On being a good expert witness in a criminal case. *Journal of Forensic Sciences, 23,* 190-200.

Langley, R., & Levy, R. (1977). *Wife beating: The silent crisis.* New York: Dutton.

Lindsay, R.C.L., & Wells, G. L. (1983). What do we reallly know about cross-race eyewitness identification? In S. Lloyd-Bostock & B. R. Clifford (Eds.), *Evaluating witness evidence: Recent psychological research and new perspectives.* New York: John Wiley.

Lindsay, R.C.L., Wells, G. L., & Rumpel, C. M. (1981). Can people detect eyewitness identification within and across situations? *Journal of Applied Psychology, 66,* 79-89.

Loftus, E. F. (1974). Reconstructing memory: The incredible eyewitness. *Psychology Today, 8,* 116-119.

Loftus, E. F. (1979). *Eyewitness testimony.* Cambridge, MA: Harvard University Press.

Loftus, E. F. (1980). Impact of expert testimony. *Journal of Applied Psychology, 65,* 9-15.

Loftus, E. F. (1982). Memory and its distortions. In A. G. Kraut (Ed.), *G. Stanley Hall Lectures.* (pp. 119-154). Washington, DC: American Psychological Association.

Loftus, E. F. (1983). Silence is not golden. *American Psychologist, 38,* 564-572.

Loftus, E. F., & Davies, G. M. (1984). Distortions in the memory of children. *Journal of Social Issues 40* (2), 51-68.

Loftus, E. F., Loftus, G. R., & Messo, J. (1984). Some facts about "weapon focus." Submitted for publication.

Loftus, E. F., Miller, D. G., & Burns, H. J. (1978). Semantic integration of verbal information into a visual memory. *Journal of Experimental Psychology: Human Learning and Memory, 4,* 19-31.

Loftus, E. F., & Monahan, J. (1980). Trial by data: Psychological research as legal evidence. *American Psychologist, 35,* 270-283.

Loftus, E. F., & Palmer, J. C. (1974). Reconstruction of automobile destruction: An example of the interaction between language and memory. *Journal of Verbal Learning and Verbal Behavior, 13,* 585-589.

Loftus, G. R., & Mackworth, N. H. (1978). Cognitive determinants of fixation location during picture viewing. *Journal of Experimental Psychology: Human Perception and Performance, 4,* 565-572.

Lower, J. S. (1978). Psychologists as expert witnesses. *Law and Psychology Review, 4,* 127-139.

Malpass, R. S. & Devine, P. G. (1983). Measuring the fairness of eyewitness identification lineups. In S. Lloyd-Bostock & B. R. Clifford (Eds.), *Evaluating witness evidence: Recent psychological research and new perspectives.* New York: John Wiley.

Malpass, R. S., & Kravitz, J. (1969). Recognition for faces of own and other race. *Journal of Personality and Social Psychology, 13,* 330-334.

McCloskey, M., & Egeth, H. (1983). What can a psychologist tell a jury? *American Psychologist, 38,* 550-563.

McCloskey, M., Egeth, H., Webb, E., Washburn, A., & McKenna, J. (1981). *Eyewitness, jurors and the issue of overbelief.* Unpublished manuscript, Johns Hopkins University.

McKenna, J., Mellott, A., & Webb, E. (1981). *Juror evaluation of eyewitness's testimony.* Paper presented at the meeting of the Eastern Psychological Association.

Munsterberg, H. (1908). *On the witness stand.* Garden City, NY: Doubleday.

Myers, M. A. (1979). Rule departures and making law: Juries and their verdicts. *Law and Society, 13,* 781-797.

Pachella, R. G. (1981). The truth and nothing but the truth (Review of "Eyewitness Testimony" by E. F. Loftus and "The Psychology of Eyewitness Testimony" by A. D. Yarmey). *Contemporary Psychology, 26,* 85-87.

Pacht, A. R., Kuehn, J. K., Bassett, H. T., & Nash, M. M. (1973). The current status of the psychologist as expert witness. *Professional Psychology, 4,* 409-413.

People v. White, 90 Ill. App. 3d 1067, 414 N.E. 2d 196 (1980).

Perlin, M. L. (1977). The legal status of the psychologist in the courtroom. *Journal of Psychiatry and Law, 5,* 41-54.

Rosenhan, D. (1983). *Psychological realities and legal policy.* Paper presented at the meeting of the Eastern Psychological Association.

Ross, J. L. (1983). The overlooked expert in rape prosecutions. *Toledo Law Review, 14,* 707-734.

Saunders, D. M., Vidmar, N., & Hewitt, E. C. (1983). Eyewitness testimony and the discrediting effect. In S. Lloyd-Bostock & B. R. Clifford (Eds.), *Evaluating witness evidence: Recent psychological research and new perspectives.* New York: John Wiley.

Schofield, W. (1956). Psychology, law, and the expert witness. *American Psychologist, 11,* 1-7.

Schooler, J. W., Gerhard, D., & Loftus, E. F. (1984). *Difference between the descriptions of memories based on perception and suggestions.* Paper presented at the Western Psychological Association, April.

Seligman, M. (1975). *Helplessness: On depression, development and death.* San Francisco: Freeman.

Smith v.State, 247 Ga. 612, 277 S.E. 2d 678 (1981).

Starkman, D. (1979). The use of eyewitness identification evidence in criminal trials. *Criminal Law Quarterly, 21,* 361-386.

State v. Chapple, 660 p. 2d 1208 (1983).

State v. Marks, 647 p. 2d 1292, Kan (1982).

State v. Saldana, 234 N.W. 2d 227 (Minn. 1982).

Sutherland, S., & Scherl, D. J. (1970). Patterns of response among victims of rape. *American Journal of Orthopsychiatry, 40,* 503-513.

Symonds, M. (1976). The rape victim: Psychological patterns of response. *American Journal of Psychoanalysis, 36,* 27-34.

Thar, A. E. (1982). The admissibility of expert testimony on battered wife syndrome: An evidentiary analysis. *Northwestern University Law Review, 77,* 348-373.

Underwood, B. J. (1948). Retroactive and proactive inhibition after five and forty-eight hours. *Journal of Experimental Psychology, 38,* 29-38.

United States v. Amaral, 448 F. 2d 1148 (1973).

Walker, L. E. (1979). *The battered woman.* New York: Harper & Row.

Walker, L. E., Thyfault, R. K., & Browne, A. (1982). Beyond the juror's ken: Battered women. *Vermont Law Review, 7,* 1-14.

Walter, P. D. (1982). Expert testimony and battered women: Conflict among the courts and a proposal. *Journal of Legal Medicine, 3,* 267-294.

Weinberg, H. I., & Baron, R. S. (1982). The discredible eyewitness. *Personality and Social Psychology Bulletin, 8,* 60-67.

Wells, G. L. (1983). *Expert psychological testimony on eyewitness issues: Empirical and conceptual analysis of effects.* Paper presented at the Johns Hopkins University Conference on Ethical Issues in Expert Testimony by Experimental Psychologists.

Wells, G. L. (1984). Reanalysis of the expert testimony issue. In G. L. Wells & E. F. Loftus (Eds.), *Eyewitness testimony: Psychological perspectives*. New York: Cambridge University Press.

Wells, G. L., Lindsay, R.C.L., & Ferguson, T. J. (1979). Accuracy, confidence and juror perceptions in eyewitness testimony. *Journal of Applied Psychology, 64,* 440-448.

Wells, G. L., Lindsay, R.C.L., & Tousignant, J. P. (1980). Effects of expert psychological advice on human performance in judging the validity of eyewitness testimony. *Law and Human Behavior, 4,* 275-285.

Woocher, F. D. (1977). Did your eyes deceive you? Expert psychological testimony on the unreliability of eyewitness identification. *Stanford Law Review, 29,* 969-1030.

Yarmey, A. D., & Jones, H. P. (1983). Is the psychology of eyewitness identification a matter of common sense? In B. R. Clifford & S. Lloyd-Bostock (Eds.), *Evaluating witness evidence: Recent psychological research and new perspectives*. New York: John Wiley.

Yarmey, A. D. & Kent, J. (1980). The relation of strength of stimulus to rapidity of habit-formation. *Journal of Comparative and Neurological Psychology, 18,* 459-482.

Younger, I. (1979). Psychological testing that might invade the province of the jury. In G. W. Holmes (Eds.), *New frontiers in litigation*. Ann Arbor, MI: Institute of Continuing Legal Education.

Ziskin, J. (1975). *Coping with psychiatric and psychological testimony*. Marina del Rey, CA: Law and Psychology Press.

PART III

TRIAL PROCEDURE

CHAPTER 9

Opening and Closing Statements

E. ALLAN LIND
GINA Y. KE

No aspect of trial procedure offers more potential for application of basic social psychological knowledge than the summary statements that counsel make before and after the presentation of evidence. Social psychologists have devoted decades to the investigation of many of the issues that arise in the construction and regulation of opening statements and closing arguments—issues such as the relative influence of arguments presented early or late in a persuasion attempt, the advisability of addressing opposing arguments in designing persuasive messages, the effects of initial impressions of a person on the interpretation of later information about that person, and the situational and stylistic factors that influence the credibility of a communicator. In this chapter we will analyze the psychology of opening and closing statements in search of both a better understanding of the processes that occur in these phases of trial and a basis for making policy and tactical recommendations concerning proper and successful conduct of these important trial events.

We begin our analysis below with a review of legal writing on opening statements and closing arguments. We note the legal constraints that govern these parts of the trial, and we point out that courts have traditionally allowed counsel more freedom to attempt to persuade in closing argument than in opening statements. We continue with a review of the tactical and strategic suggestions offered by trial practice manuals and books with respect to effective advocacy in opening and closing statements. On the basis of this review we identify the following legal issues:

(1) How much freedom to persuade should be given to counsel in opening statements?

(2) What is the relative importance of opening statements versus closing arguments as opportunities for counsel to influence the jury?
(3) How extensive should the opening statement be? Is there greater danger in overstating or understanding the case in the opening statement?
(4) What tactics and styles are most effective in counsel statements?

We then turn from writings by legal scholars and tacticians to writings by psychological theorists, examining those areas of social psychology that seem most likely to be relevant to opening and closing statements. We find in the social psychological literature answers to the second, third, and fourth of the issues just presented. In addition, we find reason to believe that the first issue—the question of the proper level of freedom to be accorded counsel—is especially problematic in the context of opening statements: The psychological literature suggests that, especially when the case turns on questions of personal characteristics or behavior, opening statements can have massive persuasive effect. Thus it appears that one of the most powerful tools of trial persuasion—the opening statement—is the one that is most restricted.

We move from the rather extensive theory available to analyze the psychology of counsel statements to the surprisingly limited body of empirical research on the topic. Fortunately, the studies that are available address precisely the issues raised in the legal literature with respect to importance, extensivity, and style of the statements. The research makes it clear that, notwithstanding the persuasive potential of opening and closing statements, jurors are properly skeptical of assertions made in these phases of the trial—a conclusion that removes some of the sting from the clash between the potential impact of truly persuasive opening statements and existing limitations on their use.

In the final section of the chapter we consider the consequences of opening statements and closing arguments from another perspective— that of their likely consequences for the apparent fairness of the trial process. Research and theory on procedural fairness suggest strongly that relatively unrestrained statements will enhance the perceived fairness of the trial and the verdict. In view of this likely consequence of unrestrained argument and remembering the research literature that shows juror skepticism about the credibility of counsel statements, we conclude that the first legal issue raised above—the question of how much freedom should be given counsel in their statements—might best be resolved in favor of more freedom than is currently allowed.

PROCEDURAL LAW ON
OPENING AND CLOSING STATEMENTS

The legal limitations on the content of opening statements are much more severe than those on closing arguments. Busch (1963), in a text on procedural law and tactics at trial, notes that the opening statement is required by rule and case law to be solely a statement of facts to be offered in evidence; it is "a relatively brief summary or outline of the substance of the evidence" (Vol. 2, p. 785). The court can allow some latitude in the content of opening statements, but there are well-recognized limits. For example, counsel are *not* allowed to argue the law or facts of the case, nor are they allowed to refer to inadmissible evidence. In fact, the assertion in an opening statement of facts not later admitted can result in reversible error.

Considerably more freedom is allowed in closing arguments. Busch summarizes the law on closing arguments as calling for "a full discussion of the issues in the case, the credibility of the several witnesses, the probability of the truth of the testimony as in harmony with or opposed to other evidence in the case, or to admitted or proven circumstances, the probative value of the evidence as satisfying or failing to satisfy the required burden of proof, the application of the law to the evidence, the question of punishment or damages, and, in general, anything properly germane to an issue of law or fact in the case" (1963, Vol. 5, p. 411). There are some limits—arguments are deemed improper if they appeal to racial or religious prejudice, sectionalism, or other motives that are clearly out of place in jury decision making—but these limits are much broader than is the case with opening statements. Indeed, this difference is the reason we refer to counsel's opening remarks as a "statement" while we may refer to closing remarks as an "argument."

Although it is difficult to find a clear articulation of the justifications for greater restriction of the content of opening statements, it seems likely that judicial rulemakers fear that jurors will be overly susceptible to arguments offered prior to the presentation of evidence and less susceptible after they have heard the evidence in the case. The differences in restrictions on argument in opening and closing statements raise the question of how much freedom should be permitted counsel in each statement. Is the current practice of greater limitation on opening statement content the wisest course? Later in this chapter we will examine some social psychological theory and research that speak to this issue.

LEGAL WRITING
ON STRATEGY AND TACTICS

The Relative Importance of Opening and Closing Statements

Lawyers generally agree that any opportunity to address the jury directly is of vital importance to a case. However, there is less agreement on the relative importance of the two arguments to the jury. Most trial practice writings pay lip service to the idea that opening statements are the means by which an attorney may inform "the jurors concerning the nature of the action and the issues involved and to give them an outline of the case so that they can better understand the testimony." However, despite the fact that the opening statement is supposed to be limited to the introduction of the nature of the controversy and is required to be free of persuasive appeals, many trial lawyers believe that the greatest gains to be made in any trial are made here. Others, relying on some of the same reasons, believe that the major opportunity to influence the jury lies in the closing argument.

Opinions regarding opening statements run the entire gamut from those which state that their usefulness is limited to those which state an opening statement is the single most influential communication the jurors will receive. Attorney Connolly (1982) states "I try lawsuits on the theory that the place to win a case is in the opening statement. If a lawyer has not won his case by the time the testimony closes, he is not going to win it in summation." (p. 159). Alfred Julien (1983), author of *Opening Statements,* lamenting the fact that opening statements have come to be viewed as a rather archaic form of introductory remarks, is of the opinion that "most trial lawyers think of summation as the most important part of the trial. It is, indeed the star attraction. But many jurors' minds, despite the admonition of the trial judge, are well made up by the time summation arrives" (p. 6). Sams (1982) agrees, stating, "You cannot avoid leaving an impression in the minds of the jurors when you make your opening statement. They will begin to lean one way or the other, even before the evidence is presented" (p. 22). He provides a telling illustration that their trust in the effectiveness of the opening statement might not be misplaced. He reports an incident in which two young lawyers in a Miami trial, having just completed their opening statements, run aground on a question over a point of law. The jury was asked to leave the courtroom while this question was discussed. When summoned by the bailiff some minutes later, the foreman announced, "We've arrived at a verdict, Your Honor" (p. 22).

The importance of the closing argument is more widely recognized. Most lawyers believe that their last chance to communicate to jurors is the most influential. It is a final chance to say what the evidence has not said for their case, a last chance to interpret the facts for the jury in the light most favorable to their client. Moreover, lawyers and judges also seem to believe that a further advantage is gained if one is the final speaker. For example, as the side that has the burden of proof is considered to be disadvantaged, the right to address the jury last is given to that side to alleviate the carrying of the burden. Attorney Langerman (1982) states, "Everyone agrees that the issue of damages is won or lost in the final argument. But I am fully convinced, despite the Chicago jury surveys, that the summation has a substantial effect on the jury's liability decision as well" (p. 124).

Among others who share this view is Crittenden (1961), who questions the necessity or desirability of making an opening statement at all. He argues that since the burden of proof rests with the plaintiff's attorney and it is his or her job to provide the attack and focus in the case, the defense is better off waiving the opening statement and maintaining the advantage of surprise.

More lawyers are beginning to realize the disproportionate attention given to closing argument both in the training of attorneys and, inevitably, in their preparation for trial. They are coming to recognize that opening statements and closing arguments are most effective when considered as a unit. The opening statement is the means by which the trial advocate sets the stage upon which he or she will present his facts, the closing argument the means by which those most telling facts are highlighted. The closing argument is most effective when it works within a context framed by the opening statement.

Even if one believes that the closing argument is of greater usefulness than an opening statement, a point that argues against waiving the right to an opening statement is the fact that in most jurisdictions, by waiving the right to open, a plaintiff's attorney also waives the right to closing argument if the defense at that later point chooses not to argue. Therefore, there is considerable support for the assertion that, at the very least, the plaintiff should never give up the opportunity to present an opening statement. "What smart lawyer wouldn't want to have two full summations?" (Julien, 1983, p. 5).

The aim of every portion of a trial is persuasion. Despite the rule prohibiting persuasive appeal, this is no less true of the opening statement than it is of the closing argument. Julien claims that the two should not be fundamentally dissimilar, that opening statements should "employ all of the techniques that have been taught for years on summation. The key to each is to be persuasive" (p. 4). The question then becomes one of preparing a persuasive opening statement that appears to be devoid of persuasive appeal.

The Extensivity of Opening Statements

A favorable first impression created by an accurate opening statement properly maintained and supported by the evidence as promised contributes appreciably to the battle of persuasion. (Morrill, 1973, p. 24)

Some legal tacticians believe that there is an advantage to giving a less than complete outline of one's case in the opening statement. One example is the case in which counsel is uncertain of the evidence he or she will later be able to provide the jury. Morrill (1973) writes that a lawyer should never overstate his or her case, that it is quite damaging to a case to promise evidence that later cannot be delivered. He states that one must be certain that evidence will be admissible before it is mentioned in the opening statement and that under no circumstances should one try to slip in evidence that one knows will later be ruled inadmissible. The justification for this advice is that the jury might later believe that the attorney has deliberately acted unfairly and will therefore doubt his or her credibility. Another case in which a less than complete opening statement might be called for is noted by Crittenden (1961). He advocates that a defense attorney who holds some really damaging piece of evidence should keep it in reserve as a surprise weapon. Others hold that delivering an incomplete opening statement provides no benefits. Julien believes that reserving an element of surprise is an outdated practice. He states that given the development of "complete discovery," the hope of complete surprise is a fairly dim one. "A wise lawyer knows what the other side will bring out. That is why it is so important to reach the minds of the jurors early." Connolly (1982), for somewhat different reasons, also espouses the view that the opening statement should be full, clear, and complete. The opening statement is the means through which the lawyer tells the jury what the case will be. "The lawyer must know what the case is about and where the witnesses are going before he enters the courtroom" (Connolly, 1982, p. 160).

The trial should be considered and prepared for as a coherent unit. The closing argument, as well as the opening statement, should be prepared before the beginning of the trial. The opening statement sets the theme for the presentation of evidence. The closing argument is the reprise. This is the only opportunity for lawyers to put the puzzle together for the jury, but the form the puzzle will take should have been decided well before the beginning of the trial. Preparation of the closing argument need not—indeed should not—be put off until after the presentation of evidence.

Tactics and Style
in Counsel Statements

After perusing a number of trial practice manuals and articles on the topic, one begins to feel that one can differentiate between good and bad opening and closing statements and even that one could oneself prepare some creditable pieces. But it would be difficult to say why specific opening statements and closing arguments are effective or persuasive. There appears to be no unified theory in legal writing on tactics for opening statements and closing arguments. Teaching how to write and present opening and closing statements reflects this deficit— it is largely anecdotal or the writer's attempt to generalize from what, in his or her experience, has worked. This is not to say that efforts in this area fly like scattershot. There appears to be a certain amount of agreement on how to and not to do the thing, but as one author notes, these "conclusions, like many others derived from legal reasoning, are based on logic and a rather haphazard study of human nature, and are totally unblemished by scientific data" (Lawson, 1970, p. 3).

This deficit can be attributed in part to a tendency on the part of a majority of lawyers to assign preparation of arguments to a back burner. Opening statements, in particular, are tricky things to prepare. The rule prohibiting argument in opening statements confines the attorney to the presentation of discrete facts—inferences, credibility, law and case theory; the drawing of conclusions constitutes impermissible argument. Therefore, when preparing for trial, lawyers are, understandably, most concerned with the collection and presentation of evidence. The opening statement introduces the case to the jurors, gives them, ideally, an overview of the evidence that each side hopes to present. The operative word here is *hope*. At the start of a trial, no lawyer can be absolutely certain what evidence will be presented, or how that evidence will be received by the jurors. Witnesses who have been carefully rehearsed may fall apart on the stand; others may, at the last minute, fail to appear.

The fundamentals in the preparation of an effective closing argument are no different from those employed in preparing an effective opening statement. Regarding both arguments to the jury, the point upon which most authors agree is that they are the most powerful, and indeed the only, means by which the attorney may personalize his or her appeal to the jury. There are several components to personalizing the case. The first of these is the use of simple courtesy. It is commonly considered expedient to preface each argument to the jury with an expression of both the attorney's own and his client's appreciation for the jurors' time and effort. Authors who advise use of this tactic further caution that this expression of thanks should never employ flattery, which may alienate the jury.

The second component is to develop a natural, seemingly spontaneous but organized personal style of delivery—that is, one should never read an argument, or deliver it extemporaneously; one should establish eye contact with each and every member of the jury. In other words, all the aspects of successful public speaking should be employed.

The final and most important component is the lawyer's use of language. Time should be taken in the opening statement to explain any technical terms or concepts, and these need not be repeated in the closing argument. Disgressions and other qualifying words and phrases should also be carefully excised from the arguments. Phrases such as "Of course, I wasn't a witness to these events," or "We will have Mr. Jones testify that . . . " may be accurate and fair but are distracting and appear to display some doubt on the attorney's part of his or her own client's case. The jury should already have been informed, either by the court or at the beginning of the opening statements, that the contents of the attorneys' arguments cannot be taken as evidence. If this has been made clear, disgressions and qualifying prefaces will be unnecessary. There is universal agreement that "legalese" should be discarded totally. Julien writes, "I find it helpful, when I go out of town to try a case, to arrive a few days early. I read the local paper and I listen to the way the people speak, by visiting bars and restaurants. That's how to pick up expressions and phrases that can later be used in court" (1983, p. 6).

The summation logically follows the points made in the opening. (Connolly, 1982, p. 160)

Connolly claims that in the opening statement, the attorney is making a bond with the jury. The function of the closing argument then is to inform the jury that the bond has been fulfilled. A major fault with most closing arguments, he claims, is that lawyers try to cover too much in them. "Remember that you have made your case before the summation" (p. 160).

A disproportionate amount of preparation and trial time is devoted to the closing argument. Even Julien, who is the major proponent of the opening statement, devotes twice as much trial time to his closing statement than to his opening. A major disadvantage to employing a short opening statement and a long closing argument is that jurors are tired by the end of a trial and their attention is easily lost. Since the opening statement is made when the jurors are more enthusiastic and alert, it, rather than the closing argument, should be the more extensive (Keeton, 1954, p. 265).

> With regard to the content of your summation, it should contain enough for you to complete a full and clear presentation of *your own case.* Ordinarily, it is not advisable to waste any time pointing out the deficiencies of your opponent's case. (Lorry, 1955, p. 121)

Some writers suggest that, as in the opening statement, the attorney should refrain from arguing during summation. They maintain that the closing argument should be used to emphasize only the best points of one's case. Although argumentation is permissible during this phase of the trial (unlike the opening statement) there are those (e.g., Keeton) who consider this tactic ill advised in the belief that bickering at this point may be perceived as taking unfair advantage of an opponent's lack of opportunity to respond, which may alienate the jury. They claim that it is more important at this point to highlight the strengths of one's own case rather than the weaknesses of the opposition's and that the greatest amount of time should be devoted to that end. It is further believed that a replaying of one's own weak points is "often a mistake if for no other reason than that these points are thereby unduly emphasized and strengthened by double exposure" (Goldstein, 1935, p. 626).

Other writers, however, believe that the closing argument should contain some mention of the weaknesses of both one's own and one's opponent's cases. They believe that attorneys should take the opportunity during the closing argument to strengthen any weaknesses in the testimony of one's own witnesses or to point out the weaknesses of their opponent's witnesses. Even Connolly, who advocates "hammering away at your best points" (1982, p. 160), takes into consideration the bond made with the jurors. What should an attorney do if he or she, or the opponent, has failed to fulfill that bond? Should one avoid argumentation even when one's opponent has promised something he has failed to provide? As we will see below, the limited research on opening and closing arguments clearly shows that one should not.

APPLICABLE SOCIAL PSYCHOLOGICAL THEORY AND RESEARCH

There are a number of areas of research and theory in social psychology that are applicable to the issues raised above. To the extent that a trial involves decisions about social events or the personal characteristics of the parties or witnesses—and this is often the case in trials where intent or defendant reputation is an issue—the substantial literature on person perception and social cognition is relevant. We review below two major theories in this area that have implications for our understanding of the psychology of counsel statements: script theory and theories of categorical processing. We also consider research and theory on the processing of information that is inconsistent with an initial impression—an issue that must arise frequently in the context of adversary trials.

The study of attitudes is the second major area of research and theory that has fairly straightforward application to procedural, tactical, and stylistic concerns in counsel statements. Trials involve judgments about issues and beliefs, as well as decisions about people and social events, and there is much in the literature on persuasion and attitude formation that is relevant to opening statements and closing arguments. We consider, in particular, theory and research on effects of the order and timing of persuasive arguments, on the relative effectiveness of "one-sided" and "two-sided" arguments, and on factors affecting the credibility of communicators.

The third major area of research and theory applicable to counsel statements—the study of procedural fairness—addresses a different set of issues, and we will defer discussion of it until later in the chapter. By way of preview, however, we note that the question of how effective counsel statements are in influencing jurors is only one question that might be taken into account in regulating these phases of trial. Procedural fairness research suggests that counsel statements may play a critical role in determining the extent to which the trial itself is perceived by those involved and by those observing it to have been fair and to have done justice.

Person Perception and Social Cognition

In many civil and criminal trials the major questions concern such issues as how a set of circumstances arose or whether some action was committed intentionally. It is reasonable to look to psychological theory on judgments of people and the interpretation of social events to discover the role that might be played by opening statements and closing arguments in such cases. For example, script theory (Abelson, 1981; Schank & Abelson, 1977) is based on the assertion that social information processing relies heavily on common understandings about the likely sequence of events in a given situation. Thus one's impressions of what occurred in the course of a particular dinner in a restaurant are heavily influenced by what typically occurs in the course of dinners in restaurants. Where only partial information is available, the recipient of the information supplies additional facts and inter-pretations based on the "script" for the situation in question.

A typical example of the way in which people use scripts to interpret their social world is provided by the following story: "John was seated in the restaurant. He looked at the menu and decided to order lobster. Later, when he had paid his waiter, he left immediately" (Fiske & Taylor, 1983, p. 167). Fiske and Taylor suggest that most people exposed to this story will later recall that John ate lobster, although this is not actually stated in the story. However, because eating what one has decided to order is a standard intermediate step between ordering and paying, people exposed to the story will themselves supply that information without realizing that they are adding anything to the story.

The phenomena described by script theory have several important implications for counsel statements. First, they suggest that opening statements can have quite substantial effects, by suggesting to jurors a certain script for the events addressed by the evidence. Further, they imply that careful invocation of particular scripts by counsel can lead jurors to supply by themselves information favorable to the attorney's clients. Note that these implications hold only for situations that are sufficiently universal to carry the common understandings on which scripts are based. An attorney could invoke a restaurant script in an opening statement, but there would be little point in trying to invoke for these purposes a computer design script. As there is little common knowledge of the latter situation, one would not expect the decision makers to introduce information of their own.

This is not to say that there is never reason to invoke uncommon scripts. Even when perceivers are not actually creating information, they may pay more attention to some later evidence because it fits with a script and perspective they have adopted. For example, it has been shown that if one can induce people to adopt mentally the visual perspective of one party in an accident, they are more likely to recall details and events available to that party (Fiske, Taylor, Etcoff, & Laufer, 1979). This suggests that there might be value to counsel presenting in opening argument a script for even an unfamiliar context if doing so might induce jurors to adopt a particular mental perspective and therefore be more attentive to favorable evidence available only to the party or witness with that perspective. Thus, even if the series of events in an accident is fairly bizarre, there might be value in describing the series from the point of view of one's client in order to induce the jurors to adopt the client's perspective and to be more sensitive to evidence that was available to that perspective.

There is one danger in using scripts in opening statements, however. Research has shown quite clearly that information inconsistent with a script (or any other type of cognitive social schema) is remembered better than is information consistent with the script (Hastie, 1980). Further, it appears that inconsistent information provokes more active cognitive processing as the perceiver seeks an explanation for the inconsistency. If no favorable explanation is readily available, this may lead jurors to assign greater weight to evidence contrary to the scripted explanation provided by the opening statement. This in turn suggests that counsel must take great care in selecting the script they present in opening argument: the purported series of events must fit very well indeed with the evidence, both favorable and unfavorable, or a ready, favorable explanation for inconsistent events must be provided to the jurors.

Most of our remarks to this point have focused on the implications of script theory and schema research for opening statements. It is almost certainly the case that the effects we have described will be strongest when the script is invoked prior to the presentation of evidence because the script can then affect not only the recall of case information but its initial perception as well (see Fiske & Taylor, 1983). However, it is likely that script-based arguments are effective in closing statements as well, and their use should be considered there.

Another concept from theory on social cognition has important implications for opening and closing statements at trial. Theories of category accessibility (e.g., Wyer & Srull, 1980) predict that the activation of a particular category of judgment, termed *priming*, increases the propensity to classify ambiguous information according to that category. In an example suggestive of the sort of persuasive techniques attorneys might use in an opening statement, Srull and Wyer (1979) primed some subjects by exposing them repeatedly to words associated with hostility. When subjects were later presented with a description of a person's actions that was ambiguous with respect to the primed trait, those who had been primed using this procedure were substantially more likely to rate the person's actions as hostile. One might expect that a prosecuting attorney who made frequent references to violent actions, whether they were the violent actions of the defendant or not, might increase the likelihood that jurors would interpret ambiguous behavior by the defendant as violent. As was the case with script theory, one implication of category accessibility theory is that opening statements may have quite substantial effects on jurors' judgments about the case, especially when impressions of persons are important. This implication would seem to vindicate the rationale courts have offered for placing greater restrictions on opening statements than on closing arguments.

Srull and Wyer (1980) make it clear that the priming effect is strongest when priming occurs immediately before the presentation of ambiguous information and when there is some delay between presentation of the ambiguous information and its retrieval for use by the perceiver. When priming occurs prior to receiving information, the interpretation of the incoming information is affected by the primed category. When there is some delay between the receipt of the later information and its use, the priming can work through memory processes as well as through perceptual processes. On the other hand, delay between the priming and the presentation of the ambiguous information allows other categories to be used, decreasing the power of the primed category. One implication of this phenomenon is that the defense in criminal and civil trials may benefit more from their opening statements than do their opponents.

It should be noted that category accessibility effects can occur even if the information that produces the effect is later discredited or forgotten. The interpretation of information generally takes place as the information is received and stored, and later removal of a source of bias does not necessarily result in a wholesale reassessment of previously stored information. At least one study (Wyer, personal communication) has shown that the subsequent discrediting of evidence does not remove its effects on trait judgments. One might apply this concept to counsel statements by recommending that counsel walk as near the edge of overstatement as is ethical in the hopes that assertions made in an opening statement might influence jurors' interpretations of admitted evidence even if the evidence directly supporting the questionable assertion is not itself admitted. As we will see below, however, there is research that casts doubt on this prescription for effective opening statements.

One final point should be made with respect to the potential problems of biased information processing as a result of the invocation of scripts or priming in opening statements. There is research (Lind, Thibaut, & Walker, 1976; Thibaut, Walker, & Lind, 1972) that shows that expectancy bias of the sort posited to account for some of these script and priming effects is inhibited by adversary presentation of information. It appears that the presence of attorneys for both sides in a case serves to remind jurors of the necessity of considering both sides, and this in turn leads to an active avoidance of expectancy bias. This is not to say that priming and script effects do not occur in the courtroom—we would hardly have devoted so much space to the description of such effects if we did not think them relevant to our topic. But neither would we suggest that such effects are always a threat to the reasonableness of jury decision making.

Attitude Theory and Research

The theories described above are unanimous in predicting that information presented early will be more influential—that opening statements have more potential for influence than do closing statements. In social psychological terms this is termed a *primacy* effect, and it stands in contrast to the *recency* effects, in which later information has greater influence, observed in many studies of the effects of persuasive communication on attitudes. We have suggested elsewhere (Lind, 1982) that primacy effects, which have been observed most often in studies of person perception, are most likely to occur in trials that turn on impressions of parties or witnesses, and that recency effects are most likely to occur in trials that turn on values and beliefs.

Recency effects are predicted by several theories of attitude formation and change that relate attitudes to memory of the persuasive arguments or to memory of thoughts about the persuasive arguments (Hovland, Janis, & Kelley, 1953; Insko, 1964; Miller & Campbell, 1959). The reasoning shared by these theories is most easily presented in the context of theories that state that attitudes, at any given time, are a function of the number of favorable and unfavorable facts and arguments remembered at that time. Because persuasive arguments presented early are likely to be remembered less well than persuasive arguments presented later, later arguments will have more influence; and the magnitude of this recency effect will increase as the time between the two arguments increases (with use of the attitude immediately after the second argument).

A common assumption of these theories is that persuasive arguments, like most other verbal material, are forgotten at a decelerating rate (see Figure 9.1). This results in a diminution of the recency effect as the time between presentation of the later argument and use of the attitude (e.g., in deliberation and decision making) increases. Figure 9.1 shows the recency effects that might result from evenly matched opening and closing statements in a simplified trial situation in which the prosecution and then the defense make opening statements at the beginning of the trial and in which the defense and then the prosecution make closing statements. In the figure, line O(P) represents memory of the material contained in the prosecution's opening statement, line O(D) the memory of the defense's opening statement, line C(D) the memory of the defense's closing statement, and line C(P) the memory of the prosecution's closing statement. The two vertical lines D1 and D2 represent two hypothetical points during the jury's deliberation when the attitude in question might be called upon to aid in a juror's decision. According to attitude-memory theories, the critical variable is the amount of persuasive material recalled, which is represented in the figure by the bar graphs that show the total amount of recalled material favorable to each side.

Among the implications of attitude-memory theories are the predictions that closing arguments will generally be more influential on trial attitudes than are opening statements, that the recency effects that occur *between* closing arguments will be more powerful than are the recency effects that occur *between* opening statements, and that all of these effects will be less powerful when lengthy deliberation or other delays increase the time interval between presentation of the statement and use of the attitude during deliberation to decide on a verdict. Similar predictions are made by a related theory linking attitudes to salience of thoughts about the persuasive arguments (Greenwald, 1968; Insko, Lind, & LaTour, 1976; Love & Greenwald, 1978), but according to this theory the predicted effects of the timing and order of statements could be negated or reversed if one statement provoked more thoughts or rendered thoughts more salient than did another. The Greenwald theory has the advantage that it can deal with the often weak relation between attitude and recall of persuasive arguments.

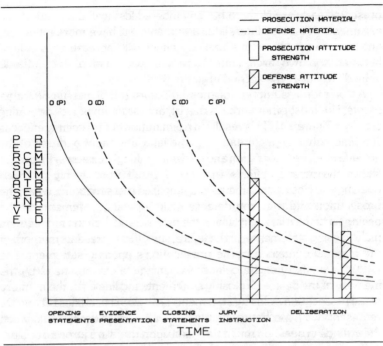

Figure 9.1   Theoretical Relationships Between Timing of Statements, Time During Trial, and Attitudes Favorable to Plaintiff and Defense

The attitude-memory theories give a clear indication of the value of presenting arguments last when the case involves issues of belief or value, but they say little about what sort of persuasive messages should be included in the arguments. Attitude researchers have examined this issue, however. For example, one of the relatively early findings in attitude-change research concerns the relative merits of one-sided and two-sided persuasive communications (Hovland, Lumsdaine, & Sheffield, 1949)—precisely the issue raised by legal tacticians who discuss the merits of referring to the opposing side's case in opening and closing statements. The early studies showed that two-sided communications (i.e., communications that included mention of opposing views) are more effective in persuading educated persons or those initially opposed to the position being advocated and that one-sided communications (i.e., communications that include only favorable arguments) are more effective in persuading less educated persons or those initially favoring the position being advocated. Lawson (1970) has reviewed more recent findings on one- and two-sided communication, including a study by Insko (1962) that used legal materials, and he concluded that two-sided communications are best in closing arguments to juries because such arguments are most effective when the targets of persuasion have some prior familiarity with the topic of persuasion. Work in what is termed *inoculation theory* (McGuire, 1964) is also relevant to this topic. It appears that it is advisable to expose people to the opposing side's arguments and to refutations of those arguments if they will ultimately be exposed to persuasion attempts by that side and if the issues involved include cultural truisms (Cialdini, Petty, & Cacioppo, 1981). Such exposure can "inoculate" against the persuasive impact of the opposing arguments. It is sometimes necessary to supply the listener with counterarguments against the opposing side as well as simply confronting him or her with that side's arguments (Cialdini et al., 1981). There is evidence that a full refutation is less necessary when the beliefs involved are not cultural truisms, but it is almost always the case that a warning that a communicator (an opposing communicator) will attempt to persuade reduces the effectiveness of that communicator's message (e.g., Petty & Cacioppo, 1979). The implication of this area of research and theory for counsel preparing opening and closing statements seems to be that issues of beliefs and values are best argued with reference to the opposition's likely arguments, but only if jurors are provided with counterarguments in the course of their exposure to the opposing arguments. In any event it is wise to point out the attitude issues on which the opposing party will attempt to influence the jury.

One additional area of attitude research that has important implications for the psychology of counsel statements is that which deals with persuasion and communicator credibility. Early research on this topic showed that a message was less persuasive when it was clear that the communicator had a definite intention to persuade (Hovland, Janis, & Kelley, 1953). Later research confirmed this finding, but suggested that the reduction in persuasion might be counteracted if the communicator is attractive and if the intention to persuade is admitted overtly (Mills, 1966; Mills & Aronson, 1965). Theory and research on communicator credibility has focused on the effects of perceived competence (knowledge of the topic of the communication) and perceived trustworthiness (desire to persuade because of vested interests in the recipient's decision). Obviously, counsel in an adversary system have much to worry about on the second count—jurors may be inclined to discount much of what they say because it is seen as motivated by a desire to win a favorable verdict.

The style of presentation of counsel statements may also affect the perceived competence of the speaker, and thereby the effectiveness of his or her speech. An indication of how this might occur is seen in a study by Erickson, Lind, Johnson, and O'Barr (1978) examining the effects of speech styles on the credibility and persuasiveness of witnesses. Erickson et al. manipulated the use of such speech forms as hedges, hesitations, qualifiers, and intensifiers and found that witnesses using these forms were perceived to be less competent and less credible and were in fact less persuasive than were witnesses who used a more straightforward style of speech. It seems likely that an attorney using these speech forms would also suffer some loss of perceived competence, credibility, and persuasiveness.

RESEARCH ON COUNSEL STATEMENTS

As mentioned earlier, there is surprisingly little empirical research that addresses directly the psychology of counsel statements. However, the research that does exist addresses some of the most important questions raised by legal writing and social psychological theory. As will be seen as we review the studies, for the most part the empirical findings confirm the predictions we have made from our analysis of relevant theory on social cognition and attitudes.

In one of the earliest studies of juror reactions to statements and testimony, Weld and Danzig (1940) had mock jurors repeatedly, as the trial unfolded, record their opinions about liability in a simulated civil trial. On the basis of observing only slight movement toward the position advocated by each attorney in opening statements, Weld and Danzig concluded that jurors remained reasonably open-minded following that phase of trial. They observed much stronger movement following the defense's closing argument, and conclude that this might well have been the most influential phase of their trial.

The two studies that are most relevant to the psychological analysis of counsel statements were conducted by Pyszczynski and Wrightsman (1981) and Pyszczynski, Greenberg, Mack and Wrightsman (1981). Both studies tested hypotheses drawn from legal and social psychological analyses of opening statements using mock jurors. The Pyszczynski and Wrightsman study tested the effects of extensive versus brief previews of the case in both prosecution and defense opening statements. The extensive previews provided definite, detailed summaries of the evidence to be introduced by each attorney along with statements of how the attorney believed the evidence should be interpreted. The brief previews provided little or no detail about the evidence.

Pyszczynski and Wrightsman found that these variations in opening statements did affect jurors' beliefs and verdicts. Specifically, they found that extensive opening previews by the prosecution resulted in more guilty verdicts and that extensive opening previews by the defense counteracted this effect by reducing the number of guilty verdicts when the prosecution also used extensive opening previews. An analysis of the jurors' changing opinions over the course of trial revealed that the amount of preview in the opening statement had a rather substantial effect on opinions throughout the trial. Thus, the results of this study favor those legal tacticians who have argued that greater attention and effort be devoted to the opening statement. The results also favor the general prediction of social cognition theories that early information can profoundly affect the interpretation of later information.

Pyszczynski et al. (1981) sought to extend this finding by examining the effects of overstatement in opening statements. They exposed mock jurors to one of three conditions: an opening statement that promised more than was actually delivered by the evidence, an opening statement that promised more than was delivered *plus* a reminder in opposing counsel's closing statement that the promise had not been fulfilled; and a control condition with the same evidence but with neither the unfulfilled promise nor the reminder about it. They found that unfulfilled promises in opening statements appear to have positive effects when they are not remarked upon by one's opponent, but that this positive effect is cancelled when such remarks are present. These findings provide support for the idea that initial information, even if not proven accurate, can influence subsequent judgments—a prediction of social cognition theories—but they provide no support for the idea that an overtly discredited piece of initial information can have effects that endure beyond its discrediting.

Finally, we should mention the results of a very recent study by Lapping and Lind (1984). Building on the speech style study mentioned in the previous section (Erickson et al., 1978), this experiment examined the ability of counsel to "explain away" a credibility-harming witness speech style either before or after the witness had testified. The results suggested that jurors are cautious in accepting counsel assertions in opening statements. In this study, mock jurors seemed willing to believe counsel if the assertion was inherently credible and if it fit well with the jurors' own assessment of the witness' personality, but they were unwilling to accept assertions that did not match their own ideas. This result is congruent with the considerable literature, described above, on credibility and persuasion, and it suggests that fears about massive biasing of jurors by opening statements may be unfounded.

COUNSEL STATEMENTS
AND PROCEDURAL FAIRNESS

Implicit in most of our discussion of counsel statements to this point has been an evaluation of the psychology of statements from the perspective of counsel. That is, we have been most concerned with an analysis of the effects of the statements on the impressions, beliefs, and attitudes of jurors, and we have often viewed the effectiveness of statements in terms of their capacity to aid in achieving a favorable verdict. If we move back to view the psychology of counsel statements from a broader, more policy-oriented perspective, we must be concerned with the fairness of the procedures and practices that govern these phases of trial. There are two aspects of the fairness question that are amenable to psychological analysis. First, what statement procedures are most likely to engender, among litigants and observers, the belief that the trial has been fair? Second, which of the effects of the various procedures are likely to result in undue bias or inaccurate decision making? We examine these two questions in this section.

Counsel Statements and Perceived Fairness

The past ten years has produced a substantial literature on the factors that affect litigant and observer perceptions of procedural fairness (for reviews see Lind, 1982; Thibaut & Walker, 1975; Walker & Lind, 1984). Among the most potent features of procedures with respect to the enhancement of perceived fairness is what has come to be termed *litigant process control*, the vesting of substantial control over the content and form of the presentation of evidence and arguments in the hands of the attorneys and litigants. Research in perceived procedural fairness has shown repeatedly that procedures that include this feature are judged to be fairer and are believed to produce fairer verdicts than are procedures that limit litigant process control in favor of judge process control (e.g., Houlden, LaTour, Walker, & Thibaut, 1978; LaTour, 1978; Lind, Kurtz, Musante, Walker, & Thibaut, 1980; Lind, Lissak, & Conlon, 1983; Walker, LaTour, Lind,

& Thibaut, 1974). Additional research has shown that procedural fairness judgments have substantial effects of the perceived fairness of the court (Tyler, 1984).

This process control effect on procedural fairness judgments has been explained by Thibaut and Walker (1978) in their theory of the psychology of legal procedure. Thibaut and Walker contend that the major goal of most trials is the resolution of the case along lines that conform to what social psychologists have termed the equity norm. The equity norm specifies that the positive or negative outcome a person receives should depend on his or her contributions to the positive or negative situation that creates the case. According to the equity norm punishment or reward should be proportional to individual, personal responsibility for the events. Thibaut and Walker point out that valid application of the equity norm requires that the decision maker, the judge or jury, have full information on the individual circumstances of each involved party. They argue that this information is best supplied by the parties themselves, both because they are best acquainted with the information and because investigators other than the parties will be likely to underestimate the effects of the environment on the parties' behavior—a social cognition bias termed the *fundamental attributional error* (Ross, 1977). To assume, as do Thibaut and Walker, that litigants and observers intuit this line of argument explains why procedures with high litigant process control are preferred.

This literature suggests that relatively unrestricted opening and closing statements will be seen as more fair than statements that are limited by rules and procedures. Given that closing arguments are already relatively free of restriction, one might expect that any efforts to enhance the apparent fairness of trials and courts should be directed to freeing up opening arguments. If Thibaut and Walker are correct in their analysis, then allowing greater freedom in opening arguments will lead litigants and observers to believe that more individual information is reaching the jury and that justice is more likely to be done.

Counsel Statements and Potential Bias

We have just argued that the literature on the psychology of perceived justice suggests that counsel statements, both at the opening and closing of trial, should be relatively unfettered in order to maximize the apparent fairness of the trial. But would this *apparent* fairness be achieved at the cost of a reduction in objective fairness? We examine this question in this final section. As we noted above, the principal policy question raised by research and theory on perceived procedural fairness concerns the extent to which opening statements should be less restrictive than is now the case. For this reason we will focus below on the possible negative and positive consequences for juror decision making bias of less restrictive opening statements.

Our review of social psychological theory and research suggests that there is at least some reason for concern about the potential biasing effects of unrestricted opening statements. The literature from social cognition makes it clear that opening statements could have substantial effects through the operation of priming or script processes. The experiments by Pyszczynski, Wrightsman, and their colleagues show effects that support this concern but that also suggest that if both sides are making maximum use of the opening statement only minimal bias will occur. The possibility that adversary processes might lessen the biasing effects that uncontested opening statements might have is also suggested by the results of the Thibaut et al. (1972) study that showed that adversary presentation lessens expectancy bias. And the literature on communicator credibility, together with the findings of the Lapping and Lind (1984) study, gives us even more reason to believe that relatively free opening statements would be less biasing than is feared.

Of course, more research is needed to provide a more definite basis for enlightened analyses of the wisdom of freeing the present restraints on opening arguments. The tension between possible bias and perceived fairness, which we have seen in the conflicting implications of the procedural justice literature and the social cognition literatures, makes this an area worthy of further investigation. Our reading of the research that does exist, however, suggests that the likely gains of more liberal opening statement rules outweigh the likely problems. We suggest that pending the outcome of further research it might be wise to consider changing opening *statements* to opening *arguments*.

REFERENCES

Abelson, R. P. (1981). The psychological status of the script concept. *American Psychologist, 36,* 715-729.

Busch, F. X. (1963). *Law and tactics in jury trials.* Indianapolis, IN: Bobbs-Merrill.

Cialdini, R. B., Petty, R. E., & Cacioppo, J. T. (1981). Attitude and attitude change. *Annual Review of Psychology, 32,* 357-404.

Connolly, P. R. (1982). Persuasion in the closing argument: The defendant's approach. In G. W. Holmes (Ed.), *Opening statements and closing arguments.* Ann Arbor, MI: The Institute of Continuing Legal Education.

Crittenden, R. (1961). The opening statement. In N. Cohen (Ed.), *Criminal law seminar.* Brooklyn, NY: Central Book Company.

Erickson, B. E., Lind, E. A., Johnson, B. C., & O'Barr, W. M. (1978). Speech style and impression formation in a court setting: The effects of "powerful" and "powerless" speech. *Journal of Experimental Social Psychology, 14,* 693-752.

Fiske, S. T., & Taylor, S. E. (1983). *Social cognition.* Reading, MA: Addison-Wesley.

Fiske, S. T., Taylor, S. E., Etcoff, N. L., & Laufer, J. K. (1979). Imaging, empathy, and causal attribution. *Journal of Experimental Social Psychology, 15,* 356-377.

Goldstein, I. (1935). *Trial technique.* Chicago, IL: Callaghan & Company.

Greenwald, A. G. (1968). Cognitive learning, cognitive response to persuasion, and attitude change. In A. Greenwald, T. Brock, & T. Ostrom (Eds.), *Psychological foundations of attitudes.* New York: Academic Press.

Hastie, R. (1980). Memory for behavioral information that confirms or contradicts a personality impression. In R. Hastie, T. Ostrom, E. Ebbesen, R. Wyer, D. Hamilton, & D. Carlston (Eds.), *Person memory: the cognitive basis of social perception* (pp. 155-178). Hillsdale, NJ: Lawrence J. Erlbaum.

Holmes, G. W. (Ed.) (1982). *Opening statements and closing arguments.* Ann Arbor, MI: The Institute of Continuing Legal Education.

Houlden, P., LaTour, S., Walker, L., & Thibaut, J. (1978). Preferences for modes of dispute resolution as a function of process and decision control. *Journal of Experimental Social Psychology, 14,* 13-22.

Hovland, C. I., Janis, I. L., & Kelley, H. H. (1953). *Communication and persuasion.* New Haven, CT: Yale University Press.

Hovland, C. I., Lumsdaine, A. A., & Sheffield, F. D. (1949). *Experiments on mass communication.* Princeton, NJ: Princeton University Press.

Insko, C. A. (1962). One-sided versus two-sided communications and countercommunications. *Journal of Abnormal and Social Psychology, 65,* 203-206.

Insko, C. A. (1964). Primacy versus recency as a function of the timing of arguments and measures. *Journal of Abnormal and Social Psychology, 69,* 381-391.

Insko, C., Lind, E. A., & LaTour, S. (1976). Persuasion, recall and thoughts. *Representative Research in Social Psychology 7,* 67-78.

Julien, A. (1983). Interview with Alfred Julien—Author of *Opening Statements. Trial Diplomacy Journal, 6,* 4-8.

Kalven, Jr., H., & Zeisel, H. (1966). *The American jury.* Boston, MA: Little, Brown.

Keeton, R. E. (1954). *Trial tactics and methods.* Boston, MA: Little, Brown.

Langerman, S. (1982). Persuasion in the closing argument: The plaintiff's approach. In G. W. Holmes (Ed.), *Opening statements and closing arguments.* Ann Arbor, MI: The Institute of Continuing Legal Education.

Lapping, J., & Lind, E. A. (1984). Mitigating the effects of witness speech style. Unpublished Bachelor's Honors Thesis, University of Illinois.

LaTour, S. (1978). Determinants of participant and observer satisfaction with adversary and inquisitorial modes of adjudication. *Journal of Personality and Social Psychology, 36,* 1531-1545.

Lawson, R. G. (1970). Relative effectiveness of one-sided and two-sided communications in courtroom persuasion. *The Journal of General Psychology, 82,* 3-16.

Lind, E. A. (1982). The psychology of courtoom procedure. In R. Bray & N. Kerr (Eds.), *Psychology of the courtroom.* New York: Academic Press.

Lind, E. A., Kurtz, S., Musante, L., Walker, L., & Thibaut, J. (1978). Procedure and outcome effects on reactions to adjudicated resolution of conflicts of interests. *Journal of Personality and Social Psychology, 39,* 643-653.

Lind, E. A., Lissak, R. I., & Conlon, D. E. (1983). Decision control and process control effects on procedural fairness judgments. *Journal of Applied Social Psychology, 4,* 338-350.

Lind, E. A., Thibaut, J., & Walker, L. (1976). A cross-cultural comparison of the effect of adversary and nonadversary processes on bias in legal decision making. *Virginia Law Review, 62,* 271-283.

Lorry, W. (1955). *A civil action, the trial.* Philadelphia, PA: American Law Institute

Love, R. E., & Greenwald, A. G. (1978). Cognitive responses to persuasion as media of opinion change. *Journal of Social Psychology, 104,* 231-241.

McGuire, W. J. (1964). Inducing resistance to persuasion: Some contemp approaches. *Advances in Experimental Social Psychology, 1,* 192-229.

Miller, N., & Campbell, D. T. (1959). Recency and primacy in persuasion as a function of the timing of speeches and measurements. *Journal of Abnormal and Social Psychology, 59,* 1-9.

Mills, J. (1966). Opinion change as a function of the communicator's desire to influence and liking for the audience. *Journal of Experimental Social Psychology, 2,* 152-159.

Mills, J., & Aronson, E. (1965). Opinion change as a function of the communicator's attractiveness and desire to influence. *Journal of Personality and Social Psychology, 1,* 173-177.

Morrill, A. E. (1973). *Trial diplomacy.* Chicago: Court Practice Institute.

Petty, R. E., & Cacioppo, J. T. (1979). Effects of forewarning of persuasive intent and involvement on cognitive responses and persuasion. *Personality and Social Psychology Bulletin, 5,* 173-176.

Pyszczynski, T., & Wrightsman, L. S. (1981). Effects of opening statements on mock jurors. *Journal of Applied Social Psychology, 11,* 301-313.

Pyszczynski, T., Greenberg, J., Mack, D., & Wrightsman, L. S. (1981). Opening statements in a jury trial: The effect of promising more than the evidence can show. *Journal of Applied Social Psychology, 11,* 434-444.

Ross, L. (1977). The intuitive psychologist and his shortcomings: Distortions in the attribution process. In L. Berkowitz (Ed.), *Advances in the experimental social psychology* (Vol. 10). New York: Academic Press.

Sams, Jr., M. My approach to opening statements for the plaintiff. In G. W. Holmes (Ed.), *Opening statements and closing arguments.* Ann Arbor, MI: The Institute of Continuing Legal Education, 1982.

Schank, R. C., & Abelson, R. P. (1977). *Scripts, plans, goals, and understanding.* Hillsdale, NJ: Lawrence J. Erlbaum.

Srull, T. K., & Wyer, R. S. (1979). The role of category accessibility in the interpretation of information about persons: Some determinants and implications. *Journal of Personality and Social Psychology, 37,* 1660-1672.

Srull, T. K., & Wyer, R. S. (1980). Category accessibility and social perception: Some implications for the study of person memory and interpersonal judgments. *Journal of Personality and Social Psychology, 38,* 841-856.

Thibaut, J., & Walker, L. (1975). *Procedural justice: A psychological analysis.* Hillsdale, NJ: Lawrence J. Erlbaum.

Thibaut, J., & Walker, L. (1978). A theory of procedure. *California Law Review, 66,* 541-566.

Thibaut, J., Walker, L., & Lind, E. A. (1972). Adversary presentation and bias in legal decision making. *Harvard Law Review, 86,* 386-401.

Tyler, T. R. (1984). The role of perceived injustice in defendants' evaluations of their courtroom experience. *Law and Society Review, 18,* 51-74.

Walker, L., LaTour, S., Lind, E. A., & Thibaut, J. W. (1974). Reactions of participants and observers to modes of adjudication. *Journal of Applied Social Psychology, 4,* 295-310.

Walker, L., & Lind, E. A. (1984). Psychological studies of procedural models. In G. Stephenson & J. Davis (Eds.), *Progress in applied social psychology* (pp. 393-414). New York: John Wiley.

Weld, H. P., & Danzig, E. R. A study of the way in which a verdict is reached by a jury. *American Journal of Psychology,* 1940, *53,* 518-536.

Wyer, R. S., & Srull, T. K. (1980). The processing of social stimulus information: A conceptual integration. In R. Hastie, T. Ostrom, E. Ebbesen, & R. Wyer, D. Hamilton, & D. Carlston (Eds.), *Person memory: The cognitive basis of social perception* (pp. 227-300). Hillsdale, NJ: Lawrence J. Erlbaum.

CHAPTER 10

Questioning Witnesses

ELIZABETH F. LOFTUS
JANE GOODMAN

EVIDENCE AND PURPOSES OF WITNESS EXAMINATIONS

Both trial lawyers and psychologists are eager to know what factors are most important in determining the outcome of a trial. A great deal of research has been conducted to explore this issue, and recently, reviewers of jury behavior research have claimed that the nature of the evidence introduced during a trial has a more vital impact on the fact finder than does any other factor (Saks & Hastie, 1978). For example, McGaffey (1983) notes that the weight of the evidence and a clear presentation of the evidence are more important than the composition of the jury. Then, in summarizing the results of the body of empirical work on this topic, Simon (1983) states that, on the whole, social scientists have reported that jurors decide cases on the basis of evidence rather than on the basis of extraneous factors such as the attractiveness of defendant. Evaluations along these lines highlight the importance of the nature and mode of presentation of evidence to the fact finder in the courtroom. As the primary means of presenting evidence in court is via witness examinations, the psychology of human questioning has been the subject of renewed interest among lawyers and psychologists alike.

The posing and answering of questions is fundamental to the entire trial process. Questioning begins the moment a client first contacts an attorney, continues during client interviews, is formalized in written interrogatories and depositions of potential witnesses, and culminates in the direct and cross-examinations of witnesses in court before a judge or jury. While the quintessential purpose of the question-and-answer process is undeniably to uncover pertinent information about the dispute in question (particularly during the discovery phase), this is by no means the sole function of witness interrogation.

The emphasis in the question-and-answer process shifts continuously throughout the trial. During direct examination, attention is focused on the witness who receives the questions and the responses provided. During cross-examination, however, the emphasis shifts to the form of the question and the asker. From time to time, the process will focus on the perceptions of the observers (Zimmerman, 1983). For example, questions in the courtroom may be posed primarily to educate and instruct the jurors about the alleged facts, to familiarize them with the parties to the dispute, and to socialize them regarding topics about which they may have little personal experience (McGovern & Davis, 1983). Subsidiary goals of questioning may be to present a theory or cohesive story to the jury, to establish a basis for closing arguments, to persuade the jury through repetition of significant facts, or to enhance the credibility of certain witnesses by asking questions which elicit answers corroborative of other evidence or character-building questions. The purpose most frequently served by cross-examination is the creation of distrust and skepticism about the testimony of a witness. This is often accomplished by asking questions that tend to show that a witness is biased or prejudiced, or has ulterior motives in testifying before the court. Questions may also be asked with the intent of distracting or confusing jurors—for example, by persistently inquiring about details that have only secondary or minimal importance in the dispute.

Throughout the witness examination, both the form of the questions and the content of the answers are limited by the rules of evidence (Tanford, 1983). For example, the hearsay rule generally prohibits witnesses from relating words that they claim to have heard uttered by someone else. This is because the jurors would have no opportunity to observe that speaker and form an opinion as to the credibility of the statements, and because the statements were not originally made under oath or subjected to cross-examination—procedural mechanisms designed to safeguard the veracity of the evidence. Thus, courtroom testimony differs in a number of ways from statements acceptable in everyday conversation. First, there is no turn-taking insofar as asking and answering of questions is concerned between the lawyer and the witness: The witnesses may not interrogate the attorneys. Second, witnesses' responses tend to be fragmented because lengthy, narrative answers that may invite the inclusion of information irrelevant to case at hand can be objected to as "nonresponsive" and thus are discouraged. Third, the fact that topics originally raised during direct examination by one examining attorney are later explored by another examiner during cross-examination means that a single issue is rarely explored fully at one particular time, a factor that exacerbates the fragmented nature of the testimony.

THE PSYCHOLOGY OF QUESTIONING

Despite the many purposes of the questioning process, basically only two forms of questions are used: open-ended questions and closed-ended questions. Open-ended questions, which elicit a narrative response, are typically used during direct examination. At the turn of the century, the French psychologist, Binet, identified these questions as "expectative" in nature (Whipple, 1909). Closed-ended questions, which seek confirmation or denial, are typically used during cross-examination. Binet identified these as "implicative" questions because they assume the existence of something.

Thus, from a theoretical perspective the psychology of questioning is not a new pursuit. Early psychological investigations of the relationship between the form of the question and the witness's memory for an event established that narrative questioning techniques were useful in obtaining accurate information about an event (Whipple, 1909). Long ago, people recognized that the narrative form of questioning had "the advantage of freedom from suggestion, of spontaneity and individuality" (Whipple, 1909, p. 157). However, subjects who gave narrative answers to open-ended questions frequently omitted mention of many details associated with the event they witnessed. Conversely, closed-ended questions probing for specific information were useful in eliciting more details about an event, although the number of recall errors increased dramatically when this questioning technique was used. Despite early acknowledgment of the limitations of using only one form of questioning to gather reliable information about past events, in a nonlegal context interviewers have been slow to implement more than one type of interrogative technique. For example, interviews conducted by the National Center for Health of persons known to have been injured by motor vehicles in the past year revealed that as many as 14 percent of 590 respondents failed to recall the accident in response to open-ended questions (Loftus, 1982).

In the courtroom, while it is generally thought that the narrative questioning technique produces a more accurate but less complete account, there are actually some instances in which something akin to a narrative question produces a more complete answer. This can occur when a lawyer questions potential jurors. In advising lawyers on this topic, one leading attorney notes, "The more a juror talks, the better you will come to know him or her" (Fahringer, 1980, p. 130). He advises that lawyers ask open-ended rather than closed-ended questions to achieve this goal. Thus, "How far did you go in school?" is better than "Did you attend college?" "How do you feel about the presumption of innocence?" is preferred to "Do you agree with the proposition that a defendant should be presumed to be innocent?" The objective in asking open-ended questions, then, is to gain more—not less—information. But this is rather a different situation from witness examinations.

CONTROVERSIES IN WITNESS EXAMINATION

Insofar as the questioning of witnesses as opposed to jurors is concerned, the adoption by the courts of a witness examination process that permits both open- and closed-ended questioning techniques reflects concerns for accuracy in the first place and completeness in the second. A third element of concern pervades the entire witness examination process—namely, the credibility of the witness's responses. Put another way, questions need to be asked so that the answers given are believed by the trier of fact. These three topics—accuracy, completeness, and credibility—have been the focus of renewed psychological inquiry into the theory of human question-answering.

As research findings on these three topics have accumulated, a number of controversial issues concerning the questioning process have arisen. Foremost among the controversies is the issue as to whether or not new information contained in a question can become integrated with the respondent's prior recollections and modify them, and the conditions under which this is more or less likely to occur (Loftus, 1983). From a theoretical standpoint, three phases of information-processing are pertinent to the questioning of witnesses: acquisition, retention, and retrieval. First, during the acquisition or encoding phase, the witness observes an event, and represents or encodes information about that event. Second is the retention phase, during which the encoded information is stored in memory. During the third phase—retrieval—the encoded information is retrieved from memory. Implications of recent research into the questioning process are that variations in retrieval strategy may influence the accuracy of recall. For example, in response to a question that contains a series of presuppositions that conflict with the encoded information, a subject may compromise by blending the recollected and the new information.

GENERAL PSYCHOLOCIAL UNDERPINNINGS OF WITNESS EXAMINATIONS

How can laboratory experiments that simulate the courtroom experience assist the trial practitioner in determining which witness examination techniques to use? To answer this question, we began by examining a variety of sources of advice to lawyers on how best to examine a witness. By scrutinizing the available lawyers' lore on the topic we hoped to assess the viability of advice commonly given to lawyers in light of current theories about the psychology of questioning and to determine which items of advice should be followed and which should be discarded.

The sources of advice we examined included Wellman's classic book, *The Art of Cross-Examination* (1936), and a panoply of more recent trial manuals, replete with the anecdotal wisdom of successful attorneys. We found advice on how to examine a hostile witness, an expert witness, a "know-it-all," and a child (Mauet, 1980). We found advice for prosecutors (Ficaro, 1982), defense lawyers (Bailey & Rothblatt, 1971), and civil lawyers (Norton, 1981). However, few guidelines were provided to distinguish intuition or superstition from sound principle. Some general items of advice could not reasonably be disputed, such as "Don't be boring" and "Be prepared." Other items were more intruiging, such as "Reveal any negative information yourself" and "Put the witness with the more details on the stand after—and not before—the witness with fewer details." We divided the advice into three broad categories: general advice applicable to all forms of witness examination; advice specific to direct examination; advice specific to cross-examination.

Preparing Your Witness

Accuracy, Confidence, and Credibility

Lawyers are typically advised not to put a witness on the stand without some preparation (Oliphant, 1978) on the supposition that a prepared witness will appear more confident and, hence, more credible to the jury. However, not all attorneys prepare their witnesses for cross-examination. An experiment to investigate the relationship between confidence and credibility was conducted by Wells, Lindsay, and Ferguson (1979). Half the witnesses were briefed for seven minutes about the upcoming cross-examination by the defense attorney. Other witnesses received no preparation. Prior to the examination, all witnesses saw a staged theft, and then identified a suspect from a six-person photo lineup. The examination included both open-ended and closed-ended questions. Subject-jurors viewed videotapes of the examinations and rated the witnesses for confidence and credibility. Witness confidence was perceived to be higher for briefed than for nonbriefed witnesses and, accordingly, the percentage of guilty verdicts among jurors who rated prepared witnesses was higher (50.5 percent) than that among jurors who rated unprepared witnesses (30.5 percent). What is most interesting about this study is the finding that preparation increased the credibility ratings of inaccurate witnesses far more than those of accurate witnesses (28 percent versus 5 percent). Consequently, a lawyer may wish to submit a cautionary instruction to jurors explaining that witness confidence is not necessarily correlated with accuracy.

Language Variation

Although attorneys tend to think of witness preparation as an opportunity to remind a witness of the content of the expected testimony, preparation can have a beneficial impact on the *form* of the testimony. The style and patterns in a witness's speech are more significant in determining the credibility of the testimony than most attorneys realize. The language variety used by a speaker significantly influences the listeners' subjective reactions (Labov, 1982; Lambert, 1981). Researchers who have specifically investigated the impact of language variation in the courtroom have confirmed the persuasive importance of speech style. Cramer (1979) interviewed more than a thousand jurors following their service on civil or criminal cases and found that they disapproved of attorneys who used jargon, slang, or extreme informality while questioning witnesses. Similarly, Parkinson (1981) found that defendants who were more polite and who spoke in more grammatically complete sentences were acquitted more often than other defendants.[1] Witness credibility is enhanced by the use of standard formal English as opposed to jargon, and use of the standard American dialect results in a more positive response than does use of a regional or accented dialect of English (Giles & Powesland, 1975).

Hypercorrect Speech

O'Barr (1981) discerned four distinct registers of speech commonly used in the course of many trials: formal legal language, containing much professional jargon; standard American English, used most frequently by lawyers and witnesses; colloquial English (closer to everyday language), used by some lawyers and witnesses; and subcultural dialects, such as black English. Analyses along these lines exposed the fact that many adult witnesses who have little or no experience with the courtroom situation speak in an aberrant way while testifying in court. Platt (1978) studied trial transcripts and isolated four distinctive anomalous lexical and syntactic features in the courtroom speech or "register" of lay people: (a) legal terminology—terms such as "allegedly" or other elaborate forms of expression, including the use of alternates ("residing or living"); (b) apologetic explanations or justifications; (c) hedges—for example, "as I recall," "I believe," "I think," "supposedly"; and (d) use of proper nouns to refer to other parties to the lawsuit.

Some investigators have wondered what impression is created by a witness who uses "hypercorrect speech," attempting to talk up to the courtroom audience by emulating the formal speech style used by judges and some lawyers. For example, a slightly injured patient was described by a witness as "in less than dire condition" and the period of three days was expressed as "seventy-two hours" (Mauet, 1980). Polite talk—a form of hypercorrect speech—further illustrates this phenomenon. Compare "The suspect exited his vehicle" with "The man got out of his car" (Charrow & Charrow, 1979). In an experiment designed specifically to measure the impact of these speech variations, it was found that subject-jurors were sensitive to linguistic subtleties, perceiving the hypercorrect speakers as significantly less convincing, less competent, less qualified, and less intelligent than speakers using standard formal English (Conley, O'Barr, & Lind, 1978).

Powerful and Powerless Speech

Further analyses of courtroom discourse conducted by Conley et al. (1978) helped delineate other variables in speech patterns that influence the credibility of a witness—namely "powerful" versus "powerless" speech styles. A powerful speech style is one in which the witness speaks without hedging ("I think," "it seemed like," "kind of," "sort of"); without hesitation ("well," "uhm," "er"); without overpoliteness ("sir," "please"); without overusing adverbial intensifiers ("surely," "definitely," "very"); and without a questioning intonation. In an experiment in which the power of these speech styles was manipulated, men and women who testified by omitting these "powerless" features from their own speech were rated as more credible, more competent, more intelligent, and more trustworthy than men and women who included these features in their responses. This finding implies that lawyers should advise their witnesses to avoid using these undesirable speech characteristics in the courtroom. Of course, hedges such as "I think" or "I guess" may call for objection under the rules of evidence as indicative of speculative or incompetent testimony (testimony that is not based on the personal knowledge of the witness).

In the past, trial lawyers have been advised not to interrupt a witness, particularly during cross-examination, on the theory that this can give the impression that the attorney is trying to prevent the witness from providing an accurate and complete response to the questions (Belli, 1982). The validity of this advice was tested by researchers who examined the effects on observers, such as jurors, of simultaneous speech in the courtroom—instances in which the witness and the examining or objecting attorney interrupt each other. Conley et al. (1978) compared conditions in which there were no witness-lawyer interruptions, instances in which the lawyer interrupted the witness, instances in which the witness interrupted the lawyer, and instances in which interruptions were generated equally by witness and lawyer. Observers' assessments of the lawyers in all three latter conditions were negative. In any of the interruption conditions, lawyers were rated as less intelligent, and observers considered their conduct to be unfair to the witnesses. Consequently, witnesses should be instructed not to interrupt their lawyers—and lawyers who wish to be favorably received should keep their own interruptions to a minimum.

Parkinson (1981) found that successful prosecutors employed different speech styles from successful defense lawyers. He compared the speech patterns of each in 19 criminal cases, studying the correlation of linguistic strategy and trial outcome. Prosecutors who included detailed questions enjoyed an advantage over those who did not. On the other hand, successful defense attorneys tended to use fewer afferent words and minimized the use of questions containing references to concepts sensed with the five senses. He found that defense lawyers who used more abstract and ambiguous language were more successful.

Formulate Questions Carefully

Many factors can influence the recall of events. Variations in the identity of the asker, the topic in issue, the voice intonation used, the length of the question, and the wording of the question have all been shown to affect the respondent in retrieving information from memory (see Loftus, 1979, for specific references). For example, studies by Harris (1973) and Loftus (1975) showed that subtle variations in the wording of a question can influence the range of possible answers. When subjects were asked how many items they recalled, the number they gave in response to the question increased in accordance with changes in the range of possible responses. When the response set was phrased in terms of small increments (1, 2, or 3 items), the mean number recalled was considerably less than that cited when the response set included greater increments of size (1, 5, or 10 items). Related research has indicated that when asked how fast a car was travelling when it "smashed" into another car, subjects were more likely to recall that they had seen broken glass at the scene of an accident than subjects who were asked how fast the cars were going when they "collided." Research along these lines has served to emphasize the importance of careful question formulation in persuading both the witness and the factfinder to adopt a particular theory of the case.

Semantic Persuasion

Danet (1980) argues that the questioning process is the central means by which reality is constructed and negotiated in the courtroom. She concludes that the outcome of the examination is as much a function of the verbal strategies and choices of the participants as it is of the supposed facts of the case. This theory is borne out of Danet's (1980) study of a controversial manslaughter trial in connection with a late abortion in which as many as 40 competing terms were used to refer to that "result of pregnancy." Danet examined the trial transcript to determine the extent to which a given witness was susceptible to "semantic contagion," tending to adopt language used by counsel for the opposition during the questioning process. Resistance to semantic contagion is clearly demonstrated by the following interchange between the prosecuting attorney and the defendant in this case:

Q: You didn't tell us, Doctor, whether you determined that the baby was alive or dead, did you, Doctor?

A: The *fetus* had no signs of life.

Danet found the witness was most susceptible to semantic contagion when questioned about the specific operation in issue. Resistance might have been greater if the witness had been specifically cautioned on the use of certain words. In this case, semantic persuasion was considered so important that the defense attorney sought an order to prevent the use of prejudicial words. As a result, the judge disallowed the words *smother*, *murder*, and *baby boy*.

Of course, lawyers who semantically depict events in terms that are never adopted or endorsed by the witnesses may undermine their cases by appearing unreasonable. For example, in a recent police misconduct case, persistent use by the prosecuting attorney of the word *tickets* to describe printed materials seized at the scene of an outdoor party, in the face of adamance by more than 20 witnesses that these were in fact invitations, probably had an effect opposite to that intended (*Baldwin v. Solheim*, 1984).

Avoid Negative Constructions

Lawyers are generally advised to avoid the use of negative constructions in question formulation (Kestler, 1982) to guard against ambiguity. Confusing questions containing multiple negatives may be generated when an attorney attempts to frame a closed-ended question during cross-examination by appending a question tag to an existing question, as in "So you never left the city that day, is that not correct?" (Grady, 1979). However, psycholinguistic research has established another reason to avoid negatives in that many people have difficulty comprehending negative constructions. This point was illustrated in a study of airline passengers presented with emergency landing instructions while waiting in an airport for a call to board their holiday flight (File & Jew, 1973). Subject-passengers who agreed to participate in the experiment were told to try to remember as much as possible about the emergency procedures, and that they would have five minutes following presentation of the instructions to write down all the details they could recall. The passage used was based closely on the actual instructions used by the airline. Some subjects were presented with statements phrased affirmatively while others were presented with negatively phrased statements. (Compare "When using the slides, remove your shoes, straighten your legs, and place hands on knees" with "When using the slides, do not keep your shoes on, do not bend your legs, nor fail to place hands on knees.") Performance was signficantly worse when instructions were negatively phrased. These results are consistent with the earlier laboratory work of Mehler (1963), who found that subjects who performed a rote-learning task recalled affirmative sentences better than negative sentences.

While there is evidence that all negative sentences take longer to process than affirmative sentences (Wason, 1961) and are more difficult to remember, some types of negative sentences are more difficult than others. For example, Vosniadou (1982) found that subjects took longer to verify syntactic negative sentences, such as "She hasn't remembered," than semantic negative sentences, such as "She has forgotten."

Pragmatic Implications

Carefully formulated questions may contain pragmatic implications that are influential in leading jurors to draw intended inferences. A pragmatic implication is simply a remark that causes the hearer to expect something that is neither explicitly stated nor necessarily logically implied in a sentence. For example, the sentence "The fugitive was able to leave the country" leads people to think he left, but it does not say he left, and he may not have. Similarly, the statement "The karate champion hit the cement block" pragmatically implies "The karate champion broke the cement block." The statement does not mention that the cement block was broken, but people tend to infer that this happened, and later on they actually misremember the statement, thinking that they heard what was only inferred by them.

Harris and Monaco (1978) and Harris, Teske and Ginns (1975) have effectively shown the power of pragmatic implications in courtroom testimony. In one study, subject-jurors heard an excerpt of a mock courtroom testimony and were later asked to indicate whether particular statements were true, false, or indeterminate based on that testimony. Half the subjects heard a given piece of information asserted directly, as in "I rang the burglar alarm," while the other half heard the same information, only pragmatically implied or suggested, as in "I ran up to the burglar alarm." Later on, even when subjects were specifically warned not to regard implications as definite facts, they generally included the implications among the facts.

The tendency of observers to draw pragmatic implications from implicit suggestions in a sentence is not dependent upon any particular syntactical arrangement. This occurs whether the evidence is presented in question form or in the form of an assertion or denial. For example, researchers found that observers inferred guilt on the part of the agent, Maxwell, assuming he was guilty, when either a question or a negative statement was used: "Did Maxwell strike his teacher?" versus "Maxwell did not strike his teacher" (Wegner, Wenclaff, Kerker, & Beattie, 1981).

Why do pragmatic implications cause distortions in memory? Related research has demonstrated that if the existence of an active item is assumed in a question, subjects will be more likely to affirm the existence of that item when questioned directly about it at a later stage (Loftus, 1979). Thus the earlier questions appear to alter memory. Questions that contain pragmatic implications may work in a similar manner. The implication causes a person to draw an inference that then becomes part of memory. Often the mere fact that a question is asked is sufficient to generate a new dimension of inquiry in the minds of the jurors. For example, in a study in which factors such as the history of the victim, the strength of the evidence, and the type of rape were varied, it was found that questions that cast aspersions on the sexual experience of the victim resulted in a less severe sentence for the defendant, irrespective of the strength of the evidence (Feild, 1980).

Strong Beginning and End

Almost without exception, attorneys are advised to start their case with a strong witness, to position a weak witness between two strong witnesses, and to end with a strong witness (Bellow & Moulton, 1981). The same basic principle is advocated for the examination of each witness. While some advocates stress the importance of a strong beginning, advising lawyers to cover the important facts early in the direct examination (Goldstein & Lane, 1969), others place more emphasis on a powerful finale. The well-known lawyer, Irving Younger, specifically recommends that examinations be ended on an "up-tick" and that the same procedure be observed before the court adjourns for every recess (Oliphant, 1978). Similarly, Belli (1982) endorses the tactic of ending cross-examinations on a high note.

Primacy and Recency Effects

Advice of this sort invokes what psychologists have called primacy and recency effects, based on studies of learning and memory. Classic work has shown that when people are given a list of items to remember, items at the beginning and at the end of the list are remembered well, while items from the middle of the list are remembered poorly (Baddeley, 1976; Loftus, 1980a). The primacy effect refers to the fact that the first few items have a greater chance of being remembered, while the recency effect refers to the fact that the last few items have a greater chance of being remembered. Psychologists describe the relationship between the moment when information is presented and how well that information is remembered as "the serial position effect."

While these phenomena have been extensively investigated by many experimental psychologists, few studies have adequately simulated the typical trial structure, in which the testimony of witnesses is alternately presented favorably on direct examination, and then subjected to critical scrutiny on cross-examination. Instead, the contrasting information has generally been presented in univalent blocks (Padilla, 1974). As a consequence, results from the laboratory have limited generalizability to the courtroom. A second problem in applying these theories to trial practice is that a great many other variables may be confounded with the timing of the presentation of information—factors such as juror competence or the amount of time between presentation of information and jury deliberation. In some cases jury instructions alone may take several hours to deliver. During the intervening time, jurors may forget either the information itself or its source (Litigation Sciences, 1981). Lawyers who follow the serial position advice should take note of the negative results obtained by Padilla (1974). In a carefully controlled study in which testimony was presented via both direct and cross-examination and closing arguments were given, Padilla found no significant primacy or recency effects when the order of information was varied.

DIRECT EXAMINATION TECHNIQUES

The More Complete the Description, the More Convincing

Compare the following two questions about a witness's morning activities: "You say in describing your morning activities that you awoke from sleep and dressed?" and "You awoke, rolled over, swung both of your legs over the bed, put your weight on your right leg, then the left, lifted yourself off the bed, and walked to the dresser? You removed your pajama top, the bottoms, then reached out with your left hand, and opened the drawer?" Is the latter version, by virtue of its completeness, more persuasive? Prosecutor Michael Picaro (1982) notes that, through the inclusion of many details in questions asked of an eyewitness, an event that took place in a few seconds can "be made to seem like hours to the jury" (p. 9). Then, if the witness is asked to identify the defendant in court, the jury will be more persuaded of accuracy of the identification. One study that bears indirectly on this issue was conducted by Parkinson (1981). He found that prosecutors who were more verbally assertive, thus whose witness examinations lasted for a long time as a result of the greater number of questions posed to witnesses, were more successful. We know of no research that has attempted to replicate this finding.

Is it generally the case that the more detailed description is better? Assuming the examiner does not violate other advice to lawyers— namely, "Don't supply too many details on peripheral matters," nor the umbrella advice, "Don't be boring"—this advice makes sense under one condition. If the detailed account is a more vivid account, the advice is supported by a host of studies on the persuasive power of vivid information.

Vividness Effects

Vivid information reaches us in a way that nonvivid information cannot. One study of the power of vivid information was conducted in the context of a simulated legal trial (Reyes, Thompson, & Bower,

1980). Subjects read testimony from a hypothetical trial of a man accused of drunk driving. Some subjects read pallid prosecution testimony and vivid, more detailed defense testimony, while others read vivid and detailed prosecution and pallid defense testimony. For example, one item of prosecution evidence was intended to establish that the defendant was drunk shortly before leaving a party to drive home. In the pallid version, the defendant staggered against a table, knocking a bowl to the floor. The vivid version of the item stated that his action knocked "a bowl of guacamole dip" to the floor "splattering guacamole all over the white shag carpet." Similarly, an item of defense evidence was designed to establish that the defendant had not been drunk. It described his ability to leap out of the way of an approaching "car" in the pallid version, or a "bright orange Volkswagen" in the vivid version.

Subjects had to recall information from the trial and then render a verdict. For subjects who rendered their verdict one day after the trial testimony, the power of vivid information was substantial. Those exposed to vivid prosecution testimony were more likely to render guilty verdicts while those exposed to vivid defense testimony were more likely to acquit. Based upon these and other findings, Nisbett and Ross (1980) concluded that vivid information—that is, concrete sensory, and personally relevant information—may have a disproportionate impact on beliefs and inferences. On the contrary, pale and dull statistical information, which is often a more accurate reflection of the truth, can be totally ignored. A leading explanation for the greater impact of vivid information is that it is better remembered and thus is more available to the subject-juror in reaching the verdict (Taylor & Thompson, 1982). Although some investigators have comforted us with the ideas that the power of vivid information is much weaker that Nisbett and Ross (1980) would have us believe, the potential for great influence still remains. One consequence of the vividness effect on advice for direct examination is that the more detailed and vivid account will be more persuasive.

Ficaro (1982) also recommends placing the witness who sees, hears, or remembers less about an event on the stand before the witness who can offer more detailed testimony. His reasoning: This will avoid potential impeachment of one witness by reference to information provided by the other. We know of no psychological studies that bear directly on this advice.

Use Loopback Questions

Lawyers are prohibited by evidentiary rules from repeating testimony, or presenting cumulative evidence. Tanford (1983) distinguished three ways in which testimony can be repeated: repetition by one witness; repetition by different witnesses; and repetition by the examining attorney. He notes that the latter form should particularly be avoided because it is most objectionable and boring. However, an important point can be hammered home if prior answers are occasionally included in a question. Jeans (1975), for example, recommends that key phrases should be selected from the witnesses' testimony and repeated to educate the jurors. This technique is referred to as "loopback questioning" or "back-tracking" and entails forming a question by incorporating part or all of a witness's previous answer into a subsequent question. For example:

Q: What happened next?

A: I opened the door.

Q: When you opened the door, what did you see?

Loopback questions are recommended for a variety of reasons, including emphasis of a favorable answer (Mauet, 1980). A loopback can also provide variation in the question format, make transitions in a line of questioning, or conclude an examination. Alternatively, loopbacks are useful to regain control of a witness who is slipping away, permitting the examiner to refer to a question that the witness answered favorably and to continue from there (Kestler, 1982).

Repetition and Recall

As a device to produce repetition of important points, loopback questions are undoubtedly a valuable technique. The importance of repetition memory is so well documented that at least one textbook on human learning and memory devotes an entire chapter to the topic (Crowder, 1976). Information that is repeated is more likely to be stored in jurors' memories, and thus increases the likelihood they will recall it during their review of the evidence during deliberation.

High Versus Low Credibility and Forgetting

Whether the use of a loopback question will also increase the persuasive nature of a particular point is still an open question. We know of no experiment to test this hypothesis, although a trial simulation study on the "sleeper effect" has some bearing on this question (Litigation Sciences, 1981). The number of times that certain testimony was repeated was varied to assess the effect on the beliefs of jurors. Intervals of up to four weeks between the presentation of evidence and the final belief measures were used. A major finding was that repetition made a significant difference in the case of a witness with high credibility but not in the case of a witness with low credibility. What is especially interesting is the finding that the subject-jurors did not remember which party had introduced the evidence. The fact that the evidence was recalled at all after the longest intervals of time emphasizes the usefulness of repetition.

Raise Unpleasant Facts on Direct

Keeton (1973) warns lawyers that when their witnesses are vulnerable to attack from unfavorable facts directly related to central issues in the case, it is usually better to reveal these facts on direct examination. One's attitude toward this weakness should be matter of fact, for if the lawyers acts positively, the jury is less likely to believe that any confidence in the witness is shaken. Advice to concede weaknesses in the witnesses' testimony is so fundamental that some lawyers have called it "a cardinal rule of direct examination," stating that a sincere disclosure of the weaknesses will make the witness a "human being to the jury and will protect the witness from attack on cross-examination" (Kadish & Brofman, 1980). Of course, from a procedural standpoint, if one elects to introduce harmful evidence oneself, this may raise the problem of impeaching one's own witness if there is no other basis for admissibility of the testimony.

Attitude Change and Inoculation

When a lawyer raises a damaging fact on direct examination, does this have the effect of "inoculating" the jury against its ultimate exposure by an opposing party? In other words, can it immunize? One research paradigm that may be relevant is that used in traditional studies of attitude change. For example, in a study conducted well before the Russians had produced their first atomic bomb, subjects were given one- and two-sided arguments in support of the view that the Russians would not be able to produce the bomb in the next five years (Lumsdaine & Janis, 1953). The two-sided argument also included a few opposing points, such as the fact that there were large uranium mines in Siberia. After hearing either the one-sided or the two-sided view, subjects heard a counter-argument to the effect that the Russians would produce the bomb in less than five years. The results were clear: Subjects who first heard the two-sided argument were less persuaded by the counterargument than those who initially heard the one-sided argument. In writing about inoculation, McGuire (1964) has used a medical analogy. He argues that people develop many beliefs over their lives that are never seriously challenged. For example, we believe we should brush our teeth twice a day, or that we should not go outside without a jacket if we have a cold. Just as a person builds up immunity to a disease (like smallpox) when given a small dose of the disease-causing germs (smallpox vaccination), so these cultural truisms will be more resistant to challenges if people are made aware of arguments against them. In a more empirical vein, McGuire and Papageorgis (1963) tested two methods for producing resistance in people to persuasive communication. Subjects read a cultural truism, followed by either supportive arguments or by a refutational defense (arguments against the truism followed by a defense against these arguments). Several days later, subjects received information attacking the cultural truism. Who was less persuaded by this attack? A refutational defense was clearly superior to a supportive defense in protecting the individual's beliefs against subsequent counterarguments.

Although the effects of inoculation may be clear in the attitude change studies, it must be kept in mind that the materials used in these studies differ from the types of arguments that jurors hear in a courtroom. Two social psychologists have warned that "there is little evidence to support any generalization of inoculation effects to the more controversial opinions and issues that serve as the content of most persuasive communications in everyday life" (Tedeschi & Lindskold, 1976). In other words, the attitude studies hint that innoculation may work, but it remains for further researchers to confirm the beneficial effects of this technique in a courtroom situation.

In-Court Identification
at the Beginning of the Testimony

Although individual styles may lead lawyers to differ as to the most effective moment in the examination to call for the in-court identification of a suspect by a witness, Ficaro (1982) advises prosecutors to do it early. This has an important psychological advantage, he argues. Once the witness has pointed out the defendant as the offender, the prosecutor may assume this fact in phrasing subsequent questions:

"When did you first notice the defendant?" "What was the first thing that the defendant said to you?" "Where did the defendant point the gun?" This is calculated to produce in the jurors' minds a running picture of the defendant committing the crime, as opposed to their visualizing an abstract, faceless assailant.

Imagination and Persuasion

Some interesting new psychological work suggests that causing people to imagine an event in a particular way will also lead them to think that the event is more likely (Carroll, 1978; Gregory, Cialdini, & Carpenter, 1982). Imagining that a tornado will strike the coast of Florida, or that Ted Kennedy will win the next presidential election, makes these events seem subjectively to be more likely. Imagining good things (like winning a contest) or bad things (like being arrested for armed robbery) makes us more likely to believe that these things could happen to us. Why does this occur? According to Anderson (1983), in everyday natural settings people engage in imagination processes such as reflecting and ruminating. Decisions about what we or other people are likely to do are often made on the basis of how easy it is to imagine a sequence of actions occurring. When we create a scenario for all or part of the actions in a given situation, the sequence becomes more available in our minds. Put another way, because these mental images have already formed, upon any subsequent consideration they may be more readily pictured than before. Another possibility, however, is that the initial mental construction of an event happening in a particular way creates a cognitive "set" that impairs the ability to see the event in competing ways (Gregory et al., 1982). Whatever the precise psychological mechanism that is responsible for the "imagining effect," these ideas lend support to Ficaro's advice.

CROSS-EXAMINATION TECHNIQUES

Cross-examination of a witness may accomplish a number of different purposes. In some instances, the witness's responses are crucial—for example, when the objective is to discredit a witness by revealing biases and prejudices, or to impeach a witness by exposing prior inconsistent statements. At other times, the witness's response is considerably less vital, for the witness merely provides a vehicle by means of which the attorney can testify. In this case, the objective is to elicit admissions from the witness that tend to corroborate or credit the opponent's case, thereby creating a record to which the attorney can refer in substantiation of arguments at the close of the trial. Since the opposing attorneys can assert their views of the facts in their own words only through the questions that they ask, control of the witness is crucial in eliciting brief answers to the questions posed (Danet, Hoffman, Kermish, Rafn, & Stayman, 1980).

No matter what the particular purpose of the cross-examination, success usually depends on the ability of the attorney to maintain control of the situation. Consequently, during cross-examination attorneys concentrate on posing questions that can be answered in only one way by the witness on the stand. The question form is structured to restrict the opportunity for the witness to give extensive explanations in response.

Ask Leading Questions

In discussing cross-examination techniques, Hupy (1982) explicitly states, "You should ask leading questions and suggest the answer you want whenever possible." The rationale permitting leading questions is based on the theory that testing a witnesses' memory, veracity, and accuracy is facilitated by the narrow structure of the leading question (Marshall, 1980).

Definitional Problems

How do we identify a leading question? Even experts agree that the definition of a leading question is far from precise (Marshall, 1980). The prevailing legal standard is found in *United States v. Durham* (1963, p. 592), describing a leading question as one which "so suggests to the witness the specific tenor of the reply desired by counsel that such a reply is likely to be given irrespective of an actual memory." Questions can be leading in certain contexts, or leading by virtue of the inclusion of suggestive details—such as "Was the getaway car a red 1978 Firebird with whitewalls and a pair of dice hanging from the rearview mirror?"

Support for the view that the leading nature of a question cannot be found exclusively in the syntactical formula that the question follows comes from Dunstan (1980), who advocates consideration of other communication variables in the courtroom. He finds coercion in the ability of attorneys to use specific conversational rules of the courtroom to advantage, while a witness, unwittingly following normal social rules, is put at a distinct disadvantage. For example, in a normal social situation, when someone asks a question, he or she is often looking for information. By comparison, in the courtroom, the attorney usually knows the answer to the question he or she is posing. (Wellman, 1936, quoted a successful cross-examiner who said "A lawyer should never ask a witness on cross-examination a question unless in the first place he knew what the answer would be, or, in the second place, he didn't care.") In the courtroom, requests for information are in fact commands that the witness cannot disobey. Conventions to avoid embarrassment and humiliation do not apply. Normal turn-taking rules of conversation are inoperant as the attorney controls the conversation and also the pauses between conversation. In short, the conversational rules of the courtroom coerce the witness regardless of the syntax of the questions. This analysis suggests that we might profitably keep the rules of the courtroom in mind when deciding whether or not a question is leading.

Credibility, Accuracy, and Leading Questions

Whatever the precise definition of a leading question, our concern here is with the impact of such questions on jurors. In an experiment by Wells, Lindsay, and Ferguson (1979) subject-jurors observed witnesses who were examined by means of either leading or nonleading questions. Leading questions were characterized by the occasional assertion of a false premise and by efforts to elicit contradictions and short responses. For example, the question, "The person you saw had a jacket, didn't she?" was later followed by "Was the jacket she had on tan or brown?" when, in fact, the suspect had not been wearing a jacket. Nonleading questions included no false premises, and were largely open-ended in nature—for example, "Describe what the person was wearing." Irrespective of witness accuracy, there was a slight trend of diminished witness credibility in the leading question condition (73 percent versus 81 percent belief). However, when the data were broken down by witness accuracy, inaccurate witnesses were more credible when nonleading questions were used, while accurate witnesses were more credible when leading questions were used.

Standardized Implicature

A sophisticated theoretical analysis of leading questions was postulated by Swann, Guiliano, and Wegner (1982). They hypothesized that observers such as jurors would use their knowledge of conversational rules to infer that an examiner has an evidentiary basis to include certain information in leading questions. Once observers accept the validity of the premises, they may go further and make corresponding inferences about the respondent. In this way, premises embedded in leading questions may quickly become foregone conclusions in the minds of jurors. Support for these hypotheses was provided in two studies in which some observers heard questions that suggested a person was an extravert (e.g., "What would you do if you wanted to liven things up at a party?" or "In what situations are you most talkative?"). Other observers heard questions suggesting that the respondent was an introvert (e.g., "In what situations do you wish you could be more outgoing?" and "Tell me about sometime when you felt left out from some social group."). Subsequently, the observers had to rate the person on a number of bipolar scales (extravert-introvert, talkative-quiet). The leading questions biased the ratings. Swann et al. concluded that the underlying premises in the leading questions were treated as conjectural evidence by the observers in forming impressions of the respondents. Even when the observers were told that the questions were randomly selected, their impressions of the respondents were still swayed by the presuppositions in the questions. These results suggest that the presuppositions contained in leading questions can attain legitimacy in the minds of jurors and induce them to misperceive the witnesses. This may be precisely what is intended by many cross-examiners.

Elicit Yes or No Answers

In almost any trial manual that addresses cross-examination, tacticians will advise attorneys to ask questions that elicit yes or no answers (Goldstein & Lane, 1969; Kestler, 1982). In this way, the witnesses can be prevented from providing unanticipated answers. By confining the witness's responses, the attorney can more readily discredit the witness (Kestler, 1982). For example, an examiner who elicits a succession of yes answers may appear to be obtaining concessions from a witness (Jeans, 1975). In other words, cross-examination can also be a rehabilitative process if, in trying to repair or undo any damage created by the direct examination, an attorney eliminates the opportunity for the witness to further damage the case (Oliphant, 1978).

Inducing Agreement

A special form of a yes/no question, the *tag question*, is useful in eliciting agreement. In an analysis of tag questions, Loftus (1980b) explained how agreement is generally obtained. In her experiment, subjects watched one of two versions of a film. One contained a bicycle and the other did not. After viewing the film, half of the subjects received the question: "Did you see a bicycle?" The other half received the question: "You did see a bicycle, didn't you?" The findings confirmed that tag questions do produce more yes answers than other questions—irrespective of whether the bicycle was actually present. Loftus noted that the tag functions by expressing the likelihood that the subject of the question exists. She concluded that when a person is asked about a recollection in a tag question form it is implied that the speaker expects a certain response. As this experiment indicated, it is most probable that the speaker will receive the expected response.

Credibility of Fragmented Testimony

Effects of limiting a witness's responses to yes or no answers were investigated in a series of studies on language in the courtroom (Conley, O'Barr, & Lind, 1978) in which fragmented (brief) and narrative (lengthy) answers were given by witnesses. Subject-jurors listened to audiotapes of the testimony and rated both the witnesses and the lawyers. The researchers predicted that the narrative style of presentation would be more persuasive than the fragmented style. This hypothesis was confirmed. The major effect, however, was the fact that the subject-jurors tended to evaluate a witness in terms of the way they perceived the lawyer's evaluation of a witness (Abbey & O'Barr, 1981). If the lawyer constrained the witness by asking many questions that called for only brief answers (as opposed to asking a few questions that allowed for expansive answers) the lawyer was perceived to have little faith in that witness. Accordingly, the subject-jurors rated that witness as less competent, less intelligent, and less assertive.

In general, advice to elicit yes or no answers is supported by the psychological literature. In fact, this trial technique can accomplish far more than the mere protection of a lawyer's case from unexpected answers during cross-examination.

Elicit Answers of "I Don't Recall"

Ficaro advised, "The more times you can get a defendant to say, 'I don't recall,' 'I don't know,' 'I can't remember,' the closer you are to conviction" (1982). Although this statement refers specifically to criminal trials, there is no reason why this advice cannot apply to civil litigation. To mitigate the impact of a series of 'I don't remember' or 'I don't know' responses on cross-examination, lawyers are often advised to encourage their clients to include a few 'I don't know' responses during the direct examination (Keeton, 1973). This tactic is designed to enhance witness credibility for "every juror will view with suspicion the witness who remembers everything on direct examination, and can remember nothing on cross examination" (Goldstein & Lane, 1969, p. 54).

The Desire for Consistency

In discussing properties of courtroom questions, Dunstan provides some insight into the practical applications of this advice (1980). He illustrated how efforts of a witness to appear consistent can be used advantageously by lawyers. In the following example, after eliciting a response from a witness who agreed to a vague description that an evening was quite warm, the attorney then shifted the focus to the issue of how warm it was:

> Q: . . . and . . . you rolled down the window of your car . . .
> A: [It] was rolled down.
> Q: . . . [it] was a warm evening?
> A: Yeah.
> Q: . . . 'bout how warm was it? [Do you] remember?
> A: No, I don't.
> Q: Seventies? Eighties?
> A: I don't remember!

Once the witness had committed herself to the position that she did not know how warm it was, when the question was repeated, she reemphasized that she did not remember the temperature. Dunstan argued that if the witness followed her first "I don't know" by conceding that the temperature was in the seventies or eighties, she would seem inconsistent and unreliable. Thus, the witness elected to appear consistent at the expense of appearing unreasonable. Despite the fact that "quite warm" and "seventies or eighties" are close in meaning, the witness appears unreasonable when she repeats "I don't know."

Attorneys who exploit a witness's desire to appear consistent by structuring cross-examination questions to elicit "I don't know" answers may diminish the witness's credibility if the response becomes more unreasonable with every repetition. Alternatively, a witness who constantly responds in this manner may lose credibility because the response is perceived as a form of a hedge, or powerless speech. However, these explanations may be too simplistic. For example, if the response is given following a question irrelevant to the central issues in the case, witness credibility may not be diminished. The matter requires empirical investigation.

Accuracy and Memory for Details

Some recent psychological findings tend to contradict a belief commonly held by jurors. Many jurors believe that an eyewitness who can supply many details observed at the scene of a crime must be more reliable than an eyewitness whose memory for trivial details is poor. In a study in which accurate and inaccurate eyewitnesses were cross-examined on their ability to recollect eleven details peripheral to the scene of the crime, witnesses who identified an innocent person as the thief recalled 8.5 items, whereas witnesses who identified the true culprit recalled an average of 6.36 trivial details on cross-examination (Wells & Leippe, 1981). As such, subject-jurors were more readily persuaded by inaccurate than accurate eyewitnesses (58.3 percent versus 37.5 percent). Thus, a witness who frequently answers "I don't know" may, in fact, have accurately identified the suspect. In light of these findings, lawyers may wish to submit a cautionary instruction to jurors noting that there is not necessarily a positive correlation between accurate identification and memory for peripheral details.

CONCLUSIONS

Advice to trial lawyers on how best to conduct a direct or cross-examination is freely offered. Some of this advice is supported by existing psychological literature. Although it is difficult to isolate a piece of advice that is blatantly erroneous, it is common to find example for which there is no empirical justification. Moreover, in many instances the proffered advice is extremely simplistic. Based upon existing empirical evidence, far more sophisticated suggestions could profitably be made and followed.

NOTE

1. Of course, this correlation does not necessarily imply that a causal relationship exists between the defendant's speech style and the outcome of the trial.

REFERENCES

Abbey, M., & O'Barr, W. M. (1981). Law and language: The Duke University studies. *Trial Diplomacy Journal*, 26-29.

Anderson, C. (1983). Imagination and expectation: The effect of imagining behavioral scripts on personal intentions. *Journal of Personality and Social Psychology, 45:* 293-305.

Baddeley, A. D. (1976). *The psychology of memory.* New York: Basic Books.

Bailey, F. L., & Rothblatt, H. B. (1971). *Successful techniques for criminal trials.* Rochester, NY: Lawyers Cooperative Publishing Co.

Baldwin v. Solheim C81-616(T)C. (W. Wash D.C., June 4, 1984).

Belli, M. M., Sr. (1982). *Modern Trials* (2nd ed.). St. Paul, MN: West.

Bellow, G., & Moulton, B. (1981). *The lawyering process: Preparing and presenting the case.* Mineola, NY: Foundation Press.

Carroll, J. C. (1978). The effect of imagining an event on expectations for the event: An interpretation in terms of the availability heuristic. *Journal of Experimental Social Psychology, 14,* 88-96.

Charrow, R. P., & Charrow, V. (1979). Making legal language understandable: A psycholinguistic study of jury instructions. *Columbia Law Review, 79,* 1306-1374.

Conley, J. M., O'Barr, W. M., & Lind, E. A. (1978). The power of language: Presentational style in the courtroom. *Duke Law Journal, 6,* 1375-1399.

Cramer, M. M. (1979). Trial balloon: A view from the jury box. *Litigation, 6,* 3-4.

Crowder, R. G. (1976). *Principles of learning and memory.* Hillsdale, NJ: Lawrence J. Erlbaum.

Danet, B. (1980). 'Baby' or 'Fetus'?: Language and the construction of reality in a manslaughter trial. *Semiotica, 32,* 187-219.

Danet, B., Hoffman, K. B., Kermish, N. C., Rafn, H. J., & Stayman, D. G. (1980). An ethnography of questioning in the courtroom. In R. W. Shuy & A. Shnukal (Eds.), *Language use and the uses of language* (pp. 222-234). Washington, DC: Georgetown University Press.

Dunstan, R. (1980). Context for coercion: Analyzing properties of courtroom "questions." *British Journal of Law and Social Psychology, 7,* 61-77.

Fahringer, H. P. (1980). In the valley of the blind: A primer on jury selection in a criminal case. *Law and Contemporary Problems, 43* (4), 116-136.

Ficaro, M. (1982). *Prosecution of violent crimes.* Paper presented in a seminar to the National College of District Attorneys, Colorado Springs, CO.

Feild, S. (1980). Rape trials and jurors' decisions: A psychological analysis of the effects of victim, defendant and the case characteristics. *Law and Human Behavior, 3,* 261-262.

File, S. E., & Jew, A. (1973). Syntax and the recall of instructions in a realistic situation. *British Journal of Psychology, 64,* 65-70.

Giles, H., & Powesland, P. F. (1975). *Speech style and social evaluation.* New York: Academic Press.

Goldstein, I., & Lane, F. (1969). *Goldstein's trial techniques* (2nd ed.). Callaghan & Co.

Grady, J. F. (1979). From the bench. *Litigation, 6,* 62-63.

Gregory, W. L., Cialdini, R. B., & Carpenter, K. M. (1982). Self relevant scenarios as mediators of likelihood estimates and compliance: Does imagining make it so? *Journal of Personality and Social Psychology, 43,* 89-99.

Harris, R. J. (1973). Answering questions containing marked and unmarked adjectives and adverbs. *Journal of Experimental Psychology, 97,* 399-401.

Harris, R. J., & Monaco, G. E. (1978). The psychology of pragmatic implication: Information processing between the lines. *Journal of Experimental Psychology: General, 107,* 1-22.

Harris, R. J., Teske, R. R., & Ginns, M. J. (1975). Memory for pragmatic implications from courtroom testimony. *Bulletin of the Psychonomic Society, 6,* 494-496.

Hupy, M. F. (1982). Preparation for and cross-examination of identification witnesses at trial. *Wisconsin Bar Bulletin,* 14-17.

Jeans, W. (1975). *Trial advocacy.* St. Paul, MN: West.

Johnson, H. H., & Watkins, T. A. (1971). The effects of message repetitions on immediate and delayed attitude change. *Psychonomic Society, 22,* 101-103.

Kadish, M. J., & Brofman, R. A. (1980). Direct examination techniques for the criminal defense attorney. *Trial Diplomacy Journal, 3,* 41.

Kearsley, G. P. (1976). Questions and question asking in verbal discourse: A cross-disciplinary review. *Journal of Psycholinguistic Research, 5,* 355-375.

Keeton, R. E. (1973). *Trial tactics and methods.* (2nd ed.). Boston: Little, Brown.

Kestler, J. L. (1982). *Questioning techniques and tactics.* New York: McGraw-Hill.
Labov, W. (1982). Objectivity and commitment in linguistic science: The case of the Black English trial in Ann Arbor. *Languages in Society, 11,* 165-201.
Lambert, W. E. (1981). The social psychology of language: A perspective for the 1980s. *Focus, 5,* 1-8.
Litigation Sciences. (1981). Witness credibility: An application of psychological data. *For the Defense, 23,* 28-20.
Loftus, E. F. (1975). Leading questions and the eyewitness report. *Cognitive Psychology, 7,* 560-572.
Loftus, E. F. (1979). *Eyewitness testimony.* Cambridge, MA: Harvard University Press.
Loftus, E. F. (1980a). *Memory.* Reading, MA: Addison-Wesley.
Loftus, E. F. (1980b). Language and memories in the judicial system. In R. Shuy & A. Shnukal (Eds.), *Language use and the uses of language* (pp. 257-268). Washington, DC: Georgetown University Press.
Loftus, E.F. (1982). Memory and its distortions. In A. G. Kraut (Ed.), *The G. Stanley Hall lecture series* (pp. 119-154). Washington, DC: American Psychological Association.
Loftus, E. F. (1983). Misfortunes of memory. *Philosophical Transactions of the Royal Society, 302,* 413-421.
Lumsdaine, A. A., & Janis, I. L. (1953). Resistance to "counterpropoganda" produced by one-sided and two-sided "propoganda" presentations. *Public Opinion Quarterly, 17,* 311-318.
Marshall, J. (1980). *Law and psychology in conflict* (2nd ed.). Indianapolis, IN: Bobbs-Merrill.
Mauet, T. A. (1980). *Fundamentals of trial techniques.* Boston: Little, Brown.
McGaffey, R. (1983). Communication strategies and research needs in selecting juries. In R. J. Matlon & R. J. Crawford (Eds.), *Communication strategies in the practice of lawyering* (pp. 250-273). Annandale, VA: Speech Communication Association.
McGovern, F. E. & Davis, J. H. (1983). From the legal professions: Legal strategies and research needs in direct and cross examination. In R. J. Matlon & R. J. Crawford (Eds.), *Communication strategies in the practice of lawyering* (pp. 318-342). Annandale, VA: Speech Communication Association.
McGuire, W. J. (1964). Inducing resistance to persuasion: Some contemporary approaches. In L. Berkowitz (Ed.), *Advances in experimental social psychology* (pp. 191-229). New York: Academic Press.
McGuire, W. J., & Papageorgis, D. (1963). The relative efficacy of various types of prior-belief defense in producing immunity against persuasion. *Journal of Abnormal and Social Psychology, 2,* 346-351.
Mehler, J. (1963). Some effects of grammatical transformations on the recall of English sentences. *Journal of Verbal Learning and Verbal Behavior, 2,* 346-351.
Nisbett, R., & Ross, L. (1980). *Human inference: strategies and shortcomings of social judgment.* Englewood Cliffs, NJ: Prentice-Hall.
Norton, J. E. (Ed.). (1981). *The anatomy of a personal injury lawsuit.* Washington, DC: Association of Trial Lawyers.
O'Barr, W. (1981). The language of the law. In C. A. Ferguson & S. B. Heath (Eds.), *Language in the U.S.A.* (pp. 386-406). New York: Cambridge University Press.
Ogle, R., Parkman, A., & Porter, J. (1980). Questions: Leading and otherwise. *The Judges Journal, 19,* 42-45.
Oliphant, R. E. (Ed.) (1978). *Trial techniques with Irving Younger.* Minneapolis, MN: National Practice Institute.
Padilla, E. R. (1974). *The effects of order of presentation and cognitive complexity on the decisions and perceptions of simulated jurors.* Doctoral dissertation, University of Washington. (Listed in *Dissertation Abstracts International.*)
Parkinson, M. (1981). Verbal behavior and courtroom success. *Communication Education, 30,* 22-32.

Platt, M. (1978). Language and speakers in the courtroom. In J. J. Jaeger, (Ed.), *Proceedings of the fourth annual meeting of the Berkeley Linguistics Society* (pp. 617-627).

Reyes, R. M., Thompson, W. C., & Bower, G. H. (1980). Judgmental biases resulting from differing availabilities of arguments. *Journal of Personality and Social Psychology, 39,* 2-12.

Saks, M., & Hastie, R. (1978). *Social psychology in court.* New York: Van Nostrand Reinhold.

Simon, R. J. (1983). Comments on jury selection and jury behavior papers. In R. J. Matlon & R. J. Crawford (Eds.), *Communication strategies in the practice of lawyering* (pp. 274-277). Annandale, VA: Speech Communication Association.

Swann, W. B., Guiliano, T., & Wegner, D. M. (1982). Where leading questions can lead: The power of conjecture in social interaction. *Journal of Personality and Social Psychology, 42,* 1025-1035.

Tanford, J. A. (1983). *The trial process.* Charlottesville, VA: Michie Co.

Taylor, S. E., & Thompson, S. C. (1982). Stalking the elusive "vividness" effect. *Psychological Review, 89,* 155-181.

Tedeschi, J.T., & Lindskold, S. (1976). *Social psychology.* New York: John Wiley.

Vosniadou, S. (1982). Drawing inferences from semantically positive and negative implicative predicates. *Journal of Psycholinguistic Research, 11,* 77-93.

Wason, P. (1961). Response to affirmative and negative statements. *British Journal of Psychology, 52,* 133-142.

Wegner, D. A., Wenclaff, R. Kerker, R. M., & Beattie, A. E. (1981). Incrimination through innuendo: Can media questions become public answers? *Journal of Personality and Social Psychology, 40,* 822-832.

Wellman, F. L. (1936). *The art of cross-examination,* (2nd ed.). New York: Coller.

Wells, G. L., & Leippe, M. R. (1981). How do triers of fact infer the accuracy of eyewitness identifications? Using memory for peripheral detail can be misleading. *Journal of Applied Psychology, 66,* 682-687.

Wells, G. L., Lindsay, R.C.L., & Ferguson, T. J. (1979). Accuracy, confidence, and juror perceptions in eyewitness identification. *Journal of Applied Psychology, 64,* 440-448.

Whipple, G. M. (1909). The observer as reporter: A survey of the psychology of testimony. *Psychological Bulletin, 6,* 153-170.

Zimmerman, G. I. (1983). Communication strategies and research needs in direct and cross-examination. In R. J. Matlon & R. J. Crawford (Eds.), *Communication strategies in the practice of lawyering* (pp. 343-352). Annandale, VA: Speech Communication Association.

CHAPTER 11

Jury Instructions

AMIRAM ELWORK
BRUCE D. SALES

> The purpose of trial by jury is to prevent oppression by the Government by providing a safeguard against the corrupt or overzealous prosecutor and against the compliant, biased, or eccentric judge. . . . Given this purpose, the essential feature of a jury lies in the interposition between the accused and his accuser of the common-sense judgment of a group of laymen. (*Williams v. Florida*, 1970, p. 100)

The right to the "benefits of trial by jury" was one of the justifications on which our founding fathers based the Declaration of Independence. Subsequently, they guaranteed this right in the Sixth and Seventh Amendments to the Constitution. As exemplified by the U.S. Supreme Court opinion quoted above, the jury system continues to be viewed as an essential feature of our democratic form of government. Such faith is in part based on a long-standing and strong sense of confidence in the jury's "common-sense" ability to reach a correct verdict. This chapter raises the issue of whether our present jury system, when evaluated empirically rather than intuitively, deserves such confidence.

In considering this issue we must first ask, "What is a correct verdict?" Certainly, the word *correct* can refer to both the outcome of a verdict (i.e., substantive due process) as well as the process by which it is reached (i.e., procedural due process). Within each of these categories, a long list of "correct verdict" attributes can be formulated and debated, but it is beyond the scope of this chapter to discuss all of them.

Our focus will be on one specific requirement of a correct verdict— namely, that it be reached in light of the relevant law. This principle was established in *Sparf v. United States* (1895), a case in which the U.S. Supreme Court concluded that the jury's duty is "to take a law from the court and apply the law to the facts as they find them to be from the evidence (p. 102)." As the *Sparf* case applied only to federal trials, state jurisdictions did not have to follow this rule, but most did. Today, most jurisdictions require the jury to follow the law in reaching a verdict, both in terms of process and outcome, and they prohibit the jury from behaving in ways that are contrary to the law.

There are several exceptions to this rule. For example, the laws of Georgia, Indiana, and Maryland allow juries to decide questions of law as well as of fact. This does not mean that juries are permitted to ignore the law. Even in these states, they are still required to reach their verdicts by following a legally prescribed process. However, they are given more latitude in terms of the outcomes. While it still is required for juries to reach their decisions with full knowledge of the legally prescribed verdicts, they are allowed to vary from the law in accordance with their own sense of justice. (For a fuller review of this see Jacobsohn, 1977; Scheflin & Van Dyke, 1980.)

To summarize, in most jurisdictions it is the duty of the jury to reach a verdict that conforms to what the law dictates given a particular set of facts. In some jurisdictions it is the duty of the jury to at least take the legally prescribed verdict into account before reaching its own. In all jurisdictions it is the duty of the jury to reach a verdict by following a legally prescribed process. All three duties are premised on a requirement that the judge instruct the jury on the relevant law and that such instructions be understandable.

What, however, if the latter premise is wrong? What if judges' instructions are often incomprehensible to jurors? Clearly, verdicts reached under such circumstances can be considered lawless and are subject to appeal and reversal. The state supreme courts of several jurisdictions have explicitly ruled that the judge is responsible for ensuring that jurors understand the law (e.g., *Commonwealth v. Smith*, 1908; *People v. Gonzales*, 1944; *People v. Miller*, 1959). For example, the Pennsylvania Supreme Court concluded,

> When the trial judge has not succeeded in delivering instructions on the law in such a way that they will be understood by the jury, his charge is inadequate and justly open to objection by the defendant. As the very object of the instructions is to inform the jury as to the law applicable to the facts of the case, the charge fails of its purpose when the jury are ignorant of the law applicable to any material question in the case. (*Commonwealth v. Smith*, 1908, p. 553)

The law is clear on this issue. A jury cannot be said to have reached a correct verdict unless it understands the relevant law. Yet, as we will detail below, empirical evaluations of the matter have repeatedly demonstrated that jurors' understanding of laws typically falls far short of what is required. Such evidence suggests that our intuitive confidence in the present-day jury system may not be justified, and it raises the issue of whether jury trials sometimes actually reduce litigants' rights to due process of law.

A BRIEF HISTORY OF JURY INSTRUCTIONS

The absolute necessity for instructing juries on the law is a recent phenomenon relative to the history of the jury system. Prior to the end of the nineteenth century, jurors often decided questions of both law and fact, which made it less crucial that they be instructed on the law (Nieland, 1979). As mentioned above, it was not until 1895 that the U.S. Supreme Court (*Sparf v. United States*) clearly differentiated the roles of the judge and jury. It became the jury's duty to apply the law to the facts of a case. The judge now had an affirmative duty to instruct the jury on that law.

Thereafter, judges spent many hours researching the laws applicable to each case and writing them in the form of jury instructions. Also, it became a tradition for lawyers to suggest their own instructions to the judge. In time, most judges developed personal collections of sample instructions they had used previously, which could be modified to fit various cases. Unfortunately, this system proved to be "inefficient and often dangerous" (McBride, 1969). Dramatic increases in the volume of litigation at the turn of the century made it very difficult for judges to take the necessary time to prepare carefully a set of instructions for each case. Consequently, the judiciary and the bar began to see a need for standardizing jury instructions.

The first such set of instructions, commonly referred to as pattern instructions (also referred to as standard, model, uniform, or approved instructions), took two years for a committee of California judges and lawyers to prepare and was published in 1938 (see McBride, 1969). California's experience was so positive that many other states followed suit. To date over forty states have adopted at least one set of pattern instructions, and a growing number of these states have made it mandatory for judges to use them (Nieland, 1979).

The widespread adoption of pattern instructions has been viewed as a major advance in the trial process (Corboy, 1965; Hannah, 1963; McBride, 1969; McKenzie, 1957; Nieland, 1979). A number of specific improvements have been attributed to pattern instructions: "impartiality of the charge, uniformity in the treatment of cases, time savings in the trial court, accuracy in the statement of law, reduction in appellate court workloads, and increased juror comprehension of instructions" (Nieland, 1979, p. 13). It appears that most of these improvements can be documented to have occurred, except the last one. The empirical evidence has shown that pattern instruction drafting committees have failed to make jury instructions comprehensible. Let us now turn to that evidence.

THE EVIDENCE ON JURY INSTRUCTIONS

In recent years social scientists have recognized that much of the law, legal system, and legal process are based on underlying behavioral assumptions that are amenable to empirical validation. One of the most prolific areas of study for researchers has been the jury system. Among the specific topics to have been researched is the one addressed here—namely, the extent to which jurors actually understand the laws they are supposed to apply. This research has demonstrated that jurors often fail to provide litigants with either substantive or procedural due process of law because they do not understand the judge's legal instructions. The problem lies not only in the language of the instructions but also in the manner by which they are presented.

Incomprehensible Language

Problems with the way jury instructions are worded were first investigated nearly 50 years ago (e.g., Hunter, 1935; Report of the Cincinnati Conference on Trial by Jury, 1937). This research suggested that juries often failed to follow the judge's instructions because they did not understand them. Since then, several recent research projects have repeatedly demonstrated that pattern instructions are often incomprehensible to the average juror and that this is a nationwide problem. Low comprehension levels of 50 percent and less among representative samples of jurors have demonstrated with instructions from the states of Arizona (Sigworth & Henze, 1973), California (Charrow & Charrow, 1979), Florida (Buchanan, Pryor, Taylor, & Strawn, 1978; Elwork, Sales, & Alfini, 1982; Strawn & Buchanan, 1976), Michigan (Elwork, Sales & Alfini, 1977), Nevada (Elwork et al., 1982), and Washington (Severance & Loftus, 1982).

Comprehension of crucial points of law. One of the especially alarming findings of these studies is that often the most misunderstood instructions relate to very basic and crucial points of law. For example,

Strawn and Buchanan (1976), using 116 volunteers who had been summoned for jury duty in Florida, carefully presented jurors with a 25-minute videotaped set of instructions taken from the Florida Standard Jury Instructions in Criminal Cases. The findings included the following:

> Only 57 percent of the veniremen correctly believed circumstantial evidence to be legal evidence or believed that a crime could be proved by such evidence. The remaining 43 percent either flatly refused to accept circumstantial evidence or said they would view it with "extreme suspicion," said they would not consider it seriously, or were simply "uncertain."
>
> Only 50 percent of the instructed jurors understood that the defendant did not have to present any evidence of his innocence, and that the state had to establish his guilt, with evidence, beyond a reasonable doubt. (p. 481)

It could be argued that this study, as well as several of the other studies cited above, may be inaccurate because the comprehension levels reported were based on instructions that were presented outside the context of a trial. That is, in real trials jurors are exposed to specific evidence, the arguments and comments of counsel, and a full deliberation. It is logical to suggest that there are many corrective forces acting on jurors in the context of real trials and that perhaps they understand the judge's instructions much better than these studies suggest. This would be a plausible hypothesis were it not for the fact that it has been shown to be false by Elwork et. al. (1982).

In one study, Elwork et al. (1982, chap. 1) showed representative samples of volunteer jurors from Lancaster County, Nebraska, a videotaped mock civil trial containing actual instructions used in Michigan. Jurors were allowed to deliberate in groups of six until they reached a verdict. After their deliberations they were asked to complete a questionnaire designed to test their understanding of the judge's instructions. On the average jurors answered only 42 percent of the questions correctly.

In another study, Elwork et al. (1982, chap. 3) used a videotape of an actual trial in Nevada and presented it to a representative sample of volunteer jurors in Lancaster County, Nebraska. Again jurors were allowed to deliberate in groups of six and reach a verdict. A post-deliberation questionnaire on the law in the case yielded an average 40 percent correct response rate. Furthermore, it was shown that jurors misunderstood many of the most crucial points of law. For example, the charge in this case was attempted murder and included several lesser offenses. Even though the real jury in the trial found the defendant guilty of battery with intent to kill, the researchers found that only 6 percent of the volunteer jurors were able to accurately differentiate this verdict from attempted murder. Given that the study was shown to have external validity along several dimensions (see Elwork et al., 1982, pp. 57-69), the researchers concluded that the real jury probably did not understand the distinction between these alternative verdicts either.

Impact on application of law. Another of the alarming findings has been that incomprehensible instructions have a significantly negative impact on both the process and outcome of jury deliberations. This was demonstrated in a study by the authors. A representative sample of the jury pool in Lancaster County, Nebraska was recruited to come to a local federal district courthouse and view a four hour videotape of a mock automobile accident trial, that had been used for other research by Miller, Bender, Florence, and Nicholson (1974). The videotape was based on a real case tried in Michigan, and depicted the suit of Mrs. Nugent (plaintiff) against Mr. Clark (defendant) for damages (costs and pain and suffering) that resulted from an automobile accident. Each party claimed that the other had been negligent and solely responsible for the accident.

The paid volunteer jurors were randomly divided into 31 six-member juries and asked to deliberate and reach a verdict. Of the juries, 16 received the original Michigan instructions, while the other 15 received a rewritten set of instructions designed to be more understandable. The juror did not know that their deliberations were being videotaped. Upon fully disclosing the videotapings and acquiring informed consents from each volunteer juror, the videotaped deliberations were then transcribed onto paper and analyzed for their content.

A comprehensive coding system of 63 content categories was developed. To ensure reliability and validity, the group of scorers—14 undergraduate students of the University of Nebraska-Lincoln—received intensive training and were given an opportunity to practice their codings on several deliberations that were videotaped solely for this purpose. Each scorer were then asked to analyze the content of two more deliberations independently, and the extent of agreement among scorers was checked using an intraclass reliability correlation (see Guilford, 1965, p. 299). For the first and second deliberations, the intraclass reliabilities were high (r's = .89 and .91, respectively).

The scorers were then divided into seven teams of two and randomly assigned an equal number of different deliberations to code. None of the scorers were told which set of instructions their assigned juries had received. Each member of a team scored each assigned deliberation independently, and kappa coefficients (see Cohen, 1960) were calculated to measure intercoder reliabilities. The mean kappa coefficient for the 31 deliberations was .82. Fortunately, the agreement rates between coders were sufficiently high so that none of the content analyses had to be discarded. In order to further ensure reliability, all of the teams were again asked to analyze a third jury deliberation as a group after the completion of their individually assigned deliberations. The intraclass reliability of the group at this point was .97.

The results of the study were as follows. It was found that the less comprehensible instructions had several types of adverse effects on the deliberation process. First, by causing more confusion the less comprehensible instructions made it more likely for one or two individuals to proclaim expertise and dominate the deliberation. This type of deference was often exemplified by the way in which the juries chose a foreman. A significantly[1] greater proportion of juries receiving the original instructions expressed a need to choose someone who had previous experience as either a foreman or a juror (37.5 percent versus 6.7 percent, respectively). The following comments were more likely to be made in such juries:

> I'm not exactly a good chairman. I would like to suggest the gentleman down here because he's got experience. He's already been in a case.
>
> I was going to say since you've been on a jury before . . .
>
> Who has been on a jury before? How do you go about this electing a foreman?

Furthermore, the incomprehensibility of the instructions affected the content of the deliberations. Compared to juries who had received the rewritten instructions, those who had received the original instructions were more likely to discuss legally inappropriate topics. For example, according to the judge's instructions the issue of whether awarded damages would be paid by the defendant's insurance company was forbidden from being discussed. Yet, juries who had received the original instructions were significantly more likely to act contrary to this rule in that they made more comments with regard to this inappropriate issue (Ms = 9.32 and 4.66, respectively). These included comments such as the following:

> Well, he has got insurance you know. It ain't going to cost him anything except his premiums will go up. But, I mean, his insurance will pay. And I

imagine the attorney with him there was again an insurance attorney. He was not somebody he went out and hired.

Actually what they are doing is suing Mr. Clark's insurance company for the balance. They're really not suing Mr. Clark because he's got insurance on this car and the insurance company will pay that.

You know, if his insurance, he would surely have insurance, you know, to help cover it, then that would be the thing to do. His insurance company could help cover the cost that theirs didn't.

In addition, a significantly greater proportion of the juries receiving the original instructions failed to discuss one of the most important points of law—namely, that the case was governed by a "contributory negligence" standard (73 percent and 25 percent, respectively). That is, according to the legal instructions, if both parties were negligent to any degree then neither could collect *any* money from the other. Yet jurors who had received the original instructions said,

We don't think that he's completely to blame or we'd give her more.

We've already agreed to that [that she was negligent too]. That's why we have reduced the amount she's asking for.

I think that they were both at fault. So I don't think that she should be getting a large amount because she was at fault too.

In contrast, jurors who had received the rewritten instructions were more likely to make comments such as these:

That is what it is saying. If both of them did wrong, therefore neither one has to pay the other guy's bill.

If you say that they are both at fault, then there is no case.

The way that I understood it is if she has any negligence whatsoever, the decision has to be in his favor.

It should be noted that on a postdeliberation questionnaire, jurors who had received the original instructions were still significantly less likely to know that they were supposed to have used the contributory negligence standard in this case (41 percent and 29 percent, respectively). Thus, the deliberation process did not eliminate jurors' misunderstandings of the law, as is often believed.

It was predicted that a greater understanding of the contributory negligence standard would in turn affect the content of jurors' discussions regarding who was negligent. Specifically, it was predicted that jurors who understood the concept of contributory negligence (that if the plaintiff was at all negligent then she could not collect any damages) would be more likely to debate the plaintiff's degree of negligence. This is indeed what happened. Those juries that were aware of and understood the contributory negligence standard, discussed whether the plaintiff was negligent just as often as they discussed whether the defendant was negligent (M = 16.35 versus M = 15.57 statements per jury). In contrast, juries that demonstrated no awareness of the contributory negligence standard during their deliberations made significantly more—in fact twice as many—statements regarding the defendant's possible negligence as they did regarding the plaintiff's possible negligence (M = 19.94 versus M = 9.81 statements per jury).

Impact on verdicts. The extent to which the comprehensibility of the jury instructions affected verdicts was also tested in the study described above (Cohen, 1960). Of the 16 juries that had received the original instructions, 1 (6 percent) reached a verdict for the defendant, 3 (19 percent) awarded the plaintiff money for costs (e.g., hospital bills), and 12 (75 percent) awarded the plaintiff money for costs and for pain and suffering. Of the 15 juries that had received the rewritten instructions, 4 (27 percent) reached a verdict for the defendant, 5 (33 percent) awarded the plaintiff money for costs, and 6 (40 percent) awarded the plaintiff money for costs and for pain and suffering. Given the small number of juries involved, all we can conclude is that the presentation of the original instructions was significantly more likely to lead to awards to the plaintiff for pain and suffering (67 percent and 40 percent, respectively).

Even though this last finding demonstrated that a clearer understanding of the law did have some impact on verdicts, fewer juries than anticipated reached a verdict for the defendant. That is, all of the juries had made statements indicating a belief that the plaintiff was partially negligent. To conform to the law, those who understood the concept of contributory negligence should have reached a verdict for the defendant. However, this is not what occurred. Of the 15 juries 10 (67 percent) that had expressed an awareness of the contributory negligence standard during their deliberations still awarded some money to the plaintiff. This pattern of results raised the possibility that the trial contained law (contributory negligence standard) that jurors considered unfair and felt had to be nullified.

To investigate this possibility, we conducted several post hoc analyses designed to uncover how the above mentioned juries justified their verdicts. One of the analyses was particularly revealing. The frequency of statements regarding who was negligent, broken down by whether such statements were either consistent or inconsistent with a verdict for the plaintiff,[2] was measured as a function of when the law on contributory negligence was first introduced into the deliberations. It was found that prior to the discussion of contributory negligence during the deliberations, there were approximately an equal number of pro-defendant and pro-plaintiff statements made (the mean ratio of one to the other was found to be 1.06). After contributory negligence was discussed, however, the ratio of pro-defendant to pro-plaintiff statements was cut significantly (the mean ratio diminished to .614). Expressed in other terms, whereas 52 percent of the statements made prior to the discussion of contributory negligence were legally inconsistent with a verdict for the plaintiff, after the concept of contributory negligence was mentioned only 38 percent of the statements were legally inconsistent with such a verdict.

These data suggest the following hypothesis: Jurors wanted to both follow the law and their own sense of equity. When confronted with a law that implied a verdict that was inconsistent with their own sense of justice, they preferred not to disregard the law. Instead, they changed their interpretations of the facts (either consciously or unconsciously) so that both the legal mandate and their own moral mandate could be satisfied.

It should be stressed that the latter hypothesis is speculative because the study was not designed to test it properly and lacked certain methodological controls. Nevertheless, the data did support the plausibility of such a hypothesis. If true, this finding would have major implications for the effectiveness of the contributory negligence standard in particular, and for how jury nullification operates in general. Thus, it should be researched further.

Manner of Presentation

The problems created by the incomprehensibility of jury instructions are further complicated by two procedures often used in presenting them. First, it is typical for a judge only to read his or her instructions to the jury and usually to do so only once. That is, jurors are usually not given written copies of the instructions to read and study. Second, most of the substantive points of law are not read to jurors until the very end of the trial, just before they begin their deliberations. It is suspected that both of these procedures reduce the jury's ability to apply the law as given to them by the instructions.

Not presenting written copies. For many years, some commentators on the jury system have advocated that jurors should be given a written set of instructions in addition to having them read by the judge (e.g., Cunningham, 1958). The argument is that jurors are not likely to comprehend or remember a set of instructions, which are often 50 to 100 pages long, when they are only read in court. This conclusion is certainly supported by many studies performed by educational psychologists, demonstrating that written materials are comprehended and remembered better than lectures (see Sales, Elwork, & Alfini, 1977). Even though this has never been proven empirically with jury instructions, it is logical to assume that jurors are just as likely to forget portions of long instructions on the law as they are to forget lectures on any other matter. One group of researchers (Elwork et al., 1982, chap. 1) has reported that when instructions were only read to subject-jurors, the comprehension levels were so low that the research had to be stopped and redesigned. The new experimental procedure, which allowed jurors time to read the instructions, had a dramatic impact on their comprehension and allowed the researchers to complete their study.

The explanation for the greater efficacy of such a procedure is obvious. Giving jurors instructions in writing allows them to review any portions that were unclear when initially delivered by the judge. Thus, without doubt, part of the reason many juries fail to understand and follow their judge's instructions is that they are not distributed in writing.

Timing of presentation. Jury instructions are presented at various times during the trial. Since most jurors are new to the courtroom environment, preliminary instructions are presented at the beginning of the trial to provide jurors with a general orientation to the trial process. Usually these instructions present a brief introduction to the legal and factual issues in the case, the hourly and daily schedule for the case, an overview to the trial process, an introduction to the roles of the judge, lawyers and jury, precautions and warnings about prohibited conduct, and so on. Even though the impact of presenting these types of instructions at the beginning of a trial has not been empirically studied, their timing is undoubtedly helpful in reducing confusion and in increasing jurors' ability to organize the evidence cognitively in a way that will be useful during their deliberations.

Certain unexpected or sensitive issues that can arise anytime during a trial may require a judge to present interim jury instructions. For example, the introduction of evidence that is admissible for a very limited purpose but that can be mistakenly used for an inadmissible purpose often requires immediate instructions from the judge. Although there is no empirical data on this, it is logical to assume that such instructions are properly timed. That is, these instructions are probably most effective when they are presented in the immediate context of the evidence or procedures to which they apply.

Whereas preliminary and interim instructions tend to focus on procedural issues, the final instructions given to jurors at the end of the trial focus both on procedural and substantive issues. Their substantive portions consist of comprehensive and often lengthy instructions on the specific decisions the jury needs to make and how to make them.

Several legal commentators have criticized the current practice of presenting most of the substantive instructions after all of the evidence has been entered, on the basis that this may reduce the ability of jurors to apply the law correctly (Prettyman, 1960). Presenting substantive instructions at the end of a trial probably does help jurors remember them when they begin their deliberations. Unfortunately, this practice fails to take into account the fact that jurors may forget a great deal of the evidence by the time they are told how to interpret it. In addition, it fails to consider the fact that jurors are likely to preevaluate the evidence they do remember on the basis of principles that they believe to be important but that may not be consistent with the law.

The line of reasoning suggests that the time at which the substantive jury instructions are presented may affect jurors' interpretations of the facts, and in turn their verdicts. Indeed, two groups of researchers have demonstrated that these effects do occur. In one study by Elwork et al. (1977) jurors' interpretations of the facts of a case changed as a function of whether the substantive legal instructions were presented at the beginning or the end of a trial. Another team of researchers (Kassin & Wrightsman, 1979) demonstrated that the timing of such instructions also had a significant impact on verdicts. Thus, according to the current wisdom substantive instructions known to be relevant to a trial before it begins should be presented to jurors both before and after the evidence is presented.

SOLUTIONS TO THE PROBLEMS

The evidence on the efficacy of currently used jury instructions is clear. Changes in the way jury instructions are worded and presented are urgently needed. With regard to the procedural problems, the solutions are simple: Jurors should hear a judge read his or her set of instructions, but they should also receive a copy of the same instructions to read and review during deliberation. In addition, as many substantive instructions as possible should be presented at the beginning of a trial and then repeated again at the end. Even though these procedural changes may be resisted by traditionalists within the legal community, they are practical and easy to implement.

Changing the language of jury instructions is another matter. The task requires the help of legal scholars to ensure legal accuracy, psycholinguists (or "good" writers) to ensure clarity, and behavioral researchers to ensure valid empirical procedures for testing comprehension. Thus, making jury instructions understandable is a complex task requiring the help of a variety of experts.

The task has been made somewhat less complicated by the publication of recently developed testing and writing procedures, specifically designed for use with jury instructions (see Elwork et al., 1982; also see Report of the Federal Judicial Center Committee to Study Criminal Jury Instructions, 1982). These procedures include standardized techniques for composing, administering, and scoring juror comprehension questionnaires so that incomprehensible instruction can be reliably identified. They also set forth empirically validated rules for rewriting incomprehensible jury instructions and improving their organization, grammar, and vocabulary.

With regard to organization, we advocate a combination of associational, hierarchical, and algorithmic structures. Under an associational structure topics that are connected to one other by a common concept are grouped together. Under a hierarchical structure higher-level concepts are broken down to their lower-level components. Finally, under an algorithmic structure the order of ideas presented is such that each is helpful to the understanding of the succeeding one.

With regard to grammar we advocate the use of active, short, and simple sentences instead of passive, long, or compound sentences with self-embedded clauses. For example, consider the following jury instruction:

> And, in the course of these instructions or during the trial, if I have said anything that indicates to you how I might feel or how you think I feel with respect to the evidence or some aspect of the evidence in this case, you should disregard my actions or statements and rely upon your own recollections of the evidence.

Using the author's grammatical guidelines this sentence would be rewritten as follows:

> Nothing I have said was intended to tell you what I think the evidence shows. You should ignore any feelings that you think I have about the evidence and depend on your own memory and thinking.

With regard to vocabulary the authors advocate the substitution of legal jargon with common and concrete words. For example, compare the following words used in one jury instruction with their substitutions:

Original Vocabulary	Rewritten Vocabulary
allegation	accusation
business concern	company, business
counsel	lawyers
court	judge, I
credibility of a witness	whether to believe a witness
establish proof of	prove
pursuant to an agreement	as part of an agreement
solicit	ask

Elwork et al. (1982, chap. 3) tested the efficacy of these techniques in several ways, using a set of complicated instructions from a real criminal trial that had been videotaped in Nevada. The authors were able to demonstrate that their rewriting methods yielded substantial improvements in comprehension levels among a representative sample of jurors. When jurors received the original set of instructions (both verbally and in writing), their average percentage of right answers per juror on 89 questions was 51 percent. With two rewriting efforts of the same set of instructions, the average percentage of right answers was increased to 80 percent.

To demonstrate the external validity of this methodology, Elwork et al. ran 18 mock trials using the same instructions mentioned above and measured what impact deliberations might have on comprehension of instructions. The proportion of correct responses per question on a postdeliberation questionnaire averaged 40 percent when the original instructions were presented. With the rewritten instructions the average proportion of correct responses per question was 78 percent. Thus, even with the benefit of having seen the original trial in which the instructions were used and having had the time to deliberate and reach a verdict, the rewritten instructions resulted in twice the comprehension levels yielded by the original instructions.

This and other data reported by Elwork et al. (1982) prove that their methodology is effective in substantially increasing the comprehensibility of jury instructions. Thus far, it appears that this methodology has been applied in only several isolated cases. Apparently it has not had a major impact on most jury instruction drafting committees, who continue to not deal effectively with the problem.

DIFFICULTIES IN IMPLEMENTING SOLUTIONS

Most behavioral scientists studying the legal process live with the hope that their findings will be accepted and used by the legal community to improve the system. Many are surprised and disappointed when this does not occur as quickly as expected or ever at all. Researchers of jury instructions have generally met a similar fate. Even though jurisdictions have shown some concern for the clarity of their instructions, to the best of our knowledge none has yet to adopt any of the suggested solutions to the problem.

If the situation is to change, it is clear that researchers need to take a much more active role than they have in the past to help implement their findings in the courts. The first step is to identify those variables that have been obstructing change in this area of law. Since there is no research on this topic, at this point the authors must rely on logic and their personal experiences.

Certainly one of the important reasons why this area of law has made little progress is that there is still a general disbelief that jury instructions are so incomprehensible. To some extent, the disbelief stems from the fact that most legal practitioners are not aware of the large body of research in this area. In addition, however, many of those who are aware of the research actively refuse to accept it. A common reaction the authors receive from judges is that our data may represent what happens in other jurisdictions, but certainly not in "my" courtroom. There is also a general resistance to the idea that social scientists have "trespassed" into a discipline that is not theirs, one that they cannot possibly understand or appreciate.

Another reason progress in this area has been impeded is that the rewriting of the nation's jury instructions is a very time consuming and expensive task, even with the techniques that have already been developed. The magnitude of what would be required makes it unlikely that anything will be done in the near future, especially while each jurisdiction has too many other problems competing for limited resources.

The most important factor impeding progress, however, is that this area of research raises many sticky issues that most judges and lawyers simply do not want to address. For example, many of those in the legal community who resist having jury instructions rewritten claim that it is because the instructions currently being used contain "words of art" that cannot be translated into eighth-grade English. They argue that in order to make some instructions more comprehensible, their legal accuracy would have to be sacrificed. It has been our experience that, in reality, legal concepts that are not open to a variety of interpretations are relatively easy to translate into simple English. The problem is that much of the law is unclear—not linguistically, but conceptually; the data for this are on the millions of pages of the various appellate court reporters. Thus, any attempt to rewrite the current approved jury instructions raises the fear that the existing differences in inter-pretations will come to the surface and create much disruption.

The fact that empirical procedures make it possible to measure the level of comprehension among jurors is not welcomed among many in the legal community because it raises many other thorny questions. For example, Who will decide what level of comprehensibility is necessary for jury instructions and what should it be? Is it enough for a jury to understand 75 percent of the law, or should it be 90 percent? If complete understanding of the law is not possible, which aspects are essential and which are not? These are not empirical questions. They are compli-cated public policy issues that are very difficult to face.

Finally, if we were to set comprehensibility standards for jury instructions we would be setting minimal standards for juror compe-tence as well. That is, no matter how clearly instructions are worded, there is still a high probability that not all jurors will understand them. This raises the issue of what to do with "incompetent" jurors once they are identified. In addition, it raises the possibility that certain compli-cated types of instructions (e.g., antitrust), no matter how simply they are worded, may be incomprehensible to most people. Does this mean that most jurors should be disqualified from serving in certain types of trials? If not, should we simplify laws that are this complex? How will any available option affect our democratic system of justice?

From our discussion, it should be clear that research on jury instructions offers an opportunity to progress but also introduces issues that are extremely complex and controversial. It is not difficult to imagine, therefore, why jury instructions may remain as they are long into the future.

NOTES

1. All reported effects were statistically significant at $p < .05$.

2. Two general categories of judgmental statements were possible: those consistent with a verdict for the plaintiff and those consistent with a verdict for the defendant. Under the contributory negligence standard, the former category would include any statement indicating that the plaintiff was not negligent or that the defendant was negligent, such as these:

> She [plaintiff] didn't have to stop. If there had been a stop sign, then we could have said she broke the law. But she didn't break any law.

> When you are in a hurry, you really don't watch your speed and will go a little bit over. You're not noticing that much. So I definitely think he [defendant] was speeding.

Under the contributory negligence standard, statements consistent with a verdict for the defendant would include comments indicating that both drivers were negligent, that the plaintiff was negligent, or that the defendant was not negligent:

> This is the thing. It looks like both of them are negligent when they came to that intersection. Neither one saw the other driver, which would make them, I would think, equally . . .

> I thought she [plaintiff] probably was lying when she said she came to a full stop.

> We've got the skid marks to show that he [defendant] probably wasn't going faster than the speed limit.

REFERENCES

Buchanan, R. W., Pryor, B., Taylor, K. P., & Strawn, D. V. (1978). Legal communication: An investigation of juror comprehension of pattern jury instructions. *Communication Quarterly, 26*(4), 31-35.

Charrow, R. P., & Charrow, V. R. (1979). Making legal language understandable: A psycholinguistic study of jury instructions. *Columbia Law Review, 79,* 1306-1374.

Cohen, J. (1960). A coefficient of agreement for nominal scales. *Educational and Psychological Measurement, 20*(1), 37-46.

Commonwealth v. Smith, 221 Pa. 552, 70 A. 850 (1908).

Corboy, P. H. (1965). Pattern jury instructions—their function and effectiveness. *Insurance Counsel Journal, 32,* 57-65.

Cunningham, T. J. (1958). Should instructions go into the jury room? *California State Bar Journal, 33,* 278-289.

Elwork, A., Sales, B. D., & Alfini, J. J. (1977). Juridic decisions: In ignorance of the law or in the light of it? *Law and Human Behavior, 1,* 163-189.

Elwork, A., Sales, B. D., & Alfini, J. J. (1982). *Making jury instructions understandable.* Charlottesville, VA: Michie.

Guilford, J. P. (1965). *Fundamental statistics in psychology and education.* New York: McGraw-Hill.

Hannah, H. A. (1963). Jury instructions: An appraisal by a trial judge. *University of Illinois Law Forum,* 627-643.

Hunter, R. M. (1935). Law in the jury room. *Ohio State Law Journal, 2,* 1-19.

Jacobsohn, G. (1977). Citizen participation in policy-making: The role of the jury. *Journal of Politics, 39,* 73-96.

Kassin, S. M., & Wrightsman, L. S. (1979). On the requirements of proof: The timing of judicial instruction and mock juror verdicts. *Journal of Personality and Social Psychology, 37,*1877-1887.

McBride, R. L. (1969). *The art of instructing the jury.* Cincinnati, OH: W. H. Anderson Co.

McKenzie, J. C. (1957). Standardized instructions—panacea or problem? *Illinois Bar Journal, 45,* 350-354.

Miller, G., Bender, G., Florence, T., & Nicholson, H. (1974). Real versus reel: What's the verdict? *Journal of Communication, 24,* 99-11.

Nieland, R. G. (1979). *Pattern jury instructions: A critical look at a modern movement to improve the jury system.*Chicago: American Judicature Society.

People v. Gonzales, 293 N.Y. 259, 56 N.E.2d 574 (1944).

People v. Miller, 6 N.Y.2d 152, 160 N.E.2d 74 (1959).

Prettyman, D. (1960). Jury instructions—first or last? *American Bar Association Journal, 46,* 1066.

Report of the Cincinnati Conference on Trial by Jury. (1937). *University of Cincinnati Law Review, 11,* 119-246.

Report of the Federal Judicial Center Committee to Study Criminal Jury Instructions. (1982). *Pattern criminal jury instructions.* Washington, DC: Federal Judicial Center.

Sales, B. D., Elwork, A., & Alfini, J. J. (1977). Improving comprehension for jury instructions. In B. D. Sales (Ed.), *Perspectives in law and psychology: Volume I. The criminal justice system* (pp. 23-90). New York: Plenum.

Scheflin, A., & Van Dyke, J. (1980). Jury nullification: The contours of a controversy. *Law and contemporary problems, 43*(4), 51-115.

Severance, L. J., & Loftus, E. F. (1982). Improving the ability of jurors to comprehend and apply criminal jury instructions. *Law and Society Review, 17*(1), 153-197.

Sigworth, H., & Henze, F. (1973). *Jurors' comprehension of jury instructions in southern Arizona.* Unpublished report prepared for the Committee on Uniform Instructions of the State of Arizona.

Sparf v. United States, 156 U.S. 52 (1895).

Strawn, D. U., & Buchanan, R. W. (1976). Jury confusion: A threat to justice. *Judicature, 59,* 478-483.

Williams v. Florida, 399 U.S. 78 (1970).

CHAPTER 12

Issues in Trial Management

Conducting the Voir Dire Examination

GORDON BERMANT

On February 2, 1983, Senator Howell Heflin of Alabama introduced Senate Bill 386 to the floor of the Senate, and on March 3, he introduced Senate Bill 677. Both bills proposed amendments to the federal rules of procedure: S. 386 would amend Federal Rule of Criminal Procedure 24(a), and S. 677 would amend Federal Rule of Civil Procedure 47(a). Both rules pertain to the conduct of the voir dire examination in federal district courts. An appendix to this chapter contains the language of the current rules and the proposed amendments.

The bills aim to expand the control lawyers exert over the examination by making their oral participation a matter of right. Under the current rules, the extent of the lawyers' participation is a matter of judicial discretion, although the case law is clear that, whoever asks the questions, the examination must be thorough enough to allow the intelligent exercise of peremptory challenges by trial counsel—whatever that means. The phrase "intelligent exercise" of peremptory challenges goes back at least as far as *Bal Theater Corporation v. Paramount Film Distributing Corporation* (1962), and has latent within it, still unanswered, many of the questions that cause the current controversy. In a real sense, the law and scholarship on this topic are efforts to define or determine what the limits and protections of intelligence are in the exercise of challenges to potential jurors, and

Author's Note: The opinions expressed here are my own, not those of the Federal Judicial Center. For several reasons, I have narrowed the scope of the chapter to cover only the single issue of direct lawyer participation in the voir dire. Of course there are other important issues that arise in the conduct of the examination. See, for example, the excellent work of Wallace Loh in Chapter 7 of his very recent textbook (Loh, 1984), and the commentary accompanying the studies in the Report of the Committee on Juries of the Judicial Council of the Second Circuit (Committee, 1984).

what procedures are required to produce the benefits of the exercise of that intelligence.

The most recent information available on federal practice suggests that approximately three-quarters of federal district judges do not permit lawyers to conduct oral examination, preferring instead to do it themselves, although most of these judges consult with the lawyers before the examination and accept questions from them to put to the panel as a whole and to individual panelists (Bermant, 1977). A number of state courts also restrict lawyers' participation, although others, notably California and New York, typically permit unfettered voir dire by trial counsel.

There is only a beginning of empirical research on the skills of lawyers to utilize the examination effectively. Hans Zeisel and Shari Diamond (1978) directly investigated the competence of attorneys to challenge prospective jurors who were likely to vote against the interests of their clients. Zeisel and Diamond concluded that, in general, the attorneys they studied were not effective as expert discriminators between friendly and unfriendly jurors.

As may be expected with anything as complicated as jury selection, there are some problems with interpreting Zeisel and Diamond's results for policy purposes. In regard specifically to the importance of oral participation by lawyers, for example, the data allow no conclusion because they were all collected in a federal court in which the judge conducted the examination without assistance from counsel. There are also some methodological problems, virtually unavoidable under the circumstances of the experimentation, that render confident extrapolations to a general conclusion very difficult (Bermant & Shapard, 1981). Nevertheless, this research remains the strongest available and a model for those who would seriously try to promote change in the current federal practice by bringing positive evidence to bear in favor of their position.

Absent convincing data, one is left with case law analysis and rhetoric that create confusing thickets of argumentation entangling several frames of discourse: historical, scientific, legal, and sociological. In this chapter, I attempt to review the arguments on both sides of the issue by referring to the texts of testimony recently offered to a Senate subcommittee on behalf of and against the proposed changes in the current rules. In addition to being the most recent statements on the subject, the testimony is relatively complete in its coverage of the important points, as well as exemplary of how proponents and opponents of this change frame their arguments.

I have no desire to hide my own position on the issue, which has several parts to it. I will state them now (and return to them later) so that the reader can fairly interpret the evaluation I offer while presenting the arguments of the Senate witnesses.

First, the lawyers who advocate changing the rules have brought no convincing empirical evidence to support the claim that, as a group, trial lawyers possess and can practice the skills at jury selection that require their direct oral participation in the examination.

Second, if they did bring such evidence to bear, that empirical demonstration might argue *against* permitting oral participation more strongly than for it.

Third, the only valid purpose of the examination is just the one for which lawyers' oral participation is not demonstrated to be necessary. The purposes that may be served by lawyers' oral participation are not legally protected and in fact are deleterious to the pursuit of a fair trial—hence there is no justification for changing the rules, and the current rules help guard against abuse of the examination for the purpose of achieving adversary advantage.

STATEMENTS BY
THE PROPONENTS OF CHANGE

On March 7, 1984, the Senate's Subcommittee on Courts, Committee on the Judiciary, held a hearing on S. 386 and S. 677. Proponents and opponents of these bills appeared with written statements. The texts of these statements (Committee, 1984, August) form the foundation for the descriptions and evaluations that follow.

Speaking for the National Association of Criminal Defense Lawyers (NACDL) was Mr. John F. Ackerman, of Houston, Texas. According to Mr. Ackerman's statement, the NACDL has a membership of approximately 3000 distributed across all fifty states. Mr. Ackerman spoke directly in favor of the passage of S. 386 pertaining to criminal trials, but he also endorsed S. 677. Following a recitation of the language of S. 386, Mr. Ackerman offered his claims on behalf of the bill, which I will present and discuss in the same order that he did. The subheadings that I have used are my own; they are not contained in Mr. Ackerman's text.

Setting the Stage by Reference to the Highest Principles

Mr. Ackerman began by noting that

> Our judicial system is a showcase for the world and one in which we are most often justified in taking pride. It is an example to the oppressed peoples of the world of "freedom" and a goal toward which they can strive . . . We must continue, in our fine-tuning of this system, to seek to provide accused persons with the fairest possible trials consistent with practicality. The ideal system is one in which all truly guilty persons are convicted and all truly innocent persons are found not guilty. Unfortunately, innocent persons are convicted and sentenced to prisons. This is a much more egregious breakdown in the system than when the occasional guilty party goes free.

Mr. Ackerman then quoted Chief Justice Burger on the supreme value of the right of the accused to a fair trial, and noted that the Sixth Amendment to the Constitution guarantees the accused a trial by an impartial jury.

Comment. It is not atypical for proponents of enhancing adversary influence in the courtroom to decorate their rhetoric with allusions to the loftiest principles of the republic. Inevitably, however, there is a break in the chain of the logic that follows, due to the lack of a link from the enunciated principles to the position advocated in the practical matter at issue. In the current instance, Mr. Ackerman quickly shifted his focus to a question of appearances.

The Argument from Appearances

> It is extremely important that the trial be "in fact" fair. It is equally important, however, that the trial be perceived as fair by the accused. One who is convicted in a proceeding which he or she perceives as fair will be less likely to emerge from prison with a grudge against the system which must be in some way evened out. An accused is much more likely to perceive fairness in a system in which the accused and counsel can play a meaningful role in the selection of the jury.

Comment. This paragraph is a good example of an unsubstantiated claim. Of course it is true that there is great social importance in the appearance of justice and the satisfaction of parties with the processes of the trial; in respect to jury selection, this concern is contained in Justice White's descriptions of the functions of the peremptory challenge: "The function of the challenge is not only to eliminate extremes of partiality on both sides, but to assure the parties that the jurors before whom they try the case will decide on the basis of the evidence placed before them, and not otherwise" (*Swain v. Alabama,* 1964).

The appearance of fairness extends beyond its importance for the accused to its importance for the members of the panel and the public at large. Writing for the court in the recent *Press-Enterprise* (1984) case, Chief Justice Burger said,

> No right ranks higher than the right of the accused to a fair trial. But the primacy of the accused's right is difficult to separate from the right of everyone in the community to attend the *voir dire* which promotes fairness . . . Openness thus enhances both the basic fairness of the criminal trial and the appearance of fairness so essential to public confidence in the system.

Neither the jury panel nor the public is pleased by the appearance or the actuality of interminable interrogation from attorneys whose avowed goal is empanelling a jury partial to their clients (e.g., the statement by a lawyer speaking in his role as President of the Association of Trial Lawyers of America: "[The trial lawyers'] main interest, obviously, is to obtain a jury favorable to their clients" [Begam, 1977]). An interesting rhetorical hook in Mr. Ackerman's line is the not-so-subtle threat that if his view of the importance of oral participation by counsel does not prevail, society will be faced with a group of grudge-filled released felons intending to take out their grudges on the rest of us. For my part I can accept that many convicted felons are filled with grudges, but I doubt that the percentage of grudge-filled people coming out of our institutions of total confinement would be reduced if their lawyers had had a chance to question the jurors prior to trial.

Finally, Mr. Ackerman goes so far as to imply that, absent oral participation by the lawyer, the jury selection process is not "meaningful." But what exactly does "meaningful" mean in this context? That the selection of jurors is no more advantageous to the defense than it would be without any voir dire at all? And if so, would Mr. Ackerman be willing to accept that change in procedure—namely, one that removes peremptory challenges altogether, and simply accepts the first twelve jurors picked at random from a panel already qualified for cause? Interestingly enough, there have been arguments made by writers with deep concerns for civil liberties and the rights of the accused for just such a system of jury selection (Note, 1977; Van Dyke, 1977).

The Pro-Prosecutorial Bias
of the Unfiltered Venire

Mr. Ackerman next offers the claim that jury venires (panels) contain far too many individuals who do not understand where the burden of proof lies in a criminal trial, and hence are biased against the presumed innocence of the defendant. This position has been taken before, for example, by Richard Christie and his associates in their work on behalf of the defendants in the several famed conspiracy trials held during the late 1960s and early 1970s (e.g., Christie, 1976). Those trials had some unique features: The law of conspiracy was relatively vague, and the prosecutors were apparently motivated by ideological factors that separated the stance of the government not only from the defendants but also from a sizable minority of the public as well. When a society is polarized on the issues at trial, and the law and facts are unclear, there is justification for a concern over biasing effects of subtle, covert attitudes held by potential jurors. In these circumstances, factors unrelated to the strength of the case could have an unwarranted effect on the trial's outcome. But what may have been true for these cases is not necessarily true for run-of-the-mill criminal trials or for many civil trials. Moreover, as Grofman (1981, p. 343) notes, there may be assymetrical strong effects of minority views in jury deliberations; in particular, that a minority in favor of acquittal may be more likely to hang a jury with an initial pro-conviction bias than a pro-conviction minority will be able to hang a jury with an initial pro-acquittal bias.

It is reasonable to suppose that such complexities of the deliberative process are at work, as well as explicit moves taken both by the court and counsel to work against whatever pretrial prosecutorial bias may exist. But there is no reason to assume that, to the extent that the current procedures are ineffective, allowing lawyers direct oral access to the jurors prior to trial would reduce risks of unfair conviction. Perhaps those who feel more strongly about changing the rules could mount a research project that tests this notion as directly as possible by comparing jurisdictions in which lawyers have full control with jurisdictions in which they have limited or little sway. Is it the case, for example, that in state courts that have modeled their voir dire practices on the federal rules there are more convictions, and more mistaken convictions, than in states such as New York and California that give lawyers almost unlimited opportunity for direct questioning?

Potential Jurors Will Lie to a Judge
or Misrepresent Themselves During the Examination

Some years ago, Broeder (1965) published a study based on federal court practice in the Midwest, in which he interviewed jurors following a number of trials and reported that some of them had been less than candid during the questioning by the court. The data are quite limited, but they do speak to a potentially serious problem that one would like to see eliminated. Mr. Ackerman cites these data and offers the ad hoc psychological opinion that "[the courtroom in which a judge is seated in his robe] is a setting in which honesty on behalf of jurors who may have the courage to express their doubts about their ability to be fair is met with rejection by this authority figure."

There are three questions to be addressed here. The first is whether the setting of the courtroom and an open and public voir dire have a tendency to elicit misleading or dishonest answers. The second is whether the elicitation of honest answers is affected by the role of the questioner, whether judge or counsel. And the third is the extent to which the elicitation of candid answers is affected by the interviewing skill of the questioner, irrespective of role.

No one knows, in fact, whether potential jurors lie or deceive themselves more often when questioned by judges or by lawyers. But if the image of the judge, in the eyes of most jurors, tends to discourage frank, complete answers to questions the judge asks, then the solution should be found in helping judges overcome that difficulty through explicit training in voir dire interviewing. There ought to be methods of conducting voir dire that lead to as much probative information about bias as the lawyers would normally acquire. The key ingredient here will be the judge's willingness to pursue improved voir dire methods. The benefits of this approach will come without the costs associated with unbridled attorney-conducted examinations.

Judges Do Not Know How
to Ask Questions

Perhaps the most significant and serious argument in Mr. Ackerman's arsenal is that the quality of questioning accomplished by most federal judges is not sufficiently probative to allow for the intelligent exercise of peremptory challenges. Given the difficulty of making measurements in this area, and given that the measurements that have been accomplished suggest that lawyers are not particularly skillful at eliminating jurors who would appear to be inclined against their clients' positions (I set aside here the question as to whether that is what the purpose of the voir dire should be), it is difficult to know with certainty that variations in the quality of the voir dire examination have adverse impact on trial outcome. But there appears to be a great deal of validity to that proposition, and there is no compelling reason why judges cannot and should not become as expert in the interviewing of prospective jurors, and as probing, as is required for the intelligent exercise of peremptory challenges. The Judicial Conference of the United States, through one of its subcommittees, explicitly recognized that fact and worked with the Federal Judicial Center to produce educational materials available to district judges for their consideration as a means of ensuring the success of their voir dire examinations (Bermant, 1982; Chmielewski & Bermant, 1982). Chmielewski and Bermant offer a series of eight recommendations based on the theory of interviewing, which if faithfully followed should lead to more effective questions and opportunities for open answers.

A related criticism raised by Mr. Ackerman and other commentators as well, is that judges do not know enough about the subtleties of the cases before them to ask the right sort of questions (see, e.g., *United States v. Ible*, 1980, at 395). I have never seen the claim followed with any kind of example; absent that, it remains a social psychological claim that is a little difficult to swallow—namely, that even routine criminal cases possess subtleties that are so fine that only the attorney for the defendant is capable of moving from them to a surgically precise extirpation of potential jurors who would not be suitable to sit in judgment of the defendant. As mentioned above, there are cases where the evidence is thin and the issues ideologically or politically tinged, in which variance caused by subtle characteristics of juror attitude (authoritarianism and so on) could have undue influence on outcome. But it is really a strenuous jump from that fact to a general assertion for all criminal cases and the vast number of civil trials over personal injuries, alleged contract violations, and so on. We are again faced with claims that are not justified by either persuasive argument or empirical information.

Judge-Conducted Voir Dire May Encourage Invasion of Jurors' Privacy

Mr. Ackerman argues that a judge-conducted examination increases the likelihood that attorneys with well-heeled clients will use a trained investigator to

> talk with a potential juror's friends and neighbors, take photographs of their homes, look at bumper stickers on their automobiles, or gather information from other available resources. Such information-gathering techniques, although frequently successful and helpful to the parties, involve invasions of a citizen's right to privacy. Such practices are encouraged by the limited nature of voir dire in most federal courts.

Babcock (1975) took a similar but milder position in her frequently cited article in favor of extensive, attorney-conducted voir dire. There is no way of knowing, on the basis of the information provided, how often if ever this in fact has been the case. But, in any event, it is novel to turn the tables and blame the court for the intrusive practices of some trial lawyers. The effort fails, of course, because zealous lawyers whose clients can afford it have employed, and will continue to employ, private investigators whenever they believe it will be of any value. Were lawyers to conduct the examination, the investigator's reports would serve as a *foundation* for the voir dire, not a *replacement* for it.

Two Anticipatory Counterattacks

Mr. Ackerman concludes his list of claims on behalf of changing the rules by responding to two arguments that are often made in favor of retaining strong judicial control over the examination (see below for the position of the opponents of change). The first of these is that, without judicial control, the examinations take more time than is warranted. The second is that, left to their own devices, lawyers abuse the voir dire examination by infusing it with efforts to plead their case before the opening statement.

In respect to the question of time, Mr. Ackerman is refreshingly frank:

> There is no question, but that it takes more time to allow attorney-conducted voir dire. Voir dire should take more time. It is perhaps the most crucial part of the trial. . . . And yet, when we choose the twelve

persons who are actually making guilt/innocence determinations in serious criminal trials, it is frequently done in as little as fifteen minutes with no searching inquiry whatsoever.

On the empirical side, Mr. Ackerman cites two of the studies that have measured the duration of voir dire (see Bermant, 1977, for a description of these results and others of a similar sort). In one case, the judge-conducted examination was about half the length of attorney-conducted examination (1 hour versus 2.25 hours). He also cites a study reporting that attorney-conducted voir dire took less 10 percent of total trial time. On the basis of these citations, Mr. Ackerman moves quickly to high rhetorical pitch:

> Should time be such an important factor in the conduct of trials that we should be unwilling to spend ten percent of the trial time in an attempt to get a fair and impartial jury? If time is such an important factor, why not require attorneys to submit opening statements to the judge so the judge can edit them and deliver them? Why not prohibit the attorneys from conducting the examination of the witnesses since such examinations frequently consume more time than the judge would have consumed had he or she been doing it? In short, why not do away with the adversary system of justice since it consumes so much time?

In respect to the question of adversary abuse of the examination, Mr. Ackerman repeats the maneuver he used earlier by turning the tables, blaming the court for lawyers' misbehavior:

> Why is that judges who do such a marvelous job of controlling improper questions of witnesses, improper opening statements and improper argument, cannot control improper voir dire? The argument [that lawyers abuse the voir dire] is specious.

Further consideration of these two arguments appears below in the context of other testimony.

The Position of the American Bar Association

Testifying along with Mr. Ackerman on the hearings of March 7 were William W. Greenhalgh and Adrian M. Foley, Jr., on behalf of the American Bar Association (ABA). In their presentation, Messrs. Greenhalgh and Foley reviewed the history of support the ABA has provided for efforts to give trial counsel broader participation in the federal voir dire practice. It was in fact a recommendation by the litigation section of the ABA that initially led to the effort to change the rules during the Congress of 1976 and 1977, and the language of the second edition of the ABA's *Standards for Criminal Justice* (Standard 15-2.4) and *Standards Relating to Trial Courts* (Standard 2.12) contain the seeds of S. 386 and S. 677.

Messrs. Greenhalgh and Foley had no new arguments beyond those offered by Mr. Ackerman. There are some interesting features of the positions of the ABA in respect to the arguments that are offered in this testimony, however. For example, the standards state explicitly that "it is the responsibility of the judge to prevent abuse of voir dire examination." This is the official statement of the position already described above in respect to Mr. Ackerman's testimony. It is an interesting one and deserves at least some further exploration.

To begin with, of course, it is obvious enough that it is the judge's responsibility to control abuse of the voir dire examination, just as it is the judge's responsibility to be in control of all aspects of the trial to prevent any abuse of fair procedure. So if the statement only reminds us of the obvious, then it is harmless but trivial. On the other hand, there would seem to be a stronger sense to the statement, one that extends the judge's obligation to a higher plane of responsibility and, reciprocally, frees lawyers to pursue adversary tactics to the point of abuse with no concern for self-generated restraint but only awaiting the imposition of restraint by the judge.

This attempt to codify a shift in responsibility is, perhaps, a piece of the problem voiced by Monroe Freedman in his book on adversary ethics:

> The other way of avoiding the difficult questions [of lawyers' ethics] has been by issuing statements or codifications of rules of conduct in such a way as to give lip service to basic systemic values, while ignoring the fact that some of those values are fundamentally at odds with each other. (Freedman, 1975, p. vii)

The values at odds with one another in the voir dire are the value of an impartial jury, on the one hand, versus the value of zealous adversary advocacy, on the other. The law is unequivocal in protecting the right to trial by an impartial jury, and adversary principles are equally unequivocal in moving the lawyer to create a trial environment favorable to the client. This conflict leads to particularly acute tensions between the judge and criminal defense counsel, creating a relationship that Marvin Frankel, former federal district judge, described as frankly adversary (Frankel, 1976, 1977). The federal voir dire rules are efforts to balance the weights of these values on trial practice and outcome. One can expect the trial bar to be active in efforts to enhance its opportunities and to shift the burden of restraint to the court if possible. But these efforts should be seen as what they are, rather than as objective efforts to enhance the impartiality of juries by remedying currently flawed procedures.

A less essential but still interesting portion of the ABA statement is a reassertion of the trial lawyers' sensitivity to the "nuances" of juror responses. There follows the assertion that inside knowledge of the case, and better-developed psychological antennae, guarantee that lawyer-led examination is superior. As mentioned already, belief in this proposition requires, at the least, that the run-of-the-mill case has subtleties and nuances of juror bias that are so deep yet important that precise questioning by the attorney is required to ferret them out. This was also the position taken a number of years ago by the president of the Association of Trial Lawyers of America when he said, "Trial attorneys are acutely attuned to the nuances of human behavior, which enables them to detect the minute traces of bias in ability to reach an appropriate decision" (Begam, 1977). Seven years have passed since Mr. Begam published that sentence, but there is no more evidence to support it now than there was then; indeed, to the extent that there is any evidence at all it tends to return a null verdict at best (Zeisel and Diamond, 1978).

STATEMENTS BY THE OPPONENTS OF CHANGE

Witnesses presenting statements in opposition to changing the current rules represented the Department of Justice and the Judicial Conference of the United States.

Position of
the Department of Justice

Testifying on behalf of the Department of Justice was Stephen S. Trott, Assistant Attorney General for the Criminal Division. The Department of Justice, as the government's litigator and the prose-cutor in all federal criminal trials, strongly opposed enactment of these two bills. Mr. Trott began his argument by noting that the current federal rules do not prohibit direct oral participation in the examination by lawyers; rather they vest the decision in the sound discretion of the judge. The judge is always free, when circumstances warrant it, to permit or encourage oral participation by lawyers and, indeed, a small but convinced minority of federal district judges believe that conduct of the examination by lawyers is a preferable procedure. Mr. Trott notes that most federal judges conduct the examinations entirely themselves. And it is the position of the department that "the prevailing practice has proven to be fair and economical." It is the claim of the Justice Department that the current system works well to ensure fairness. Moreover, the department argues that there is, through the process of appeal, a guarantee of a review of fairness (see Bermant & Shapard, 1981, pp. 75-76, for a list of cases up to that date).

On Questions of Time and Abuse

Mr. Trott presented the allegations against trial attorneys that Mr. Ackerman had anticipated and attempted to rebut—namely, that lawyers will abuse the examination by invading jurors' privacy, by attempting to achieve prior commitments from jurors about their votes before the trial begins, and, as Mr. Trott put it, to "engage in personality contests with opposing counsel." In short, Mr. Trott listed the several classes of abuse that together constitute the illegitimate didactic purpose of the examination (Bermant, 1977; Bermant & Shapard, 1981).

Mr. Trott suggested that experience with attorney-controlled voir dire in large state court systems, California and New York in particular, argues against changing the federal rules. He called attention specifically to a set of recommendations made in 1982 to then New York Governor Hugh Carey by the governor's Executive Advisory Commission on the Administration of Justice. With reference to trial time in New York City, the Commission reported that voir dire under the control of attorneys could consume up to a third of total trial time— quite a different figure from the 10 percent maximum claimed to be representative in the testimony of Mr. Ackerman. The courts of New York City are clogged to a degree that prevents the speedy expediting of criminal trials so that any unnecessary delays are a form of denying justice to those who are awaiting trial. Mr. Trott also made reference to some extraordinarily long voir dire examinations in California, reporting on one case in which the examination took nine calendar months (129 court days) to select a jury while in another case the examination lasted 82 days.

Comment. Regarding the two California cases, it must be noted that both were capital cases, and should therefore move into a special category in which the duration of the voir dire should be judged against a different standard than that used in less drastic cases, particularly those in which, in fairness, it must be said that there are no extraordinary circumstances.

If, as the proponents of change argue, most jury panels are predisposed to favor the prosecution, then one might respond cynically to the government prosecutor's opposition to changing the rules, believing it to be due to the prosecution's benefits from the the status quo. But as mentioned above, Grofman (1981) has shown that it is simplistic to believe that the dynamics of jury deliberation are inherently pro-prosecutorial. Moreover, because the prosecution in federal criminal trials has fewer peremptory challenges to exercise (6, against 10 for the defense in federal felony cases with a single defendant), it is really quite important to the prosecution to have as much valid information as possible in order to exercise its relatively small number of challenges with maximum intelligence. It may be, though I have no evidence to support the conjecture, that collective experience in the Department of Justice is relatively modest in its assessments of the efficacy of jury selection techniques. Because, as a matter of fact, the department does not need to impress its client with claims of great psychological skill and sensitivity to the nuances of behavior, the prosecutor's approach to the voir dire examination may end up being somewhat more humble or pragmatic.

In referring to abuse of the examination, Mr. Trott cited an appeal taken in the Court of Appeals for the Second Circuit in the case of Leroy Barnes (*United States v. Barnes*, 1979). Leroy "Nicky" Barnes and 10 other defendants had been convicted in the southern district of New York on conspiracy to violate federal narcotics laws as well as on various substantive narcotics violations, including the distribution of almost two kilograms of pure herion. The jury began in January 1978 and continued for 10 weeks. The judge, faced with this trial of considerable proportions and high publicity, and confronted with a well-known and documented history of abuse and threats against potential jurors in major narcotics prosecutions in the southern district of New York, decided to keep the names and addresses of potential jurors private during the otherwise public voir dire—jurors were assigned numbers and appeared in public in the courthouse and in the jury box, but they were not required to divulge their names or addresses. Defense counsel appealed this procedure on the grounds of an abuse of discretion by the trial judge in limiting the due process rights of the accused. The Court of Appeals rejected the claim. In general, the recitation of the history of the trial court's conduct during the voir dire examination in *Barnes* is a good example of how a well-conducted examination can be undertaken under current federal rules. In general, the published opinion in this case, with its detailed descriptions, analyses, and conclusions, is a valuable source of instruction for students of both trial management and the appellate process.

The Position of the Judicial Conference of the United States

Speaking for the Judicial Conference were Judge T. Emmet Clarie, Chief Judge of the District of Connecticut and Chairman of the Judicial Conference Committee on the Operation of the Jury System, and Judge William B. Enright of the Southern District of California and Chairman of the Voir Dire Subcommittee of the Conference's Jury Committee.

Judge Clarie stated at the outset that

> The Judiciary firmly believes this legislation will impede the administration of justice, destroy the impartiality of jury, and impose severe and unnecessary increases in the administrative expenses of the Federal courts. We strongly recommend against enactment of these bills. (*U.S. v. Barnes*, 1979)

Judge Clarie went on to review the history of Judicial Conference action in respect to the examination. As expected, the concerns of the conference have been about the excessive durations of lawyer questioning and the abuse or pretrial commitment of jurors through lawyers' didactic exercises. Judge Clarie emphasized the distinction between probative and didactic functions of the examination:

> The *only* purposes of voir dire are to determine whether prospective jurors possess necessary statutory qualifications and are fair and impartial. Voir dire does *not* exist so that litigants may select jurors favorable to their cause, and the examination process is not intended to be the first round in the adversarial presentation of evidence: "No litigant is entitled to a jury of his liking. He is only entitled to an impartial jury." [footnotes omitted]

Speaking to the claim of trial lawyers that they are particularly sensitive to the nuances of human behavior and can therefore probe more skillfully than can judges into potential bias, Judge Clarie opined simply that the proposition was "specious." He noted that juror bias is seldom specific but rather generic against classes of persons (e.g., ethnic groups), occupations (police), or institutions (insurance companies). Moreover, by the time of trial the judge has participated in enough pretrial activities (rulings on motions, conferences) to have gained a sense of what the important concerns about juror bias are. In pursuing this line of his presentation, Judge Clarie quoted part of the opinion written by Judge Learned Hand in the often-cited *United States v. Dennis* (1950):

> It is of course true that any examination on the voir dire is a clumsy and imperfect way of detecting suppressed emotional commitments to which all of us are to some extent subject, unconsciously or subconsciously. It is the nature of our deepest antipathies that often we do not admit them even to ourselves; but when that is so, nothing but an examination, utterly impracticable in a courtroom, will disclose them, an examination extending at times for months, and even then unsuccessful. No such examination is required. . . . If trial by jury is not to break down by its own weight, it is not feasible to probe more than the upper levels of a juror's mind. (p. 221)

Judge Clarie stated the Judicial Conference's view of the reality behind the claims for the advantages of changing the current rules:

> Representatives of the trial bar who claim that they desire to conduct voir dire only for the purpose of enhancing the impartiality of the jurors selected are, I respectfully submit, being less than honest. If voir dire were made a part of the adversarial process, a lawyer's opportunity, indeed his obligation, would be to seize every tactical advantage that became available. Counsel in criminal cases, in particular, who are charged with providing effective assistance to defendants under the Sixth Amendment, could ill afford to overlook an opportunity to argue their case to prospective jurors or to utilize their challenges to secure a panel favorably inclined to their position. It does not require very penetrating research to verify that this is the true desire of the trial bar. (*U.S. v. Barnes*, 1979)

Regarding the efficacy of "judicial reprimand" to control lawyers who ask improper or excessive numbers of questions, Judge Clarie noted that the damage is always done before the reprimand is issued, and that it is therefore essential that the court review the content of questions before they are asked, even if counsel is to ask them.

Among Judge Clarie's several additional criticisms of the legislation was his concern that there is a "serious flaw" in the bills stemming from an ambiguity in the language about the time limits. Different jury selection methods are used by federal judges (see, e.g., Bermant, 1982); the bills' specifications need careful interpretation for each of these.

Judge Enright seconded the positions taken by Judge Clarie and supplemented them with examples of voir dire abuse taken from

California state court proceedings. In addition to describing a California case (*People v. Wells*, 1983) in which an otherwise valid homicide conviction was reversed on appeal because the trial court had refused to allow defense counsel to put two (out of many that were permitted) questions on voir dire ("Why don't we have a black governor in California" and "Why are there so few black presidents of large corporations?"), Judge Enright submitted for the record a copy of an article from a state trial lawyers' journal that, unintentionally but more eloquently than could otherwise be done, makes the case on behalf of those who believe it unwise to change the federal voir dire rules. I will describe the substance of this article in the concluding section that follows.

CONCLUSION

At the beginning of the Chapter I stated my own position in three parts. I will conclude by recalling each of these and assessing them in the light of the intervening material.

First, the portion of the trial bar that advocates changing the rules has brought no convincing empirical evidence to support the claim that, as a group, they possess and can practice the skills at jury selection that require their direct oral participation in the examination. No information has come to light since Zeisel and Diamond published their paper in 1978 that would convince an impartial observer that lawyers' claims for their probative skills at questioning potential jurors are sufficiently greater than judges' *can be*, or that justice is served only if lawyers' oral participation is protected as a right free from the exercise of judicial discretion. As noted, several federal judges have advocated, both on and off the bench, the importance of direct oral participation by counsel—for example, Judge Fay writing the opinion for panels in the (old) Fifth Circuit *United States v. Ible* (1980) and in *United States v. Ledee* (1977); the comments of Judge Feikens in Bermant (1982); and the article by Judge Lay (1974). If, as appears to be the case, it is a minority of federal judges who believe that fairness requires direct participation by counsel, these may be the judges who have been fortunate enough to practice in jurisdictions wherein the trial bar skillfully employs the examination for its probative purpose and scruples, not to abuse the examination for illegitimate purposes. Faced with such skilled and scrupulous trial lawyers, judges might be glad to relinquish the voir dire into the lawyers' hands. It would appear, however, that the experience of most federal judges does not permit them to contemplate a sanguine vacation from their responsibilities under Rules 24(a) and 47(a); too many members of the trial bar, left to their own devices, will abuse the examination, the panel members, and the patience of the public who also await their days in court. Those remaining members of the bar whose behavior during the examination is routinely trustworthy, on the other hand, would, presumably, gain sufficient credibility that knowledgeable judges would be pleased to give them the opportunity to conduct a portion of the examination themselves.

I italicized the phrase "can be" in the previous paragraph to emphasize what we must accept as an unfortunate but plausible reality—namely, that some federal judges do not pursue the examination with the thoroughness or skill that is required to support the intelligent exercise of peremptory challenges. Surely, however, this situation can be remedied through education and training opportunities. The advantage to this approach, as opposed to acquiesence to the legislative changes now up for consideration, is the absence of the cost that is inevitably associated with increasing the adversary content of the examination.

Second, if lawyers could demonstrate that they were as skillful at the examination as they claim to be, the significance of the demonstration for the current issue might, paradoxically, work against their cause. For an ability to move juries into configurations that are sympathetic to one's client *to a degree beyond what the facts would allow* is to move from an impartial jury to a partial one, which is, of course, just what is to be avoided. And there can be no doubt that the accomplishment of this partiality is a goal of the zealous (hence ethical) trial lawyer, regardless of the rhetoric the representatives of the organized bar may present in the legislative form. Of course, if one assumes equally skilled examiners and challengers on both sides, then, presumably, the "extremes of partiality" that Justice White described in *Swain* will be eliminated—but how is one ever to measure these skills with sufficient precision to be confident that equality exists in any particular case? In the face of this uncertainty, is it better to trust luck or to design a judge-conducted voir dire that reduces any unnecessary risk? I submit that the question virtually answers itself.

Third, the only valid purpose of the examination is just the one for which lawyers' oral participation is not demonstrated to be necessary. There is no reason to accept that trial lawyering, *as a profession*, conveys uniformly on its members skills that most psychologists and psychiatrists would never lay claim to—namely, instant deep insight and predictive power, based on brief and marginal indicia, of subtle bias and its influence on group decision making under pressure. One can search law school curricula in vain for the readings or lectures where such incredibly valuable information is to be found. Of course, there are likely to be supremely gifted individuals who can, in fact, perform at very high levels of skill and adroitness in conducting the examination—there is much more to interpersonal assessments and skills, after all, than psychology can lay formal claim to having delineated, or even having grasped. But the current rules do not prevent lawyers from exercising their skills, provided the judges before whom they appear respect them sufficiently to trust them to behave according to the law.

Although law schools do not teach what trial lawyers claim to know, there is nevertheless a vast trial advocacy literature, a good portion of which is devoted to tips on how to handle potential jurors during the voir dire. It was just such an article that Judge Enright submitted along with his prepared statement to the Senate subcommittee, as an example of why the Judicial Conference is eager to leave Rules 24(a) and 47(a) just as they are.

The article, by lawyer Stanley K. Jacobs of Los Angeles, appears in the December 1983 issue of the *California Trial Lawyers Association Forum*, in the Courtroom Persuasion department, under the title "Jury Selection Tips." Contained in its brief compass is an example of just about every sort of attitude and unsubstantiated claim that leads to concern about changing the federal rules. The focus is on civil, not criminal, trials, which means that we are not faced with the awful questions of capital punishment or extended incarceration and the resultant desire to subordinate other values in deference to allowing defense counsel every avenue of zealous advocacy, even irrelevant ones. Moreover, the purely adversary nature of the article is so blatant that efforts to cover it with concern for discovering unfair jurors fail totally; and even Jacobs does not seem to take them seriously.

Mr. Jacobs begins by observing that

> often in the jury selection process, plaintiff's counsel must confront a prospective juror who had indicated a clear and unequivocal bias against the plaintiff's case. What approach should be taken toward such a juror?

Fair enough so far, for this would appear to be a genuine problem. How does Mr. Jacobs advocate solving it? By using a series of questions in the examination of this allegedly biased juror *that are intended to condition the other panelists in earshot* rather than to elucidate the questioned juror's bias. Faced with a potential juror who, Mr. Jacobs has discerned, is unfairly hostile to his client's cause, Mr. Jacobs decides to launch an essay in the form of 21 questions (having to do with insurance companies and the criteria for settling claims) even though he has already decided to challenge the panelist peremptorily. Mr. Jacobs states,

> The responses that the juror gives to those questions really do not matter. The questions serve the purpose intended in that they educate all the other prospective jurors as to the positive aspects of the plaintiff's case. Thereafter, when exercising your pre-emptory (sic) challenges, don't forget to excuse that juror and thank him for his service, no matter what answers he gives to the questions.

Following this advice and a similar prescription on how to take advantage of a potential juror favorable to one's cause, who is bound to be challenged by the other side, Mr. Jacobs offers "general rules" that reflect his social-psychological judgments:

> As a general rule, do not accept nurses on your jury. They may become too intolerant to pain and suffering even though when you question them about it they will indicate that they have great empathy for such people. . . . Do not accept people who work for the welfare services. As a rule I find them callus (sic) and indifferent and likely to view your client as if they are asking for a handout.

But as before, Mr. Jacobs advises putting nurses and social workers through a set of questions aimed at other potential jurors before challenging them peremptorily. And he concludes his article with his punch line for selling the efficacy of his advice:

> By exploring these sensitive areas with these jurors, you in essence have them testifying at the very outset of the case to the very things that you want to establish by your own witnesses. Don't miss the opportunity to turn such jurors to your own advantage.

Mr. Jacobs's article is just what Judge Enright claimed it to be, a prescription for "an abusive tactic which would promote the very court delay and congestion which we all so eagerly hope to overcome." Mr. Jacobs's clients may or may not be well served by his applications of the tactics and nostrums he proposes, but other litigants, potential jurors, and the taxpaying public surely are not. The exercise of sound judicial discretion, coupled with a serious and informed approach to enhancing judicial interviewing skills, are the best safeguards against a runaway adversary attack on the voir dire examination.

As of this writing (August 1984) S. 677 and S. 386 have been reported out of the subcommittee but appear to be stalled in the full committee due to what one reporter identifies as "lack of strong support from the organized bar" (Moreau, 1984). I believe this to be an encouraging sign because it suggests that there are many trial attorneys who, recognizing the inherent conflict between their responsibilities as zealous adversary advocates and the court's responsibilities to guard the impartiality of juries, do not wish to tamper with the delicate balance that is best preserved by resting decisions about the conduct of the examination within the sound discretion of the district judge.

Postscript (October 1984). Procrastination occasionally pays dividends. In respect to my delay in completing this chapter, three dividends accrued between August and October. First, Wallace Loh's splendid textbook, including a thorough treatment of voir dire issues, has been distributed by the Russell Sage Foundation (Loh, 1984). The chapter provides a helpful context in which to place this much narrower exposition.

The second dividend was the release by the Judicial Council of the Second Circuit (Connecticut, New York, Vermont) of a report on seven studies conducted by district court judges in the circuit, testing innovations in the typical conduct of jury trials. In addition to a study of direct attorney participation, reviewed in the next paragraph, the judges also tested the utility of questioning jury panelists out of the presence of other panelists; giving the jury instructions from the judge before counsels' opening statements ("preinstructions"); allowing jurors to put questions to witnesses by passing them in writing to the judge; affirmatively advising jurors that they may take notes; providing the jury with a written copy of the judge's charge to take with them into the deliberation room; providing the jury with a tape recording of the judge's charge to use in the deliberation room.

Perhaps it should come as no surprise that a self-conscious exploration of voir dire arose in the Second Circuit because, as noted above, the New York State trial courts allow extended voir dire by counsel and important federal cases involving voir dire disputes have also been decided there (e.g., *Barnes*). The study itself was relatively modest: Nine district judges permitted each side to ask questions for 10 minutes (or more, in multiparty cases) at the conclusion of the judge's portion of the examination. The judges used the procedure in 43 trials, both civil and criminal. Evaluation reports were distributed to the judges and the attorneys. Although the return rate from the judges was respectable (39 out of 43), the return rates from attorneys were very low (approximately one-third), creating a concern about representativeness.

Expectably, imposing a 10-minute limit on the duration of attorneys' questions held down the total duration of the examination. Also expectably, attorneys quickly moved in some cases to use the examination for adversary, didactic purposes. The report cites 10 cases of improper questioning reported by judges or attorneys in the 43 trials. In 3 of the 10 cases, the judge interrupted the examination because of the attorney's line of questioning.

Finally, in a summary evaluation, the nine participating judges were slightly more in favor of, rather than opposed to, the use of this procedure in at least some cases. Most lawyers reported favorably on the procedure. A prominent exception to the prevailing opinion was voiced by the United States Attorney for the Second Circuit, a member of the Committee, who is quoted as disapproving of the experiment and of any liberalization of lawyers' participation in the examination.

The final dividend of procrastinating for two months to complete this chapter came as an opportunity for an extended discussion about voir dire with Professor Vanessa Merton of the City University of New York School of Law at Queens College. Professor Merton is an experienced trial attorney in the State of New York as well as a scholar and teacher of trial advocacy. She disagreed vigorously with my opinion about the proper role of lawyers in the examination. In the course of her lucid account of the arguments in favor of lawyer-conducted examinations, she presented the beginning of an argument that I believe is original and deserves development and analysis. The following brief treatment is based on the germ of the idea that Professor Merton gave me. I do not know if I take the argument through the same steps as she might, but I reach her conclusion nevertheless.

The argument begins with the observation that jury trial is just one phase of an extended period of adversary activity that begins with arrest or indictment in criminal cases or the filing of a suit in civil cases and ends with winning or losing final appeals of judicial decisions. In criminal cases, advocacy is a critical feature of prosecutors' arguments to grand juries, plea arrangements, and the tactics surrounding changes of venue or challenges to the composition of the jury wheel. In civil cases, lawyers pursue pretrial motions and discovery activities in thoroughly adversary fashion. The principle that guides and sanctions these activities is that fairness to clients is best assured through frank adversary activity in the client's behalf.

How strange it is, the argument continues, to step aside from this approved commitment to adversary advocacy during the questioning of prospective jurors. How naive and hypocritical it is to limit the lawyers' approach to prospective jurors by creating an artificial distinction between testing them for bias and testing them for openness to communication from the lawyers. Juror bias against a lawyer can devastate the client's cause as easily as direct bias against the client. Fairness requires that lawyers be able to assess their rapport with potential jurors during the examination. Good advocacy requires that lawyers be perceived as credible and trustworthy by jurors; lawyers must have ample opportunity to prepare themselves and the jury for the complex communications that will follow in the trial. Regardless of how skilled a questioner the judge may be, no amount of judicial questioning will allow bias against the lawyer to surface. Hence, lawyers must be allowed to question jurors directly as well as challenge them peremptorily.

This argument, though sketchy, has at least two virtues. First, it is a step toward honesty—and away from hyprocrisy—as a justification of lawyers' efforts at ingratiation during the voir dire. Second, it rests on the reasonable assumptions that adversary advocacy begins long before trial and that juror bias against a lawyer is bad for the lawyer's client. These virtues enhance the argument's persuasiveness.

But there is something else about the argument that troubles me and leads me finally to reject it, at least partially. The argument portrays the lawyer approaching the task of communicating with jurors by trying to establish, through the voir dire, a good interpersonal climate in which to convince them of the correctness of the client's position. The imagery is of sincerity, even humility, in the lawyer's demeanor (if you will, picture Jimmy Stewart as the role model).

Unfortunately, this assumption is rudely violated by the brash confidence with which trial lawyers approach the examination and their places in it. The trial advocacy literature and congressional testimony do not in fact portray lawyers as conscientious advocates who wish to work with jurors to produce an outcome that does full justice to the client's cause. Instead they portray, unintentionally but with great clarity, lawyers as sly manipulators who think of jurors as inferior folk whose behaviors are predictable through stereotypes. A unsavory air permeates these self-promotions, wafting around the facade of zealous adversary advocacy. This reduces one's sympathy for the claims that otherwise have merit.

Finally, the truth must be that trial lawyers come in all shapes and sizes, skill levels, and degrees of sincerity and respect for the jurors they attempt to persuade. Those who approach their task in the positive spirit implied in this final argument deserve direct participation in the voir dire examination; they will benefit their clients fairly. Those who do not, do not deserve the opportunity. They lose the right when they treat the jury system cynically and jurors with contempt.

If this view is correct, then the conduct of the examination must be determined in each case. But who shall decide? There is only one plausible candidate, and that is the person responsible for managing the conduct of the trial and guaranteeing its integrity—the judge. And that is just what the current federal rules provide.

REFERENCES

Babcock, B. (1975). Voir dire: Preserving "Its wonderful power." *Stanford Law Review,* 27, 545-565.

Bal Theatre Corporation v. Paramount Film Distributing Corporation, 206 F. Supp. 708 (1962).

Begam, R. (1977). Voir dire: The attorney's job. *Trial, 13* (3).

Bermant, G. (1977). *Conduct of the voir dire examination: Practices and opinions of federal district judges.* Washington, DC: Federal Judicial Center.

Bermant, G., & Shapard, J. (1981). Voir dire, juror challenges, and adversary advocacy. in B. Sales (Ed.), *The trial process.* New York: Plenum Press.

Bermant, G. (1982). *Jury selection procedures in United States district courts.* Washington, DC: Federal Judicial Center.

Broeder, D.W. (1965). Voir dire examination: An empirical study. *Southern California Law Review, 38,* 503-528.

Chmielewski, D., & Bermant, G. (1982). Recommendations for the conduct of the voir dire examination and juror challenges. In G. Bermant (Ed.), *Jury selection procedures in United States district courts.* Washington, DC: Federal Judicial Center.

Christie, R. (1976). Probability v. precedence: The social psychology of jury selection. In G. Bermant, C. Nemeth, & N. Vidmar (Eds.), *Psychology and the law.* Lexington, MA: D.C. Heath.

Committee (1984, August). *Report of the Committee on Juries of the Judicial Conference of the Second Circuit.*

Frankel, M. E. (1975). The search for truth: An umpireal view. *University of Pennsylvania Law Review, 123,* 1031-1059.

Frankel, M. E. (1976). The adversary judge. *Texas Law Review, 54,* 465-487.

Freedman, M. (1975). *Lawyers' ethics in an adversary system.* Indianapolis, IN: Bobbs-Merrill.

Grofman, B. (1981). Mathematical models of juror and jury decision-making: The state of the art. In B. Sales (Ed.), *The trial process.* New York: Plenum.

Jacobs, S.K. (1983). Jury selection tips. *California Trial Lawyers' Association Forum,* (December), 344-355.

Lay, D. P. (1974). In a fair adversary system the lawyer should conduct the voir dire examination of the jury. *The Judges' Journal, 13*, 63-65.

Loh, W. D. (1984). *Social research in the judicial process.* New York: Russell Sage Foundation.

Moreau, D. (1984). Voir dire legislation stalled in congress. *Litigation News, 9* (1), 12.

Note (1977). Limiting the peremptory challenge: Representation of groups on petit juries. *Yale Law Journal, 86,* 1715-1741.

People v. Wells, 195 Cal. Rptr. 608 (1983).

Press-Enterprise Company v. Superior Court of California, Riverside County, 104 Sup. Ct. 819 (1984).

Swain v. Alabama, 280 U.S. 202 (1964).

United States v. Barnes, 604 F. 2d 121 (1979).

United States v. Dennis, 183 F. 2d 201 (1950).

United States v. Ible, 630 F. 2d 389 (1980).

United States v. Ledee, 549 F. 2d 990 (1977).

Van Dyke, J. M. (1977). *Jury selection procedures.* Cambridge, MA: Ballinger.

Zeisel, H., & Diamond, S. S. (1978). The effect of peremptory challenges on jury and verdict: an experiment in a federal district court. *Stanford Law Review, 30,* 491-531.

PART **IV**

CONCLUSIONS AND CONTROVERSIES

CHAPTER 13

The Evidence on Evidence

Science and Law in
Conflict and Cooperation

PETER W. SPERLICH

ANOTHER DISMAL SCIENCE?

Those who prefer their science dismal now have a choice. In addition
to economics there is the growing field of *evidentiology*—the study of
how the legal system uses evidence about the law and for the law.
Behavioral scientists have produced a large number of studies about
the operation of various aspects of the legal system: What credibility do
jurors attribute to eyewitnesses? Do jurors comprehend judicial
instructions? What are effective ways to examine witnesses? Are larger
and smaller juries functionally equivalent? Do harsh penalties deter
more than mild ones? Who shows the greatest risk of recidivism? How
do citizens feel about the legal system? How can lineups be made fair?
Are confessions trustworthy? Behavioral scientists, as well as scholars
from other fields, often provide information relevant *for* particular cases
at law. The data and/or generalizations (conclusions) may be drawn
from the accumulated knowledge of the discipline, or they may be the
results of case-specific studies: With a given amount of available light,
can the human eye distinguish blue and green? What are a community's
standards regarding sexually explicit materials? Who can be a fair juror
for this case? Was there discrimination in the selection of the grand jury

Author's Note: I wish to express sincere gratitude to the Institute of Governmental
Studies of the University of California at Berkeley for its support of my "evidentiological"
inquiries.

325

that indicted this defendant? Can the defendant get a fair trial in this venue? Do purchasers of a certain product confuse two trade names?

A very great number of topics may be investigated scientifically about the law or for the law. New academic fields (e.g., forensic psychology) and applied activities (e.g., systematic jury selection) have developed to satisfy theoretical and practical needs. An important question remains: What does the law do with the products of science? Are scientific findings used at all? Are they used correctly? Are misuses accidental or deliberate? What can be done to improve the legal use of scientific evidence? *How* the law does/might/should use scientific data and findings is the third, and probably most important, concern of the new field of inquiry.

What makes the field so dismal? Interdisciplinary cooperation is never free of problems, but jurists and scientists appear to generate by far the richest array of mutual complaints, grievances, reproaches, suspicions, aspersions, and just plain hostility (Loevinger, 1966, p. 70; Collins, 1978, p. 179). The literature contains sharp exchanges about the constitutional dangers (Cahn, 1955; Clark, 1959), seductive qualities (Sperlich, 1980b, 1980c; O'Brien, 1980, 1981), and competence (Fahr, 1961; Geis, 1962) of science. To be sure, not all jurists and not all scientists regard each other with disappointment and apprehension all of the time. Many jurists welcome and appreciate the contributions of science; many scientists gladly and optimistically offer their services. Nevertheless, there is a constant undercurrent of tension and discomfort. Some of the problems reflect temporary inadequacies. With goodwill and hard work, they will be corrected. Other problems, however, result from the fundamentally different purposes of law and science. They are not likely to be resolved, no matter how much goodwill and effort are applied (Loh, 1984, pp. 716-717). It is high time, however, to correct what can be corrected, and at least to understand the reasons for the existence of those differences that cannot be resolved.

Both sides must shoulder blame for fundamental misunderstandings, as well as for the fact that there still exist solvable problems in the production, transmission, and use of scientific evidence. The jurists, however, complain more vehemently and relentlessly. This is surprising, for they are clearly in charge. The "evidentiary" interaction of law and science takes place on legal territory and is controlled by legal rules (Loh, this volume). Jurists decide whether or not a scientific finding will be admitted into evidence, what weight and credibility will be attached to it, and what conclusions will be drawn from it. Jurists decide which scientific discipline is sufficiently trustworthy and which scientist is sufficiently expert to be allowed to offer testimony in the chambers of the law. If there is no request for his or her testimony, the most a scientist can do is to alert attorneys or judges to the existence of relevant data; he or she cannot force the jurists to use them. Indeed, the scientist does not even have an effective defense when there is massive and persistent misuse of the name and findings of science—witness the U.S. Supreme Court's recent decisions on jury size and decision rules. Indeed, as these cases show, the scientist may have to endure a substantial dose of judicial slur and disdain (Sperlich, 1980a).

Science and law are unequal partners in yet another way. Law needs science much more than science needs law. Science's need for law is merely that of any human enterprise: a regulative framework of rights and obligations, prohibited and mandatory acts, and a procedural system for the resolution of disputes. The law, however, needs science in order to perform its key task: dispute resolution. Disputes that reach the third-party stage of mediation, arbitration, or adjudication typically have two elements of contention that require authoritative rulings: issues of law and issues of fact. Not every case contains a factual dispute; not every factual dispute requires scientific evidence for its resolution. Sometimes factual issues can be resolved through the testimony of direct witnesses on case-specific facts. Frequently, however, case facts require for their proper interpretation a context of general scientific findings. Often scientific generalizations ("social facts") are directly relevant. The ever-increasing technical complexity of modern life and the parallel increases in the complexity of the factual content of lawsuits make it certain that in the future law will need science even more rather than less. The need will also increase because of the growing political role of the courts (Shapiro, 1964, 1981). The legislative and policymaking functions of the courts are controversial (Berger, 1977; Miller, 1982). Regardless of the constitutional merit of the arguments, it seems inescapable that the appellate courts will make social policy. With this, the law's need for general (i.e., empirical, systematic, scientific) knowledge reaches new heights.[1]

Law schools train jurists to resolve legal disputes: how to determine (or, at least, argue) which legal rules and precedents apply to a particular case. It is largely an exercise in deductive logic and techniques of persuasion. While many jurists majored as undergraduates in a social science field, they are generally not trained in research methodology and statistics. Systematic research training and methodological experience are generally reserved for graduate school

(Wasby, 1980, p. 15). The primary methods of science are systematic observation, inductive logic, and statistical testing. They are not usually part of a jurist's methodological repertoire. When a case requires more than direct testimony on case facts, the law has nowhere to go but to science—unless it wants to perpetuate the courts' penchant for relying on judicial intuition and common sense (Rosenblum, 1971, pp. 459-463; Kassin & Wrightsman, this volume; Wells, this volume).

From the perspective of the sciences, the law looks like this: It needs science to fulfill its key task. It controls the use of science. It forever complains about science. Frequently it ignores relevant scientific findings. Often it misuses scientific evidence and mistreats scientific experts. The question suggests itself: Why do scientists continue to cooperate?[2] Apart from the possibility of masochism (which, as an interested party, I refuse to explore), the answer may well be found in a genuine feeling of obligation (Thomas, 1974b) and the hope that cooperation will produce important social benefits (Collins, 1978, p. 146). Most intellectuals, but particularly behavioral scientists, are susceptible to appeals of reform and promises of social betterment.

In any case, there has never been a lack of scholars interested in the evidentiary problems of the law and motivated to assist jurists in the resolution of factual disputes. As do nearly all things, concern about error in direct testimony and, thus, erroneous verdicts, begins with the ancient Greeks (Konecni & Ebbesen, 1982, p. 101). Systematic psychological analysis of the factual elements in litigation dates from the work of Münsterberg (1908) and the other early forensic psychologists (Konecni & Ebbesen, 1982, p. 113). Political philosophy has always taken a strong interest in questions of law. Not surprisingly, systematic attention to legal matters is a strong component of the work of the early social scientists, such as Durkheim and Weber (Rosen, 1972, p. 40). Interestingly, the probabilistic (statistical) nature of legal rules of evidence was noted as early as Leibniz (Finkelstein, 1978, p. 2).

The data and findings of the behavioral sciences[3] saw their first major legal use in *Muller v. Oregon* (1908) as part of the innovative Brandeis brief (Rosen, 1972, pp. 75-98). A more recent case of a similar pioneering nature is *Brown v. Board of Education* (1954), with its famous footnote eleven (Rosen, 1972, pp. 134-172). *Brown* appears to have caused a major reorientation of the social sciences toward the law. The case was followed by a veritable explosion of law-related research undertakings and publications (Loh, 1984, p. 8). As the next section will indicate, it has not let up. Evidentiology may be a dismal science, but just like economics, it does not lack devotees.

SCIENTIFIC OFFERINGS

Behavioral scientists approach the law from a variety of perspectives and with a variety of interests. They also offer a variety of contributions and services to the legal community.[4] Research *about* the legal system occupies the largest niche. The various aspects of the law here are the objects of inquiry. This type of research requires the least interaction and cooperation of law and science—merely that of any science and its subject matter. It is, therefore, also the least dismal of the subfields. Scholarly motivation may simply be to know, knowledge serving as its justification. Hopes for reform and improvement, however, may also be part of the picture. If successful, inquiry will hold a mirror to the law, permitting law to know itself more accurately and objectively, exposing inadequacies and inefficiencies. *If* the jurists pay attention, there may well be improvements in the operation of the law.

Listing all the research about the law would fill more pages than are available here. A few examples, however, will demonstrate the great diversity of topics and approaches. They will also indicate the great potential for application of these studies. Many research undertakings focus on procedural matters. How do appellate courts select cases for review (Provine, 1980)? What are the effects of difference in timing and wording of jury instructions (Elwork & Sales, this volume; Kassin & Wrightsman, this volume; Wells, this volume)? What are the effects of communication styles on juror perception and memory (Farmer et al., 1976; O'Barr, 1982; Loftus & Goodman, this volume)? What are the effects of video rather than "natural" presentation of testimony (Miller & Fontes, 1979)? What techniques are effective in the direct and cross-examination of witnesses (Loftus & Goodman, this volume)? What are the procedural causes of delay (Zeisel, Kalven, & Buchholz, 1959; Zeisel & Callahan, 1963)? Some studies address a variety of procedural issues (Doob, 1976; Dorsen & Friedman, 1973; Lind, 1982; Saks, 1982).

Many research projects focus on substantive topics, for example, plea bargaining (Heinz & Kerstetter, 1980; McDonald & Cramer, 1980); comparison of judicial decisions and jury verdicts (Kalven & Zeisel, 1966); the nature of judicial attitudes, behaviors, rulings, and policies (Champagne & Nagel, 1982; Kort, 1963; Nagel, 1963; Schubert, 1963, 1965; Spaeth, 1963; Ulmer, 1967); jury deliberations and verdict choices (Grofman, 1976, 1977; Hastie, Penrod, & Pennington, 1983; Kaplan, 1982; Kessler, 1975; Nemeth, 1976; Saks, 1977; Sperlich, 1980a; Stasser, Kerr, & Bray, 1982; Van Dyke, 1977); legal socialization (Tapp

& Kohlberg, 1977; Weyrauch, 1977); popular attitudes toward the law and legal issues (Knudten, 1978; Newman, 1978); legal impact (Lempert, 1966); personality characteristics and career patterns (Fenster, 1977; Platt & Pollock, 1976); the nature of expert testimony (Loewen, 1982; Szasz, 1957; Wolfgang, 1974; Zeisel, 1956); witness credibility (Loftus, 1979; Miller & Burgoon, 1982; Greene, Schooler, & Loftus, this volume; Wells, this volume), including the credibility of defendants (Shaffer, this volume) and of their confessions (Kassin & Wrightsman, this volume); law enforcement conduct (Campbell & Ross, 1968; Wells et al., 1979); particular types of offenders and offenses (Cressey & Ward, 1969; Gebhard et al., 1965; Glueck & Glueck, 1968; Hirschi & Selvin, 1967; Murray & Cox, 1979; Newman et al., 1978; Wolfgang et al., 1972; Zahn & Snodgrass, 1978); and sentencing, deterrence, and recidivism (Austin & Utne, 1977; Barnett & Hagel, 1977; Bedau, 1982; Gross & von Hirsch, 1981; Wolfgang, 1978). In addition, a substantial number of texts are now available that deal comprehensively with the structures and processes of the legal system from the perspective of several of the behavioral sciences (Becker & Landes, 1974; Cohn & Udolf, 1979; Greenberg & Ruback, 1982; Hirsch, 1979; Hoebel, 1954; Konecni & Ebbesen, 1982; Nader, 1969; Nagel, 1969; Saks & Hastie, 1978). Regarding topics such as jury instructions, witness examination techniques, law enforcement procedures, recidivism rates, deterrence effects, and citizen attitudes, research *about* the law may also serve in an applied capacity, providing background information *for* litigation.

A considerably smaller number of scholars is engaged in primary litigation research—that is, in studies designed specifically to generate information needed *for* the resolution of a particular dispute.[5] These are typical adjudicative information needs: the effects of pretrial publicity on potential jurors in change of venue motions (Loewen, 1982; Padawer-Singer & Barton, 1975); the existence of racial or other discrimination in the formation of jury wheels (Hans & Vidmar, 1982; Sperlich & Jaspovice, 1975, 1979; Van Dyke, 1977); the determination of juror characteristics relating to fairness, impartiality, and "benign inclinations" (Bennett, 1983; Berk, 1976; Christie, 1976; Freid et al., 1975; Sperlich, 1977; Van Dyke, 1977); and, more substantively, the nature of community standards (Beckett & Bell, 1979). Survey research (Jacoby, this volume) and statistical analysis (Loewen, 1982) are primary behavioral science tools with which to respond to the information needs of the adjudicator. In addition to community standards, it would be difficult to resolve certain claims adequately— claims regarding trade mark infringements, monopolistic practices and antitrust violations, employment and salary discrimination, misleading advertisements, and school segregation—without systematic surveys of opinions or conduct and without statistical methods of analysis. Eyewitness testimony and other types of direct or circumstantial "lay" witness testimony often are inadequate to resolve factual disputes. The witness must be an "expert" with technical training and a background in the relevant scientific fields. These requirements do not change when the data needs are more modest, such as in the analysis of a particular chemical compound, in the determination of the ballistic properties of a particular gun, or in the calculation of the load capacity of a particular beam.

An important branch of scientific studies *for* litigation are those inquiries that seek to provide (scientific) evidence about (lay) evidence. The primary discipline is psychology. The present volume includes several chapters on psychological research on evidence as evidence. In some ways, of course, these are reports *about* the law. Their principal purpose, however, is to provide knowledge *for* the law. The findings have much value in informing judges and juries about the character-istics and likely veracity of various types of evidence; they also should be useful to judges and legislators when rules of legal procedure are to be designed.[6]

The presentation and examination of the oral testimony of witnesses are the primary evidentiary tools of American jury trials. Invariably, testimony has two components. The first is the strictly legal or admissible one, consisting of the case-relevant identity of the witness and the precise content of his testimony. The second component consists of a variety of extralegal or nonadmissible factors. These may include the witness' appearance, demeanor, social characteristics, reputation, and mode of speech. It is obviously important for the courts to receive evidence on the nature and strength of extralegal effects on jurors and judges. If they are understood, it may be possible to devise procedural tools to counteract them. While some of the evidence is mixed, in part because of methodological problems, there are sub-stantial indications that extralegal factors can affect the sympathy of jurors as well as attributions of credibility to the witness (Kaplan, this volume; Shaffer, this volume). The matter becomes particularly important from a constitutional perspective when the witness in question is the defendant in a criminal trial. In addition to the possibility of drawing erroneous inferences from extralegal factors, there is the danger that jurors will reach adverse conclusions if the defendant exercises his right not to testify. Jurors customarily are instructed not to draw adverse inferences. As reported by Shaffer (this volume), however, there is evidence that current instructions are not entirely successful. While not necessarily regarding the claim of Fifth Amendment privileges as an admission of guilt, jurors tend to treat it as one more piece of evidence for the guilt of the defendant. Clearly, a reconsideration of current instructions and experiments with revised versions are in order.

There may be testimony that the defendant has admitted the act of which he is accused; the jurors may even watch the defendant's confession on videotape. There is no doubt that this is perceived as the strongest possible evidence of guilt and is likely to be sufficient by itself to persuade the jurors to convict. Unfortunately, a number of studies have shown that there exist numerous ways in which persons can be manipulated or coerced into making false confessions (Kassin & Wrightsman, this volume). The question, thus, becomes under what conditions confession evidence should be trusted. Kassin and Wrightsman's review (this volume) suggests that it appears to be quite difficult to determine the trustworthiness of a confession, particularly if the person's memory has been altered (falsely coming to believe himself that he has committed the act in question) and its original content can no longer be retrieved. Moreover, juries tend to place much faith in the probative value of a confession even if doubts are raised regarding its voluntariness. This is true in particular if the alleged manipulation or coercion involved promises rather than threats. Kassin and Wrightsman (this volume) tried cautionary instructions in a number of experiments. They failed to mitigate the jurors' "positive coercion bias," though some versions were at least partially effective. Here, too, more work is needed in respect to the wording of the cautionary instructions, as well as in regard to procedural matters, especially timing. It appears, for example, that instructions received before the presentation of evidence are more effective than those that come at the end of the trial (Kassin & Wrightsman, this volume).

Adjudicators attribute high probative value to eyewitness testimony, second only to a defendant's confession. While false confessions may be relatively infrequent, mistaken eyewitness identification is not rare. Wells (this volume) notes that erroneous testimony may result from flaws in perception, decay or alteration of memory, retrieval failure, or inaccurate communication. How can jurors or judges determine the reliability of an eyewitness? What procedural devices, such as cautionary instructions or expert testimony, can be adopted to assist the adjudicator? Wells (this volume) reviews a number of studies that have shown that the expression of self-confidence is "the single most important determinant of the credibility ascribed to eyewitnesses" as it accounts for as much as 50% of the variance in the jurors' decisons to believe or not to believe the testimony.[7] Unfortunately, studies have also shown that there is "little or no relationship" between the confidence and the accuracy of an eyewitness (Wells, this volume; Greene et al., this volume). Persons *generally* overestimate eyewitness accuracy (Wells, this volume; Greene et al., this volume); they also do poorly in taking into account specific conditions under which the witnessing, information storage, or recall took place, e.g., the effects of stress, biased lineups, misleading information, or hypnosis (Wells, this volume; Greene et al., this volume). In spite of these problems, jurors do not generally receive cautionary instructions from the bench. When instructions are given, they tend not be congruent with scientific evidence (Wells, this volume).[8] Whatever assistance jurors or judges do receive largely comes through expert testimony on eyewitness reliability.[9] In addition to providing such expert testimony and helping the courts in the formulation of effective cautionary instructions, psychologists and other scientists may also have some opportunities to improve eyewitness accuracy directly. For example, they may assist police academies and police departments in developing unbiased lineup procedures. To increase the (most likely low) interest of law enforcement agencies in such efforts, courts could extend exclusionary rules to eyewitness identifications produced under biased lineup conditions (Wells, this volume).

Eyewitness accuracy and credibility have become prominent subjects of expert psychological testimony. There are many other factual issues, related to a great variety of disputes, for which scientific evidence can be helpful. Particularly since *Brown*, the courts have substantially extended the range of admissible expert testimony about human behavior and performance, as well as about social conditions and processes. As noted by Greene et al. (this volume), behavioral scientists have provided evidence regarding such matters as mental states of defendants, degree of psychological trauma suffered by victims of violent crime, effects of segregation on learning, effects of pretrial publicity, nature of community standards, employment discrimination, trademark confusion, civil remedies, and criminal sentencing. Some expert testimony derives from the clinical observation and testing of particular individuals (or other units of analysis); other testimony is based on general research of a more comprehensive and theoretical type. Clinical scientists can testify to the state or conduct of *specific* individuals; research scientists can provide evidence how people are or behave *in general* (Greene et al., this volume). The clinician is more likely to give case-specific testimony; the research scientist is more likely to offer empirical generalizations or "social facts." These generalizations of the research scientist, however, may also be required when factual disputes are purely case-specific. It is difficult to correctly interpret and draw the appropriate inferences from particular facts, unless they can be placed into the context of empirical generalizations. In respect to eyewitness testimony, scientific experts can provide crucial contextual information about the acquisition and decay of memory elements, the problem of cross-racial identification, the impact of anxiety on observation, individual differences (e.g., associated with age) in witnessing ability, and other factors (Greene et al., this volume).

Not all areas of scientific inquiry, clinical or general, are established as well as eyewitness research. Recently some courts have admitted expert testimony on the "battered woman syndrome" and "rape trauma syndrome" (Greene et al., this volume). These areas are new foci of clinical attention. It is doubtful that there exist warranted empirical generalizations. The courts are well advised to be cautious in dealing with testimony that is based largely on clinical work. Clinicians do not normally deal with representative samples of the relevant populations. The persons with whom they work usually constitute a limited and skewed selection from the relevant pool. Empirical generalizations attempted purely on the basis of clinical experience tend to be deficient and erroneous. Current admissibility rules are not sensitive to this problem. It is a standard admissibility requirement that the evidence about which the expert testifies must be scientifically reliable and generally accepted in the scientific community (Greene et al., this volume). This provides no protection against false, clinically-based, generalizations if the terms are interpreted to mean "reliable by clinical standards" and "accepted among clinicians." In the areas of battered women and rape traumas, in any case, "there has been little consensus about the validity of the research and whether that research can form the basis for an expert's opinion" (Greene et al., this volume). Without doubt, expert testimony can be highly valuable in guarding against erroneous and prejudicial "lay" testimony. Expert testimony, however, can also have a prejudicial impact. The admissibility decision requires a balancing of the likely probative and prejudicial impacts (Greene et al., this volume). It will not be easy to develop appropriate and uniform balancing criteria. Involved are not only legal and scientific issues, but also the personal values of jurists and scientists (Greene et al., this volume).

In an adversary system, lay and expert witnesses who are permitted to testify present their evidence to the adjudicators through oral examinations—direct and cross. Naturally, there are experts on how to conduct examinations most effectively. Most of them are practicing trial attorneys. Behavioral scientists also pay attention to this aspect of litigational evidence. The practitioner's experience is invaluable, but it needs to be supplemented by systematic investigations. The same is true in respect to the voir dire stage of jury selection. The practitioners' lore tends to have the weaknesses of all clinical work: it is an inadequate basis for generalization and prediction. There is no dearth of contradictory examination and voir dire advice from experienced practitioners (Loftus & Goodman, this volume; Bermant, this volume; Sperlich, 1977). Direct and cross examination have as their primary purpose the presentation and testing of pertinent information. There are other purposes, however, such as educating the jurors or confusing them, creating trust or distrust in a witness, or presenting a theory of the case (Loftus & Goodman, this volume; Bermant, this volume). Of course, the form and content of questions and answers are limited by the rules of evidence—exceedingly complex in jury trials (Loh, this volume). Behavioral scientists have provided evidence for the various aspects and purposes of witness examination. They have investigated the influence of speech style on credibility, of question wording on the recall of events and the content of the answers, and of imagining an event on the estimation of its probability. They have studied the effects of interrupting the witness, the presence of multiple negatives in questions, order of presentation (primacy and recency effects), and leading questions (if the court will allow them). Behavioral scientists also have offered advice on how to prepare a witness for cross-examination, how to obtain short answers and induce agreement, and whether or not to volunteer unpleasant facts (Loftus & Goodman, this volume). A number of recent studies have investigated the relative ease or difficulty of detecting deceptive testimony. It appears that it is particularly difficult for jurors (and others) to detect deception on the part of character witnesses (Kaplan, this volume).

Knowledge about examination techniques, of course, can be used to uncover factual truth or to obscure it. Nearly all knowledge and skills—scientific or not—have this two-sided quality. In the present case, it is more likely the scientist who will be troubled by the obscuring use of scientific knowledge. Jurists generally take the position that "the main purpose of the legal process is peaceful resolution of a dispute rather than the acquisition of information. . . . In our adjudicatory system reliability in determining the facts is an important, but not the only, ideal" (Loh, this volume, p. 36). Regardless of the lower valuation of truth in law than in science, scientists studying the use of evidence in litigation have an obligation to caution jurists and the general public about the admission of pseudo-scientific evidence. There are a variety of fields that have clad themselves in the name and trappings of science, without possessing the defining characteristics of a science. Polygraph examinations are a case in point. Yet, numerous state and federal courts admit polygraph evidence as expert testimony (Lykken, this volume). The issue is not whether a discipline or a study is perfect. If admissibility were contingent on perfect comprehensiveness and accuracy of knowledge, there would be little testimony at all. The issue is the degree of imperfection. The question is not whether a field or study has flaws, but whether these flaws are fatal (Jacoby, this volume). The flaws are fatal in such efforts as to determine truth-telling or lying via polygraph examinations, character traits via handwriting analysis, or the future via the casting of horoscopes. When scientific laypersons, such as jurists, attribute scientific validity and reliability to such enterprises, scientists should not remain silent, even if they normally shun the adversary role. It is clear that scientific studies for litigation need not limit attention to lay testimony. Expert testimony deserves equal scrutiny.

The last branch of *evidentiology* to be discussed investigates the use to which jurists put scientific evidence. Do the courts make use of the available relevant evidence or do they ignore it? Do the courts use such evidence fairly or do they misuse it? Do judges routinely gather the best evidence (if necessary, by their own efforts) and accept its message, or do they normally ignore scientific evidence and use it only when it can serve to ornament decisions reached on other grounds? The evidence on the use of evidence is quite clear; judges do all of these things. The high prevalence of nonuse and misuse, and the fact that the very products of science are involved, make this the gloomiest branch of a dismal science. Nevertheless, scholars can be found who will pursue the subject matter, persistently, and, even, with passion. It may be injured pride. It may also be the optimism that unflagging educational efforts, sooner or later, will cause the judges to mend their ways. The literature is critical of the courts, but invariably it seeks to be instructive and helpful. Members of nearly all the behavioral sciences have contributed to this branch of evidentiary inquiry (Collins, 1978; Davis,

1973; Rosen, 1972; Saks & Baron, 1980; Saks & Van Duizend, 1983; Sperlich, 1980b; Wessel, 1980; Wolf, 1981; Zeisel, 1978).

The sequence in which the three branches have been presented corresponds directly to their relative development. Studies *about* litigation are considerably more prevalent than studies *for* litigation. Studies of the *use* of scientific evidence are least frequent. The field as a whole, however, is well developed and as advanced as any of the behavioral sciences. An important indicator is the methodological sophistication of the field. Many of the available texts have strong methodological components (Baade, 1963; Loevinger, 1963; Loewen, 1982; Mannheim, 1965; Nagel, 1975; Talarico, 1980a). In addition, there is a multitude of writings that advise on and/or make use of particular technical procedures, such as survey research and other field work (Barksdale, 1957; Jacoby, this volume; McCall, 1975; Zeisel, 1960), experiments (Advisory Committee, 1981; Beutel, 1957; Campbell & Ross, 1968; Heinz & Kerstetter, 1980; Zeisel, 1956), content analysis (Kort, 1963), cost-benefit analysis (Young, 1978), operations research (Reed, 1973), modeling and simulation (Diamond, 1979; Grofman, 1977; Nagel, 1977; Ulmer, 1967), and various types of statistical analysis (Baldus & Cole, 1980; Finkelstein, 1978; Fisher, 1980; Kaye, 1982; Loewen, 1982; Lozowick, 1968; Talarico, 1980b; Zeisel & Callahan, 1963). Evidence for the advancement of the field can also be found in the increasing availability of summarizing substantive texts and readers (Bermant, Nemeth, & Vidmar, 1976; Evan, 1962; Fields & Horwitz, 1982; Flynn & Conrad, 1978; Gordon, 1975; Haward, 1981; Kerr & Bray, 1982; Lloyd-Bostock, 1981; Sales, 1977; Tapp & Levine, 1977). Most impressive for a law-related field, perhaps, is the appearance of relevant volumes in the style of law school case books (Evan, 1980a; Friedman & Macaulay, 1969; Grossman & Wells, 1972; Katz, Goldstein & Dershowitz, 1967; Loh, 1984). The offerings of the behavioral sciences to the law are substantial, diverse, important, and quite sophisticated. How do jurists approach these offerings?

COMPLAINTS ABOUT SCIENCE

With decidedly mixed feelings. Most jurists understand that science can make important contributions to their work; few appear to be particularly elated about it. There is considerable variation, of course, in the degree to which jurists welcome scientific assistance, not only among individuals, but also among the subdivisions of the profession. As a group, attorneys appear to be more open to science than judges. The criminal bar seems to be more welcoming than the civil bar. Few jurists, however, seem to be without apprehensions and complaints. Some of the charges are rather droll, e.g., that scientists are incomprehensible because they use *jargon* (Lochner, 1973, pp. 825-825). Are these the people who talk about collateral estoppel, sequestration, and ratio decedendi? There is no field of systematic inquiry or specialized activity that does not have a technical language. Neither science nor the law, neither the arts nor industry, neither politics nor sports, can work exclusively with the vocabulary of ordinary languages. Of course, one can overdo linguistic inventiveness, substituting technical expression for ordinary words without real need. Particularly, when communications are directed at persons outside the profession, there is an obligation to compose the message in an accessible language. Science has this obligation, so does the law—a field, it should be noted, notorious for the inability of judges to instruct jurors in a language that the latter can understand (Elwork & Sales, this volume).

Another amusing charge is that of the *partisan scientist*. A working assumption in the law is that while attorneys are partisan advocates, expert witnesses approach the case from a neutral perspective. Generally, reality conforms to this assumption (the science-inherent exceptions will be noted shortly). Though expert witnesses usually appear on behalf of one of the parties, most scientists, most of the time, have no personal interest in the outcome of the dispute, but provide undistorted evidence and honest opinions, as best they can (Saks & Van Duizend, 1983, pp. 71-72; Shuchman, 1979, p. 55). And who is unhappy about it? Jurists, of course. Warnings about cooptation are a recurring theme in the literature. While scientists persistently seek ways to preserve expert neutrality (Jacoby, this volume; Rosen, 1972, p. 202; Kantrowitz, 1977; Sperlich, 1980b, pp. 288-289), attorneys more likely will try to convert the expert witness into a partisan (Saks & Van Duizend, 1983, pp. 72-73; Peters, 1980, pp. 158-159; Wolf, 1981, pp. 273-274). As is true in other areas of human interaction, if the seduction is successful, the seducer is likely to view the seduced as a "whore" (Saks & Van Duizend, 1983, p. 73). "But will he respect me tomorrow morning?" seems to be a useful question even for expert witnesses.

Some scientists, of course, need not be seduced. When strong partisan commitments are joined to weak commitments to professional ethics, neutrality is likely to be lost. Disputes that involve issues of social policy are likely to attract partisan-scientists. Desegregation litigation is an obvious case-in-point (Wolf, 1981; Rist & Anson, 1977; Newby, 1969). As other persons, scientists have policy preference and ideological predilections. As citizens, they are entitled to have them. They are not entitled, however, to let their ideological choices determine the results of their scientific inquiries—whether these results are intended for publication in professional journals or for expert testimony in courts of law. Not everyone agrees with this. Some believe that scientific evenhandedness is a bias in itself, and that science should be partisan—on the "right side," of course (Loewen, 1982, pp. 48-49, 54-55; Sperlich, 1983, pp. 472-473; also see the Loewen/Sperlich exchange, 1984, in 67 *Judicature* 264). Others believe that scientific neutrality is not possible in principle. For some this means that scientific objectivity is a mere pretense, that scientific work naturally is ideological and/or partisan, permitting scientists to "discover" what they have advocated all along or what their clients want to hear (Horowitz, 1980, p. 152). For the pseudo-sciences, such as psychiatry and polygraph analysis, this may even be true—thus the "hired guns" and the "battles of the experts." More often, the rejection of the possibility of scientific neutrality means a denial that science can be *value-free* (Loh, this volume; Monahan, 1977, p. 206).

The denial of what must be the very first principle of any *science*—that its findings reflect observed reality rather than the preferences of its practitioners—involves a drastic, and perhaps even willful, mis-understanding of what claims are advanced when the term *value-free* is applied to a scientific discipline. First, the claim is a normative statement. It is not an assertion that all scientists work in the value-free mode, only that they *should*, if their inquiries are to be truly scientific. Second, the claim is a very limited statement. It refers merely to the non-relationship between a scientist's values and the results of his inquiries. The claim does *not* include any assertion that scientists don't have values, that the values that scientists hold do not influence their choice of subject matter, that science need not be concerned about values (e.g., research ethics), or that science has no interest in values as an object of inquiry. Behavioral scientists may well be committed Republican or Democratic partisans. If, however, they were to under-take studies of "presidential approval" (same time, same place, equally competent), the reported ratings for a Republican president should be the same, regardless of the fact that one scientist would like to see them low, and the other high. Were this not the case, the distinction between ideology and science would dissolve. It is plainly false to claim that scientists *cannot* work in the value-free mode. It is true that scientists *do not* always work in conformity with this principle. This lowers the

worth and reputation of science. Greater ideological self-conscious-
ness, unfailing disclosure of personal preferences, and a more rigorous
enforcement of professional ethics are among the remedies.

In respect to behavioral science, the claim of ideological contamina-
tion often takes a more specific form: *liberal* advocacy (Loh, this
volume; Moynihan, 1979, pp. 19-20). This contains an element of truth.
When there is ideological commitment, it is more often on the liberal
side. However, even in the desegregation cases, not all partisan-experts
were of this persuasion (Newby, 1969; Rist & Anson, 1977). The
argument also fails to distinguish "pure" and "applied" science. The
former aims at knowledge without being particularly interested in the
usefulness of the findings. The latter takes utility as its prime concern.
Indeed, some branches of the latter, quite self-consciously, perceive of
themselves as "therapeutic" enterprises (Weber & McCall, 1978, pp.
7-9). There is a clear commitment to "improving" society. The goals of
"improvement" flow from the values of the practitioners. While
objective studies remain possible, they are rare. Inquiry serves
implementation. At the same time, however, the "therapeutic" fields,
such as social work, community psychology, urban planning, or
business administration, do not generally claim to be value-free.

When the argument of liberal advocacy is advanced in the context of
litigation, the critics usually fail to appreciate the conditions of expert
participation. It is not necessarily the scientists who align science with
the "change-oriented" side. The intensely conservative nature of the
law favors those who want to keep things as they are; stare decisis. The
partisans of the status quo naturally have the upper hand in legal
proceedings. They do not need procedural innovations (Brandeis
brief!) new pleadings, novel interpretations, or the exploration of scientific evidence. Precedent will win the day. Not surprisingly, liberal
judges (Rosen, 1972, pp. 211-218) and attorneys for the *dis*advantaged
(Garry, 1969; Ginger, 1972; Kairys, 1982; Wells, this volume; Loh, this
volume) are more likely to consult scientists and ask them to testify,
than will their counterparts. It is not appropriate to infer liberal
ideological commitment solely from litigational association. The courtesy
enjoyed by attorneys should be extended to expert witnesses: appearing on behalf of a party does not mean approving of it, or identifying with
any of its positions.

An important complaint against the behavioral sciences is that their
use in litigation will undermine the constitution, sometimes because of
the fixed position regarding human nature to which they adhere
(Robinson, 1980), and sometimes because they are forever changing

their views (Cahn, 1955). They are said to be particularly dangerous to civil rights and civil liberties (Cahn, 1955; Dworkin, 1977a; O'Brien, 1980). As noted earlier, scientific evidence will have no effect that the law does not want it to have. Jurists have total control over the admission and use of such evidence. Scientific evidence can be "reinterpreted" by the courts, or presented merely as ornamentation (Sperlich, 1980a, 1980b). If there are changes in the construction of constitutional clauses, it will be because judges want them, not because scientists have provided expert testimony. The source of the "constitutional danger" is the alleged uncertainty (inconsistency, instability) of findings in the behavioral sciences.[10] As with the matter of "jargon," jurists denounce in science what they find unobjectionable, or even praiseworthy in the law. Uncertainty, when in the law, may even be counted as a "blessing" (Carter, 1979, pp. 35-36). It is true that scientists will disagree among themselves, but they have nothing on the jurists. Is there any human enterprise that can rival the inconsistencies of the law—from the reversals and counter-reversals at different levels in the court hierarchy, to the split-decisions of the appellate courts, to the different rulings in different federal districts? Attorneys not only "shop" for experts; they "shop" for judges and even courts (if they can)—one wonders why?

It is true, of course, that there is instability in the findings of the behavioral sciences. Different findings emerge in different places and at different times. This may be disturbing to people whose happiness is predicated on the existence of eternal and universal laws. Given the many inconsistencies in the law, it is difficult to see why jurists should be so troubled by scientific inconsistency. Human beings, in any case, are able to make choices. They are not birds, whose songs are determined by instinct. Human beings will sing different songs in different places and at different times. This is the *fundamental* misconception of the law about behavioral, or any science; that its findings will converge in *absolute truth*, in pronouncements of eternal and universal validity (Cohen & Weiss, 1977, pp. 72-75; Loh, 1984, pp. 743-744). The only possible obligation and only sensible goal of behavioral science is to record accurately all existing variety and changes, not to pretend that all human behavior fits a single mold. The instability is not in the behavioral sciences, but in the phenomena that they study. For decades in this country, of all religious groups, Jews gave the strongest support to the Democratic party. Recent years have seen a rapid decline in this support, and the realignment, probably, is not yet completed. Are the social sciences untrustworthy because they report changes in the relationship between religious affiliation and party preference?

Changes in human behavior may indeed become constitutionally relevant. It may well be that, in a given time-place context, segregated educational facilities have an effect "x" on minority students, and it may equally be true that at a later date this effect no longer occurs. Perhaps minority students have changed, gained new pride, so the presence or absence of other groups in the classroom has become irrelevant. This merely means that in the pursuit of particular constitutional guarantees, certain interventionist remedies may be required at one time, but not at the other. It decidedly does not mean that the rightful claim to constitutional protection as such has become subject to the changing findings of science. Constitutional rights are *normative*, not factual, assertions. Norms cannot be invalidated (or validated) by facts. All that science can do is to show whether current social practices prevent or aid the implementation of some norm. The muddle-headed thinking reflected in the "slippery slope" and "flimsy foundation" arguments (Loh, 1984, p. 615), is a consequence of the failure to clearly distinguish between *norms* and *facts,* or, even, of denying that they can be distinguished.[11]

COMPLAINTS ABOUT THE LAW

Forensic scientists also have grievances, though they tend to complain less than jurists. Some of the complaints encountered in the preceding section can now be found in the reverse direction: e.g., the use of jargon in the law, and the failure of jurists to understand the requirements of science (Loewen, 1982, pp. 23-24; Saks & Baron, 1980, pp. 62-81; Saks & Van Duizend, 1983, pp. 10, 57-60, 92-93; Sperlich, 1980b, pp. 282-283.) Related to this is the frequent change that jurists do not know when to use experts and how to use them. Often attorneys call much too late for scientific assistance (e.g., calling for a public opinion survey a few days before the evidence is due in court), and occasionally they hire the wrong expert (Greene et al., this volume; Loewen, 1982, pp. 15-18; Saks & Van Duizend, 1983, pp. 51-52). As noted earlier, there is substantial concern and discomfort about being pushed into a partisan role.

A recurrent theme is the discourtesy of jurists. Scientists feel that often they are treated as "hired hands," to whom one gives orders, rather than as fellow professionals, deserving of civility and of respect. The specific charges range from the attorneys' failure to prepare themselves and reserve enough time for meetings, to not informing the scientist about the outcome of the case, and to not paying bills in a timely fashion, if at all (Saks & Van Duizend, 1983, 58-60, 82). Judges also are a source of professional discourtesies (*Ballew v. Georgia*, 1978; Sperlich, 1980a, pp. 280-282). Indeed, some scientists will not provide expert testimony because they find the workings of the system personally degrading (Wolf, 1981, p. 273).

The *adversary system*, rather than personal discourtesies, is the source of most grievances. The most thorough analysis of the presentation and use of expert testimony flatly concludes that the adversary system is *not* a dependable method to arrive at factual truth in litigation (Wolf, 1981, p. 268). Jurists, of course, praise adversary proceedings. Wigmore considered cross-examination (i.e., the adversary system) to be the "greatest legal engine ever invented for the discovery of truth" (Loh, this volume, p. 34); he even argued that it is consistent with scientific principles (Saks & Hastie, 1978, p. 164).[12] Such valuations may be simple conceits, for it is doubtful that adversary proceedings are fully dependable even for the determination of case facts (Shuchman, 1979, pp. 56-60). The adversary system, in any case, is glaringly deficient in its ability to accurately determine "social fact" issues. Perhaps adversary proceedings can determine reasonably well whether or not person A committed act B. They are ill-suited, however, to determine the general causes, frequencies, and consequences of acts (Wolf, 1981, p. 262; Saks & Van Duizend, 1983, p. 70). The more complex and the more technical the subject matter, the less well suited is the question-and-answer format to a full and accurate communication of the findings.[13] Adversary proceedings present evidence in fragments, separated by substantial intervals in time. There is no logical or sequential order, greatly jeopardizing the coherence, quality, and meaning of scientific evidence (Marshall, 1969, p. 109; Wolf, 1981, p. 89. 259-262). Instructions from the bench, often not even comprehensible to the jurors, will not remedy days or weeks of confusion (Kaplan, this volume).[14]

The adversary system has been characterized as a "world of make-believe" (Marshall, 1969, p. 123) and as an exercise in "competitive lying" (Manning, 1974, p. 821). This is harsh, but not altogether wrong. The adversary system does not encourage the telling of the whole truth (Rosen, 1972, pp. 202-203; Shuchman, 1979, p. 41; Wolf, 1981, pp. 259, 272). According to Wolf (1981), the relevant evidence may not be presented fully and accurately because of differences in resources or competence among the litigants (pp. 121-123, 231, 260, 268-269).

Counter-evidence may not be made known to the court because the right experts are not called, because cross-examination is not vigorous, or even because of collusion among the parties (pp. 82, 129, 224, 263-264). The adversary system is as likely to confuse judge and jury as to educate them (pp. 85-86, 101, 108, 135, 229, 260-261). It leaves contradictions unresolved; it encourages attention to be focused on the personal characteristics of expert witnesses rather than on the quality of their evidence; it permits deliberate confusing of the witness; it obscures the distinction between expressions of value or policy preferences and factual testimony (pp. 275-277; see also Moore, 1974, p. 101; Loftus & Goodman, this volume). It also pushes experts into partisan and advocacy roles (Wolf, 1981, pp. 34, 273; Saks & Van Duizend, 1983, p. 72). The basic problem of adversary proceedings is that they assign responsibility for the presentation of factual truth to the parties least interested in it. The professional duty of an attorney is to present his client in the best possible light. Factual omissions and distortions are part of that picture. Customarily, the judge is merely a passive recipient of whatever the parties chose to offer, though current procedure would allow a more active role (Saks & Van Duizend, 1983, pp. 69-70).[15] The mythology of the law is that full truth will emerge from partial presentations, and that each party will expose the other's omissions, distortions, and lies. Scholars, such as Wolf, who have investigated the process, arrive at different conclusions.

Misuse and deliberate nonuse of scientific evidence are widespread practices in the law (Saks & Baron, 1980). Attorneys may claim mitigating circumstances for their distortions and partial accounts; they are *supposed* to be advocates. Judges have no such excuse. They, if anyone in the legal system, are expected to be interested in the emergence of a full and accurate set of facts. Unfortunately, the relationship of the bench to factual truth is no less problematic than that of the bar. The worst offenders are the justices of the higher courts, who tend to have a rather high regard for their intuitions and their apprehension of "common sense," particularly in respect to "social facts" (Sperlich, 1980a, pp. 266-274; Sperlich, 1980b, pp. 280-282). This illusion of "already knowing-it-all" diminishes interest in scientific evidence. Explicit references to such evidence in rulings is no guarantee that it was influential. Often references are merely ornamental (Doyle, 1977, p. 13; Chambers, 1977, p. 33; Coons, 1977, p. 52; Sperlich, 1980a, p. 271). They may also serve as rationalizations for decisions reached on other grounds. (Loh, 1984, p. 742; Marvell, 1978, p. 181; Rosen, 1972, pp. 204-211). Scientific findings tend to be cited when they support judicially desired outcomes and ignored when they do not. (Miller, 1969, p. 198). If the findings do not support desired outcomes, and if cognizance cannot be avoided, distortion and misuse tend to be their fate (Sperlich, 1980a, pp. 265-266; Marvell, 1980, p. 29). It is not surprising that attorneys are more concerned with victory than with truth (Loftus & Goodman, this volume; Shuchman, 1979, pp. 34, 49). It is surprising to discover open judicial approval of "fictional" evidence, as long as it "serves its purpose and produces victory" (Miller 1969, p. 192).

Scientists tend to be upset when they discover that the adversary system does not work as advertised, and that jurists take liberties with evidence. They invest much time and effort in uncovering the deficiencies of procedure and the shortcomings of the bar and bench—and cannot understand why diagnostic statements and therapeutic proposals evoke such slight interest. This is the *fundamental* misunderstanding of science about the law: that law values truth as highly as does science. Scientists would not make this error in respect to other disciplines, say medicine, or music, or literature. What misleads them about the law is the presence of the factual component in dispute resolution. When courts must resolve factual disputes, scientists assume that jurists will be just as interested in truth as they are. The assumption is wrong. This is not to say that jurists are uninterested in truth, or even opposed to it. It is to say that jurists value other principles more highly. It is to say that the law has other goals than science.

The primary purpose of the law is not the determination of factual truth, but the authoritative resolution of disputes (Loh, this volume). If speedy, authoritative, and lasting dispute resolution can be achieved with the facts, fine. There is little hesitation, however, to attain resolution without the facts, or even against them. "Facts" in the law, it should be noted, are not necessarily that which is known to be true. It may merely be what has been stipulated by an agreement of the parties, or what has been asserted from the bench (Shuchman, 1979, p. 16). The so-called "legal fictions" are a case in point. They are deliberate factual assertions, known to be false. The use of such "fictional" facts is testimony to the pre-eminence of goals and values other than truth (Ross, 1980, p. 177; Saks & Baron, 1980, pp. 176-177; Loh, 1984, pp. 721-722).

The primary *goal* of the law, as noted, is to resolve disputes. The primary *values* often are identified as "justice" and "fairness" (Wessel, 1980, p. 34). Such terms, however, are problematic. Justice and fairness are in the eye of the beholder. To the litigant, surely, they are *winning the suit.* To the judge dealing in legal fictions, they are the implementation of a certain policy—such as, that *somebody* ought to support a child (Saks & Baron, 1980, p. 177). The legal process, it may fairly be said, is not evidence-driven, but *policy-driven.* Necessarily, one who makes or implements the policy will call it "fair" and "just." Naturally, one who benefits from the policy will reach the same assessment. As Plato's Thrasymachus knew well, justice is the interest of the stronger—in Harold Lasswell's memorable phrase: politics is who gets what, when and how. Substantive as well as procedural laws are products of the political process, the contrary claims of divine and natural law scholars notwithstanding. As seen, policy choices also are part of the adjudicative process.[16]

At least two schools of legal theory, formalism and neo-formalism, have devoted their efforts to camouflaging policy choices in adjudication. The "mechanical" jurisprudence of formalism pretends that judges have no will of their own and exercise no effective influence on the disposition of cases. The correct verdict is contained in the law; judges merely find and announce it. Legal realism showed that adjudication was neither this pure, nor this simple. Neo-formalism, however, has mounted a vigorous counter-attack, urging upon judges the restraints of "principled decision-making," as well as reassuring the public that judges really find the law, not make it (Dworkin, 1977b, 1978; O'Brien, 1980). It is possible, indeed likely, that some cases are decided "mechanically" or in a "principled" manner. It is doubtful, however, that many decisions remain so "untouched by human hands." Few slogans in American politics are as misleading as the civic-class maxim that "ours is a government of laws, not of persons." Do angels make and apply our laws? It is useful to think of another motto in this context: *cui bono?* Who benefits from the denial that the legal process is part of politics, and that, as all politics, it deals in the allocation of advantages? The secondary status of truth, in any case, cannot be understood without a recognition of the political components of the law.

WHAT IS TO BE DONE?

Nothing can be done about the fundamentally different approaches of law and science to factual truth. Science *must* accord the highest value to truth, law *cannot.* Only the mutual misunderstanding can be erased. Legal reasoning is deductive and, thus, is entitled to absolute truth claims (as long as it is recognized that these claims have merely internal-logical, not external-empirical validity). Jurists expect to find similar certainty (i.e., absolutism, universalism) in the products of science. They become dissatisfied and distrustful when they do not find them. Yet, empirical-inductive fields have no right to absolutes. All they can offer are probabilities—some weaker, some stronger. The goal of science is the discovery of knowledge. Factual truth, necessarily, is the highest value. Scientists expect to find a similarly high regard for truth in the law. They become dissatisfied and distrustful when they discover how frequently law ignores the facts, and how radically it distorts them. Yet, the goals of law are the resolution of disputes and the setting of social policy. For the first task, it is more important that there is a resolution, than that the resolution has the strongest possible factual support. The second task is normative—the institutionalization of interests and the distribution of advantages—and only indirectly related to the world of facts.

Given the uncertain nature of scientific knowledge, the difficulties and inconveniences inherent in cooperation, and the ease of writing "legal fiction"—should jurists continue to seek the assistance of science? The answer must be yes. Effectively, there is no choice. Resolving factual disputes is inescapably part of the legal process. While there is no formal tribunal in which legal fictions can be challenged and declared false, there are limits to distortion. The legal system needs credibility to be effective. It will lose credibility when too many of its rules and decisions depart the company of truth (Marshall, 1969, pp. 121-122; Miller, 1969, p. 195).

Given the likelihood of the misuse of its findings, the unpalatable role demands and discourtesies associated with providing expert testimony, and the much lesser need of science for the law—should scientists continue to provide assistance to the law? The answer should be yes. Science could withdraw, but cooperation seems to be the better choice—precisely because the law cannot divorce itself altogether from the truth if it is to remain credible and effective. The particulars of the law can and must be debated. Only anarchists are likely to disagree, however, that civilized existence requires an effective and credible legal system.

The relationship between science and law is that of a "necessary but cautious alliance" (Haney, 1980, p. 193). The allies, however, should demand more of each other than has been the case in the past. Numerous reforms are possible; many have already been suggested (e.g., Konopka, 1980, pp. 133-135; Saks & Van Duizend, 1983, pp. 91-101; Sperlich, 1980b, pp. 286-289; Wessel, 1980, pp. 146-151; Wolf, 1981, pp. 280-282). They involve personal, educational, procedural, and structural changes. They require major efforts on both sides. Not all are likely to succeed, but many have an excellent chance to improve the cooperation between science and law, the use of evidence in the law, and, most importantly, the quality of dispute resolution. There will be no success, however, if each field seeks to reform itself entirely by its own wisdom. The needs as well as the knowledge of the other field must be taken into account.[17]

The first need of the law is that what is offered in its chambers as "scientific evidence" does deserve the name. This is not always the case. Jurists cannot be expected to distinguish data, generalizations, and opinions that meet scientific standards, from those that do not. They need assistance to detect non-standard operations (e.g., an experiment without a control group, or a survey with too small a sample), premature generalizations, generalizations based purely on clinical observations, ideologically motivated conclusions, the pseudo-scientific status of certain fields, as well as the (in)adequacy of particular expert witnesses. The scientific disciplines have not been sufficiently helpful in the past. They have been hampered by their customary mode of operation: collegial, voluntaristic, and rather unconcerned about intra-disciplinary disagreements—truth to be established not authoritatively or, even, persuasively, but only by reference to repeated systematic observations. Scientists also have generally shied from controversy in public fora in the (most likely correct) belief that this diminishes rather than strengthens science. Nevertheless, to improve forensic application, the sciences will have to assume greater responsibility for their own, and a greater willingness to denounce charlatans who claim the name of science.

No scientist is forced to do forensic work. If, however, he elects to apply his knowledge in the courts of law, he should meet certain standards of professional ethics and conduct. The key word is *disclosure*. Personal values and interests should be made explicit, as should be the presence of weaknesses in the evidence and the existence of alternative interpretations. Such requirements already are part of certain professional codes (Loh, 1984, p. 711). The lever available to a professional association is the certification and de-certification of its forensic specialists, already employed in some fields (Saks & Van Duizend, 1983, p. 91). The effective use of this lever will require the cooperation of the courts, admitting only certified specialists to testify as expert witnesses. The initial certification will require some demonstration of competence, by evidence of completed training and/or examination. The retention of certification will require some supervison and monitoring on part of the association. Associations must be willing to make their doubts known when testimony seems to contain technical errors, or appears to be driven by ideological concerns. Scientists, in other words, should do more of what the courts should do less—engage in adversary proceedings (Rivlin, 1973, p. 61; Levine, 1974, pp. 674-676; Loh, this volume).[18] In addition, the professional associations need to better define and promulgate the accepted standards of the field (Jacoby, this volume), including guidelines for expert testimony. What volume, consistency, and strength should findings have at a minimum, if they are to be offered as "scientific evidence" to the law?[19] "Pure" scientists will chafe under such demands, but they do not pertain to them. At stake is the organization of applied work, of the forensic sections of the various sciences. Application always has had to endure more supervision, direction, and discipline than basic scholarship.

Once the scientific disciplines have taken the necessary steps to ensure that forensic experts and testimony meet the standards of the field, ways must be found to improve access and transmission. This will require the efforts of science and of law. Education is of primary importance for the reduction of mutual incomprehension and mis-understanding. It has been advocated often enough, that law schools should broaden their horizons beyond appellate case law, and provide judges and attorneys with the variety of skills they need for successful practice. Apart from some optional courses added to the law school curricula (usually much too narrow and technical, e.g., econometrics), little progress has been made to communicate a systematic under-standing of the nature, methods, and substantive specialties of the various sciences. The professional orientation of law professors and law students, as well as the conceptual properties of the study of the law, produce powerful obstacles to a significant broadening of the cur-riculum (Loh, 1984, pp. 723-739). Fortunately, formal law school courses are but one educational avenue—one, furthermore, which will be of little use to already practicing jurists. Forensic scientists, interested legal scholars, judges, and attorneys can join forces in such ventures as special workshops, seminars, and conferences. The organizational context could be provided by law schools, academic departments, university institutes, or the professional associations of law and science. For greater permanence, it would be desirable to establish university institutes of forensic science, parallel to other academic research units. Such institutes should be staffed by jurists and scientists, and have a two-fold purpose: educating each group about the other and contributing to the development of integrated forensic research and application.[20]

In sad contrast to the remarkable record-keeping and indexing system of the law, it is difficult to locate the materials of science. The existing "abstracts" of the various disciplines are not adequate. It may be possible to develop the scientific equivalent of the West Publishing Key Number Digest System (Baron, 1980, pp. 154-155). Jurists also have problems in locating (the right) experts. It would be appropriate for the forensic fields to develop directories of experts. Bar associations might share in this task. The currently available commercial forensic-service directories are neither sufficiently comprehensive, nor sufficiently selective. The scientific fields would also perform an important service if they established panels of experts for preliminary consultation. Such panels would not provide evidence or testimony, but would direct attorneys or judges to the relevant fields and appropriate experts. Advisory panels and/or forensic institutes also could advise jurists on how to interact with scientists and assist them in assembling teams of experts in complex cases (Jacoby, this volume; Loewen, 1982, pp. 15-16). A large-scale variation of advisory panels, under the aegis of science, is the recently proposed *consensus-finding conference* (Wessel, 1980, pp. 173-183).

Scientists making their expertise more easily available to the law, is only one part of the required change. Jurists must make it easier to receive expert testimony, from the attitudinal as well as the institutional perspective. Some judges, for example, need to abandon the notion of unlimited personal competence, and acknowledge that systematic research is a better guide to factual truth than intuition and common sense. Courts also should liberalize admissibility rules, so that relevant testimony will not be kept out on technical grounds—prototypical is the relaxation of the hearsay rule to permit testimony based on opinion surveys. In the context of the adversary system, judges may have to do more than to open doors. Given the litigants' limited interest in presenting all of the facts and presenting them accurately, judges may have to step outside and actively gather the necessary evidence. Several vehicles already exist for this type of search, among them judicial notice for undisputed facts and commissioned research for contested facts (Konopka, 1980, p. 133; Marvell, 1980, p. 164; Rosen, 1980, p. 13-14; Sperlich, 1980b, pp. 285-288). Judges may appoint special masters and ad hoc panels of experts, to receive advice on the proper interpretation of court-gathered evidence (Greene et al., this volume; Lempert, 1981, pp. 125-126; Konopka, 1980, p. 133; Wessel,

1980, pp. 148-149). This may take the form of a blue-ribbon jury (which can be composed in any way) to render an advisory opinion on a disputed factual point (Konopka, 1980, p. 134; Sperlich, 1982b, pp. 416-417). In order to have a more permanent source of advice, a judge may even want to appoint a science clerk in addition to the usual law clerks.[21] The organization of a greater number of courts of special jurisdiction would produce judges with substantial scientific under-standing and competence, less needful of expert advice (Konopka, 1980, pp. 134-135; Wessel, 1980, p. 148). Judges, of course, can also return to the litigants the burden of assembling a more complete account of the facts. If the presentation of evidence is partial because of one side's lesser resources, a sharing of data may be ordered, or the court may make available additional resources to the disadvantaged party. Courts may even be able to impose on attorneys the obligation to bring to attention unfavorable as well as favorable evidence that has been encountered—analogous to the obligation to report unfavorable legal precedent (Sperlich, 1980b, p. 286, n. 34).

The reform suggestions discussed so far leave intact the courts' customary adversary proceedings. It is not certain that changes *within* the adversary system can succeed. The partisan interests of the litigants are undisputed and unquestioned. Even a more active judicial role may not be able to overcome the impact of partial and distorted presentations. Judges, in any case, produce their own distortions. Given the habitual and extensive nonuse and misuse of scientific evidence in the courts, it is not surprising that some reform suggestions aim at fact-determination *outside* the courtroom and apart from adversary proceedings. At times the establishment of government agencies has been suggested, such as Justice Cardozo's ministry of justice. Others have proposed the establishment of research offices, working independently, though attached to particular courts (Sperlich, 1980b, pp. 288-289). Best known is the idea of the science court, an entirely independent assembly of full-time scientific experts, providing factual dispute resolution and evidence evaluation for courts and other governmental agencies (Kantrowitz, 1976, 1980; Boffey, 1976; Casper, 1976; Martin, 1977; Matheny & Williams, 1981). The science court has been proposed in a variety of embodiments, differing in whether its decisions would be binding, who would appoint its members, and by what procedures it would operate.[22] The science court is the most powerful construct yet suggested. Particularly if its decisions were to be binding, its impact on law and society would be immense. Not surprisingly, doubts and opposition have been voiced (Loh, 1984, pp.

712-713; O'Brien, 1980, p. 15; Saks & Van Duizend, 1983; pp. 94-95). Strong and independent courts of evidence will not find ready acceptance. Most judges and attorneys are certain to oppose them. Prevailing popular distrust of technology and science will aid the antagonism of the jurists. To the degree, however, that reform is not possible *outside* the regular courts, it becomes imperative to improve the use of scientific evidence *inside* the current structures, with the rules and conventions of the adversary system as the primary focus of reform.

Which changes will bring improvement? The last way by which the answer to this question can be found is the method of the law— deductive reasoning. Systematic experiments, meticulous observations, and careful evaluations are needed instead (Sperlich, 1980b, p. 289; Saks & Van Duizend, 1983, pp. 97-100). Establishing the standards against which success will be measured (e.g., accuracy and completeness of testimony) is, in part, a normative undertaking. Determining to what degree different structural and procedural arrangements satisfy these standards, however, is an empirical endeavor.

Few observers are satisfied with the current state of scientific evidence in litigation; many agree that matters should not remain as they are. What is needed, however, are not simply changes, but *improvements*. The task of *evidentiology* is to identify the changes that help. Their implementation will make our science less dismal. Anyone for optimism?

NOTES

1. A similar need exists when courts have to design a *remedy*, following a verdict of "liable" (Wolf, 1981, pp. 211-238). Indeed, some commentators feel that the real value of behavioral science lies in helping judges designing remedies (Doyle, 1977, p. 15).

2. There are a number of scholars who oppose the use of scientific evidence and expert testimony in litigation. Their position, however, tends to be *not* that its grievances justify science to withhold valuable services, but that these services are lacking value (Greene et al., this volume; Wells, this volume).

3. I use the term *behavioral sciences* as a convenient shorthand for psychology and the social sciences.

4. Disciplines other than the behavioral sciences, of course, have relevance for the law. The natural sciences, for example, are important in providing empirical generalizations *for* the interpretation of case facts. The behavioral sciences, however, are the primary fields of conducting studies *about* the law.

5. Studies *for* the law require much greater law-science cooperation than studies *about* the law. The close interaction of jurists and scientists provides multiple opportunities for incomprehension and misunderstanding. Most of them are not wasted and the discipline enters into its more dismal regions. The discipline also takes on a more applied orientation. Scholarly interests tend to be practical and/or reform oriented, including, however, the "pure science" interest of testing the validity of theoretical constructs through practical application.

6. Existing procedural rules, even those of recent origin, do not generally take into account relevant scientific findings (Wells, this volume; Elwork & Sales, this volume; Kaplan, this volume).

7. Lay persons serving as jurors are not the only ones wrongly inferring credibility from certainty. Even legal professionals are subject to this error (Wells, this volume).

8. "...almost all of the current legal perspective is based on the intuition of the judges involved in the cases. ...[certain criteria] are appealing at an intuitive level but are not in general agreement with empirical findings" (Wells, this volume, p. 45).

9. Some commentators, however, object to expert assistance, fearing that jurors will become *too* skeptical of eyewitness testimony, and that conviction rates will decline (Wells, this volume; Greene et al, this volume). The fear of fewer convictions also has produced objections to behavioral science assistance in the selection of trial jurors (Etzioni, 1974).

10. Sometimes the complaint is couched in the form that the behavioral sciences, in contrast to the natural sciences, do not have "universal laws" (Robinson, 1980, p. 24). This involves at least a partial misunderstanding of the differences between natural and behavioral sciences. Not all findings of the natural sciences are universal laws; nor is all natural science knowledge correct; nor are the natural sciences free of diverse interpretations of the same phenomenon—one only needs to think of the particle and wave theories of light. Jurists should not be permitted to get away with the story that they dearly love science, just not those "soft" behavioral sciences. The uneasy reception of "hard" science evidence into the legal process bears an uncanny resemblance to the difficulties experienced by the "softer" fields (Sperlich, 1980b, p. 282).

11. None of this meant to deny the presence of knowledge instability because of technical inadequacies or simple error. This is a problem shared by all sciences. Nor is there any intent to deny that scientific findings are less than totally certain. *All* scientiific evidence is probabilistic (Loh, this volume). These matters, however, are not the points of attack in the "constitutional danger" arguments.

12. To the contrary, the scientific method is one of the two chief alternatives to the adversary system (Wessel, 1980, pp. 42-47, 141-142). The other is the inquisitorial system of Continental (civil law) jurisprudence (Abraham, 1980, pp. 105-107; Ehrmann, 1976, pp. 88-95; Merryman, 1969, pp. 120-139).

13. The opponents of trial by jury have not been slow to take advantage of the problems associated with complex litigations: Jurors do not understand the evidence? Abolish the jurors. Judges, however, do not have a much easier time with complexity than jurors. The required remedies lie in the area of pretrial and courtroom procedure, rather than in the choice of adjudicators (Sperlich, 1982a, 1982b).

14. It should also be noted that the rules of evidence, developed to control the jury (Loh, this volume), are not uniformly friendly to the search for truth; some promote it, some obstruct it (Evan, 1980b, p. 163). Here also are possibilities for reform.

15. One of the strongest current pushes for greater judicial activism is found in an area in which it is least needed—the voir dire of prospective jurors (see Bermant, this volume).

16. Adjudicative policymaking may take place in jury as well as in bench trials. Nullification is the primary manifestation of jury policy choices, even if such policymaking can apply only to the instant case (Scheflin, 1972; Kadish & Kadish, 1973; Jacobsohn, 1977; Scheflin & Van Dyke, 1980).

17. Once again, science has more to offer to the law than vice versa. Yet, the law has remained almost entirely "immune" to scientific methods and findings (Marshall, 1969, p. 119). Scientific knowledge about communication and decision-making has had practically no effect on the conduct of trials (Evan, 1980b, p. 162). Indeed, the advisory committee that prepared the new federal rules of evidence did not include a single scientist, consisting entirely of attorneys and judges (Shuchman, 1979, p. 50).

18. The idea of adversary science proceedings has already met opposition (Wessel, 1980, pp. 148-149).

19. This does not preclude testimony about lack of adequate knowledge or division among scientists. Presenting *uncertainty* to the courts can also be valuable. It may restrain judges from enacting into law purely personal certainties—usually mistaken (Haney, 1980, p. 186).

20. The primary need of jurists, it should be emphasized, is not to gain command of the substance of scientific fields. Few judges or attorneys require extensive substantive competence. Exceptions are judges of specialized courts and attorneys in specialized practice. What jurists need above all is an understanding of the procedures, methods, current capabilities, and philosophical foundations of science.

21. It should not be overlooked that jurors also can benefit from the assistance of special science masters or other court-appointed, neutral educators. Given current procedures (e.g., no transcripts, fragmented presentation, unresolved contradictions), jurors are at a particular handicap to make sense of conflicting expert testimony. At the very least, such technical innovations as edited video presentations of testimony should be employed (Miller & Fontes, 1979).

22. There is substantial disagreement whether the science court should employ adversary methods (Horowitz, 1980, pp. 153-154; Loh, 1984, p. 711; Wessel, 1980, pp. 148-149). I hold to the hypothesis that an effective science court (or similar organization) requires a shift away from pure collegiality toward adversariness. Of course, the shift should not go so far as to adopt the adversary proceedings presently employed in our courts of law.

REFERENCES

Abraham, H. J. (1980). *The judicial process* (4th ed.). New York: Oxford University Press.

Advisory Committee on Experimentation in the Law (1981). *Experimentation in the Law.* Washington, DC: Federal Judicial Center.

Austin, W., & Utne, M. K. (1977). Sentencing: Discretion and justice in judicial decision-making. In B. D. Sales (Ed.), *Psychology in the legal process.* New York: Spectrum Publications.

Baade, H. W. (Ed.). (1963). *Jurimetrics.* New York: Basic Books.

Baldus, D. G., & Cole, J.W.L. (1980). *Statistical proof of discrimination.* New York: McGraw-Hill.

Ballew v. Georgia, 435 U.S. 246 (1978).

Barksdale, H. C. (1957). *The use of survey research findings as legal evidence.* Pleasantville, NY: Printer's Ink Books.

Barnett, R. E., & Hagel, J., III (Eds.). (1977). *Assessing the criminal.* Cambridge, MA: Ballinger.

Baron, C. H. (1980). Overcoming barriers to the use of applied social research in the courts. In M. J. Saks & C. H. Baron (Eds.), *The use/nonuse/misuse of applied social research in the courts.* Cambridge, MA: Abt Books.

Becker, G. S., & Landes, W. M. (Eds.). (1974). *Essays in the economics of crime and punishment.* New York: Columbia University Press.

Beckett, J. S., & Bell, R. A. (1979). Community standards: Admitting a public opinion poll into evidence in an obscenity case. *Case and Comment, 84,* p. 18.

Bedau, H. A. (Ed.). (1982). *The death penalty in America.* (3rd ed.). New York: Oxford University Press.

Bennett, C. (1983). Jury selection: A psychological approach. *Social Action and the Law, 9,*(3), 77.

Berger, R. (1977). *Government by judiciary.* Cambridge, MA: Harvard University Press.

Berk, R. A. (1976). Social science and jury selection: A case study of a civil suit. In G. Bermant, C. Nemeth, & N. Vidmar (Eds.), *Psychology and the law: Research frontiers.* Lexington, MA: Lexington Books.

Bermant, G., Nemeth, C., & Vidmar, N. (Eds.). (1976). *Psychology and the law: Research frontiers.* Lexington, MA: Lexington Books.

Bernd, J. L. (Ed.) (1967). *Mathematical applications in political science.* Charlottesville: University Press of Virginia.

Beutel, F. K. (1957). *Some potentialities of experimental jurisprudence as a new branch of social science.* Lincoln: University of Nebraska Press.

Boffey, P. M. (1976). Science court: High official back test of controversial concept. *Science, 194,* p. 167.

Brown v. Board of Education, 347 U.S. 483 (1954).

Cahn, E. (1955). Jurisprudence. *New York University Law Review, 30,* p. 150.

Campbell, D. T., & Ross, H. L. (1968). The Connecticut crackdown on speeding: Time series data in quasi-experimental analysis. *Law and Society Review, 3,* p. 33.

Carter, L. H. (1979). *Reason in law.* Boston: Little, Brown.

Casper, B. M. (1976). Technology policy and democracy: Is the proposed science court what we need? *Science, 194,* p. 29.

Chambers, J. L. (1977). Implementing the promise of *Brown*: Social science and the courts in future school litigation. In R. C. Rist & R. J. Anson (Eds.), *Education, social science, and the judicial process.* New York: Teachers College Press.

Champagne, A., & Nagel, S. (1982). The psychology of judging. In N. L. Kerr & R. M. Bray (Eds.), *The psychology of the courtroom.* New York: Academic Press.

Christie, R. (1976). Probability v. precedence: The social psychology of jury selection. In G. Bermant, C. Nemeth, & N. Vidmar (Eds.), *Psychology and the law: Research frontiers.* Lexington, MA: Lexington Books.

Clark, K. B. (1959). The desegregation cases: Criticism of the social scientist's role. *Villanova Law Review, 5,* p. 224.

Cohen, D. K., & Weiss, J. A. (1977). Social science and social policy: Schools and race. In R. C. Rist & R. J. Anson (Eds.), *Education, social science, and the judicial process.* New York: Teachers College Press.

Cohn, A., & Udolf, R. (1979). *The criminal justice system and its psychology.* New York: Van Nostrand Reinhold Co.

Collins, S. M. (1978). The use of social research in the courts. In L. E. Lynn, Jr. (Ed.), *Knowledge and policy: The uncertain connection.* Washington, DC: National Academy of Sciences.

Coons, J. E. (1977). Recent trends in science fiction: Serrano among the people of number. In R. C. Rist & R. J. Anson (Eds.), *Education, social science, and the judicial process.* New York: Teachers College Press.

Cressey, D. R., & Ward, D. A. (1969). *Delinquency, crime, and social process.* New York: Harper & Row.

Davis, A. L. (1973). *The United States Supreme Court and the use of social science data.* New York: MSS Information Co.

Diamond, S. S. (Ed.). (1979). Simulation research and the law. *Law and Human Behavior, 3,* p. 1.

Doob, A. N. (1976). Evidence, procedure, and psychological research. In G. Bermant, C. Nemeth, & N. Vidmar (Eds.), *Psychology and the law: Research frontiers.* Lexington, MA: Lexington Books.

Dorsen, N., & Friedman, L. (1973). *Disorder in the court.* New York: Pantheon Books.

Doyle, W. E. (1977). Social science evidence in court cases. In R. C. Rist & R. J. Anson (Eds.), *Education, social science, and the judicial process.* New York: Teachers College Press.

Dworkin, R. (1977a). Social sciences and constitutional rights: The consequences of uncertainty. In R. C. Rist & R. J. Anson (Eds.), *Education, social science, and the judicial process.* New York: Teachers College Press.

Dworkin, R. (1977b). *Taking rights seriously.* London: Duckworth.

Dworkin, R. (1978). No right answer? *New York University Law Review, 53,* p. 1.

Ehrmann, H. W. (1976). *Comparative legal cultures.* Englewood Cliffs, NJ: Prentice-Hall.
Etzioni, A. (1974). Creating an imbalance. *Trial,* 10, p. 28.
Evan, W. M. (Ed.). (1962). *Law and sociology.* New York: Free Press.
Evan, W. M. (Ed.). (1980a). *The sociology of law.* New York: Free Press.
Evan, W. M. (1980b). Value conflicts in the law of evidence. In W. M. Evan (Ed.), *The sociology of law.* New York: Free Press.
Fahr, S. M. (1961). Why lawyers are dissatisfied with the social sciences. *Washburn Law Journal,* 1, p. 161.
Farmer, L. C., et al. (1976). Juror perception of trial testimony as a function of the method of presentation. In G. Bermant, C. Nemeth, & N. Vidmar (Eds.), *Psychology and the law: Research frontiers.* Lexington, MA: Lexington Books.
Fenster, C. A. et al. (1977). Police personality: Social science folklore and psychological measurement. In B. D. Sales (Ed.), *Psychology in the legal process.* New York: Spectrum Publications.
Fields, F. R., & Horwitz, R. J. (Eds.). (1982). *Psychology and professional practice: The interface of psychology and the law.* New York: Quorum Books.
Finkelstein, M. O. (1978). *Qualitative methods in law.* New York: Free Press.
Fisher, F. M. (1980). Multiple regression in legal proceedings. *Columbia Law Review,* 80, p. 702.
Flynn, E. E., & Conrad, J. P. (Eds.). (1978). *The new and the old criminology.* New York: Praeger.
Freid, M., et al. (1975). Juror selection: An analysis of voir dire. In R. J. Simon (Ed.), *The jury system in America.* Beverly Hills, CA: Sage.
Friedman, L. M., & Macaulay, S. (1969). *Law and the behavioral sciences.* Indianapolis, IN: Bobbs-Merrill.
Garry, C. R. (1969). Attacking racism in court before trial. *The Guild Practitioner,* 28, p. 86.
Gebhard, P. H. et al. (1965). *Sex offenders: An analysis of types.* New York: Harper & Row.
Geis, G. (1962). The social sciences and the law: Reply to Samuel M. Fahr. *Washburn Law Journal,* 1, p. 569.
Ginger, A. F. (1972). *The relevant lawyers.* New York: Simon & Schuster.
Glueck, S., & Glueck, E. (1968). *Delinquents and nondelinquents in perspective.* Cambridge, MA: Harvard University Press.
Gordon, R. (1975). *Forensic psychology.* Tucson, AZ: Lawyers and Judges Publishing Co.
Greenberg, M. S. & Ruback, R. B. (1982). *Social psychology of the criminal justice system.* Monterey, CA: Brooks/Cole.
Grofman, B. (1976). Not necessarily twelve and not necessarily unanimous. In G. Bermant, C. Nemeth, & N. Vidmar (Eds.), *Psychology and the law: Research frontiers.* Lexington, MA: Lexington Books.
Grofman, B. (1977). Jury decision-making models. In S. S. Nagel (Ed.), *Modeling the criminal justice system.* Beverly Hills, CA: Sage.
Gross, H., & von Hirsch, A. (Eds.). (1981). *Sentencing.* New York: Oxford University Press.
Grossman, J. B., & Wells, R. S. (1972). *Constitutional law and judicial policy making.* New York: John Wiley.
Haney, C. (1980). Psychology and legal change: On the limits of a factual jurisprudence. *Law and Human Behavior,* 4, p. 147.
Hans, V. P., & Vidmar, N. (1982). Jury selection. In N. L. Kerr & R. M. Bray (Eds.), *The psychology of the courtroom.* New York: Academic Press.
Hastie, R., Penrod, S. D., & Pennington, N. (1983). *Inside the jury.* Cambridge, MA: Harvard University Press.
Haward, L.R.C. (1981). *Forensic psychology.* London: Batsford Academic and Educational Ltd.

Heinz, A. M., & Kerstetter, W. A. (1980). Victim participation in plea-bargaining: A field experiment. In W. F. McDonald & J. A. Cramer (Eds.), *Plea-bargaining*. Lexington, MA: Lexington Books.

Hirsch, W. Z. (1979). *Law and economics*. New York: Academic Press.

Hirschi, T., & Selvin, H. C. (1967). *Delinquency research: An appraisal of analytical methods*. New York: Free Press.

Hoebel, E. A. (1954). *The law of primitive man*. Cambridge, MA: Harvard University Press.

Horowitz, D. L. (1980). Overcoming barriers to the use of applied social research in the courts. In M. J. Saks & C. H. Baron (Eds.), *The use/nonuse/misuse of applied social science research in the courts*. Cambridge, MA: Abt Books.

Jacobsohn, G. J. (1977). Citizen participation in policy-making: the role of the jury. *Journal of Politics, 39*, p. 75.

Kadish, M. R., & Kadish, S. H. (1973). *Discretion to disobey*. Palo Alto, CA: Stanford University Press.

Kairys, D. (Ed.). (1982). *The politics of law: A progressive critique*. New York: Pantheon.

Kalven, H., Jr., & Zeisel, H. (1966). *The American jury*. Boston: Little, Brown.

Kantrowitz, A., et al. (1976). The science court experiment: An interim report. *Science, 193*, p. 653.

Kantrowitz, A. (1977). The science court experiment. *Trial, 13*, p. 48.

Kaplan, M. F. (1982). Cognitive processes in the individual juror. In N. L. Kerr & R. M. Bray (Eds.), *The psychology of the courtroom*. New York: Academic Press.

Katz, J., Goldstein, J., & Dershowitz, A. M. (1967). *Psychoanalysis, psychiatry, and law*. New York: Free Press.

Kaye, D. (1982). The limits of the preponderance of the evidence standard: Justifiably naked statistical evidence and multiple causation. *American Bar Foundation Research Journal*, p. 487.

Kerr, N. L., & Bray, R. M., (Eds.). (1982). *The psychology of the courtroom*. New York: Academic Press.

Kessler, J. B. (1975). The social psychology of jury deliberations. In R. J. Simon (Ed.), *The jury system in America*. Beverly Hills, CA: Sage.

Knudten, M. S. et al. (1978). Will anyone be left to testify? Disenchantment with the criminal justice system. In E. E. Flynn & J. P. Conrad (Eds.), *The new and the old criminology*. New York: Praeger.

Konecni, V. J., & Ebbesen, E. B. (Eds.). (1982). *The criminal justice system: a social-psychological analysis*. San Francisco: Freeman.

Konopka, A. F. (1980). Applied social research as evidence in litigation. In M. J. Saks & C. H. Baron (Eds.), *The use/nonuse/misuse of applied social research in the courts*. Cambridge, MA: Abt Books.

Kort, F. (1963). Content analysis of judicial opinions and rules of law. In G. Schubert (Ed.), *Judicial decision-making*. New York: Free Press.

Lasswell, H. D. (1958). *Politics: Who gets what, when, how*. New York: Meridian Books.

Lempert, R. (1966). Strategies of research design in the legal impact study: the control of plausible rival hypotheses. *Law and Society Review, 1*, p. 111.

Lempert, R. O. (1981). Civil juries and complex cases: Let's not rush to judgment. *Michigan Law Review, 80* p. 68.

Levine, M. (1974). Scientific method and the adversary model. *American Psychologist, 29*, p. 661.

Lind, E. A. (1982). The psychology of courtroom procedure. In N. L. Kerr & R. M. Bray (Eds.), *The psychology of the courtroom*. New York: Academic Press.

Lloyd-Bostock, S.M.A. (Ed.). (1981). *Psychology in legal contexts: Applications and limitations*. New York: Macmillan.

Lochner, P. R., Jr. (1973). Some limits on the application of social science research in the legal process. *Law and the Social Order*, p. 815.

Loevinger, L. (1963). Jurimetrics: The methodology of legal inquiry. In H. W. Baade (Ed.), *Jurimetrics*. New York: Basic Books.

Loevinger, L. (1966). Law and science as rival systems. *Jurimetrics, 8,* p. 63.
Loewen, J. W. (1982). *Social science in the courtroom: Statistical techniques and research methods for winning class-action suits.* Lexington, MA: Lexington Books.
Loftus, E. F. (1979). *Eyewitness testimony.* Cambridge, MA: Harvard University Press.
Loh, W. D. (1984). *Social research in the judicial process.* New York: Russell Sage Foundation.
Lozowick, A. H., et al. (1968). Law and quantitative multivariate analysis. *Michigan Law Review, 66,* p. 1641.
Lynn, L. E., Jr. (Ed.). (1978). *Knowledge and policy: The uncertain connection.* Washington, DC: National Academy of Sciences.
Mannheim, H. (1965). *Comparative criminology.* Boston: Houghton Mifflin.
Manning, B. (1974). If lawyers were angels: A sermon in one canon. *American Bar Association Journal, 60,* p. 821.
Marshall, J. (1969). *Law and psychology in conflict.* Garden City, NY: Anchor/Doubleday.
Martin, J. A. (1977). The proposed "science" court. *Michigan Law Review, 75,* p. 1058.
Marvell, T. (1980). Misuse of applied social research. In M. J. Saks & C. H. Baron (Eds.), *The use/nonuse/misuse of applied social research in the courts.* Cambridge, MA: Abt Books.
Marvell, T. B. (1978). *Appellate courts and lawyers.* Westport, CT: Greenwood Press.
Matheny, A. R., & Williams, B. A. (1981). Scientific disputes and adversary procedures in policy-making: An evaluation of the science court. *Law and Policy Quarterly, 3,* p. 341.
McCall, G. J. (1975). *Observing the law: Applications of field methods to the study of the criminal justice system.* Washington, DC: National Institute of Mental Health.
McDonald, W. F., & Cramer, J. A. (Eds.). (1980). *Plea-bargaining.* Lexington, MA: Lexington Books.
Merryman, J. H. (1969). *The civil law tradition.* Palo Alto, CA: Stanford University Press.
Miller, A. S. (1982). *Toward increased judicial activism: The political role of the Supreme Court.* Westport, CT: Greenwood Press.
Miller, C. A. (1969). *The Supreme Court and the uses of history.* Cambridge, MA: Harvard University Press.
Miller G. R., & Burgoon, J. K. (1982). Factors affecting assessment of witness credibility. In N. L. Kerr & R. M. Bray (Eds.), *The psychology of the courtroom.* New York: Academic Press.
Miller, G. R., & Fontes, N. E. (1979). *Videotape on trial.* Beverly Hills, CA: Sage.
Monahan, J. (1977). Community psychology and public policy: The promise and the pitfalls. In B. D. Sales (Ed.), *Psychology in the legal process.* New York: Spectrum Publications.
Moore, D. R. (1974). Scientists as suppliers of facts: Do lawyers listen? In W. A. Thomas (Ed.), *Scientists in the legal system: Tolerated meddlers or essential contributors?* Ann Arbor, MI: Science Publications.
Moynihan, D. P. (1979). Social science and the courts. *The Public Interest, 54,* p. 12.
Muller v. Oregon, 208 U.S. 412 (1908).
Munsterberg, H. (1908). *On the witness stand: Essays on psychology and crime.* Garden City, NY: Doubleday.
Murray, C. A., & Cox, L. A., Jr. (1979). *Beyond probation: Juvenile corrections and the chronic delinquent.* Beverly Hills, CA: Sage.
Nader, L. (Ed.). (1969). *Law in culture and society.* Boston: Aldine.
Nagel, S. S. (1963). Off-the-bench judicial attitudes. In G. Schubert (Ed.), *Judicial decision-making.* New York: Free Press.
Nagel, S. S. (1969). *The legal process from a behavioral perspective.* Homewood, IL: Dorsey.
Nagel, S. S. (1975). *Improving the legal process: Effects of alternatives.* Lexington, MA: Lexington Books.

Nagel, S. S. (Ed.). (1977). *Modeling the criminal justice system.* Beverly Hills, CA: Sage.
Nemeth, C. (1976). Rules governing jury deliberations: A consideration of recent changes. In G. Bermant, C. Nemeth, & N. Vidmar (Eds.), *Psychology and the law: Research frontiers.* Lexington, MA: Lexington Books.
Newby, I. A. (1969). *Challenge to the court: Social scientists and the defense of segregation, 1954-1966* (rev. ed.). Baton Rouge: Louisiana State University Press.
Newman, G. R. (1978). Criminalization and decriminalization of deviant behavior: A cross-national opinion survey. In E. E. Flynn & J. P. Conrad (Eds.), *The new and the old criminology.* New York: Praeger.
Newman, G. R., et al. (1978). A structural analysis of fraud. In E. E. Flynn & J. P. Conrad (Eds.), *The new and the old criminology.* New York: Praeger.
O'Barr, W. M. (1982). *Linguistic evidence: Language, power, and strategy in the courtroom.* New York: Academic Press.
O'Brien, D. M. (1980). The seduction of the judiciary: Social science and the courts. *Judicature,* 64, p. 8.
O'Brien, D. M. (1981). Of judicial myths, motivations, and justifications: A postscript on social science and the law. *Judicature,* 64, p. 285.
Padawer-Singer, A. M., & Barton, A. H. (1975). The impact of pretrial publicity on jurors' verdicts. In R. J. Simon (Ed.), *The jury system in America.* Beverly Hills, CA: Sage.
Peters, G. W. (1980). Overcoming the barriers to the use of applied social research in the courts. In M. J. Saks & C. H. Baron (Eds.), *The use/nonuse/misuse of applied social science research in the courts.* Cambridge, MA: Abt Books.
Plato, (1982). *The republic.* New York: Modern Library.
Platt, A., & Pollock, R. (1976). Channeling lawyers: The careers of public defenders. In G. Bermant, C. Nemeth, & N. Vidmar (Eds.), *Psychology and the law: Research frontiers.* Lexington, MA: Lexington Books.
Provine, D. M. (1980). *Case selection in the United States Supreme Court.* Chicago: University of Chicago Press.
Reed, J. H. (1973). *The application of operations research to court delay.* New York: Praeger.
Rist, R. C., & Anson, R. J. (Eds.). (1977). *Education, social science, and the judicial process.* New York: Teachers College Press.
Rivlin, A. M. (1973). Forensic social science. *Harvard Educational Review,* 43, p. 61.
Robinson, D. N. (1980). *Psychology and law: Can justice survive the social sciences?* New York: Oxford University Press.
Rosen, P. L. (1972). *The Supreme Court and social science.* Urbana: University of Illinois Press.
Rosenblum, V. G. (1971). A place for social science along the judiciary's constitutional law frontier. *Northwest University Law Review,* 66, p. 455.
Ross, H. L. (1980). Legal concepts and applied social research concepts: Translation problems. In M. J. Saks & C. H. Baron (Eds.), *The use/nonuse/misuse of applied social research in the courts.* Cambridge, MA: Abt Books.
Saks, M. J. (1977). *Jury verdicts: The role of group size and social decision rule.* Lexington, MA: Lexington Books.
Saks, M. J. (1982). Innovation and change in the courtroom. In N. L. Kerr & R. M. Bray (Eds.), *The psychology of the courtroom.* New York: Academic Press.
Saks, M. J., & Baron, C. H. (Eds.). (1980). *The use/nonuse/misuse of applied social science research in the courts.* Cambridge, MA: Abt Books.
Saks, M. J., & Hastie, R. (1978). *Social psychology in court.* New York: Van Nostrand Reinhold Co.
Saks, M. J., & Van Duizend, R. (1983). *The use of scientific evidence in litigation.* Washington, DC: National Center for State Courts.
Sales, B. D. (Ed.). (1977). *Psychology in the legal process.* New York: Spectrum Publications.

Scheflin, A. W. (1972). Jury nullification: The right to say no. *Southern California Law Review, 45*, p. 168.

Scheflin, A. W., & Van Dyke, J. (1980). Jury nullification: The contours of a controversy. *Law and Contemporary Problems, 43*, p. 51.

Schubert, G. (Ed.). (1963). *Judicial decision-making.* New York: Free Press.

Schubert, G. (1965). *Judicial policy-making.* Chicago: Scott, Foresman.

Shapiro, M. (1964). *Law and politics in the Supreme Court: New approaches to political jurisprudence.* New York: Free Press.

Shapiro, M. (1981). *Courts: A comparative and political analysis.* Chicago: University of Chicago Press.

Shuchman, P. (1979). *Problems of knowledge in legal scholarship.* West Hartford: University of Connecticut School of Law Press.

Simon, R. J. (Ed.). (1975). *The jury system in America.* Beverly Hills, CA: Sage.

Spaeth, H. J. (1963). Warren Court attitudes toward business. In G. Schubert (Ed.), *Judicial decision-making.* New York. Free Press.

Sperlich, P. W. (1977). *Scientific methods for the selection of trial jurors: Practical and ethical considerations.* Paper presented at the Annual Meeting of the Western Political Science Association, Phoenix, Arizona, March.

Sperlich, P. W. (1980a). . . . And then there were six: The decline of the American jury. *Judicature, 63*, p. 262.

Sperlich, P. W. (1980b). Social science evidence in the courts: Reaching beyond the adversary process. *Judicature, 63*, p. 280.

Sperlich, P. W. (1980c). Postrealism: Should ignorance be elevated to a principle of adjudication? *Judicature, 64*, p. 93.

Sperlich, P. W. (1982a). The case for preserving trial by jury in complex civil litigation. *Judicature, 65*, p. 394.

Sperlich, P. W. (1982b). Better judicial management: The best remedy for complex cases. *Judicature, 65*, p. 415.

Sperlich, P. W. (1983). Scientific evidence in the courts: the disutility of adversary proceedings, a review essay. *Judicature, 66*, p. 472.

Sperlich, P. W., & Jaspovice, M. L. (1974). Grand juries, grand jurors, and the Constitution. *Hastings Congressional Law Quarterly, 1*, p. 63.

Sperlich, P. W., & Jaspovice, M. L. (1975). Statistical decision theory and the selection of grand jurors: Testing for discrimination in a single panel. *Hastings Congressional Law Quarterly, 2*, p. 75.

Sperlich, P. W., & Jaspovice, M. L. (1979). Methods for the analysis of jury panel selections: Testing for discrimination in a series of panels. *Hastings Congressional Law Quarterly, 6*, p. 787.

Stasser, G., Kerr, N. L., & Bray, R. M. (1982). The social psychology of jury deliberations. In N. L. Kerr & R. M. Bray (Eds.), *The psychology of the courtroom.* New York: Academic Press.

Szasz, T. S. (1957). Psychiatric expert testimony: Its covert meaning and social function. *Psychiatry, 20*, p. 313.

Talarico, S. M. (Ed.). (1980a). *Criminal justice research.* Cincinnati: Anderson.

Talarico, S. M. (1980b). An application of discriminant analysis in criminal justice research. In S. M. Talarico (Ed.), *Criminal justice research.* Cincinnati: Anderson.

Tapp, J. L., & Kohlberg, L. (1977). Developing senses of law and legal justice. In J. L. Tapp & F. J. Levine (Eds.), *Law, justice, and the individual in society: Psychology and legal issues.* New York: Holt, Rinehart & Winston.

Tapp, J. L., & Levine, F. J. (Eds.). (1977). *Law, justice, and the individual in society: Psychology and legal issues.* New York: Holt, Rinehart & Winston.

Thomas, W. A. (Ed.). (1974a). *Scientists in the legal system: Tolerated meddlers or essential contributors?* Ann Arbor, MI: Science Publications.

Thomas, W. A. (1974b). Scientists and lawyers: Their obligation to cooperate. In W. A. Thomas (Ed.), *Scientists in the legal system.* Ann Arbor, MI: Science Publications.

Ulmer, S. S. (1967). Mathematical models for predicting judicial behavior. In J. L. Bernd (Ed.), *Mathematical applications in political science*. Charlottesville: University Press of Virginia.

Van Dyke, J. M. (1977). *Jury selection procedures*. Cambridge, MA: Abt Books.

Wasby, S. L. (1980). History and state of the art of applied social research in the courts. In M. J. Saks & C. H. Baron (Eds.), *The use/nonuse/misuse of applied social research in the courts*. Cambridge, MA: Abt Books.

Weber, G. H., & McCall, G. J. (1978). *Social scientists as advocates: Views from the applied disciplines*. Beverly Hills, CA: Sage.

Wells, G. L., et al. (1979) Guidelines for empirically assessing the fairness of a lineup. *Law and Human Behavior, 3*, p. 285.

Wessel, M. R. (1980). *Science and conscience*. New York: Columbia University Press.

Weyrauch, W. O. (1977). The "basic law" or "constitution" of a small group. In J. L. Tapp & F. J. Levine (Eds.), *Law, justice, and the individual in society: Psychology and legal issues*. New York: Holt, Rinehart & Winston.

Wolf, E. P. (1981). *Trial and error: The Detroit school segregation case*. Detroit, MI: Wayne State University Press.

Wolfgang, M. E. (1974). The social scientist in court. *Journal of Criminal Law and Criminology, 65*, p. 239.

Wolfgang, M. E. (1978). The death penalty: Social philosophy and social science research. *Criminal Law Bulletin, 14*, p. 18.

Wolfgang, M. E., et al. (1972). *Delinquency in a birth cohort*. Chicago: University of Chicago Press.

Young, D. R. (1978). Cost-benefit analysis: A component and stimulant to criminal justice research. In S. M. Talarico (Ed.), *Criminal justice research*. Cincinnati: Anderson.

Zahn, M. A., & Snodgrass, G. (1978). Drug use and the structure of homicide in two U.S. cities. In E. E. Flynn & J. P. Conrad (Eds.), *The new and the old criminology*. New York: Praeger.

Zeisel, H. (1956). The New York expert testimony project: Some reflections on legal experiments. *Stanford Law Review, 8*, p. 730.

Zeisel, H. (1960). The uniqueness of survey research. *Cornell Law Quarterly, 45*, p. 322.

Zeisel, H. (1978). Statistics as legal evidence. In W. H. Kruskal & J. M. Tanur (Eds.), *International encyclopedia of statistics* (Vol. 2). New York: Free Press.

Zeisel, H., & Callahan, T. (1963). Split trials and time saving: A statistical analysis. *Harvard Law Review, 76*, p. 1606.

Zeisel, H., Kalven, H., Jr., & Buchholz, B. (1959). *Delay in court*. Boston: Little, Brown.

NAME INDEX

Abbell, M. 95, 121
Abbey, M. 274, 276
Abelson, R. P. 239, 250
Abraham, H. J. 353, 354
Abrams, S. 79, 94
Alfini, J. J. 86, 92, 283, 284, 290, 291, 292, 293, 294, 296
Allport, G. W. 205, 222
Anderson, C. 270, 276
Anderson, C. A. 161, 174
Anderson, N. H. 157, 169, 171
Anson, R. J. 338, 340, 359
Andreoli, V. 22, 39
Andriks, J. L. 48, 65
Antes, J. R. 216, 222
Arnolds, E. B. 202, 222
Aronson, E. 166, 173, 245, 252
Ash, P. 109, 122
Aubry, A. 73, 92
Austin, W. 35, 38, 167, 171, 330, 354
Ayres, R. 74, 75, 91, 94

Baade, H. W. 337, 354
Babcock, B. 306, 321
Backster, C. 103-104, 121
Baddeley, A. D. 49, 63, 264, 276
Bailey, F. L. 257, 277
Baldus, D. G. 337, 354
Balloun, K. S. 121
Barksdale, H. C. 337, 354
Barland, G. 109, 110, 111, 122
Barnaby, H. B. 177, 200
Barnett, F. J. 114, 122
Barnett, R. E. 330, 354
Baron, C. H. 337, 342, 344, 345, 346, 350, 354, 359
Baron, R. S. 212, 225
Barthel, J. 76, 78, 92

Bartlett, F. C. 50, 63, 205, 222
Barton, A. H. 330, 359
Bassett, H. T. 221, 225
Bauchner, J. E. 139, 148
Baumeister, R. F. 125, 147
Bazelon, D. 36-37, 38
Beattie, A. E. 263, 279
Beck, E. L. 61, 64, 212, 218, 224
Becker, G. S. 330, 354
Becker, L. A. 142, 147
Beckett, J. S. 330, 354
Bedau, H. A. 330, 354
Begam, R. 302, 309, 321
Bekerian, D. A. 54-55, 63
Bell, R. A. 330, 354
Belli, M. M., Sr. 260, 264, 277
Bellow, G. 264, 277
Bem, D. J. 79-80, 92
Bender, G. 285, 297
Bennett, C. 330, 354
Berger, M. 127, 128, 141, 147
Berger, M. A. 23, 39, 177, 200
Berger, R. 327, 354
Berk, R. A. 330, 354
Berman, J. J. 130, 149
Bermant, G. 298-322, 335, 337, 353, 355
Bernd, J. L. 355
Bersh, P. A. 109, 122
Beutel, F. K. 337, 355
Block, G. 134, 147
Boal, R. B. 194, 198
Boffey, P. M. 351, 355
Boisvenu, G. A. 106, 121, 122
Boone, J. S. 136, 147
Borchard, E. M. 67, 76, 92
Borgida, E. 131, 149, 166, 171, 214, 223
Boster, F. J. 68, 93
Bothwell, R. K. 60, 63, 211, 223

Bower, G. H. 49, 63, 265-266, 279
Bowers, J. M. 54-55, 63
Bowers, W. 125, 147
Bradley, M. T. 121, 122
Bramel, D. 83, 92
Brandt, D. R. 139, 148
Brannen, L. 143, 144, 149
Bransford, J. D. 205, 223
Bray, R. M. 8, 26, 39, 167, 168, 171, 329, 337, 357, 360
Breen, J. P. 121, 123
Brekke, N. 214, 223
Brigham, J. C. 37, 38, 58, 60, 61, 63, 204, 211, 223
Brock, T. C. 142, 147
Brodsky, S. 203, 223
Broeder, D. W. 304, 321
Brofman, R. A. 268, 277
Brown, E. L. 51, 56, 63
Browne, A. 202, 225
Bruce, A. 57, 64
Brunk, C. G. 91, 92
Bruner, J. S. 49, 63, 64, 162, 172
Buchanan, R. W. 283, 284, 296, 297
Buchholz, B. 329, 361
Buckhout, R. 44, 64
Buckley, J. 109, 122
Burgess, A. 208, 209, 210, 223
Burgoon, J. K. 136, 137, 139, 148, 165, 173, 330, 358
Burns, H. J. 51, 54, 64, 205, 224
Busch, F. X. 231, 250
Byrne, D. 161, 167, 173

Cacioppo, J. T. 245, 250, 252
Cahn, E. 326, 341, 355
Caldwell, C. 161, 174
Callahan, T. 329, 337, 361
Campbell, D. T. 242, 252, 330, 337, 355
Campbell, J. J. 135, 147
Campbell, J. L. 134, 149
Camper, P. M. 222, 223
Cantril, H. 48, 64
Caputo, R. 73, 92
Carlson, S. C. 115, 122
Carpenter, K. M. 270, 277
Carroll, J. C. 270, 277
Carroll, K. R. 134, 147

Carroll, W. K. 202, 222
Carter, L. H. 341, 355
Case, T. 143, 144, 145, 146, 149
Casper, B. M. 351, 355
Cavoukian, A. 115, 116, 122, 206, 223
Chambers, J. L. 344, 355
Chamblin, M. H. 125, 147
Champagne, A. 329, 355
Charrow, R. P. 259, 277, 283, 296
Charrow, V. 259, 277, 283, 296
Chen, H. T. 219, 223
Chmielewski, D. 305, 321
Christie, R. 303, 321, 330, 355
Cialdini, R. B. 245, 250, 270, 277
Cimerman, A. 104, 122
Clark, K. B. 326, 355
Clary, E. G. 131, 145, 147
Cleary, E. W. 14, 38, 152, 153, 154, 155, 159, 161, 162, 172
Clifford, B. R. 205, 223
Cofer, C. N. 205, 223
Cohen, D. K. 341, 355
Cohen, J. 286, 288, 296
Cohn, A. 330, 355
Cole, J.W.L. 337, 354
Collins, S. M. 326, 328, 336, 355
Conley, J. M. 138, 148, 259, 260, 274, 277
Conlon, D. E. 248, 251
Connolly, P. R. 232, 234, 236-237, 250
Conrad, J. P. 337, 356
Coons, J. E. 344, 355
Corboy, P. H. 282, 296
Cornish, W. R. 26, 27, 38, 131, 145, 147, 166, 174
Cox, L. A., Jr. 330, 358
Cramer, J. A. 329, 358
Cramer, M. M. 258, 277
Cressey, D. R. 124, 149, 330, 355
Crittenden, R. 233, 234, 250
Cronbach, L. J. 196, 198
Cross, M. B. 206, 223
Crowder, R. G. 267, 277
Cunningham, T. J. 290, 296

Dane, F. C. 125, 147, 171, 172
Danet, B. 261, 271, 277
Danzig, E. R. 246, 252
Darley, J. M. 125, 147

Davidson, P. O. 121, 122
Davies, G. M. 50, 53, 65, 205, 224
Davis, A. L. 336-337, 355
Davis, J. 26, 39, 254, 278
Deffenbacher, K. A. 51, 56, 63, 204, 205, 211, 223
DePaulo, B. M. 137, 149
Dershowitz, A. M. 337, 357
Devine, P. G. 56, 60, 64, 205, 224
DeVitt, E. J. 85, 93
Diamond, B. L. 221, 223
Diamond, S. S. 299, 309, 314, 322, 337, 355
Dinges, D. F. 57, 60, 65
Doob, A. N. 25, 27, 39, 131, 135, 137, 147, 148, 166, 172
Dorsen, N. 329, 355
Doyle, W. E. 344, 352, 355
Dreilinger, E. A. 134, 148
Dristas, W. J. 48, 64
Driver, E. D. 80, 92
Dunstan, R. 271, 275, 277
Dworkin, R. 341, 346, 355

Ebbesen, E. B. 127, 147, 328, 330, 357
Ebbinghaus, H. E. 50, 64, 205, 223
Efran, M. G. 167, 172
Egeth, H. 61, 62, 65, 202, 204, 211, 212, 213, 216, 218, 219, 220, 224
Ehrmann, H. W. 353, 356
Ekehammar, B. 163, 172
Elliott, E. S. 49, 64
Ellis, H. D. 49, 50, 53, 57, 64, 65
Ellison, K. W. 44, 64
Elwork, A. 86, 92, 161, 172, 280-297, 329, 338, 353
Endler, N. S. 163, 172
Erickson, B. E. 138, 148, 246, 247, 251
Etcoff, N. L. 240, 251
Etzioni, A. 353, 356
Evan, W. M. 337, 353, 356

Fahr, S. M. 326, 356
Fahringer, H. P. 256, 277
Fairley, W. B. 31, 39
Fallot, R. D. 160, 172
Farmer, L. C. 329, 356
Feild, S. 264, 277
Fenster, C. A. 330, 356

Ferguson, T. J. 56, 57, 58, 65, 205, 212, 218, 226, 257, 272, 279
Ficaro, M. 257, 266, 269, 270, 274, 277
Fields, F. R. 337, 356
File, S. E. 262, 277
Finkelstein, M. O. 31, 39, 328, 337, 356
Fisher, F. M. 337, 356
Fishman, L. 166, 172
Fiske, S. T. 88, 94, 239, 240, 251
Flagg, P. W. 205, 223
Fleming, J. A. 106, 121, 122
Florence, T. 285, 297
Flynn, E. E. 337, 356
Foley, L. A. 125, 147
Fontaine, G. 135, 148
Fontes, N. E. 139, 148, 165, 173, 354, 358
Forkosch, M. D. 114, 122
Fortenberry, J. H. 125, 147
Foster, H. H. 76, 78, 92
Frank, B. 68, 76, 92
Frank, J. 68, 76, 92
Frankel, A. 130, 148
Frankel, M. E. 309, 321
Frankfurter, F. 71, 94
Franks, J. J. 205, 223
Frazier, P. 223
Freedman, M. 308, 321
Freid, M. 330, 356
Friedman, L. 329, 337, 355, 356
Funder, D. C. 163, 172

Garry, C. R. 340, 356
Gebhard, P. H. 330, 356
Geis, G. 326, 356
Gelles, R. J. 207, 223
Gerard, H. 37, 39
Gerhard, D. 205, 225
Gershman, B. L. 89, 92
Gibbons, D. 79, 94
Giesen, M. 121, 122
Gilbert, R. 161, 174
Giles, H. 258, 277
Ginger, A. F. 340, 356
Ginns, M. J. 263, 277
Giuliano, T. 272, 273, 279
Gleser, G. 196, 198
Glueck, E. 330, 356
Glueck, S. 330, 356

Goldstein, A. G. 49, 64
Goldstein, I. 237, 251, 264, 273, 275, 277
Goldstein, J. 337, 357
Goodman, J. 253-279, 329, 335, 344, 345
Goodstein, R. K. 207, 223
Gordon, R. 337, 356
Grady, J. F. 262, 277
Greenberg, J. 246, 247, 250, 252
Greenberg, M. S. 330, 356
Greene, E. 50, 61, 64, 201-226, 333, 342, 350, 352
Greenwald, A. G. 243, 251
Gregory, W. L. 270, 277
Griswold, E. N. 141, 148
Grofman, B. 303, 311, 321, 329, 337, 356
Gross, H. 330, 356
Grossman, J. B. 337, 356
Guilford, J. P. 285, 296
Guttmacher, M. 77, 92

Hagan, J. 125, 148
Hagel, J. III 330, 354
Hamel, I. Z. 82, 93
Hamilton, D. L. 160, 172
Hamilton, V. L. 48, 64
Handler, M. 176, 199
Haney, C. 347, 354, 356
Hannah, H. A. 282, 296
Hans, V. P. 25, 27, 39, 131, 148, 166, 172, 330, 356
Hansen, D. A. 161, 172
Harris, R. J. 260, 263, 277
Harris, V. A. 82, 93
Hartshorne, H. 158, 172
Hastie, R. 22, 25-26, 39, 158, 174, 240, 251, 253, 279, 329, 330, 343, 356, 359
Hastorf, A. H. 48, 64
Hatvany, N. 61, 64
Haward, L. 215, 223, 337, 356
Heider, F. 142, 148
Heinz, A. M. 329, 337, 357
Heisse, J. 108, 122
Helmsley, G. D. 137, 148
Hendrick, C. 129, 130, 149
Henze, F. 283, 297
Hermann, D.H.J. 132, 148
Heslegrave, R. J. 115, 116, 122
Hess, D. W. 74, 75, 91, 94

Hewitt, E. C. 61, 64, 206, 212, 225
Hilberman, E. 208, 209, 224
Hilgard, E. R. 79, 92
Hilgendorf, E. L. 57, 64
Hinkle, S. 82, 93
Hirsch, W. Z. 330, 357
Hirschi, T. 330, 357
Hocking, J. E. 139, 148
Hodges, B. H. 160, 172
Hoebel, E. A. 330, 357
Hoffman, K. B. 271, 277
Holmes, D. S. 121
Holmes, G. W. 251
Holmstrom, L. 208, 209, 210, 223
Holt, R. 26, 39
Hook, S. 141, 148
Horowitz, D. L. 339, 354, 357
Horowitz, I. A. 224
Horrath, F. 108, 110-111, 122
Horwitz, R. J. 337, 356
Hosch, H. M. 61, 64, 212, 218, 224
Houlden, P. 248, 251
Hovland, C. I. 242, 244, 245, 251
Hryciw, B. 55, 65
Hunter, F. 108, 109, 122, 123
Hunter, R. M. 283, 296
Hupy, M. F. 271, 277
Hutchins, R. M. 8

Iacono, W. G. 106, 121, 122
Inbau, F. E. 73, 75, 90, 92, 101, 103, 111, 123
Insko, C. A. 242, 243, 251
Irvine, A. A. 88, 93
Irving, B. L. 57, 64
Izzett, R. R. 166, 167, 168, 172

Jackson, P. 160, 174
Jacobs, S. K. 316, 317, 321
Jacobsohn, G. J. 281, 297, 353, 357
Jacoby, J. 175-200, 330, 336, 337, 338, 349, 350
Janis, I. L. 242, 245, 251, 268, 278
Jannuzzo, J. A. 115, 122
Jaspovice, M. L. 330, 360
Jeans, W. 267, 273, 277
Jew, A. 262, 277
Johnson, B. C. 246, 247, 251
Johnson, C. 224

Johnson, H. H. 277
Jones, E. A., Jr. 95, 122
Jones, E. E. 82, 93, 160, 172
Jones, H. P. 204, 216, 217, 226
Jones, H.P.T. 58, 59, 66
Julien, A. 232, 233, 234, 236, 237, 251

Kadish, M. J. 268, 277
Kadish, M. R. 353, 357
Kadish, S. H. 353, 357
Kahneman, S. 159, 174
Kairys, D. 340, 357
Kalven, H., Jr. 8, 67, 86, 89, 93, 124, 125, 126, 127, 128, 131, 132, 133, 141, 145, 148, 165, 172, 209, 224, 251, 329, 357, 361
Kaminski, E. P. 139, 148
Kantrowitz, A. 338, 351, 357
Kaplan, M. F. 86, 93, 125, 148, 150-174, 329, 331, 335, 343, 353, 357
Karlin, M. B. 49, 63
Kassin, S. M. 59, 60, 64, 67-94, 291, 297, 328, 329, 330-332
Katz, J. 337, 357
Kaufman, I. 67, 93
Kaye, D. 337, 357
Kearsley, G. P. 277
Keeton, R. E. 138, 148, 237, 251, 268, 274, 277
Kelley, H. H. 82, 83, 93, 129, 148, 156, 173, 242, 245, 251
Kelman, H. C. 77, 93
Kemmerick, G. D. 161, 167, 172
Kent, J. 205, 211, 226
Kerber, R. M. 263, 279
Kermish, N. C. 271, 277
Kerr, N. L. 8, 125, 148, 329, 337, 357, 360
Kerstetter, W. A. 329, 337, 357
Kessler, J. B. 329, 357
Kestler, J. L. 262, 267, 273, 278
Kidd, R. F. 32, 39
Kiger, R. 135, 148
Kirschenbaum, H. M. 166, 172
Kleinmuntz, B. 110-111, 122
Knudten, M. S. 330, 357
Koffler, J. M. 114, 122
Kogan, J. D. 221, 224
Kohlberg, L. 329-330, 360

Konecni, V. J. 127, 147, 328, 330, 357
Konopka, A. F. 347, 350, 351, 357
Kort, F. 329, 337, 357
Kraut, R. E. 136, 138, 148
Kravitz, J. 49, 64, 205, 224
Kruglanski, A. W. 82, 93
Kuehn, J. K. 221, 225
Kurtz, S. 248, 251

Labov, W. 258, 278
LaBuy, W. J. 85, 93
LaFave, W. R. 89, 93, 133, 148
Lambert, W. E. 258, 278
Landes, W. M. 330, 354
Landy, D. 166, 173
Lane, F. 264, 273, 275, 277
Langerman, S. 233, 251
Langley, R. 207, 224
Lapping, J. 247, 250, 251
Larson, J. A. 100, 122
Lassiter, G. D. 88, 93
Lasswell, H. D. 346, 357
LaTour, S. 243, 248, 251, 252
Laufer, J. K. 240, 251
Lawson, R. G. 235, 244, 251
Lay, D. P. 314, 322
Leginski, W. 167, 168, 172
Leippe, M. R. 48, 59, 64, 276, 279
Lempert, R. O. 157, 158, 173, 330, 350, 357
Lepper, M. R. 77, 93
Levine, F. J. 337, 360
Levine, M. 349, 357
Levy, R. 207, 224
Lind, E. A. 137, 138, 148, 242, 246, 247, 248, 249, 250, 251, 259, 260, 274, 277, 329, 357
Lindsay, R.C.L. 54, 56, 57, 58, 59, 61, 64, 65, 66, 205, 212, 218, 219, 221, 224, 225, 226, 257, 272, 279
Lindskold, S. 269, 279
Lissak, R. I. 248, 251
Litigation Sciences 265, 268, 278
Lloyd-Bostock, S.M.A. 337, 357
Lochner, P. R., Jr. 338, 357
Loevinger, L. 326, 337, 357
Loewen, J. W. 175, 199, 330, 337, 339, 342, 350, 358

Loftus, E. 7, 30, 39, 44, 48, 50, 51, 54, 61, 62, 64, 66, 201-226, 253-279, 283, 297, 329, 330, 335, 344, 345
Loftus, G. R. 205, 224
Loh, W. D. 13-39, 156, 160, 173, 298, 318, 322, 326, 328, 335, 336, 337, 339, 340, 341, 342, 343, 344, 345, 348, 349, 351-352, 353, 354, 358
Lorge, I. 187, 200
Lorry, W. 237, 252
Love, R. E. 243, 252
Lower, J. S. 224
Lozowick, A. H. 337, 358
Lumsdaine, A. A. 244, 251, 268, 278
Lykken, D. T. 95-123, 336
Lynch, B. E. 116, 123
Lynn, L. E., Jr. 358

Mack, D. 246, 247, 250, 252
Mackworth, N. H. 216, 224
Macaulay, S. 337, 356
Magnusson, D. 163, 172
Mahan, L. 29, 39, 81, 94
Maides, S. 82, 93
Maier, N.R.F. 165, 173
Malpass, R. S. 49, 54, 56, 60, 64, 205, 224
Mannheim, H. 337, 358
Manning, B. 343, 358
Markwart, A. 116, 123
Marquis, K. H. 53, 65
Marshall, J. 53, 65, 271, 278, 343, 347, 353, 358
Marston, W. M. 8
Martin, J. A. 351, 358
Marvell, T. B. 344, 345, 350, 358
Matheny, A. R. 351, 357
Mathes, W. C. 85, 93
Mauet, T. A. 257, 259, 267, 278
May, M. 158, 172
McArthur, L. Z. 156, 173
McBride, R. L. 282, 297
McCall, G. J. 337, 340, 358, 361
McCarthy, J. T. 180, 191, 199
McClelland, L. 160, 174
McCloskey, M. 61, 62, 65, 202, 204, 211, 212, 213, 216, 218, 219, 220, 224
McCormick, C. T. 28, 29, 39, 67, 68, 70, 91, 93, 126, 140, 141, 148, 161, 162

McDonald, W. F. 329, 358
McGaffey, R. 253, 278
McGlynn, R. P. 134, 148
McGovern, F. E. 254, 278
McGuire, W. J. 245, 252, 269, 278
McIntyre, P. 61, 64, 212, 218, 224
McKenna, J. 212, 224
McKenzie, J. C. 282, 297
McMurran, M. 50, 65
Mehler, J. 262, 278
Mellott, A. 212, 225
Merryman, J. H. 353, 358
Messo, J. 205, 224
Miller, A. G. 82, 93
Miller, A. S. 327, 358
Miller, C. A. 345, 347, 358
Miller, C. E. 170, 171, 173
Miller, D. G. 51, 54, 64, 205, 224
Miller, G. R. 68, 93, 136, 137, 139, 148, 165, 173, 285, 297, 330, 354, 358
Miller, L. E. 86, 93, 163, 168, 169, 171, 173
Miller, N. 242, 252
Mills, J. 245, 252
Mischel, W. 158, 173
Mitchell, H. E. 161, 167, 173
Monaco, G. E. 263, 277
Monahan, J. 7, 202, 224, 339, 358
Moore, D. R. 344, 358
Morlau, D. 318, 322
Morrill, A. E. 234, 252
Morris, W. N. 130, 148
Moulton, B. 264, 277
Moynihan, D. P. 340, 358
Munsterberg, H. 7, 76, 79, 93, 202, 225, 328, 358
Murray, C. A. 330, 358
Murray, D. M. 47, 57, 61, 66
Musante, L. 248, 251
Myers, G. C. 48, 65
Myers, M. A. 125, 127, 129, 130, 144, 148, 219, 225

Nader, L. 330, 358
Nagel, S. S. 329, 330, 337, 355, 358
Nanda, H. 196, 198
Nash, M. M. 221, 225
Nelson, C. 162, 174
Nemeth, C. 166, 173, 329, 337, 355, 359

Nesson, C. R. 32, 39
Newby, I. A. 338, 340, 359
Newcomb, T. 162, 173
Newman, G. R. 330, 359
Nicholson, H. 285, 297
Nieland, R. G. 282, 283, 297
Nisbett, R. 159, 173, 266, 278
Noble, A. M. 167, 168, 171
Norman, W. T. 162, 173
Norton, J. E. 257, 278

O'Barr, W. M. 137, 138, 148, 246, 247, 251,
    258, 259, 260, 274, 276, 277, 278, 329,
    359
O'Brien, D. M. 326, 341, 346, 352, 359
Ogle, R. 278
O'Hara, C. E. 73, 94
O'Hara, G. L. 73, 94
Oliphant, R. E. 257, 264, 273, 278
Orne, E. C. 57, 60, 65
Orne, M. T. 57, 60, 65, 97, 123
Osgood, C. E. 162, 173
Oskamp, S. 53, 65
Ostrom, T. M. 48, 59, 64
Ostrove, N. 167, 174
OTA Report. 97, 107, 123

Pachella, R. G. 225
Pacht, A. R. 221, 225
Packer, H. L. 141, 148
Padawer-Singer, A. M. 330, 359
Padilla, E. R. 264, 265, 278
Page, A. W. 207, 223
Palmer, J. C. 205, 224
Papageorgis, D. 269, 278
Park, D. 89, 94
Parkinson, M. G. 136, 149, 258, 260, 265,
    278
Parkman, A. 278
Pasano, M. S. 115, 122
Passini, F. T. 162, 173
Paulsen, M. G. 70, 94
Pennington, D. C. 23, 39
Pennington, N. 329, 356
Penrod, S. 131, 149, 166, 174, 329, 356
Perlin, M. L. 203, 221, 225
Perry, B. S. 121, 123
Peters, G. W. 338, 359

Petty, R. E. 245, 250, 252
Picaro, M. 265
Pickett, C. 176, 199
Pierce, G. 125, 147
Plato, 346, 359
Platt, A. 330, 359
Platt, M. 259, 279
Podlesny, J. A. 121, 123
Pollock, R. 330, 359
Porter, J. 278
Postman, L. J. 49, 63, 64, 205, 222
Potts, G. R. 205, 223
Powers, P. A. 48, 65
Powesland, P. F. 258, 277
Prettyman, D. 291, 297
Provine, D. M. 329, 359
Pryor, B. 283, 296
Putnam, W. H. 60, 65
Pyszczynski, T. 246, 247, 250, 252

Rafn, H. J. 271, 277
Rajaratnam, N. 196, 198
Raskin, D. 109, 110, 111, 121, 122, 123
Reed, J. H. 337, 359
Reid, J. E. 73, 75, 90, 92, 101, 102-103, 108,
    112, 122, 123
Reidel, M. 125, 149
Reik, T. 76, 94
Reiner, J. P. 180, 182, 200
Reyes, R. M. 265-266, 279
Reynolds, A. G. 205, 223
Richardson, D. 134, 149
Richey, M. H. 160, 174
Rist, R. C. 338, 340, 359
Rivlin, A. M. 38, 39, 349, 359
Robey, A. 203, 223
Robin, A. 177, 200
Robinson, D. N. 340, 353, 359
Rodrigues, J. 49, 64
Rollison, M. A. 121, 122
Roper, R. S. 117, 123
Rosen, P. L. 328, 337, 338, 340, 343, 344,
    350, 359
Rosenberg, S. 162, 174
Rosenblum, V. G. 328, 359
Rosenhan, D. 201, 202, 221, 225
Rosenthal, R. 137, 149
Ross, H. L. 330, 337, 345, 355, 359

Ross, J. L. 208, 225
Ross, L. 82, 94, 159, 161, 173, 174, 249, 252, 266, 278
Rothblatt, H. B. 135, 149, 257, 277
Ruback, R. B. 330, 356
Rumpel, C. 56, 58, 59, 64, 218, 224

Sadowski, C. 129, 130, 143, 149
Saks, M. J. 22, 25-26, 32, 39, 131, 149, 158, 166, 168, 174, 253, 279, 329, 330, 337, 338, 342, 343, 344, 345, 346, 347, 348, 352, 359
Sales, B. D. 8, 86, 92, 161, 172, 280-297, 329, 337, 338, 353, 359
Saltzburg, S. A. 157, 158, 173
Salvan, S. A. 88, 94
Sams, Jr., M. 232, 252
Saunders, D. M. 61, 65, 206, 212, 225
Savitsky, J. C. 136, 149, 167, 174
Schank, R. C. 239, 252
Schantz, M. 74, 75, 91, 94
Scheflin, A. W. 281, 297, 353, 360
Scherl, D. J. 210, 225
Schersching, C. 125, 148, 168, 169, 170, 173
Schneider, D. J. 162, 174
Schofield, W. 221, 225
Schooler, J. W. 201-226
Schubert, G. 329, 360
Schwartz, J. M. 82, 93
Schwarzer, W. W. 29, 39
Scott, A. 89, 93
Scott, A. W. 133, 148
Scott, B. 224
Scott, J. 223
Sealy, A. P. 26, 27, 38, 131, 145, 147, 166, 174
Seligman, M. 208, 225
Selvin, H. C. 330, 357
Seng, M. P. 202, 222
Severance, L. J. 30, 39, 283, 297
Shaffer, D. R. 124-149, 331, 332
Shapard, J. 299, 310, 321
Shapiro, M. 327, 360
Sheffield, F. D. 244, 251
Shephard, R. N. 50, 65
Shepherd, J. W. 50, 53, 57, 65
Shimkunas, A. M. 160, 174

Shuchman, P. 338, 343, 345, 353, 360
Siegel, D. 35, 38
Sigall, H. J. 167, 174
Sigworth, H. 283, 297
Sim, M. E. 136, 149, 167, 174
Simon, R. 29, 39, 81, 94, 134, 149, 253, 279, 360
Slesinger, H. 8
Slough, M. C. 69, 94
Slowick, S. 109, 122
Smith, R. S. 161, 174
Snodgrass, G. 330, 361
Snyder, M. 82, 94
Sosis, R. H. 166, 173
Soskis, D. A. 57, 60, 64
Spaeth, H. J. 329, 360
Sperlich, P. W. 325-361
Srull, T. K. 240, 241, 252
Starkman, D. 225
Stasser, G. 329, 360
Stayman, D. G. 271, 277
Stephens, O. H. 69, 94
Stern, R. M. 121, 123
Stewart, J. E. 125, 149
Stone, G. R. 71, 94
Strack, F. 61, 64
Strawn, D. U. 283, 284, 296, 297
Sturgill, W. 51, 56, 63
Sue, S. 161, 174
Suggs, D. 130, 149
Sutherland, A. E. 76, 94
Sutherland, E. H. 124, 149
Sutherland, S. 210, 225
Swann, W. B. 272, 273, 279
Symonds, M. 208, 209, 225
Szasz, T. S. 330, 360
Szucko, J. J. 110-111, 122

Taqiuri, R. 162, 172
Talarico, S. M. 337, 360
Tanford, J. A. 254, 267, 279
Tanford, S. 166, 174
Tannenbaum, P. H. 162, 173
Tapp, J. L. 7, 329-330, 337, 360
Taylor, K. P. 283, 296
Taylor, S. E. 88, 94, 239, 240, 251, 266, 279
Tedeschi, J. T. 269, 279
Teske, R. R. 263, 277

Thar, A. E. 202, 225
Thayer, J. 18, 39
Thibaut, J. 22, 35, 39, 242, 248, 249, 250, 251, 252
Thomas, W. A. 328, 360
Thomson, D. M. 54, 65
Thompson, S. C. 266, 279
Thompson, W. C. 265-266, 279
Thorndike, E. L. 162, 174, 187, 200
Thurber, J. A. 165, 173
Thyfault, R. K. 202, 225
Tousignant, J. P. 58, 59, 66, 205, 212, 218, 221, 226
Tribe, L. H. 32, 39, 99, 123
Tulving, E. 52, 54, 65
Tversky, A. 159, 174
Tyler, T. R. 249, 252

Udolf, R. 330, 355
Ulmer, S. S. 329, 337, 361
Underwood, B. J. 205, 225
Utne, M. K. 167, 171, 330, 354

Van Duizend, R. 337, 338, 342, 343, 344, 347, 348, 352, 359
Van Dyke, J. M. 281, 297, 302, 322, 329, 330, 353, 360, 361
Veblen, T. 38
Vidmar, N. J. 61, 64, 140, 149, 206, 212, 225, 330, 337, 355, 356
Vivekananthan, P. S. 162, 174
von Hirsch, A. 330, 356
Vosniadou, S. 262, 279

Wald, M. 74, 75, 91, 94
Walker, L. 22, 35, 39, 242, 248, 249, 250, 251, 252
Walker, L. E. 202, 206, 207, 225
Walster, E. 167, 171
Walter, P. D. 225
Waltz, J. R. 150, 152, 154, 157, 162, 174
Ward, D. A. 330, 355
Warfield, J. F. 121, 122
Warner, T. 86, 87, 93
Warr, P. 160, 174
Wasby, S. L. 328, 361
Washburn, A. 212, 224
Wason, P. 262, 279
Watanabe, T. 121, 123

Watkins, O. C. 52, 65
Watkins, T. A. 277
Webb, E. 212, 224, 225
Weber, G. H. 340, 361
Wegner, D. A. 263, 272, 273, 279
Weihofen, H. 77, 92
Weinberg, H. I. 212, 225
Weinstein, E. 79, 94
Weinstein, J. B. 23, 39, 177, 200
Weiss, J. A. 341, 355
Weiten, W. 166, 174
Weld, H. P. 246, 252
Wellman, F. L. 257, 272, 279
Wells, G. L. 44, 47, 50, 53, 54, 55, 56, 57, 58, 59, 60, 61, 62, 63, 64, 65, 66, 83, 87, 90, 94, 204, 205, 211, 212, 213, 218, 219, 220, 221, 224, 225, 226, 257, 272, 276, 279, 328, 329, 330, 332-333, 340, 352, 353, 361
Wells, R. S. 337, 356
Wenclaff, R. 263, 279
Wentzel, A. 35, 38
Wessel, M. R. 337, 345, 347, 350, 351, 353, 354, 361
Weyrauch, W. O. 330, 361
Whipple, G. M. 8, 52, 66, 255, 279
White, W. S. 72, 76, 94
Whitebread, C. H. 74, 75, 91, 94
Wicklander, D. 109, 122
Wigmore, J. H. 15, 16, 34, 39, 67, 68, 69, 70, 72, 76, 77, 94
Will, G. 141, 149
Willging, T. E. 224
Williams, B. A. 351, 358
Williams, T. 35, 38
Wills, E. J. 49, 64
Winograd, E. 49, 66
Wissler, R. L. 131, 149, 166, 168, 174
Wolf, E. P. 337, 338, 343, 344, 347, 352, 361
Wolfgang, M. E. 125, 149, 330, 361
Wolfskiel, M. P. 58, 61, 63
Woocher, F. D. 226
Worchel, S. 35, 38
Worley, A. E. 138, 149
Wrightsman, L. S. 8, 67-94, 125, 147, 171, 172, 246, 247, 250, 252, 291, 297, 328, 329, 330, 332
Wyer, R. S. 240, 241, 252

Yandell, B. 129, 149
Yarmey, A. D. 58, 59, 66, 204, 205, 211, 216, 217, 226
Young, D. R. 337, 361
Younger, E. J. 67, 94
Younger, I. 97, 123, 201, 202, 221, 226, 264

Zahn, M. A. 330, 361
Zanna, M. P. 160, 172

Zeisel, H. 8, 67, 86, 89, 93, 124, 125, 126, 127, 128, 131, 132, 133, 141, 145, 148, 165, 172, 183, 200, 209, 224, 251, 299, 309, 314, 322, 329, 330, 337, 357, 361
Zimbardo, P. G. 74, 76, 94
Zimmerman, G. I. 254, 279
Ziskin, J. 203, 226
Zuckerman, M. 163, 174

SUBJECT INDEX

Abscam, 88-89
Admissibility
  of character testimony, 150-155
  of a confession, 70-72
  of evidence in general, 23-27, 331
  limits of, 15
  of testimony by expert witnesses, 210,
    217-220
  of testimony by polygraphers, 95, 336
Adversarial method, 33-35, 335, 343-346,
  351-352
  and expert witnesses, 343, 351-352
Attorneys
  closing arguments, 229-252
  credibility, 245-246
  examination of witnesses, 253-279
  opening statements, 19-20, 229-252
  relationship to and treatment of expert
    witness, 342-343
  role in voir dire, 298-321
  speech style, 247
  statements, 246-250

Battered woman syndrome, 206-208, 214,
  217, 219, 222, 334
Burden of proof, 27

Category accessibility, 241
Character testimony, 150-174
  admissibility of, 150-155
  detecting credibility of, 164-165
  general versus specific issue, 161-164
  harmful possibilities, 159-161
  impact of, on jurors, 164-171
  psychological assumptions in, 155-164
  purposes of, 150
  truthfulness and, 158-159
  types of, 150

Closing arguments, 20-21, 229-252
  legal aspects and limits of, 231-232
  relative importance of, 232-234
  research on, 238-250
  tactics and style in, 235-238
Communicator credibility, 245-246, 267
  attorneys and, 245-246
  and character testimony, 158-159
  defendants and, 127, 134-140
  detection of, 164-165
  expert witnesses and, 215, 217-220
  eyewitnesses and, 48-57, 333
Confessions, as evidence, 67-94, 332
  accuracy of, 90
  and entrapment, 88-89
  extent of, 67
  false confessions and, 76-78
  jurors' reactions to, 80, 83-88, 90
  positive coercion bias in relation to, 84-
    86
  promises versus threats in inducing,
    87-88
  research on, 83-88
  rules regarding, 68-72
  validity of, 76-80
  voluntariness, as criterion, 70-72

Defendant, as witness, 22, 124-149
  appearance and demeanor, 135-136
  credibility of, 127, 134-140
  denial by, 129-130
  failure to testify, 140-145
  inadvertent conduct, as defense, 133
  insanity, as defense, 132, 133, 134
  intoxication, as defense, 132
  necessity, or duress, as defense, 133
  nonverbal behavior, 136-138
  versus other witness testifying to alibi,
    130

373

prior record, 131
reputation and, 154-155
rights and privileges of, 126-128
self-defense, as defense, 132-133
Defendant testifying in own behalf, 22, 129-130
and past record, 154-158
and speech style, 137-138
Deliberations, 15
and confessions evidence, 87
role in reducing effects of juror bias, 170-171
Discounting principle, 83-88, 129, 130

Entrapment, 88-89, 91
jurors' reactions to, 89
Evidence (see also Evidence law)
admissibility of, 15
as determinant of verdicts, 8
evidence on evidence, 325-359
the law on, 13-39
order of presentation of, 19-23, 238, 242-245
types of
character testimony, 150-174
confession evidence, 67-94
defendant's testimony, 124-149
expert witnesses, 201-228
eyewitness evidence, 43-66
lie detector evidence, 95-123
survey evidence, 175-200
Evidence law
admissibility of evidence, 23-27, 81-83
Federal Rules of Evidence on, 19, 23
order of presentation of evidence, 19-23
procedural justice and, 18
rationale of, 15-16
structure of, 14-19
sufficiency of evidence, 27-33
and survey admissibility, 177-179
Evidentiology, 325-329, 336, 352
Examination of witnesses, 253-279
complaints about, 342-343
controversies in courtroom, 256
in cross-examination, 270-276
in direct examination, 264, 265-270

and influence on their memory processes, 48-57
by police, 72-76
of polygraphers, 98-99
preparing for, 257-264
psychology of questioning, 255-256, 257, 260-264
and rules of evidence, 254-255
Expert witnesses, 201-226, 333
admissibility of, 210
on battered woman syndrome, 206-208, 214, 217, 222
on eyewitness reliability, 61-62, 204-206, 211-213, 216, 217-218
as "hired hands," 220-221, 342
history of, 201-202
neutrality of (and problems re), 220-221, 338-339, 343, 351
polygraphers as, 98-99
probative value of, 217-220
proper role for, 220-222
qualifications of, 215
on rape trauma syndrome, 208-210, 214, 217, 222
scientific basis of, 215-217, 218-219
treatment by judges and attorneys, 342-343, 350
types of, 202-203, 333-334
Extralegal factors, 8, 331
in jury decisions, 124-125
Eyewitnesses, testimony of, 43-66, 332-333
accuracy of, 48-57
confidence of, 44, 56-57
expert witness on, 61-62
errors in, 44-46, 51, 52, 53
jurors' and judges' reactions, 45-46, 57-61
legal perspectives on, 46-48
memory processes of, 48-57
police practices on, 45, 53, 54
testing conditions, 60
witnessing conditions, 59-60

Fifth Amendment pleas, 140-145
Forensic social science, 38, 349
"Fundamental attribution error," 82, 249

Geter, Lenell, 44

Hearsay rule, 15
Hypnosis, 57, 59

Information-integration theory, 169-170
Inoculation theory, 245, 268-269
Inquisitorial method (see Adversarial method)
Insanity plea, 132, 133, 134
Instructions by the judge, 21, 280-297
    comprehensibility of, 29-31, 283-288
    effect on jury, 25-27, 85-87, 280
    history of, 282-283
    impact on verdicts, 288-289
    incomprehensibility of language of, 283
    manner of presentation, 289-290
    solutions to problems in, 30, 291-295
    timing of presentation, 290-291
    on voluntariness of confession evidence, 85-87
Intoxication, 132

Jury, 7, 8, 15, 16, 25, 114-117, 135, 140-145, 201, 214
    its ability to detect deception, 138-140, 164-165
    and entrapment, 88-89
    history of, 16
    instructions to, 280-297
    judgments of credibility, 134-140, 164-165
    nullification, 17, 280-282
    reactions to character testimony, 164-171
    reactions to confession evidence, 80, 83-88, 90
    reactions to defendant's failure to testify, 141-145
    reactions to eyewitness testimony, 57-61
    reactions to polygraph evidence, 114-117
    sovereignty, 17
    understanding of rape trauma, 214
    voir dire of, 298-323
Jury nullification (see Nullification)
Jury selection (see Voir dire)

Learned helplessness, 207-208

Lie-detector (see Polygraph)
Limited-use instructions (also "limiting" instructions), 25-27, 161, 170
Litigant process control, 248-249
Lovejoy, Maurice, 44

Memory processes, in eyewitnesses, 48-57, 263
    acquisition, 48-50
    communication, 55-57
    questioning, effects on, 263
    retrieval, 52-55
    storage, 50-51

Nullification, 17, 280-282

Opening statements, 19-20, 229-252
    legal aspects and limits of, 231-232
    length of, 234-235
    relative importance of, 232-234
    research on, 238-250
    tactics and style in, 235-238
Opinion rule, 15
Order of presentation of evidence, 19-23
    research on order effects, 22-23, 238, 242-245
"Other crimes evidence" rule, 24-27, 161, 170

Pagano, Father, 44
Police
    and biased lineups, 60
    and confessions, 72-76
    and eyewitnesses, 45, 46
    interrogation, 72-76
    "Mutt and Jeff" routine by, 74
    training of, 63
Polygraph, 95-123, 336
    accuracy of, 107-121
    admissibility of, 95, 336
    Backster zone comparison test, 103-104
    claims of accuracy, 96, 121
    control question test, 102-103, 110-113, 120
    credibility of, 114-117
    description of tests, 99-107
    examiners as expert witnesses, 98-99

examiners, types of, 96-98
guilty knowledge test, 106-107, 117-119
pre-employment screening test, 104-106
Primacy versus recency, 242-245, 264-265
   in direct examination of witnesses, 264-265
Priming, 240-241
Privilege rule, 15
Procedural fairness, 248-250
Procedure, trial, 9, 18, 19, 36, 37, 68, 70-72, 126
   defendant's testifying, 140-145
   instructions to jury in, 253-279
   opening statements in, 229-252
   questioning witnesses in, 253-279
   regarding confessions, 68-72
   as related to evidence, 14-15
   rules of evidence, 8, 23
   voir dire, 298-323
Psychological stress evaluator, 108
Psychology and the law (see also Science and the law), 13-14, 325-361
   adversarial possibility of each, 221-222
   historical nature of, 7-8
   interface of, 7, 326

Quantification of evidence and standards of proof, 31-33

Rape trauma syndrome, 208-210, 214, 217, 219, 222, 334
Relevance rule, 15

Science and the law, 325-361
   complaints about the law, 342-346
   complaints about science, 337-342
   in conflict over eyewitness testimony, 47-48
   examples of scientific research on the law, 329-331
   history of the relationship, 328
   interface of, 326, 346-348
   methods of science and, 328
   reasons for misunderstandings between, 326-328
   reform in the relationship, 346-352
   scientific research on the law, 329-337

values in conflict, 346-347
"science court," 351-352
Script theory, 239
Self-defense, 132-133
Self-incrimination, privilege against, 127
Self-perception theory, 79-80
Standard of proof, 28-29, 31-33
"Station house syndrome," 78
Summation (see Closing arguments)
Surveys and field experiments, as evidence, 175-200
   authenticity in, 193-194
   case law relevant to, 179-193
   factors used in establishing admissibility of, 177-179
   history of, 176-177
   surveys versus experiments, 194-195
"Sympathy hypothesis," 86

Taylor, Erwin, 44
Trials, 7, 8, 9, 16, 32, 34
   conceptions of, 16
   inquisitorial versus adversarial method, 33-35

Values
   in deciding to be an expert witness, 221
   of expert witnesses, 221, 338-341
   liberal advocacy, 340
   in psychological research, 36-38
   of science versus the law, 346-347
   "value-free" science, 340
Verdicts, 8, 87, 116
   alibi testimony and, 130
   and attractiveness of defendant, 166, 167
   character testimony, 165-171
   defendant's appearance and demeanor, 135-136
   defendant's failure to testify, 140-145
   evidence as the determinant of, 8, 9
   extralegal determinants of, 8, 124-125
   insanity as a defense and, 132, 134
   judge's instructions as influence on, 30, 288-289
Voir dire, 298-322
   arguments for changing, 300-309, 319-320

arguments for status quo, 309-314, 320-321

Voluntariness, of confessions, 70-72

Witnesses (see also Examination of witnesses)
accuracy for details, 276

credibility of, 257-260, 273-274, 275
desire for consistency, 275-276
examination of, 253-279
preparing of, 257-264
speech style of, 137-138, 258-260, 273-274, 275

ABOUT THE CONTRIBUTORS

Gordon Bermant is the Director of the Division of Innovations and Systems Development at the Federal Judicial Center. The center is the research and development organization of the federal courts. Bermant has been with the center since 1976, acting as Senior Research Psychologist and Deputy Director of the Research Division before assuming his current responsibilities. He received a Ph.D. in psychology from Harvard University in 1961, and spent three years doing post-doctoral work at Harvard and the University of California at Berkeley before moving to the the Psychology Department at the University of California at Davis. He remained at Davis as an Associate Professor until 1969, when he moved to Seattle to become Center Fellow for Behavioral and Social Sciences at the Battelle Seattle Research Center. He remained with Battelle, and with the University of Washington as Affiliate Professor of Psychology, until 1976. Bermant has written or edited six books and more than 60 articles and reviews. He is Past President of the American Psychology-Law Society, a Fellow of the American Psychological Association, and a member of the Executive Committee of the APA's Division of Psychology and Law.

Amiram Elwork, Ph.D., is the Director of the Law-Psychology (J.D./-Ph.D.) Graduate Program administered by Hahnemann and Villanova Universities. He has written extensively on the jury and trial process, but is best known for his research on the incomprehensibility of jury instructions, having coauthored the book, *Making Jury Instructions Understandable*. In recent years his interests have shifted toward issues involving mental health and law. Currently he is conducting research on the efficacy of divorce mediation.

Jane Goodman is a trial attorney with the Equal Employment Opportunity Commission, and is a doctoral candidate at the University of Washington. She received her bachelor's degree from the University of

Witwatersrand in Johannesburg, and her TTHD (master's) degree in education from the Johannesburg College of Education and the University of Witwatersrand, jointly. Goodman received her J.D. (cum laude) from the University of Puget Sound Law School in 1983 and became a member of the Washington State Bar Association in 1983. She recently presented a paper entitled "Constitutional Protection for Linguistic Minorities" to the National Association of Bilingual Education in Washington, D.C.

Edith Greene is a Research Associate in the Department of Psychology at the University of Washington. She received a B.A. in psychology from Stanford University in 1975; an M.A. in experimental psychology from the University of Colorado in 1977; and a Ph.D. in psychology and law from the University of Washington in 1983. Her primary research interests are in the areas of jury decision making and eyewitness testimony. She has authored papers pertaining to jurors' comprehension of judicial instructions, their use of extralegal evidence, and their decisionmaking in eyewitness cases. She is presently coprincipal investigator of an NSF grant to study the use by hypnosis in court. Dr. Greene is also Senior Editorial Assistant for *Criminology*, the journal of the American Criminology Society.

Jacob Jacoby received his B.A. and M.A. in psychology from Brooklyn College, and his Ph.D. in social psychology from Michigan State University. He served with the Air Force from 1965 through 1968. From 1968 to 1981 he was at Purdue University, where he went from Assistant Professor to Professor and head of the Consumer Psychology Program in the Department of Psychological Sciences. In September 1981 he assumed the Merchants Council Chair in Marketing at New York University. Dr. Jacoby is Past President of both the Association for Consumer Research and the American Psychological Association's Division of Consumer Psychology. He has published more than 100 chapters and articles, 10 books and monographs, and given more than 150 talks at professional conferences, universities, and before industry audiences. He has received grants from the National Science Foundation, the Consumer Research Institute, the Federal Trade Commission, and the American Association of Advertising Agencies. Dr. Jacoby has served as a consultant to government agencies, and has also provided expert opinion and testimony in more than 30 cases involving federal and state trials and hearings on consumer issues.

Martin F. Kaplan earned his bachelor's and master's degrees at the City College of New York in 1960 and 1962, respectively, and his Ph.D. at the University of Iowa in 1965. He has been at Northern Illinois University since then, and is currently Professor of Psychology. He has served as a Visiting Scientist at the University of California, San Diego, and the University of North Carolina, Chapel Hill. Current research programs include modes of influence in jury deliberation; sex differences in influence during group discussion, juror bias; and moral reasoning. Dr. Kaplan is a member of the Society of Experimental Social Psychologists and the Association of Trial Behavior Consultants, and is a Fellow of the Division of Psychology and Law and of the Division of Personality and Social Psychology of the American Psychological Association. He has contributed regularly to journals and edited issues in social psychology and in psychology and law, and has also edited several books, including *Human Judgment and Decision Processes in Applied Settings* (1977) and *The Impact of Social Psychology on Procedural Justice* (1985).

Saul M. Kassin is Assistant Professor of Psychology at Williams College. He received his Ph.D. in personality and social psychology at the University of Connecticut after which he served as a postdoctoral research fellow at the University of Kansas and on the faculty at Purdue University. He is the author of numerous journal articles and book chapters, and has coedited *Developmental Social Psychology: Theory and Research* (with S. Brehm and F. Gibbons, 1981). Interested in various aspects of jury decision making, Kassin is currently on leave from Williams, having been awarded a Judicial Fellowship at the U.S. Supreme Court (1984-1985) and an NIMH Postdoctoral Research position at Stanford University (1985-1986).

Gina Y. Ke is a graduate student in Social Psychology at the University of Illnois at Urbana-Champaign She received her B.A. from Swarthmore College. Her current interests include the study of attributional processes in marital conflict, and information transfer and decision making in organizations.

E. Allan Lind is an Associate Professor of Psychology at the University of Illinois at Urbana-Champaign. He received his Ph.D. in social psychology from the University of North Carolina. He was previously an Assistant Professor of Psychology at the Univerity of New Hampshire and a Research Associate at the Federal Judicial Center. His current research interests include the psychology of procedural fairness in legal and organizational settings, third-party dispute resolution procedures, and the effects of speech style on credibility and perceived power.

Elizabeth F. Loftus is Professor of Psychology at the University of Washington, Seattle, where she has taught since 1973. She is also on the faculty of the National Judicial College, where hs has taught since 1975. She received her Ph.D. from Stanford University in 1970. Dr. Loftus serves on the editorial boards of nine journals, including *Law and Society Review* and *Law and Human Behavior*; she is also President of the Division of Psychology and Law of the American Psychological Association, Past President of the Western National Academy of Sciences, and has served on three committees of the National Academy of Sciences. In January 1983 she was invited to present her research, which focuses on eyewitness testimony and courtroom procedure, before the Royal Society of London. Dr. Loftus has published eight books and over 100 scientific articles.

Wallace D. Loh is Professor of Law and Adjunct Professor of Psychology at the University of Washington. A graduate of Grinnell College, he received his Ph.D. in social psychology from the University of Michigan and his J.D. from Yale Law School (where he was a Russell Sage Fellow in Law and Social Science and an editor of the law journal). He has been a Research Fellow at the Universiteit te Leuven (Belgium) and a Visiting Professor of law at Vanderbilt, Texas, Emory, and Houston. In 1984 he published *Social Research in the Judicial Process: Cases, Readings and Text.*

David T. Lykken is a Professor of Psychiatry and Psychology at the University of Minnesota where he began as a college freshman in 1946 and has remained ever since. Trained originally as a clinical psychologist, his research has been mostly in the areas of psychopathology, psychophysiology, and human behavior genetics. He is a Past-President of the Society for Psychophysiological Research, Director of the Minnesota Twin Study, and Codirector of the Minnesota Center for Twin and Adoption Research. Polygraphic interrogation is a form of applied psychophysiology and therefore a natural interest for Dr. Lykken, whose first paper on the polygraph was published in 1959. He is perhaps the leading scientific critic of the lie detector industry, with a total of more than 30 articles and one monograph devoted to this topic.

He has been asked to testify on lie detection before committees of state legislatures, of both the U.S. House and Senate, and as an expert witness in state and federal courts from Alaska to Florida.

Bruce D. Sales, J.D., Ph.D., is Professor of Psychology and Sociology, and Director of the Law-Psychology Program at the University of Arizona. He is coauthor of the books *Making Jury Instructions Understandable, American Trial Judges,* and *Disabled Persons and the Law,* and editor of the book *The Trial Process* amongst several others. He is editor of the journal *Law and Human Behavior* and the book series *Perspectives in Law and Psychology,* and coeditor of the book series *Law, Society and Policy.*

Jonathan W. Schooler is a doctoral student at the University of Washington. He received a B.S. in psychology from Hamilton College in 1981 and an M.S. in human experimental psychology from the University of Washington in 1984. He is a cognitive psychologist interested in human memory, particularly in memory distortions and episodic-semantic memory distinctions. He is presently working on survey questionnaire design and has research interests in eyewitness testimony.

David R. Shaffer is a Professor of Psychology at the University of Georgia and currently Associate Editor of the *Journal of Personality.* His psycholegal research interests center on the defendant and the impact of the defendant's testimony on juridic decisions. He is also coordinator of the Developmental Psychology program at the University of Georgia, and is the author of *Social and Personality Development* (1979) and *Developmental Psychology: Theory, Research, and Applications* (1985).

Peter W. Sperlich received his Ph.D. in political science from the University of Michigan. He has been a Professor in the Department of Political Science of the University of California at Berkeley since 1963. He has also been a visiting professor at the school of law of the University of California at Berkeley. He is the author of *Conflict and Harmony in Human Affairs* (Rand McNally, 1971) and numerous research monographs and articles on science and law.

Gary L. Wells is a Professor in the Department of Psychology at the University of Alberta. He received his B.S. in psychology from Kansas

State University, and his Ph.D. in experimental social psychology from Ohio State University. Wells is Consulting Editor for the *Journal of Applied Psychology* and is a member of the American Psychological Association, Division of Personality and Social Psychology, Division of Psychology and Law, and the Society of Experimental Social Psychology. He serves as a reviewer for 19 journals. He has published widely in professional journals on eyewitness testimony, attribution, attitudes, and human judgment. His most recent book is *Eyewitness Testimony: Psychological Perspectives* (coedited with Elizabeth F. Loftus; Cambridge University Press, 1984).

Lawrence S. Wrightsman is Professor of Psychology at the University of Kansas, where he served as department chairperson from 1976 to 1981. For the academic year 1981-1982 he was Intra-University Visiting Professor at the University of Kansas School of Law. He received a B.A. and an M.A. from Southern Methodist University and a Ph.D. in social psychology from the University of Minnesota. He has previously taught at Hamline University, the University of Hawaii, and George Peabody College for Teachers. The author of eight books and numerous journal articles, he has also served as President of the Society for the Psychological Study of Social Issues (SPSSI) and the Society of Personality and Social Psychology (Division 8 of the American Psychological Association). He currently directs the Kansas Jury Research Project and teaches a course on jury decision making to law students there.